Children's Britannica

CHILDREN'S BRITANNICA

Volume 11

LONDON—MOSS

ENCYCLOPÆDIA BRITANNICA INTERNATIONAL, LTD
LONDON

First edition 1960

Second edition 1969

Third edition 1973

© Encyclopædia Britannica International, Limited 1975

ISBN 0 85229 126 4

Printed in England by
Hazell Watson & Viney Limited, Aylesbury,
Hazells Offset Limited, Slough
and bound by
Hazell Watson & Viney Limited, Aylesbury & Cymmer

Tower Bridge was completed in 1894. It is a bascule bridge, which opens to allow ships to pass through. The next bridge upstream is London Bridge, which ships cannot pass unless their superstructure is designed for river work, with masts and funnels that can be lowered. Beyond the lifting of Tower Bridge can be seen the central keep of the Tower of London—the square White Tower built by William the Conqueror to keep the people of London in awe.

LONDON is the capital of the United Kingdom and one of the three largest cities in the world. (Tokyo and New York are the other two.) Greater London has an area of 622 square miles and a population of about 7,380,000.

London is also interesting because of its history, which reaches back to Roman times and is recorded in the names of many of its streets. It possesses some of the greatest treasures in the world, among them the rare books in the British Museum and the paintings in the National Gallery. Like other great cities, it has hotels, hospitals, theatres, schools, tall office buildings, libraries, shops, houses and flats.

So much goes on in London that the remark made by Dr. Samuel Johnson about 18th-cen-

tury London is still true : "When a man is tired of London, he is tired of life; for there is in London all that life can afford."

London is situated on the River Thames, in what is called the London Basin. This "basin" is really more like a shallow saucer with a floor of clay resting upon chalk. The Thames, known to Londoners as "the river", winds its way through this saucer, dividing London into north and south. (See THAMES RIVER.) The Romans probably built the first bridge. Then came Old London Bridge, built in stone and begun in 1176. This was removed in 1832 and replaced by another about 100 feet upstream built by John Rennie. Rennie's bridge was in 1968 sold to a town in Arizona, United States, for re-erec-

1

tion as a tourist attraction. It was replaced by a six-lane bridge.

London has plenty of places of entertainment, ranging from Madame Tussaud's collection of waxworks in Marylebone Road to the cinemas in the West End. There are also beautiful parks and squares. They include St. James's Park, known for the ducks, geese, pelicans and other water birds on its ponds; Kensington Gardens with its Round Pond; Hyde Park, where at Speakers' Corner people with something to say get up and say it to anyone who will listen; and Green Park. All these are fairly close together. There is also Regent's Park, with the famous London Zoo.

Other places of interest are the big railway stations of Victoria, Waterloo, Paddington, Charing Cross, St. Pancras, King's Cross, Liverpool Street and the rebuilt Euston Station—one of the most modern in Europe. Sports grounds include the two where Test and county cricket matches are played, Lord's and the Kennington Oval; Wembley Stadium; and the grounds of the big London football teams.

When talking about London, it is important to remember that there are three Londons—the City of London, the London boroughs and Greater London. Together, the City and the boroughs make up Greater London. The remainder of this section of the article describes them and explains the differences between them.

The City covers only about a square mile and is the oldest part of London. It extends from Temple Bar in the west to Aldgate in the east and from City Road in the north to Southwark, across the Thames, in the south. The City is administered, or managed, by the Corporation of the City of London, headed by the Lord Mayor. A new Lord Mayor is elected each year and drives in a procession known as the Lord Mayor's Show, to the Guildhall. The Lord Mayor's Show is a great occasion; so is the banquet which he gives to members of the cabinet and other important people. The Lord Mayor lives in the Mansion House during his period of office.

In the City are the great domed church of St. Paul's, the Bank of England, sometimes called the "Old Lady of Threadneedle Street", the Stock Exchange and the Royal Exchange, and the Old Bailey, where important criminal trials take place. There too is the church of St. Mary-le-Bow. Anyone born within sound of its bells is said to be a cockney (a true Londoner).

By the Thames is the Tower of London, one of the oldest and most famous buildings in Britain. It has been used as a royal palace, a fortress and a prison. Between Tower Bridge and London Bridge is the fish market of Billingsgate. (See BILLINGSGATE MARKET; TOWER OF LONDON.)

A few remains of the wall which encircled London in Roman times can still be seen in the City. The "seven gates to London" include six points at which Roman roads pierced the wall, and seven streets are still called after them: Aldgate, Bishopsgate, Moorgate, Cripplegate, Aldersgate, Newgate and Ludgate. Moorgate, was not one of the original Roman gates.

The City is the business centre of London. During the day it is full of people, but at night the City becomes silent and almost empty. Much of the work done in the City is concerned with banking, insurance and stocks and shares, while elsewhere people are at work selling and buying all kinds of goods. Mostly the people who buy and sell the same things do business near to one another. For instance, the diamond merchants are grouped together in Hatton Garden.

The London Boroughs surround the City and with it make up Greater London, which is administered by the Greater London Council. In 1965, the 28 old metropolitan boroughs and the county of Middlesex ceased to exist. Most of Middlesex became part of the new Greater London, which also took in parts of Hertfordshire, Essex, Kent and Surrey. The metropolitan boroughs were replaced by 12 inner London boroughs and the outlying parts of London were divided into 20 outer London boroughs.

The inner London boroughs are: City of Westminster, Camden, Islington, Hackney, Tower Hamlets, Greenwich, Lewisham, Southwark, Lambeth, Wandsworth, Hammersmith, and the Royal Borough of Kensington and Chelsea. Of these, Greenwich, Lewisham, Southwark, Lambeth and Wandsworth are south of the Thames. The outer London

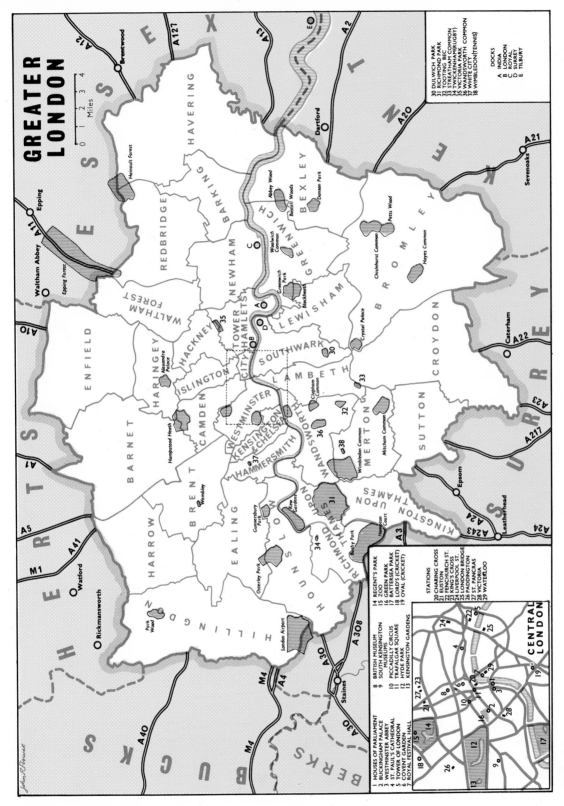

GREATER LONDON

Miles
0 1 2 3 4

1 HOUSES OF PARLIAMENT
2 BUCKINGHAM PALACE
3 WESTMINSTER ABBEY
4 ST. PAUL'S CATHEDRAL
5 TOWER OF LONDON
6 COVENT GARDEN
7 ROYAL FESTIVAL HALL
8 BRITISH MUSEUM
9 SOUTH KENSINGTON MUSEUMS
10 PICCADILLY CIRCUS
11 TRAFALGAR SQUARE
12 HYDE PARK
13 KENSINGTON GARDENS
14 REGENT'S PARK
15 ZOO
16 GREEN PARK
17 BATTERSEA PARK
18 LORD'S (CRICKET)
19 OVAL (CRICKET)

STATIONS
20 CHARING CROSS
21 EUSTON
22 FENCHURCH ST.
23 KING'S CROSS
24 LIVERPOOL ST.
25 LONDON BRIDGE
26 PADDINGTON
27 ST. PANCRAS
28 VICTORIA
29 WATERLOO

30 DULWICH PARK
31 RICHMOND PARK
32 TOOTING BEC
33 STREATHAM COMMON
34 TWICKENHAM (RUGBY)
35 VICTORIA PARK
36 WANDSWORTH COMMON
37 WHITE CITY
38 WIMBLEDON (TENNIS)

DOCKS
A INDIA
B LONDON
C ROYAL
D SURREY
E TILBURY

CENTRAL LONDON

3

Feeding the pigeons in Trafalgar Square. The church in the background is St. Martin's in the Fields.

boroughs north of the Thames are Hounslow, Hillingdon, Ealing, Brent, Harrow, Barnet, Haringey, Enfield, Waltham Forest, Redbridge, Havering, Barking and Newham. Those south of the Thames are Bexley, Bromley, Croydon, Sutton, Merton and the Royal Borough of Kingston upon Thames, while Richmond upon Thames lies on both banks.

Although Greater London is the area with which local government is concerned (see LOCAL GOVERNMENT), some other things in and around the capital are not arranged to fit in with the Greater London boundaries. For example, the Metropolitan Police District stretches some distance north and south of Greater London and the City has its own police force. The London Postal District, which includes all places for which the word "London" is part of the address, is a great deal smaller than Greater London, but the London Telecommunications Region (for telephone and telegram services) is a good deal larger. The Underground railways which London Transport manages on behalf of the Greater London Council stretch well beyond the boundaries of London.

The Centre of Government

Today, Charing Cross on the north side of the Thames is taken to be the centre of London. Around it are the buildings which show that London is the centre of Britain's government.

The Queen lives in Buckingham Palace for much of the year, but there are other royal palaces in London as well. St. James's Palace, Kensington Palace, the Tower, Clarence House, Marlborough House and Hampton Court, all belong to the sovereign. Even the Houses of Parliament are officially a royal palace, called the Palace of Westminster. (See BUCKINGHAM PALACE; HAMPTON COURT; WESTMINSTER, PALACE OF.)

If you stand beside the Houses of Parliament you can look down the street called Whitehall flanked by the main government offices, including the Home Office, the Foreign Office and the Treasury. (See WHITEHALL.) Off Whitehall is a narrow, rather dull-looking street called Downing Street. (See DOWNING STREET.) The Prime Minister lives at No. 10.

Not all the business of governing Britain is carried on in this small area of London, but it is here that great and important decisions are made and have been made for centuries. The statues of many great figures of English history —Cromwell and Charles I, Gladstone and Disraeli, Nelson and Florence Nightingale—can be seen standing in the streets of this part of London. Lambeth Palace, the home of the Archbishop of Canterbury, is just across the river.

The West End

West of Charing Cross is the West End. In this area are to be found stores and shops in streets such as Oxford Street, Regent Street and Bond Street. This part of London also contains many hotels and, above all, theatres. No city in the world has more to offer people who love the theatre than has London.

North of Oxford Street is London's tallest building, the 620-foot Post Office Tower, which is a centre for radio and telephone communications.

Trafalgar Square, known for its fountains, pigeons and the towering Nelson's Column, is close to Charing Cross. It is overlooked by the National Gallery. Meetings of people who wish to make public protests are often held in Trafalgar Square. To the west is Piccadilly Circus, gay with advertisements and lights. North of Piccadilly Circus is the area known as Soho, a colourful region of narrow streets, markets, shops and restaurants.

A mile or two to the west of Piccadilly is Kensington, a residential district with broad streets and big houses, many of which are divided up into flats. At the eastern end of the district, just off Kensington Road, is the Royal Albert Hall, where concerts, meetings and boxing matches are held. Farther west are Earls Court and Olympia, which are big exhibition halls; and the Commonwealth Institute, which has permanent displays showing the scenery, natural resources, life and development in the Commonwealth countries. In South Kensington are some of the most famous museums in London, including the Science Museum and the Natural History Museum.

To the south of Kensington and bordering on

the river is Chelsea, another residential district. Chelsea used to be famous as a place where artists and writers lived. They still do live there, but in recent years Chelsea has tended to become what Mayfair used to be, a fashionable district, while Mayfair (the district at the eastern end of Hyde Park) now consists more of offices. Changes of this kind in the character of different parts of London are always going on. A flower show is held each year in the grounds of Chelsea Hospital, the home of the scarlet-coated Chelsea pensioners. (See CHELSEA PENSIONERS.)

Attractions for children are the London Zoo in Regent's Park in the northwest; and, not far off in the Marylebone Road, Madame Tussaud's waxworks, which also include a planetarium. (See WAXWORKS; ZOO.)

Learning, the Law and Newspapers

North of New Oxford Street is a district known as Bloomsbury. It is the centre of books and learning in London and its most important building is the British Museum. Visitors go to the British Museum to see the strange and curious things there, from the preserved bodies (mummies) of ancient Egyptians to the beautiful Portland Vase, and scholars study in the great domed reading room of the British Museum Library, which contains about 7,000,000 books of all kinds. In the streets around the British Museum are publishing houses and bookshops.

Near the British Museum is a tall, handsome, white building which is the main building of the University of London. London University has about 34,000 students and is divided into a number of colleges and schools scattered about in different parts of London, with one or two in neighbouring counties. The medical schools of the London hospitals are part of the University.

To the southeast of London University and the British Museum is the legal centre of London, containing the four Inns of Court, which are concerned with training barristers. They are the Inner and Middle Temple, Lincoln's Inn and Gray's Inn.

Fleet Street, where the newspapers of London are written and printed, runs eastwards from the Inns of Court. It gets its name from a stream called the Fleet which once flowed from High-gate Ponds to Blackfriars but has now disappeared beneath streets and buildings. Today the stream flows through two large sewers under Blackfriars Bridge. Temple Bar is at the western end of Fleet Street. (See TEMPLE BAR.)

The East End and the Port

The East End is the part of London east of the City. It lies between Aldgate Pump on the west and the River Lea on the east. Hackney is to the north and the Thames to the south.

This area of London is poor and crowded but also busy and varied. Many Jews settled in the East End, particularly in the Whitechapel Road. In Middlesex Street is a fascinating market, generally known as Petticoat Lane, which is held on Sundays. Limehouse became famous as London's Chinatown.

The smells of the River Thames and of the cargoes unloaded from ships hang over the East End, and many people there work in the docks. The Port of London, of which the docks form a part, is one of the world's greatest ports. Down-river in Essex, Tilbury Docks are used by the largest ships that call at the port. Tilbury has modern deep water berths, including container berths. Tilbury also has a large dry dock (see DOCK AND WHARF) and is the passenger terminal for ocean liners. All these docks are managed by the Port of London Authority, which controls the River Thames from Teddington Lock to far out in the estuary—a river distance of 92 miles.

South of the Thames

Most of the historic buildings of London and its centres of business, pleasure and learning are on the north side of the Thames. Nevertheless, the south side has interesting and pleasant areas.

In Greenwich, for example, are the beautiful buildings of the Royal Naval College, built by Sir Christopher Wren. Greenwich also possesses a beautiful park in which stand the buildings of Greenwich Observatory. (See GREENWICH.) Unfortunately, as London grew its air became so smoky that it was difficult to see the stars properly, and so the observatory was moved to Herstmonceux in Sussex. In the National Maritime Museum of Greenwich are exhibits showing the history of Britain's ships, and in a specially built dry dock lies the famous clipper ship "Cutty Sark". Near by is Sir Francis Chichester's 53-foot yacht "Gipsy Moth IV", which he sailed single-handed round the world in 1966–67. Near Greenwich are the attractive village and common of Blackheath.

Two of the greatest hospitals in London are on the south side of the Thames. One of them is St. Thomas's Hospital, which was founded in the 13th century in Southwark but was removed to Lambeth in the 19th century. The other, Guy's Hospital, was founded in the 18th century and still stands in Southwark.

Near Waterloo Station is the site of the National Theatre, which used the former Old Vic theatre until its new Thameside home was ready. The Royal Festival Hall, which is used for concerts, conferences and exhibitions, was built for the Festival of Britain in 1951. Next to it stands a group of massive concrete buildings containing two other concert halls (the Queen Elizabeth Hall and Purcell Room) and the Hayward Gallery.

Farther Afield

London has suburbs with characters of their own. On the northern heights overlooking the city stand Hampstead, the home of many artists and writers, and Highgate, with a quieter village atmosphere. Between them stretches Hampstead Heath. Beside the Thames on the west side of London are Richmond, with its great park, and Kew, where there are gardens with plants from all over the world. (See KEW GARDENS.) To the north, wild fallow deer live in Epping Forest, the southern tip of which is in Greater London.

Throughout London, most people travel by buses or by Underground trains. The Underground forms a huge and busy network running under London's streets and buildings. The Underground system also runs in the open far out into the suburbs. (See UNDERGROUND RAILWAYS.) London's Heathrow Airport, the chief airport of Britain, is on the western outskirts.

Besides all its offices, London has many factories. It is the main centre in Britain for the food and drink industries, and for printing, publishing and the manufacture of clothes and furni-ture. Industrial estates on the outskirts of London produce machinery, electrical and radio goods and aircraft parts. At Dagenham in the borough of Barking is a huge factory making motor cars, starting from the iron ore unloaded at the riverside. It has its own power station.

The Growth of London

London was first built on two low, gravel-topped hills on the north bank of the Thames. They were too high to be flooded, but the river came right underneath them so it was handy for boats. Also, although the river was just shallow enough to ford (to cross on foot), its south side was marshy and enemies found it difficult to launch a surprise attack. So a settlement grew up on these two hills, and this became the town which the Romans called Londinium. On one of these hills St. Paul's Cathedral now stands and on the other the Bank of England.

At first, the town was protected only by the fort at Cripplegate, and when the British tribe known as the Iceni rebelled against the Romans in A.D. 60, they were able to burn down most of Londinium. At about the end of the 2nd century, the Romans built a wall around the city.

Although Londinium was quite an important Roman town, it was Winchester that was the capital of Anglo-Saxon England. By the 11th century, however, London was the largest town in England. William the Conqueror made it his capital and was crowned king there.

During the middle ages London was divided into two parts—the court part and the merchants' part. The court part had moved west to Westminster, the "Church in the West", while the merchants remained in the City and made money which they used to increase their power. The kings in the middle ages often tried to get money from the merchants, and the merchants often provided it. However, in return they demanded some privilege or freedom which made them even richer and more powerful.

Both because of its money and because of the courage of its leaders, the City of London has been able to deal with kings and parliament as an equal, and it is for this reason above all that London is at the very heart of the history of England. Today, when the Queen visits the City she stops at Temple Bar, where she is offered the City Sword. This shows that even the sovereign is not able to enter the City of London if the citizens do not wish it. Also, when the Lord Mayor of London visits parliament officially, it stops work to receive him—a thing it will not do for anyone else except the sovereign.

The Londoners of the middle ages must have taken for granted many things which seem terrible to us today. Among them was the sight of prisoners being dragged through the streets on frames called hurdles to be hanged at Tyburn Tree, the gallows named after another lost stream, the Tyburn. Near Marble Arch, at the beginning of Oxford Street, is a small tablet which marks the site of Tyburn Tree. However, the people had their share of amusements. At Smoothfield (Smithfield), where horses were sold, races also took place. The baiting (teasing) of bulls and bears was popular, also cock-fighting, wrestling and archery.

The mediaeval Londoners were used to filth, bad smells and disease, including a deadly disease called bubonic plague. This broke out at intervals in London, for it is a disease that thrives in dirty conditions, and the streets of London were filthy.

In 1664, during the reign of Charles II, London was attacked by an outbreak of plague which was so fearful that it is always referred to as the "Great Plague of London". In the summer of 1665 people were dying at the rate of thousands a week within a few hours of being taken ill. Carts were taken round the streets when the plague was at its height, and the drivers called, "Bring out your dead!" The bodies of plague victims were buried in great pits.

When the plague was past its worst, another disaster fell upon London. Fire broke out in a house in Pudding Lane, near London Bridge, in September 1666. The crowded wooden houses round about burned very easily, and the fire spread until most of London was a sea of flames. After four days, when it was over at last, a large part of London was a smoking wilderness. The greatest loss was St. Paul's Cathedral. (See FIRES OF LONDON.)

Terrible as it was, the Great Fire had some good results, for it destroyed the crowded and dirty streets which were breeding places for the plague and it gave people the opportunity to build a new and healthier London. Unfortunately, even though the great architect Sir Christopher Wren was given the job, he was not able to carry it out completely, as people who had lost their houses and shops wanted to have them rebuilt as they had been before. Wren was, however, allowed to rebuild St. Paul's and a large number of parish churches which are amongst the most beautiful in the world.

In the 18th century London began to spread into the open countryside round about, though Islington, Deptford, Battersea, Paddington and Chelsea were still villages. Gradually, however, the villages became part of the town.

London in the 19th century was better drained than before and therefore more healthy. Railways began to be built and factories grew up. At night the streets were lit, first by gas and then by electricity. In many ways London was a better place to live in, but the air was full of grime which blackened the buildings, and it seemed as though the town would never stop growing.

World War II and after. London suffered greatly in World War II. In September 1940 the German Air Force sent its aircraft over the capital and bombed it every night for nearly two months. This attack was known as the "blitz", from *Blitzkrieg*, a German word meaning "lightning war". In December 1940 so many fires were started one night from bombs being dropped that something like a second great fire of London started. St. Paul's and Westminster Abbey were hit by bombs, and the debating chamber of the House of Commons was altogether destroyed. Later in the war London was attacked again by pilotless aircraft (which Londoners nicknamed "doodlebugs" and "buzzbombs") and by rockets.

At the end of the war, although London had been hit in very many places, few parts were completely flattened. One of these was the area around St. Paul's. The ruins remained for years afterwards, long enough for a few plane trees to grow among them. It took London some time to recover from the war and some signs of the bombing still remain, but by about 1955 most of the damage had been repaired.

There are many parts of London which have not been mentioned in this article because of lack of space. There are, however, separate articles BIG BEN; COVENT GARDEN; LEADENHALL MARKET; LLOYD'S; OLD BAILEY; SCOTLAND YARD; SMITHFIELD MARKET; TEMPLE BAR; TOWER OF LONDON; WESTMINSTER, PALACE OF; WEMBLEY STADIUM; WHITEHALL.

LONDONDERRY is a county in Northern Ireland. Its chief city, which is the most important town in Northern Ireland after Belfast, is also called Londonderry, but is sometimes also called by its ancient name of Derry. Londonderry is bounded on the north by the Atlantic Ocean, on the west by Lough Foyle and County Donegal, which belongs to the Republic of Ireland, on the east by County Antrim and on the south by County Tyrone. Lough Neagh, which is the largest lake in the British Isles, borders Londonderry on the southeast.

Londonderry has wide areas of mountains, including the Sperrin Mountains in the south, and moorland, particularly in the south and centre. There is rich farmland eastward in the Bann Valley and westward in the Roe Valley and near the Foyle.

Most of the people of Londonderry earn their living by farming, but some work in factories. In Coleraine in the northeast linen and synthetic (artificial) fabrics are manufactured, and underwear is made at Limavady. There are fisheries on the Bann and on the north coast. Portstewart and Castlerock are holiday resorts. At Coleraine is the New University of Ulster.

Londonderry was given to the merchant companies of London in the 17th century, and large numbers of Protestants from Britain made their homes there. The little town of Derry was rebuilt and given the new name of Londonderry, which was also given to the county.

The city of Londonderry is best known for the part it played in the attempts of the Roman Catholic King James II to return to the throne of Britain in 1689. His army besieged Londonderry and ships were prevented from coming up the Foyle, but the citizens, though starving, refused to give in. After 105 days a ship succeeded in reaching the city and ended the siege.

Roaring Meg

fishing

linen

Derry city gate

Today Londonderry is an industrial city, specializing in making shirts, and more than 50,000 people live there. It has two cathedrals and a university college. The famous city walls and their cannon can still be seen. During the bitter conflict which broke out in Northern Ireland, the city was the scene of violence and disorder.

LONGFORD is a county in the west of Leinster, in the Republic of Ireland. It contains both bog and grazing land, as well as several lakes and rivers. (See LEINSTER.)

LORD CHANCELLOR. In the House of Commons is a man, known as the Speaker, who does not belong to any of the political parties there but who makes sure that order is kept during debates. In the House of Lords there is also a speaker, but he is called the Lord Chancellor. He sits on a seat known as the Woolsack. (See WOOLSACK.)

The Lord Chancellor is always a lawyer and is highest in position of all the judges in England. He is entitled to sit as a judge when legal members of the House of Lords hear appeals from the courts of appeal of England, Scotland and Northern Ireland. He is also a member of the Cabinet, and has under his charge a government department which deals with legal appointments and the management of the courts. Besides these jobs, he gives advice upon which men should be appointed Church of England bishops and he can also appoint rectors or vicars to a number of parishes.

Unlike the Speaker of the House of Commons, the Lord Chancellor belongs to whichever party is in power at that time, and so he resigns when the government is changed.

Central Press

The Lord Chancellor (left) and the Lord Chief Justice arriving at Westminster Abbey for the annual judges' service.

LORD CHIEF JUSTICE.
Second only to the Lord Chancellor among English judges is the Lord Chief Justice. He is always a peer, although he could hold his office without being one, and so he sits in the House of Lords when it is acting as the highest court of the country. He is also a member of the Court of Appeal. (See COURTS.)

His chief duty, however, is to sit as a judge of the Queen's Bench Division and to arrange all its business. The divisional court of the Queen's Bench Division hears appeals on points of law against decisions of the magistrate's courts.

The Lord Chief Justice is appointed by the Queen, who is advised by the Prime Minister.

LORD LIEUTENANT.
In each county of the United Kingdom the sovereign has a representative, who is called the lord lieutenant. In Tudor times the lord lieutenant was chief among the county justices and an important military figure. It was his duty to raise and lead the

county militia. (This consisted of civilians who were called upon to fight in times of emergency.) Today the lord lieutenant no longer has any fighting duties but he is often connected in some way with the Territorial and Army Volunteer Reserve in his county.

More important is his part in choosing the justices of the peace in his county—though not in those of the larger boroughs that have justices of their own. (See JUSTICE OF THE PEACE.) With the help of a local advisory committee he puts forward to the Lord Chancellor the names of people who are suitable to become justices. He is usually the official keeper of the records of those law courts in the county that are presided over by justices. (See COURTS.) With the sovereign's approval the lord lieutenant may appoint deputy lieutenants to help him.

LORD'S CRICKET GROUND
in London is the headquarters of cricket. It is the home of the Marylebone Cricket Club (M.C.C.) which is the highest authority in the game and makes the rules. (See MARYLEBONE CRICKET CLUB.)

The present ground is the third home of Lord's. In 1787 Thomas Lord, one of the ground staff of the White Conduit Club, rented

Every cricketer dreams of making a century at Lord's.

some land in Marylebone, London, where Dorset Square is now. He persuaded the club to move there but some 20 years later the ground became too expensive and Lord was forced to move north. The second ground had to be given up because it was planned that the Regent's Canal should run through it and in 1813 Lord bought the present ground at St. John's Wood. He spent the winter lifting and relaying the turf from the original ground for the second time and opened in June 1814 with a match between the M.C.C. and Hertfordshire.

One of the Test matches of every series against a touring team is always played at Lord's and appearing in a Test match at the headquarters of cricket is a high spot in a player's career. Lord's is also the headquarters of the Middlesex County Cricket Club. In the Lord's grounds are the Imperial Cricket Memorial Gallery and an indoor school for young cricketers.

LORELEI.

On the east bank of the River Rhine near St. Goar in Germany there is a steep cliff 140 metres high which has a strange echo. A legend says that this cliff was the home of a beautiful siren (an evil spirit) called Lorelei who lured sailors to destruction. As a girl she had drowned herself in the river because her lover proved faithless. She was changed into a siren and sat on the cliff combing her long hair with a golden comb and singing so beautifully that sailors forgot to watch their course and their boats were dashed upon the rocks. This legend, which was invented in 1802 by Clemens Brentano, is told in a poem called "The Lorelei" by the German poet Heinrich Heine. The poem was set to music by P. F. Silcher.

LOTUS.

The lovely lotus flower, which is mentioned in many myths and legends of different lands, is a kind of water lily. One of these lilies, called the Egyptian lotus, grows in the tropics. The floating leaflets are thick and very large, sometimes 60 centimetres across. They have toothed edges and a waxy bloom on their upper surface which throws off water like quicksilver. The lower surface is hairy. The flowers are verg big and rounded with thick white petals.

In Indian and Chinese religious paintings, Buddha can often be seen sitting in a large lotus flower. This is the Indian lotus, also known as the Indian sacred bean. It grows in bogs and shallow water in part of India and China and in these countries has been looked upon as sacred from very ancient times. The flowers of the Indian lotus are a pale pink and both the leaves and flowers open about 1 metre above the water. In Kashmir the seeds of the Indian lotus are eaten.

The Indian lotus grows about 1 metre above the water.

A very near relation of the Indian lotus in America is the American lotus, which has yellow flowers that also come up out of the water.

These three lotuses belong to the water-lily family, Nymphaeaceae. In England they can be grown in a tank in a warm greenhouse.

In Homer's poem the *Odyssey* the hero Ulysses (Odysseus) and his men come to a sleepy land where the people feed on a plant called lotus, or lotos. They offer it to Ulysses' men, who after eating it wish only to remain there, and Ulysses has much difficulty in dragging his men away from the lotus-eaters and persuading them to continue on their way home again.

This lotus is thought to have been a small, prickly shrub which bears a sweet-tasting, sloe-like fruit, from which both bread and a kind of wine can be made. It is no relation to the lotus lilies.

LOUIS XIV

(1638–1715), King of France, had a longer reign and greater power than any other French king. His subjects called him "The Sun King", because he dazzled them with his splendour and, in a sense, made everything revolve round himself. However, he fought so

LOUIS, JOE

many wars and lived so extravagantly that he left his country ruined when he died.

Louis was born at Saint-Germain-en-Laye (west of Paris) on September 5, 1638, and was the son of Louis XIII and Anne of Austria. As he was only four when his father died, his mother ruled France with her minister, Cardinal Mazarin; and later Mazarin ruled alone. Soon after Louis was crowned Mazarin died and Louis announced that he was going to be his own first minister, making every part of the government answerable to him personally. He worked hard and took his duties as supreme ruler very seriously. He could be charming and gracious, and impressed all France—even all Europe —with gorgeous royal ceremonies and elaborate court life. He built the vast palace of Versailles, near Paris, and had it richly decorated and furnished. He weakened the turbulent French nobles who had so often been strong enough to defy earlier kings. He made them attend his court and encouraged them to be extravagant so that they would ruin themselves.

In foreign affairs his aim was to increase French power and in the first years of his reign he was successful, partly by crafty diplomacy (the management of relations with other countries) and partly by war. From 1667 until 1713 he was almost constantly at war and this proved to be his undoing. He fought against the Netherlands, England, Spain and Austria, and although he gained small territories for France he ended by losing more than he gained. The wars were so costly, both in lives and money, that he left France loaded with debt and her farmlands only half cultivated. He made one of his greatest mistakes in 1685 when he revoked (cancelled) a law known as the Edict of Nantes, under which the Protestants, or Huguenots, had been granted freedom to worship in their own way. When the Edict was revoked Protestantism became illegal and thousands of the Huguenots fled abroad, many to England and Prussia. They were a great loss to France because they were hard-working and skilled craftsmen. (See HUGUENOTS.)

LOUIS, Joe (born 1914). This great American boxer, of mixed Negro, American Indian and white blood, held the heavyweight championship of the world from 1937 to 1949 and defended his title 25 times, more often than any previous holder. His real name was Joseph Louis Barrow and he was born in Alabama. He began his boxing career as an amateur and when he was 20 won the American amateur light heavyweight championship. In the same year he turned professional and in his first fight knocked out his opponent in one round. In his first year as a professional he scored 10 knockouts in 12 fights.

He won the world's heavyweight title from James J. Braddock, whom he knocked out in eight rounds, in June 1937. Among those who

Planet News

Joe Louis in his fight with Tommy Farr in 1937.

tried without success to take the title from him were the Welshman Tommy Farr (one of the few whom Louis failed to knock out), the German Max Schmeling, Tony Galento, Bob Pastor, Billy Conn, Tami Mauriello and Jersey Joe Walcott.

From 1942 to 1945 Louis served in the army and during this time gave exhibitions of boxing at army and navy camps. After World War II he returned to the defence of his title, and on March 1, 1949, he retired as undefeated champion. A fast and clever boxer, Louis was usually regarded as one of the most powerful hitters in the history of boxing. His height was 6 feet 2 inches and he usually weighed in at more than 200 pounds.

Louis made a comeback to the ring and tried to regain the title from Ezzard Charles in 1950 but lost in 15 rounds.

LOURDES is a town in southwest France at the foot of the Pyrenees. Until the middle of the 19th century it was of no great importance, but it has become a great centre of pilgrimage for Roman Catholics.

Marie-Bernarde Soubirous (usually called Bernadette) was the 14-year-old daughter of a poor miller of Lourdes. On February 11, 1858, she went to gather firewood outside the town. Afterwards she said that at the foot of a rocky hill called Massabielle she heard a sound, turned and in a grotto (cave) in the rock, beheld a lady who smiled at her. The lady seemed only 15 or 16 years old. She was of great beauty and surrounded by light, and wore a white dress, with a blue sash whose ends nearly reached the ground and a long white veil. Bernadette was sure the lady came from heaven and knelt to say some prayers. The lady made the Sign of the Cross and seemed to join in the prayers.

Bernadette visited the grotto again and saw the vision of the lady 18 times altogether, although no one else saw anything. The lady made it clear she was the Virgin Mary, the Mother of God. She told Bernadette that she must "do penance for herself first and then for others". When Bernadette scratched the ground where the lady told her, a spring began to flow and flows to this day. Bernadette was told to ask the priest to arrange for a chapel to be built at the grotto, but he sent her away.

On Bernadette's later visits to the grotto, great crowds went with her, some of them merely out of curiosity and others to pray. The police feared disorder and tried to close the grotto, but in the end the Emperor Napoleon III said that people might go there if they wished.

There were a few cases of remarkable cures of sick people and cripples who bathed in the water from the spring or drank it, although it was found to be quite ordinary water. The bishop of the diocese in which Bernadette lived ordered an inquiry. In 1862 the Pope ruled that the visions had been genuine and that the Mother of God had appeared to Bernadette.

Lourdes gradually became a place of pilgrimage, and not all the pilgrims were Roman Catholics. There is a statue of the Virgin Mary in the grotto and the pilgrims pray there and attend services in the four churches near by. The largest church is a huge boat-shaped building of bare concrete, built underground and able to hold 20,000 people. Many thousands of sick pilgrims come to Lourdes and are bathed in the water from the spring. Every now and then (although very seldom) there is a cure that doctors cannot explain. The greatest miracle of Lourdes, however, is that so many people from all over the world should come there to pray. About 3,000,000 come every year and there have been more than 4,500,000 in a year. There are over 600 hotels and boarding houses in Lourdes and on a hillside outside the city there are big dormitories and a dining hall for use by groups of poor pilgrims.

Bernadette herself became a nun and was happy in helping others, especially looking after the sick. She had much common sense, love of God and love of others and a strong sense of humour. Her health was very poor and she suffered terribly from asthma (an illness that makes breathing difficult). She died in 1879 at the age of 35. In 1933 she was canonized, or declared to be a saint, by Pope Pius XI.

The population of Lourdes is about 17,000.

LOUSE. The word "louse" (its plural is "lice") is given to many different kinds of crawling creatures. Generally, however, it means the small, wingless grey insects found in the hair and clothes of people who are either very dirty or have been unlucky enough to get too close to people who have lice.

These insects are what are known as sucking lice, for they suck blood from their hosts; that is, the people on whom they live. Their bites cause much irritation and sometimes disease. If many people are crowded close together, as sometimes happens during wars or other disturbances, and some have lice, they spread very quickly from person to person. They may carry the germs of typhus fever, and have been the cause of many outbreaks of it among soldiers and in crowded prisons.

Body lice quickly die if they are removed from the warmth of the body, so one way of getting rid of them is to throw away the lice-infested clothes or expose them to heat so as to kill the lice eggs. Head lice are killed

The common louse magnified nine times.

by washing the hair with various preparations, including paraffin, but the eggs, also known as nits, stick to the hair and have to be removed with a fine comb.

Nowadays, as people grow more clean and live in healthier houses, body and head lice are becoming much rarer.

Besides sucking lice, there are also biting or bird-lice, which are found on birds. More than 2,000 kinds of lice are now known and nearly every mammal and bird has its own particular kind—sometimes several different kinds.

Other lice are book-lice, most of which have wings, and plant-lice, which are better known as aphids or greenfly. There are also wood-lice, which, unlike the others, are not insects, being related to crabs and shrimps. (See APHID; BOOK-LOUSE; WOOD-LOUSE.)

LOUTH, the smallest county in Ireland, is in the province of Leinster. Its chief towns are Dundalk and Drogheda. (See LEINSTER.)

LUCERNE is a plant related to beans, peas and clovers and, like those plants (legumes), it enriches the soil by means of nitrogen. (See NITROGEN.) It is a useful fodder plant and resists drought. During a dry, hot summer, the fields become dry and parched, but lucerne remains green and thriving because it has a long root that can reach far below the surface to where the ground is moist.

Lucerne has many stems, with leaves divided

into three parts. The flowers are small and grow in close clusters. Those of common lucerne are purple in colour, but there is also yellow lucerne and variegated lucerne, which is a cross between the other two. (Variegated is a word meaning "marked with different colours".)

Lucerne is grown throughout the world, especially in dry climates where the land can be irrigated (watered). It is called alfalfa in the United States, where nearly half the world's output is grown. Lucerne is also widely cultivated in Argentina. In Britain it has been grown in parts of Kent and Essex since the 17th century and recently has become increasingly important.

The original home of lucerne was the Caspian Basin in Asia Minor (now Turkey), an area where many valuable plants were first grown.

Lucerne.

It was taken by early traders to China, Europe and North Africa, and it was the Moors of North Africa who gave it the name alfalfa. After the Moors conquered Spain in the 8th century, they planted lucerne there, and Spanish settlers later took it to South America. From there it spread to North America.

The Roman farmers used lucerne a good deal, and they probably brought the plant to Britain. The lucerne grown in Britain today, however, originally came from Flanders, which is the name given to what are now parts of Belgium and France.

LUDDITES. The Luddites were workers who broke up factory machinery as a protest against the hardships brought about by the beginnings of the Industrial Revolution in England. (See INDUSTRIAL REVOLUTION.) They took their name from their leader "King Ludd".

The Luddite movement began in the textile

industry around Nottingham in 1811 and spread to other areas, as hand workers protested at the lowering of their wages and the poor quality of machine-made goods. In 1812 a group of Luddites were shot by soldiers and the factory owner who had ordered the shooting was murdered. Lord Liverpool's government took strong measures against the Luddites. Many were hanged or transported following a mass trial at York.

There were further outbreaks of Luddite machine-breaking in 1816 but after that harsh government action and better economic conditions brought the movement to an end.

LUKE, Saint. Saint Luke wrote two books of the New Testament—the third Gospel and the Acts of the Apostles. He was a doctor and St. Paul wrote of him as "the Beloved Physician". Not much is known about him but it is thought that he may have been born in Philippi (north-eastern Greece) and he was certainly a Gentile (not a Jew). Of all the writers of the Gospels, he was by far the most educated and his books are the best written. He accompanied St. Paul on several of his missionary journeys and in the Acts of the Apostles it is possible to detect when he is speaking of journeys he himself has made, for at such times he uses the personal pronoun "we" Thus he writes, "Setting sail therefore from Troas, we made a straight course to Samothrace". (Troas was a town on the northwest coast of Asia Minor, and Samothrace is an island in the Aegean Sea.) It is possible that Luke first came to take part in this missionary work because of St. Paul's constant need of medical attention, Luke being invited to go on the journeys to look after him when he was ill. Whatever the reason, there is no doubt that Luke became as keen on proclaiming the good news about Christ as the rest of the disciples.

St. Luke's Gospel was meant especially for the Gentiles and was probably written about 20 years after that of St. Mark. When writing it, Luke made use of St. Mark's account but added to it from other books and from stories about Jesus, some of them coming from people who also had known Jesus. He tells of many things that are not to be found in the other Gospels. For example, he alone gives the famous parables of the Good Samaritan, the Prodigal Son, the Pharisee and the Publican and the story of the Ten Lepers.

St. Luke also shows how Jesus tried to give women a high place among His followers. He tells how Our Lord allowed the two sisters, Mary and Martha, to provide Him with a home where He could rest when he was tired out by His work. Luke gives us the story of the Widow of Nain whose son was raised from the dead. He also tells us of the women of Jerusalem who wept as Our Lord passed them carrying His Cross. Only Luke gives the name of the women who accompanied Jesus on His travels.

There are other ways in which St. Luke's Gospel differs from the others. Its first two chapters give a great deal of information about John the Baptist and about the birth and childhood of Jesus. Here we can read of John's parents, Zacharias and Elisabeth (a relation of the Virgin Mary), and of how the Angel Gabriel announced to Mary that she was to be the mother of Jesus; how, when Mary heard this news, she sang the song "My soul doth magnify the Lord", which is known as the Magnificat; how the shepherds kept watch at night; and how the infant Jesus was presented to the Lord in the Temple.

St. Luke is sometimes regarded as the patron saint of doctors and nurses because he was "the beloved physician". His day is October 18.

LULLABY. Children usually hear their first music when their mother sings as she rocks them to sleep. The song she sings is a lullaby, or cradle song, written especially to lull babies to sleep.

William Byrd, the English composer of the 16th century, wrote two of the earliest lullabies that we still know. Later the Austrian composers Mozart and Schubert wrote the *Wiegenlieder* (this is the German word for lullabies), and the French composer Gounod wrote a lullaby called "Quand tu chantes" (When you sing). However, these are lullabies only in name. They show how very simple forms of music have been used by composers for some of their most beautiful works. A famous example of this type is Frédéric Chopin's *Berceuse* for the piano. (This is the French word for lullaby.)

Lullabies are usually written in 6/8 time with

a gently rocking rhythm. When words are set to the music they, too, are in a rocking rhythm, as in this verse from a song by Lord Tennyson :

Sweet and low, sweet and low,
  Wind of the western sea,
Low, low, breathe and blow,
  Wind of the western sea !
Over the rolling waters go,
Come from the dying moon, and blow,
  Blow him again to me;
While my little one, while my pretty one, sleeps.

LUMPSUCKER.
The lumpsucker is an ugly fish which gets its name from having a lumpy body, rather swollen in appearance, and a large, vividly coloured sucking-disc on its underside. The female lumpsucker may grow to a length of 60 centimetres, although it is usually much smaller than this. The male lumpsucker makes up for his looks by being a most devoted father who will suffer death rather than desert his eggs. He is about half the size and more brightly coloured than the female, and his under-surface becomes brick-red during the breeding season.

The female lays her eggs among the rocks between the lines of seaweed which mark the points

A pair of lumpsuckers. The male is shown on the left.

reached by various tides. The male attaches himself to a rock in front of the eggs by means of his sucking-disc, and it would be very hard to pull him away. He fans the eggs with his large pectoral (front) fins so that the water flows continually over the eggs and keeps them supplied with oxygen.

The father's real troubles, however, begin when at certain tides he and the eggs are left uncovered on the shore, for then he is likely to be attacked by sea birds and by crows and rats. Moreover, in some places in Europe lumpsuckers are used as food and the fishermen spear them while they are on guard. Sometimes, too, a storm will wash the eggs higher up the shore, and then many anxious fathers will be seen searching for their charges. In order to live out of water the lumpsucker keeps its gills moist by keeping the gill chambers closed so that the gills do not dry up. It is also probable that it takes in oxygen from the water stored in the stomach.

As though these trials were not enough, it appears that the lumpsucker is unable to feed during the breeding season, for the stomach is then filled with water.

Lumpsuckers are found in British waters, particularly on the coasts of Lancashire and Wales. Because of their habits they are also known as hen-fishes or sea-hens.

LUNGFISH.
The lungfishes are found in the fresh waters of South America, Africa and Australia, and it seems that they have lived there, in very similar forms to the ones they have now, since the time when the three continents were joined together.

Lungfishes show how amphibians (which include the frogs, toads and newts) evolved, or developed, from fishes, and how lung-breathers came from gill-breathers. They all have an air bladder which they use as a breathing organ, and the African ones have a double bladder. Their nostrils are connected with the mouth and their young are very much like tadpoles. They can also breathe through their gills like other fishes.

The lungfish of Queensland (Australia), is a heavily built fish with very large scales and a gristly backbone. It sometimes rises to the surface to breathe through its air-bladder, and its breathing can be heard quite easily. The Australian aborigines used to eat it and the early settlers called it "Burnett salmon" (after the Burnett River) but it is now protected by law.

The African lungfishes are slender with small scales and long, thin pectoral and pelvic fins. They lay their eggs in burrows in the river bank, where the male guards them. As the swamp dries up in the dry season, the lungfishes burrow in the mud and lie motionless in a muddy, slime-lined cocoon until the rain comes again. The cocoons can be dug out and sent long distances without

The lungfish has strong, well developed fins.

harming the fish. Lungfishes have been received in their cocoons in Great Britain : the cocoons are put into water and as the mud walls collapse the fish swim out very sluggishly.

LUPIN. The lupin grows in tall spikes of flower-heads crowded together on a central stalk. They are many different colours, including blue, purple, yellow, pink and white, and in some cases the flowers are two separate colours. They are rather like the flowers of the pea plant and they belong to the same family, Leguminosae. Wild lupins grow in America and round the Mediterranean.

The kind of lupin most often grown in English gardens today is the Russell lupin. It has the widest variety of colour and the flowers are crowded more closely than those of other lupins.

Tree lupins, which are usually yellow or white, have smaller flowers than the other kinds.

The ancient Egyptians cultivated one kind of lupin and ate the seeds after soaking them to get rid of the bitterness. Another kind was grown by the Greeks and Romans, who also ate the seeds and grew the plants to feed their animals. They also used them to enrich the soil. (See LEGUMINOUS PLANTS.)

The leaves of the lupin are made up of many narrow leaflets which radiate out from the top of the leaf stalk like a star. At night each leaflet folds in half and they all either hang down or stand up, according to the species.

There is no nectar in the flowers, but bees visit them for pollen, and they have a special arrangement called the piston-mechanism which makes certain that pollen is carried by the bee from one flower to another. When the bee stands on the flower the stigma comes shooting out and brushes against the bee's underside, collecting the pollen which the insect has brought from another flower. Then the flower's own pollen, which is tightly packed inside it, is squeezed out by the weight of the bee, through a little opening, on to the under surface of the insect's body. When the bee has gone the flower goes back to its normal position.

The pods of lupins are often covered with silky hairs, and when the seeds are ripe the pod explodes. The two halves twist and the seeds are thrown off.

Reginald A. Malby

The Russell lupin is very common in English gardens.

LUTE FAMILY.

LUTE FAMILY. The members of the lute family, which includes the guitar, are stringed instruments with a body shaped like a pear cut in half and ending in a broad neck. The strings stretch the whole length of the instrument from the broader end of the body to the neck and are usually plucked by the fingers. The greatest difference between the various members is that of size; they vary from the six-feet-long chitar-

A lute.

rone (no longer in existence) to the little mando-line that is only two feet long. (See MANDOLINE.) The ordinary treble lute is about 20 inches long.

The lute came to Europe from Asia, where it is still popular. It was much used in England during the 16th and 17th centuries and the English composer John Dowland wrote songs of great beauty which were accompanied by the lute. Among the last composers to write for the lute were J. S. Bach and Franz Joseph Haydn. The lute fell out of favour in the 19th century but in recent years several professional musicians have played it again.

LUTHER, Martin (1483–1546).

LUTHER, Martin (1483–1546). Martin Luther was the first of the Protestant reformers of the 16th century. (These reformers brought in the religious beliefs known as Protestantism, which are explained in the article REFORMA-TION.) Luther was born at Eisleben (west of Leipzig, Germany) on November 10, 1483, and was brought up at Mansfeld near by, where his father became a copper miner. He went to school at Mansfeld and at Magdeburg and entered the University of Erfurt in 1501. He be-came a Master of Arts in 1505 and his father then persuaded him to study law, but no sooner had he begun his new studies than he dropped

them and joined the Order of Augustinian Friars, for during a terrible thunderstorm he had feared he was going to be killed and had vowed to enter monastic life. In 1507 he was ordained as a priest and in 1512 was appointed Professor of Scripture at the University of Wittenberg (north of Leipzig). He soon became the leader of a group of men who were beginning to hold religious ideas that were very different from the accepted religious ideas of the time. Luther and his companions thought the accepted ideas had strayed too far away from the teaching of the Bible. They therefore followed the teaching of St. Augustine of Hippo, which they believed was based on that of St. Paul, and they taught that man could be saved only by relying on God's mercy. Anything else he might do counted for nothing. (See AUGUSTINE OF HIPPO, SAINT.)

In 1517 his ideas caused him to make a strong protest when a friar named Tetzel arrived near Wittenberg selling what were known as indulgences. It was thought at this time that even after God had forgiven a man's sins the man still had to be punished for them in this world or in purgatory. (Purgatory is explained in the article HEAVEN AND HELL.) Indulgences were issued by the pope and it was claimed that they cancelled out the punishment for forgiven sin. Men could obtain indulgences by good works such as giving money to church funds.

Luther saw that this did not agree at all with his belief about the way in which God saved man —believing, as he did, that it was by forgiveness only. Therefore he posted on a church door in Wittenberg a list of criticisms of the idea of in-dulgences. This began a great quarrel and Luther was ordered by the church to take back what he had said. He refused to do so and was excommunicated (expelled from the church) in 1521. By this time he had stated publicly that the church was wrong in many other ways than in its teaching about indulgences. He took no notice of the excommunication and when he was summoned to appear before the Emperor's Diet (council) at Worms he still refused to take back what he had said, and was outlawed. (See WORMS, DIET OF.) His prince, the Elector of Saxony, hid him in his castle, from which he re-turned to Wittenberg in 1522. Out in the world once more, he found that some people had been changing religious practices more than he approved. He restored order, but himself gradually began to accept the changes that others had started. He had already rejected Catholic ideas about the Mass and the sacraments, and he now altered church services so that they expressed his new beliefs. He gave up monastic life, which he came to think was wrong, and in 1525 married a former nun, Catherine von Bora.

For the rest of his life Luther was occupied in spreading and defending the ideas of the Protestant Reformation. He had a gift for writing and his works fill about 70 large volumes; besides

Luther made a list of 95 arguments against indulgences, and nailed it to a church door where all might see it.

this he translated the Bible into German. He was also a great preacher. However, he failed to persuade all Germany to follow him. At the time of his revolt against the church he enjoyed great popularity, for nearly all Germans were discontented with the pope's control over Germany and with his demands for money. However, many people were alarmed at what Luther's ideas had helped to cause. The Peasants' Revolt of 1524–1526 had broken out largely because the peasants used his ideas—which they misunderstood—to claim freedom from their masters, just as they thought he had claimed freedom from the authority of the pope. When Luther approved the crushing of their revolt, even though it was done most brutally, the peasants also lost faith in him. Luther's marriage, and his permission for Count Philip of Hesse to have two wives at once, shocked many other people. His disagreement with Ulrich Zwingli, the Swiss religious reformer, also weakened the success of the Reformation. So Germany did not become a wholly Protestant country, and indeed the Catholics and Protestants separated into two hostile groups.

By the time of Luther's death, at Eisleben on February 18, 1546, civil war was beginning between the two sides, which was ended only in 1555 by the peace of Augsburg. This treaty laid it down that the princes of Germany should have the right to decide whether their states should be Catholic or Lutheran. During Luther's last years religious disputes broke out between his own followers, which caused much trouble after his death.

LUTINE BELL. The Lutine Bell hangs in the Underwriting Room at Lloyd's (see LLOYD'S) in the City of London and is rung when important news is to be announced. It is rung twice before good news and once before bad news. For a very long time Lloyd's has been closely connected with the insurance of ships and their cargoes, and in the past bad news was usually news of ships that were overdue (had not arrived at their destination) and good news was the report of their safe arrival. Since ships have carried wireless and other aids to navigation their position is usually known and so the news

The Lutine Bell in the Underwriting Room at Lloyd's.

psalms at all. One series shows men ploughing, sowing, harrowing and harvesting; another shows people preparing meals and having dinner. There are pictures of a man feeding his pigs from an oak tree, of archery practice, of a lady at her toilet and a boy stealing cherries. One picture of Constantinople makes it look like an English city of the time with inn and shop signs. In addition to the pictures the pages are also decorated with paintings of imaginary and horrifying beasts. The Luttrell Psalter is now in the British Museum in London.

LUXEMBOURG.
The little inland country of Luxembourg is only about the size of the English county of Dorset. Luxembourg's neighbours are Belgium to the west and north, Germany to the east and France to the south. Northern Luxembourg is part of the forest of the Ardennes. The south is part of the Lorraine plateau (tableland) and is good farmland. The streams in the deep valleys run into the River Moselle which for some distance forms the frontier with Germany.

The people of Luxembourg are of peasant stock, hard-working, thrifty and patriotic. Three languages are spoken in the country—French, German, and a German dialect called *Letzeburgesch*. Schooling is free between the ages of 6 and 15 and children must attend school during this time. Nearly all the people are Roman Catholics. The only large town is the capital, also called Luxembourg. It was once a very strong fortress on a plateau surrounded by steep cliffs on three sides, and contains two fine old churches, Notre Dame and St. Michael's, as well as the royal palace. Flights of steps and narrow winding streets connect it with the new town in the valley below.

About one-quarter of the people work on the farms, most of which are in the southern part of the country. The main crops are oats, potatoes, and roots and clover for the animals. Most of the farms keep dairy cattle and pigs. There are important vineyards in the Moselle valley. More important than agriculture, however, is the little country's huge output of iron and steel. There are big supplies of iron ore (the earth from which iron is obtained) in the southwest corner of

of overdue ships scarcely ever has to be announced. An occasion when the bell was rung for news not connected with shipping was at the announcement of the death of King George VI in 1952.

From 1799 to 1859 the Lutine Bell lay at the bottom of the sea, for it was the ship's bell of H.M.S. "Lutine" which was sunk in a gale off the Dutch coast in 1799. H.M.S. "Lutine" was originally a French ship that was captured by the British during fighting between Great Britain and France.

LUTTRELL PSALTER.
The manuscript, or handwritten book, called the Luttrell Psalter is a collection of the psalms which was made for Sir Geoffrey Luttrell of Lincoln's Inn, London, in about 1340. Psalter simply means a book of psalms, but this one is so beautifully illustrated that it is more like a picture gallery of English life in the middle ages.

Most of the pictures do not illustrate the

Luxembourg, and the manufacture of iron and steel are the chief industries of the country. Luxembourg has good roads and its railways connect it with the rest of Europe. Some goods are carried in barges on the Moselle. The busy airport at Findel, near the capital, links Luxembourg with the rest of Europe. Radio Luxem-

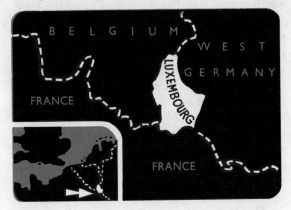

bourg broadcasts are beamed over a wide area.

Luxembourg was once part of the Holy Roman Empire, on which there is a separate article. It was then much larger than now and included part of Belgium. In 1442 it was bought by the King of Burgundy and in later years it was held by Austria, Spain and France. Under the Emperor Napoleon I, Luxembourg was a French *département*, or district. The Congress of Vienna in 1815 made Luxembourg a grand duchy under King William I of the Netherlands. When William's Belgian provinces rebelled against him most of Luxembourg joined with

FACTS ABOUT LUXEMBOURG

AREA: 2,586 square kilometres.
POPULATION: 339,900.
KIND OF COUNTRY: Independent grand duchy.
CAPITAL: Luxembourg.
GEOGRAPHICAL FEATURES: The country forms part of the plateau of the Ardennes forest and is hilly and well-wooded. It is watered by the Sûre (Sauer) and Alzette rivers.
CHIEF PRODUCTS: Oats, potatoes, wheat, grapes; iron ore.
CHIEF EXPORTS: Iron and steel; textiles; machinery.
IMPORTANT TOWNS: Luxembourg, Esch-sur-Alzette, Differdange.
EDUCATION: Children must attend school between the ages of 6 and 15.

them, and in 1831 the country was divided into two parts. The larger part became the Belgian province of Luxembourg and the smaller part (the present grand duchy) remained under William's rule.

The Treaty of London in 1867 guaranteed the neutrality of the grand duchy of Luxembourg, which means that the powerful countries of Europe agreed that they would defend Luxembourg if it were attacked. In fact, it was invaded and occupied by the Germans in both World Wars. In 1942 the Germans forced the grand duchy to become a part of their country, in spite of the protests of the people. Luxembourg was freed by the Allied armies in 1944 and its ruler, the Grand Duchess Charlotte, received a warm welcome when she returned.

Since 1945 Luxembourg has done much to work together with other European countries. It is a member of the defensive alliance called the North Atlantic Treaty Organization (Nato) and a founder member of the European Economic Community (the Common Market). The city of Luxembourg is the headquarters of the European Coal and Steel Community. (See COMMON MARKET.)

LYNX. The lynx was once believed to have better eyesight than almost any other animal, and so the phrase "lynx-eyed" came to be used for people with particularly sharp eyes. It is a member of the cat family and various forms live in Europe (including Russia) and in America.

The lynx is generally about 1 metre long with a tail up to 20 centimetres long. It can at once be recognized by the long, erect tufts of hair on its ears. It has long legs and is able to make great leaps. Lynxes are active climbers and when they live in forests they spend much of their time in trees. They are also found in rocky places.

Lynxes hunt only at night, stalking their prey and pouncing on it. They catch all kinds of birds and small mammals, frequently more than they can eat, and sometimes kill sheep and goats. Very occasionally a lynx will attack a human being. Though lynxes are savage and snarling animals, the cubs can be tamed and will follow their masters like dogs.

There are several species, or kinds, of lynxes.

The northern or European lynx, which lives in Scandinavia, Russia and northern Asia, is a thickset animal with a square head, large paws and a grey coat spotted with brown. The handsome Spanish lynx of several Mediterranean

The Canadian lynx has thick, mottled grey fur.

countries is smaller, reddish and more distinctly spotted.

In America the Canadian lynx of the forest country of southern Canada and the United States is often trapped for its thick, mottled grey fur. It is a timid creature and seldom approaches towns. Farther south its place is taken by the bobcat, often called the bay or red lynx or wild cat. This animal has reddish grey fur, with a few black spots. It is smaller than the Canadian lynx, with small ear tufts. It is now much rarer than it once was, but it still does serious damage on poultry farms from time to time.

In Africa and southern Asia lives the caracal, also called the Persian or black-eared lynx. Its body is about the same size as a fox's, with a tail of ten inches. Its fur is reddish-brown above and whitish beneath and there are two white spots above each eye. The ear tufts are black. Caracals, which live among grass and bushes, are able to leap into the air and catch low-flying birds, such as pigeons.

LYONS or LYON. The third largest city of France is Lyons (in French, Lyon) in the southeast of the country. It lies where the River Rhône flowing from the east joins the River Saône flowing from the north. With the help of canals linking the Rhône to other waterways, Lyons

has become a great centre for water, rail and road traffic between Paris and the south of France. It is also important because it stands on the routes to Switzerland and Italy.

Lyons is especially noted as the centre of the French silk industry, which was introduced from Italy in the 15th century. Much of the artificial silk industry, too, has developed around Lyons, which is also important as a centre for dyeing silk and other materials and for making dyes and chemicals. There are many other industries in the eastern district called Villeurbanne, including the most important, the metal industry.

In the old town west of the Saône the big white marble church of Notre Dame, splendidly decorated, stands on top of a hill, but it is quite modern. Below it at the water's edge is the beautiful Gothic cathedral of St. Jean, which was begun in 1175 and has some fine stained-glass windows. Lyons has many other fine churches and old buildings, in addition to a large university and medical school, and no less than 21 museums. Most of the hotels and shops are on the peninsula between the two rivers. The population of Lyons is about 535,000.

LYRE. The lyre was a musical instrument much used by the ancient Greeks, although it was probably invented in Asia. It consisted of a hollow body, or sound-chest, from the top of which two arms stretched upwards and outwards. They were connected near the top by a cross-bar. Four, seven or ten strings were attached to another bar on the body of the lyre and were stretched from there to the cross-bar. The strings were plucked with a plectrum, a small piece of wood or metal. The cithara was a larger instrument but in many ways it was like the lyre.

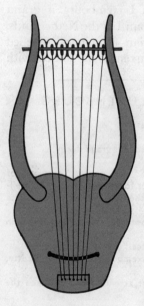

Ancient Greek lyre

22

LYREBIRD. The lyrebird was given its name because the tail of the cock bird has a wonderful resemblance to the lyre, a stringed instrument which was played by the ancient Greeks. The "lyre" has 16 feathers. Two broad ones, curved outwards at the tip, form the outline, two

In the mating season, the male lyrebird courts the female by showing off his magnificent lyre-shaped tail, raising it and spreading it above his back like a peacock. The female has a much less remarkable wedge-shaped tail.

stiff, long ones shoot up through the centre and the other 12 spread out fanwise in a delicate tracery, like the strings.

There are two kinds of lyrebird, and both live in Australia. They are brown in colour and the female's tail is in the shape of a long wedge. Lyrebirds live in scrub and woods, feeding on insects and snails. They run very fast along the ground and seldom fly. They are good singers and mimics, or imitators.

The male lyrebird is about the size of a farmyard rooster and has the same grand manner of strutting around. When he is courting he gathers together sticks and leaves to make a platform. On this he displays to the female, sweeping his tail upwards and forwards so that it covers his head. Lyrebirds mate for life but it is the female that builds a large dome-shaped nest. She lays only one egg, which is dark in colour and blotched as if with ink. Throughout the time that the female remains in the nest the male sings and roams nearby but does not visit her. The young bird remains with its parents until it is three or four years old, so a family party may have two or three youngsters of different ages.

LYRIC. A lyric is a short song-like poem which is written because of some personal feeling or experience of the poet's. Usually a lyric is divided up into stanzas, or verses, with lines that rhyme and with a musical flow or rhythm. Unlike a ballad or an epic, a lyric does not tell a story. A good lyric often seems as if it had been made up on the spur of the moment to pour out the poet's feelings, but the feelings themselves may not be at all simple and the poem may have a very complicated pattern. Today the songs in musical shows are also usually called lyrics.

Lyric comes from the same Greek word as *lyre,* which was a musical instrument a little like a harp. In ancient Greek the idea of a lyric poem was that it should be sung to the accompaniment of the lyre. In England in Elizabethan times too lyrics were generally written to be set to music. They had to be simple and short because the listener had to give some of his attention to the music as well as to the words. So although they were always about feelings they were not always the private feelings of the poet, for a poem written for someone else to sing cannot "belong" to the poet who writes it in quite the same way as a poem meant to be read in quiet and solitude.

Many of the most beautiful were published in song books and no one knows who wrote them. Here is one, about tears :

> Weep you no more, sad fountains;
>   What need you flow so fast?
> Look how the snowy mountains
>   Heaven's sun doth gently waste!
> But my Sun's heavenly eyes
>   View not your weeping
>   That now lies sleeping
> Softly, now softly lies
>   Sleeping.

After this time, it gradually became less common to write poems to be set to music, and so lyrics came to be more serious and full of deep feeling. William Wordsworth, Percy Bysshe Shelley, John Keats and Lord Tennyson (all of whom have separate articles) wrote fine lyrics.

MAC. The word *Mac* means "son" in the Gaelic language of Scotland and Ireland, and it comes at the beginning of many Scottish and Irish family names. Often it is shortened to Mc, or M'.

The King of the Picts in the 8th century was Angus Mac Fergus (son of Fergus), and the first king of a united Scotland was Kenneth Mac Alpin (son of Alpin).

Many of today's names beginning with Mac have a long history themselves. Macaulay, for example, may have begun as a combination of Mac and the Norse name of Olaf or Olave, dating from the days of the Viking invasions of Britain.

Some groups of different names today go back to a single ancient one, as McInnes, McNeish and McGuinness all come from Mac Aonghais (son of Angus). Sometimes Mac was put in front of a word describing a profession or job, or a person's appearance. McDougall, for instance, is from the ancient words *dubh ghal,* and means "son of the dark stranger"; MacIntyre is son of the carpenter, MacIntosh son of the chief.

In Ireland the "O" in names like O'Donnell and O'Connor also means "son of", and so does the Welsh "Ap", as in Ap Rhys. "Fitz" is another similar word, coming from the French word for son, *fils,* as in Fitzroy and Fitzwilliam.

McADAM, John Loudon (1756–1836). The man who did most to build good roads in place of the narrow muddy tracks that covered Great Britain in the 18th century was John Loudon McAdam. He was born at Ayr in Scotland and went to school at Maybole near by. In 1770 his father died and he went to live with an uncle who was a merchant in New York, where he made a fortune. In 1783 he returned to settle in Ayrshire and there began to try out new ways of road making. He continued these experiments when in 1798 he took a government post at Falmouth. In 1815 he was put in charge of the roads near Bristol and began to put his ideas into practice.

Before McAdam's time engineers copied the old Roman method of laying a foundation of large heavy stones under their roads. McAdam said this was unnecessary and even harmful because it increased the wear on carriages and horses using the road. He preferred to cover the subsoil, or earth beneath the surface, with a ten-inch layer of broken stone, using pieces no bigger than would go in a man's mouth. This layer was covered with smaller stones down to coarse sand in size. The traffic passing over a road of this kind, helped by the rain, bound the whole surface together. The road was laid with a slight camber, which means that the surface was arched so that

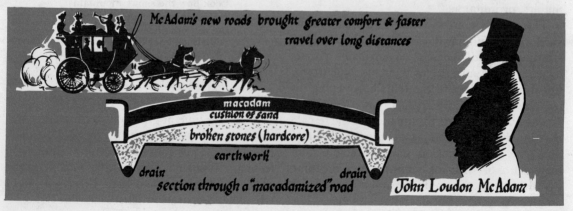

McAdam's new roads brought greater comfort & faster travel over long distances

macadam
cushion of sand
broken stones (hardcore)
earthwork
drain   drain
section through a "macadamized" road

John Loudon McAdam

the centre was a few inches higher than the edges, and where necessary drains were dug along each side.

It was found that McAdam's roads lasted a long time and that coach horses, which were usually worn out after three years on ordinary roads, could work for much longer on the new highways with their springy surfaces. McAdam became famous and in 1827 the government appointed him to a post that allowed him to introduce his method—now called "macadamizing"—all over Great Britain. The new network of good roads did much to increase prosperity.

MACARONI, vermicelli, spaghetti and other similar foods are made from a special kind of wheat grown in southern Europe and North America. This wheat contains more of the sticky substance known as gluten and is harder than the ordinary kind of wheat.

The first stage in the manufacture of these foods is the grinding of the wheat. This produces the large particles known as semolina (see FLOUR) which are then mixed with water and

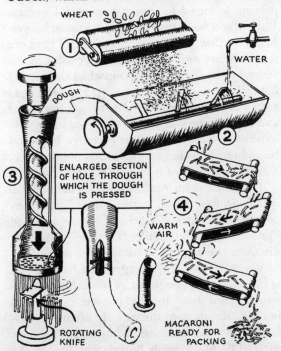

(1) Hard wheat is ground into semolina. (2) Dough is made. (3) The dough is forced through holes which are fitted with tiny bullet-shaped formers, so that it comes out as long pipes of macaroni. (4) The macaroni is dried.

kneaded by a machine into a stiff, smooth dough. After this it is put through something rather like a mincing machine, which forces the dough out through holes at one end. The size of the holes determines whether it will be called macaroni, spaghetti or vermicelli: macaroni is fairly thick and has therefore come through a machine with the biggest holes, the thinner spaghetti has come through smaller holes and the thinnest of all—vermicelli—through still smaller holes.

As the sticks come out of the machine they are cut into lengths and put into cabinets, where warm air dries them hard. The temperature of the air has to be carefully regulated, for the quality of the macaroni, spaghetti or vermicelli can easily be spoiled at this stage.

Italians are particularly fond of macaroni and the other forms of *pasta*.

MACARTHUR, John (1767–1834). The pioneer of the Australian wool industry, John Macarthur, was born near Plymouth (Devon) and went to Sydney in New South Wales as a lieutenant in the army in 1789. He obtained land at Parramatta and began breeding sheep for wool. He bought a flock bred from Merino sheep originally brought from South Africa, obtained sheep from the royal stud in England and built up flocks from which many fine-woolled sheep were bred. In 1801 he went to England and after leaving the army he returned to New South Wales in 1805 with some merinos from the royal flock. He had serious quarrels with the governor, William Bligh (see BOUNTY, MUTINY OF THE) who opposed the wealthy sheep-owners and favoured the small settlers. Macarthur was in England from 1809 until 1817 when he returned to attend to his increasing flocks. He was an important figure in New South Wales, and a member of its government from 1825 until he became insane in 1832. (See also AUSTRALIAN PIONEERS.)

MACAULAY, THOMAS BABINGTON MACAULAY, BARON (1800–1859). One of the poems written by Thomas Macaulay tells the story of the Roman hero Horatius who kept the bridge over the River Tiber against a horde of foes. The story of Horatius is one of a series of poems called *Lays of Ancient Rome*; and another poem of Macaulay's tells of the coming of the Armada from Spain and the lighting of the warning beacons all across England. Thomas Macaulay also wrote essays and articles of various kinds and a great *History of England*.

He once said of himself, "When I sit down to work, I work harder and faster than any person I ever knew", and his life showed that this boast was true. He began very young, too, for at seven years old he was busy writing a history of the world! His father later sent Thomas to Cambridge University, where he studied law, but it was not long before he decided to make his career in politics instead. From his father Thomas inherited a determination to work for laws that would put an end to slavery, and he made his first public speech on this subject. In 1830 he became a member of parliament and remained a member, except for one period of five years, until 1857, when he was given the title of Baron Macaulay. At one time he was one of the men responsible for government in India, where he organized a scheme of national education and worked out the system of Indian law.

This busy public life did not prevent Macaulay from carrying on writing, and sometimes he used to get up at five o'clock in the morning to compose articles and poems. He had finished the first volumes of the *History of England* by 1848, but was still working on the last parts when he died in 1859. He was buried in the Poets' Corner in Westminster Abbey.

Macaulay was a kindly, honest and generous person, but he was also very set in his own opinions and despised people who disagreed with him. This meant that often he did not write fairly about the events and people of the past.

MACE. Maces were originally used as weapons in battle—and with their short handles and heavy knobs were no doubt very effective, especially against chain mail. They were among the weapons of the serjeants-at-arms who protected the king, and when no longer used as weapons they gradually became the symbols (signs) of the authority of these officers when carrying out his commands. By a similar process, the maces which are carried in front of mayors

and other city officials have become the symbols of their authority and of that of the bodies which they represent.

Each of the British Houses of Parliament has a mace which is carried into the House at the start of each day's debate by a servant of the sovereign—the serjeant-at-arms. The mace used by the House of Commons is the more famous; it is lent by the sovereign as a sign of the importance that he or she attaches to all that the Commons do. This royal mace, of highly decorated silver gilt, is the symbol of order and power. Without it the Commons cannot meet. That is why, when Oliver Cromwell lost his temper with parliament in 1653 and called in soldiers to drive out the members of the Commons, he pointed to the mace on the table and told his soldiers to take it away. (See CROMWELL, OLIVER; and also SPEAKER, which explains other facts about the mace used in the House of Commons.)

MACHIAVELLI, Niccolo (1469–1527). Although he became famous as a writer, little is known of Machiavelli's early life. Both his parents belonged to the city state of Florence, Italy, where his father was a well known lawyer. Machiavelli was an important official of Florence for 18 years and was highly successful in his work, but he fell out of favour when the Medici family returned to power in 1512. (See FLORENCE; MEDICI FAMILY.) After being imprisoned and tortured he was allowed to retire to his villa outside the city where, in the evenings, he put on his old official robes and spent his time writing. The most famous of his works is *The Prince*.

This book is an examination of the ways in which princes rise to power and of how they govern their states. (Machiavelli uses the word "prince" to mean the ruler of a state.) The book discusses the art of government in an entirely new way. In the middle ages men had written about how rulers *ought* to govern; Machiavelli wrote about how they *did* govern. He had noticed that the two things were often very different. Having examined what makes a prince successful, Machiavelli hoped that one of the young Medicis would profit from his book and act accordingly. At that time Italy consisted of many separate states which were often at war with one another and did not combine even against foreign invaders. He thought a strong man was needed to unite Italy and save it from destruction—a man who would stop at nothing in order to bring success.

Machiavelli had a poor opinion of mankind and seems at first glance cold and cynical. But by nature he was passionate, generous and basically religious, although he despised a church which taught men to reject ambition and accept mediocrity or misery without question. For him success was what mattered, not the means used to gain it. In a wicked world he felt justified in teaching that princes were entitled to deceive. From these ideas comes the word "Machiavellian", which is used to describe people who seek to gain success by a mixture of force and fraud.

MACHINE.
A machine is a device that makes work easier either by reducing the effort needed or by making it easier to use effort. Although we often think of a machine as a complicated arrangement of wheels and gears and rods and all sorts of moving parts, a basic, or true, machine is quite a simple thing. Prehistoric man invented and used machines, and in the eyes of the engineer and scientist there are only six kinds of basic machine. These are : the lever, the pulley, the wheel and axle, the inclined (sloping) plane, the wedge and the screw. As the pulley and the wheel and axle are special kinds of levers and the screw and the wedge are special kinds of inclined planes, there are really only two main kinds of basic machine—levers and inclined planes.

An example of the lever is the "crowbar", a long bar used for "levering up" or lifting a heavy weight such as a paving stone from the ground.

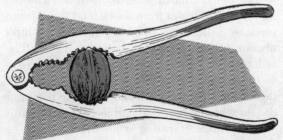

A pair of nutcrackers is a lever of the second class.

The fulcrum is the point about which the lever pivots or turns. In what is called a lever of the first class, such as the crowbar, the fulcrum is

This crowbar is being used as a lever of the first class.

between the effort and the load to be moved. A pair of scissors is another lever of the first class. A pair of nutcrackers, in which the load (the nut whose shell must be cracked) is between the fulcrum and the effort applied by the hand, is a lever of the second class. Another example of a lever of the second class is the wheelbarrow. In the third class of lever the effort is applied between the fulcrum and the load. An example of a lever of the third class is a pair of sugar tongs. The lifting of a fish from the water with a rod and line is another example of the use of a lever of the third class.

The Law of Machines

The law of machines of all kinds can be explained most easily by considering the lever. In a lever of the first class, where the man is lifting a heavy stone block with a crowbar, it can be seen that the effort (the force given by the man's hand) moves through quite a large distance in order to obtain a small movement of the load (the stone block). The law is that the effort needed to lift the load multiplied by the distance moved by the effort, is equal to the weight of the load multiplied by the distance through which it is lifted. Therefore, if the distance between the man's hand and the fulcrum on the ground where the lever is pivoted is 20 metres, and the distance between fulcrum and stone is 2 metres, then (since 20 metres is ten times 2

MACHINE

metres) the lifting force moves ten times more than the effort applied by the man. This means that the lifting force is ten times greater than the effort and this particular crowbar is said to have a *mechanical advantage* of ten. As the man can easily apply an effort of 100 kilograms, he can make the crowbar exert a lifting force of $100 \times 10 = 1,000$ kilograms, or a tonne. By choosing a lever with a very large mechanical advantage, quite a small effort can be made to lift a huge load. Archimedes, a Greek inventor who lived in the 3rd century B.C., was thinking of a lever of this sort when he said: "Give me a place to stand and I will move the earth".

No machine, however, can give out more *work* than is put into it. Work is defined as force times the distance it acts; thus in the case of the man with the crowbar the law of machines tells us that the man's hand must move ten inches for every inch he lifts the stone. This is another way of saying that the effort moves ten times as fast as the load.

The crowbar used as a lever is, therefore, a very simple machine which increases the force applied by the man, but moves the load more slowly and through a smaller distance. Notice also that the crowbar reverses the direction of the force, since the man presses down on his end of the crowbar to lift the stone at the other end.

The Pulley and the Wheel and Axle

Pulleys are very useful machines. A single pulley turning on a fixed axle, or spindle, does not give greater mechanical advantage, but it is useful for changing the direction of a force—for example, for lifting a load by means of a downward pull. A lifting tackle, or "purchase" as it

The capstan uses the principle of the wheel and axle.

is sometimes called, does, however, give greater mechanical advantage. In it there may be one

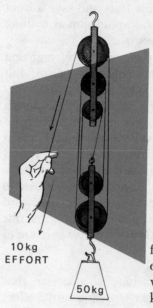

10 kg EFFORT

50 kg

A tackle with a mechanical advantage of five.

or more fixed pulleys and one or more movable ones with one continuous rope or chain passing round them all. Since there is only one rope and the force in it must be the same everywhere, the mechanical advantage is the total number of lengths of the rope between the fixed and moving pulleys. If there are five such lengths, an effort of 10 kilograms will lift a load of 50 kilograms, if there is no friction. Friction (on which there is a separate article) causes pulleys to resist being turned on their spindles. To overcome friction extra force must be used. The same law of machines that is true of the lever holds good for lifting tackle. Thus if it has (in theory) a mechanical advantage of five, the load is lifted only 1 metre for every 5 metres of movement of the rope at the effort. Also, the load is lifted at

Gearing is an example of the wheel and axle.

only one-fifth the speed at which the effort moves the rope.

The old-fashioned windlass used for winding up buckets of water from a well, and the capstan used by sailors for weighing (lifting) a ship's anchor, are examples of the wheel and axle. The sailors push on long bars (the ends of the spokes of the wheel) fitting into holes in the barrel of the capstan (the axle). The longer the bars and the thinner the barrel, the greater the mechanical advantage. Gearing is another example of the wheel and axle, in which one wheel is made to turn another by means of teeth cut around the outside of both wheels. The teeth of one wheel fit between the teeth of the other, so that the second wheel is forced to turn when the first does. The mechanical advantage depends on the number of teeth on the two wheels. If the driving wheel has 20 teeth and the driven wheel 80, the mechanical advantage is (in theory) $\frac{80}{20}$, which is 4. (See also the article GEARS.)

Inclined Planes, Wedges and Screws

The inclined plane is the simplest of all machines and is sometimes called a ramp. A heavy box can be loaded into a lorry quite easily by pushing it up a sloping plank, but it would be very difficult to lift it bodily. The actual work done would be the same in each case if there were no friction, but in actual practice more work is needed when using the inclined plane because of friction. The huge blocks of stone used for building the pyramids in Egypt were probably lifted into place by being hauled up ramps (see PYRAMID). In any inclined plane, the mechanical advantage decreases with the steepness of the slope, or gradient as it is sometimes called.

The wedge is a special kind of inclined plane. The blade of a pocket-knife and the point of a needle are both wedges, but the wedge which is easiest to understand is the kind used for splitting logs of wood. The wedge is driven downwards by the effort of hammering it and forces apart the wood through which it travels. The load is

Using an inclined plane to load a heavy box into a lorry.

represented by the resistance to splitting offered by the wood and is usually much greater than the effort. The use of a wedge, however, wastes a lot of the effort in overcoming friction.

The screw has an inclined plane (the thread) that, instead of going straight, travels round and round a bolt or spindle like a "spiral" staircase.

A wood-screw's thread is a fairly steep inclined plane.

When a wood-screw is turned by a screwdriver, it travels into the wood for a distance which depends on the steepness of the thread. The common nut and bolt used for fixing parts of engines and machinery together works in the same way. The grooves called screw-threads formed on the outside of the bolt fit into similar threads formed inside the hole through the nut. Thus when the nut is turned it travels slowly along the bolt. The vice used on a workshop bench for gripping a piece of wood or metal is another example of the screw.

A further example is the screw-jack used for lifting a motor car when changing a wheel. This usually gives a very great mechanical advantage. For example, the end of the jack-handle may move through a distance of 15 centimetres in lifting the car only 1 millimetre. This would mean a mechanical advantage (in theory) of 150. Thus, supposing a man could exert a pull of 100 kilograms on the handle, he could in

A wedge is a special kind of inclined plane.

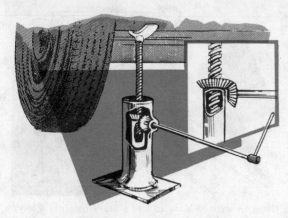

A screw-jack gives a great mechanical advantage.

theory lift a mass of 15,000 kilograms, or 15 tonnes. In practice, however, friction would probably reduce this to about 10 tonnes.

MACHINE TOOLS

can be used to shape nearly any material. Machine tools are usually driven by electricity because it is easy to control and also because it provides a relatively compact and fume-free source of power.

The *power saw* may be either a circular saw or a straight-bladed saw. Circular saws are often, but not exclusively, used in woodworking. Straight-bladed saws can be either a power-driven version of a hacksaw or a band saw, where the working part of the saw is straight but is made of steel sufficiently flexible to be bent round in a large endless loop.

Holes are made by a *drilling machine* which has a driven spindle to which the drill is fixed. The part that makes the hole is called a twist drill. It is a pointed rod of hard steel, fluted with spiral grooves along which escapes the material as it is cut from the bottom of the hole by the drill. This cut material is known as "swarf". Drilling machines have a handle that moves the spindle to advance the twist drill into the material. Some machines have several spindles and so can drill several holes at once.

A *boring machine* is a robust drilling machine used to make large holes. When a large hole is required a starting hole is made either by the largest twist drill available or by initially casting it into the material. This hole is expanded sideways but not deepened by a boring machine.

The cutting tool protrudes from the side of the spindle while it is rotated inside the hole. A *jig-borer* is a boring machine in which the table on which the work is carried can be moved forwards or sideways with great accuracy. Thus the positions of the holes in relation to each other can be controlled very exactly.

Very large holes are made by a *boring mill*. The piece to be bored is clamped to a circular table which is rotated. The cutting tools are held stationary so that material is shaved off as the piece rotates.

A *lathe*, on which there is a separate article, is used to make parts which are either cylindrical or flat, for instance bolts or rollers. Shaping with a lathe is called "turning" because the piece to be shaped is rotated or turned in front of the cutting tool. An automatic lathe, once set, will go on making articles such as bolts so long as it is fed with bars of metal. A lathe is perhaps the basic machine tool for it is possible, though sometimes difficult, to use a lathe to make any other machine tool.

In a *shaping machine* the piece of work (or workpiece) is held stationary while the tool is moved in a straight line along it. On the return stroke the tool moves fractionally sideways, and the next cut is made alongside and slightly overlapping its predecessor. A *planing machine* is like a shaping machine, although usually larger. Its tool remains still while the piece being planed moves to and fro. A *slotting machine* holds the workpiece on a horizontal table while the tool moves up and down to make a slot.

A *milling machine* uses a special cylindrical tool with a number of identical cutting edges. This tool is rotated above a slowly moving table to which the workpiece is fixed. The cutter can only remove a limited amount of material in a single pass above the table, which may have to be moved a number of times to complete the operation.

Grinding machines are very important machine tools. Instead of a tool that cuts or shaves, they carry a fast-spinning wheel made of artificial abrasive (gritty) stone. Grinding machines produce parts with a very smooth finish and of exactly the size required, and there are very many types. A *surface grinder* works like a milling machine and produces flat surfaces. A *cylindrical grinder* can be used to make either a roller-shaped article or a round hole. In some grinders the piece being ground (if made of iron or steel) is held by a magnetic chuck (see MAGNETISM). Other grinding machines are used for gear-cutting and for cutting the threads, or spiral grooves, of screws.

The cutting tool on all machine tools must possess special qualities. All the power of the machine is concentrated at the point of contact between the tool and the workpiece. Therefore this cutting edge must not only be sharp, and remain sharp, but it must also be very strong. In addition it must also retain these properties while hot. (Sometimes liquid coolants are used to control the temperature.) If the machine is not large and the tool can be conveniently re-sharpened special tool steels can be used. However, in many machines the cutting edge is made from a carbide, often tungsten carbide, a material which is almost as hard as a diamond.

Machine tools have made possible mass production of identical goods. Once they have been set the latest machines are able to make complicated shapes with little skilled attention, and can inspect the parts they make and sort out the ones that are not correctly made.

MACKENZIE RIVER.

Over 4,200 kilometres long, the Mackenzie River is the second longest in North America. With its tributaries it drains the eastern slope of the Canadian Rocky Mountains and takes the overflow from three huge lakes—Athabasca, Great Slave and Great Bear. The head streams of the Mackenzie are the Athabasca and Peace Rivers (see ALBERTA). North of Lake Athabasca they join to form the Slave River. Along this stretch there are difficult rapids between Fitzgerald (Alberta) and Fort Smith and barges are carried overland by road between these two places. After leaving Great Slave Lake the river is called the Mackenzie and flows though "muskeg", which is swampy lowland forested with spruce, birch and pine trees. The Mackenzie flows into the Arctic Ocean through a large delta (see DELTA). The whole region is frozen in winter and the spring thaw sends vast quantities of water downstream.

In the late summer, steamers and boats can use the river between the Arctic and Fort Smith and above Fitzgerald.

Radium and uranium (on which there are separate articles) are obtained near Great Bear Lake, as well as silver and other metals. West of the lake, oil wells near Norman Wells are connected by pipe line to Whitehorse on the Alaska Highway (see ALASKA HIGHWAY).

The river was first navigated in 1789 by Alexander Mackenzie, a young Scotsman. He started from Fort Chipewyan on Lake Athabasca and with a few Indians in three canoes followed the river to its mouth.

MACKEREL.

The mackerel is a handsome streamlined fish whose second dorsal fin and the anal fin are divided into a number of small separate "finlets" above and below the tail. These control the flow of water over the tail as the fish swims, so that eddies do not form and slow the fish down. That is why the mackerel and its relatives, the bonitos and tunnies, are among the fastest of fishes, and are able to move quickly for long periods. They roam the ocean in great shoals, feeding on the small fishes, crustacea and other creatures near the surface.

The common mackerel is about 30 centimetres long, with silvery underparts, dark bars and gleaming blue-green bands on its sides, and

"Finlets" near its tail help the mackerel to swim fast.

a large mouth. It is caught for the sake of its oily, richly flavoured flesh and tastes best if eaten shortly after it has been caught.

Mackerel spawn in summer, in the open sea, up to 80 kilometres away from the land. The eggs float at first, then after about two days they sink slowly to the bottom. The female mackerel produces about 500,000 eggs.

The chub mackerel is different from the true

mackerel in having an air-bladder, some enlarged scales on the shoulder and spots on the side. It usually lives in warmer seas but sometimes appears off the British coast, where it is called the Spanish mackerel.

The bonitos, which are caught in large numbers in America, France and West Africa, are very much like large mackerel but with the dorsal fins less widely separated and with no scales on the body behind the shoulder. Occasionally they appear off Great Britain. They are beautifully marked fishes, shaped rather like small tunny (see TUNNY), and are caught on baited hooks on a row of lines trailed from long booms or "tangons" set out on each side of small, fast boats.

MACMILLAN, Maurice Harold (born

1894), became Prime Minister of Great Britain in January 1957. He was born in London on February 10, 1894, and was educated at Eton College and at Oxford University. During World War I he served in the Grenadier Guards and in 1920 entered his family's book-publishing business of Macmillan and Company. He married Lady Dorothy Cavendish, a daughter of the Duke of Devonshire.

Camera Press
Harold Macmillan.

Macmillan began his political career in 1924 when he was elected Conservative M.P. for Stockton-on-Tees, Durham. He was outspoken in his opinions, and became rather unpopular in the House of Commons during the 1930s because of the way he criticized British politicians for not opposing more strongly the warlike policies of Germany and Italy. However, he was given a government post when Winston Churchill formed a government in 1940.

At the general election of 1945 Macmillan was defeated at Stockton-on-Tees but was soon afterwards elected for Bromley (Kent). When the Conservatives won the 1951 election Macmillan became Minister of Housing and Local Government and reached the government's target of building 300,000 houses a year. In 1954 he was Minister of Defence and in 1955 was Foreign Secretary for nine months. From 1955 to 1957 he was Chancellor of the Exchequer and introduced the Premium Savings Bond scheme. When Sir Anthony Eden resigned as Prime Minister in January 1957 Macmillan took his place.

As Prime Minister he won respect for his unruffled manner, his quick wit at question time and the courage of his speeches—as when in 1960 he warned the South African Parliament of the "wind of change" in Africa and asserted Britain's dislike of the policy of *apartheid* (see SOUTH AFRICA).

One of Macmillan's chief concerns was to strengthen relations between Britain and the United States and he had several fruitful meetings with Presidents Eisenhower and Kennedy. He also visited the Russian premier Nikita Khrushchev in Moscow. Although he was a firm supporter of European unity and tried hard to bring Britain into the European Economic Community (see COMMON MARKET), he failed because of French opposition. During his term as Prime Minister Macmillan visited most of the other Commonwealth countries and was the first British Prime Minister to visit India since its independence.

At home Macmillan had to deal with unemployment, which increased even while Britain was prosperous. There were difficulties, too, in obtaining new defence weapons and in maintaining security against spies. In October 1963 Macmillan became ill and resigned. He was succeeded by Lord Home (see DOUGLAS-HOME).

MADAGASCAR is an island five times as

large as England and Wales, separated from the east coast of southern Africa by the Mozambique channel. The first European to see Madagascar was the Portuguese seaman Diogo Dias in 1500. From 1896 until 1958 Madagascar was a French colony or under French control. Madagascar became independent as the Malagasy Republic. (See MALAGASY REPUBLIC.)

MADEIRA ISLANDS.

In the North Atlantic, about 640 kilometres from the coast of northwest Africa, lie the islands called the Madeiras. The largest is Madeira itself, northwest of which is the small island of Porto Santo.

There are also two groups of uninhabited rocks called Desertas and Selvagens. The Madeiras, which are Portuguese, have a land area somewhat larger than the Welsh island of Anglesey. They are the tops of great volcanic mountains that rest on the floor of the ocean. The highest peak, in the centre of Madeira, is 1,861 metres above sea level. From the rugged ridges, deep narrow valleys run down to the steep cliffs around the coast.

The Madeiras have a pleasant warm climate and are popular as a winter resort with people from northern Europe. Madeira was once thickly wooded and gets its name from the Portuguese word *madera*, meaning "timber", but most of the higher parts are now covered with whortleberry and heath plants, with belts of Spanish chestnut and pine trees on the lower slopes. There are no wild animals larger than rabbits although goats have been introduced. The surrounding sea is rich in fish such as mackerel, tunny and whitebait.

The people are mainly of Portuguese stock and most of them live in the towns and villages along the coast. Their plots of land are arranged in terraces like steps. Water for these plots is taken from the mountain streams and brought through winding stone-built channels. Each farmer is allowed to run the water through the channel to his plot for so many hours in the day or night. The chief crops are sugar cane, bananas, grapes from which Madeira wine is made, and on the higher ground potatoes, vegetables and fruits.

Besides farming and fishing, the people of Madeira work at making wicker chairs, furniture and baskets from the stems of osiers (a kind of willow). Many of the women make lace and fine embroidery, now more important as an industry than wickerwork. The only large town and seaport is Funchal, built on the slopes overlooking a bay in the south of Madeira. The gardens of its white villas are bright with tropical flowers and plants. Many of the streets are too steep and narrow for wheeled traffic other than bicycles, but roads connect Funchal with most coastal villages. In some places, however, goods are carried in sledges called *carros* drawn by oxen or mules along cobbled tracks.

When it was discovered by a Portuguese explorers in 1420, Madeira was uninhabited. The Portuguese soon made large settlements, cut down forests and cultivated the land. The history of the Madeiras has been one of peaceful agricultural development. The islands form the Funchal district of Portugal and send members to the Portuguese *Cortes*, or parliament. The population is about 269,000.

MADONNA AND CHILD.

Madonna is the Italian word for "Lady" and the Madonna and Child is a familiar title for the Virgin Mary and the infant Jesus. This subject has inspired artists since the earliest days of Christianity and has been represented in art more often than any other except the Crucifixion. These representations vary from the most primitive doll-like figures to the sophisticated works of the Old Masters, and are in every conceivable material, from drawings that are little more than scratchings on walls to sculptures in stone, wood and metal, paintings in tempera and oils, engraving, embroidery, stained glass, and mosaic, down to the Christmas cards and plastic materials of today.

It is not difficult to see why this was, and is still, such a popular subject. It records a tremendous event in history, the birth of Christ, and also the love of a mother for her child—

which is an experience common to all mankind.

The theme has been illustrated in an infinite variety of ways, ranging from treatments of the Bible stories of the Nativity (the familiar Christmas crib) and the Flight into Egypt, to those depicting delightful legends, such as that of the cherry tree which bowed its branches so that the Madonna could pick some fruit when she was hungry. Some artists have shown both mother and child as royal personages wearing

Courtesy, Trustees of the National Gallery
"Madonna of the Meadow", by Giovanni Bellini.

crowns; others, such as Rembrandt, have painted them in a homely, realistic manner.

The illustration is of a picture, now in the National Gallery, which was painted by Giovanni Bellini early in the 16th century. The Madonna, gazing with tenderness and wonder at her child, is seated in an Italian landscape amid oxen, birds and scenes of familiar everyday life, to show how natural was the artist's devotion to his subject.

MADRAS.

Madras, now known as Tamil Nadu, is a state in southern India. The people of Madras are mostly Tamils, who are darker than the peoples of northern India and speak a different language. Most of them are Hindus (see HINDUS AND HINDUISM). All over the country are great Hindu temples with lofty gateways, covered with images of the Hindu gods. Agriculture is the main occupation and the chief crops are rice, millet, cotton, sugar and groundnuts.

The southern part of the Indian peninsula was the first to be visited by European traders seeking spices, precious stones and gold. Owing to the work of Christian missionaries, far more people in Madras can read or write than in other parts of India. In the northeast of the state is the capital, Madras City, which is a busy seaport with a large artificial harbour. During the 18th century France and Britain fought for possession of Madras. It had been under British rule for nearly 200 years when India became independent in 1947.

MADRID.

In 1561 King Philip II chose Madrid as the capital of Spain chiefly because it lay almost exactly in the middle of the country. It is set on a barren, sandy plateau, or tableland, more than 2,000 feet above sea level, exposed to the merciless glare of the summer sun and, in winter, to the piercing winds from the snow-clad mountains north of it. Only hardy people like the Madrilenos (as the inhabitants of Madrid are called) could stand the climate. The soil of the surrounding country is too poor for growing crops or grazing cattle and Madrid therefore depends for its food on the distant coast towns.

The Gran Via, with its smart shops and skyscrapers, runs past a sordid low-lying district reaching down to the ridiculous little river called the Manzanares. (The great Spanish writer Miguel de Cervantes, who lived and died in Madrid, started the fashion for poking fun at the Manzanares.) The ten main streets of the newer part of the city fan out from the Puerta del Sol. In this part, the buildings are pleasantly separated by parks, squares and gardens. The most beautiful street is the Paseo del Prado, on one side of which is the Retiro Park with gardens, ponds, fountains and a zoo. Between the Paseo del Prado and the park is the famous Prado museum, containing the paintings collected by Spanish monarchs since the 15th century.

Among the famous buildings of Madrid are the National Library and the Royal Armoury.

Other notable buildings are those of the university, which were rebuilt after having been severely damaged by bombardment during the Spanish Civil War (1936–1939).

Modern developments in Madrid include the building of a large number of dwellings for poorer people on the banks of the Manzanares, the completion of a ring-road round the city and the construction of the Barajas airport linked with the city by a fine highway. The main railways and roads of Spain were designed to radiate from Madrid like the spokes of a

Courtesy, Spanish National Tourist Office
The Prado in Madrid contains many famous paintings.

wheel, and the city itself has an underground railway. Madrid is an important industrial centre and has factories making aircraft, lorries, machinery, radio and electrical equipment and many other goods.

The population is about 3,150,000.

MADRIGAL. A madrigal is an unaccompanied part-song. It became a custom in the 16th century to hand round song books after supper and for all the members of the family, and any guests they might have, to join in the singing of madrigals.

Madrigals began in Italy in the 14th century and came to England during the 16th century. In 1588 and 1597 Nicholas Yonge made them especially popular when he published a collection of Italian madrigals with English words under the title *Musica Transalpina* (Music from

across the Alps). He and his friends sang these in their homes and the finest musicians of the time began to write similar pieces for from two to six voices.

Among the greatest English composers of madrigals were Thomas Bateson, William Byrd (see BYRD, WILLIAM), Orlando Gibbons, Thomas Morley, Thomas Vautor, Thomas Weelkes and John Wilbye. In 1601 as many as 26 composers joined together to publish a set of madrigals in praise of Queen Elizabeth I. It was known as *The Triumphs of Oriana* (this was a romantic name for Queen Elizabeth) and each ended with the words, "Long live fair Oriana". Unfortunately the Queen died just before the collection was published.

The old Elizabethan madrigals are still frequently sung. The Madrigal Society, which was founded in 1741 and is the oldest English musical club, still has regular meetings. There are many other madrigal clubs at schools and universities.

MAFEKING NIGHT. At 9.35 p.m. on May 18, 1900, the news reached London that Mafeking had been relieved the day before. Mafeking, a town in the north of what was then the Cape Colony (a British colony in South Africa) had been besieged by the Boers since October 12, 1899, and had held out under the command of Colonel Robert Baden-Powell, on whom there is a separate article. Great crowds sang and cheered in the streets all over Great Britain and the Empire, and a new verb "to maffick" was invented to describe this kind of rejoicing.

MAGAZINES FOR CHILDREN have been published in England since as long ago as 1788 and they are still very popular today. Besides some magazines published monthly, there are weekly children's papers of all sorts containing stories and articles on many different subjects of interest. Many of the most popular (though not necessarily the best) of these papers are "comics" or picture papers, in which the stories are told in strips of small pictures and all the articles are very fully illustrated, usually in colour.

Certain types of articles and stories have

The Greyfriars stories of Frank Richards were published weekly in the *Magnet*.

Radio Times Hulton Picture Library

The first magazine in the English language intended for children seems to have been *The Juvenile Magazine, or an Instructive and Entertaining Miscellany for Youth of Both Sexes,* which began in 1788. Its title shows that it was a very much more serious paper than the comics of today, and in the first number the editor was careful to explain that nothing would appear in it which could possibly be disrespectful to parents or make them look ridiculous. The contents included tales, essays on such subjects as geography and natural history, puzzles, poetry, short one-act plays, pictures and four pages of news.

Eleven years later, in 1799, the first number of another magazine appeared in London, *The Children's Magazine*. It too was very serious, and in fact had fewer stories and pictures in it.

Slowly the number of magazines began to grow. In Great Britain in the first 50 years of the 19th century 21 children's magazines were published—most of them probably intended for Sunday reading—but in the next 50 years the number of new magazines increased rapidly to over 160. It was in 1862 that the first magazine to appeal specially to boys at boarding schools came out, *Every Boy's Magazine*. In the first volume there were reviews of two exceptionally popular school stories—*Tom Brown's Schooldays* and *Eric, or, Little by Little*—many articles on cricket, football, hockey and athletic sports and a serial by R. M. Ballantyne.

A very different paper was *Boys of England. A Magazine of Sport, Sensation, Fun, and Instruction*. It was a weekly paper of 16 pages, printed on thin paper and sold at one penny. The first number appeared in 1866 and contained the opening of a serial tale, *Alone in the Pirates' Lair*, that became very popular. Sensational stories, illustrated with large pictures that were even more sensational, were the chief contents of this magazine, and after only a few months 150,000 copies a week were being sold.

About the same time as *Boys of England*, two other illustrated weekly magazines appeared for younger boys and girls. They were *Chatterbox*, which cost one half-penny, and *Little Folks*, which cost one penny. In another magazine, *Young Folks*, there were tales of warlike adventure—Robert Louis Stevenson's book *Treasure*

always been popular in children's comics and magazines. They include the life stories of famous men and women, articles about sports and hobbies and illustrated explanations of how ships, aircraft, rockets and other mechanical things work. Natural history, travel and adventure, entertainment and books, and letters to the editor are other popular features. Also very popular are quizzes and competitions, as well as articles about well known sportsmen, film stars and other people in the news. There are a number of comics in which the stories are all of one type—school stories, for instance, or science fiction or westerns.

There are magazines specially designed for young children, including those too young to go to school. These contain articles telling children how to make things as well as easy-to-read stories and simple puzzles. For older children, particularly those in their teens, there are magazines which resemble magazines for adults. For example, they include articles about fashion.

Island was published as a serial in this magazine, and so were *The Black Arrow* and *Kidnapped*. Perhaps the best known magazine of all, however, the *Boy's Own Paper*, began in 1879. It was to continue for more than 70 years. Its special contents were long serials of adventure, school stories, and tales and articles about sport. The opening number contained the first of three articles entitled *How I swam the Channel*, by Captain Matthew Webb (he was the first person to do this), and in the second volume were ten articles on cricket by W. G. Grace. Many contributions were made by the author

One of the most famous magazine detectives was Sexton Blake.

T. B. Reed, including the popular school story *The Fifth Form at St. Dominic's.*

Because of the success of the *Boy's Own Paper* the publishers brought out, in 1880, a companion magazine, the *Girls' Own Paper*. To-wards the end of the 19th century, two other magazines of high standard appeared : *Chums* in 1892 and *The Captain*. *The Captain* contained school stories by P. G. Wodehouse and articles on cricket and other sports by C. B. Fry.

In the 20th century more and more new children's magazines continued to be published, although there were changes in the kind of tales that were most popular. Detectives became the fashion, the chief among them being Sexton Blake. He first appeared in 1893 in the *Halfpenny Marvel* and continued his career in several other magazines, including the *Boys' Herald,* the *Jester* and, from 1933, the *Detective Weekly*. Perhaps the most famous of all the school story characters was Billy Bunter of Greyfriars.

MAGELLAN STRAIT. The mainland of South America is separated from the island of Tierra del Fuego south of it by the bleak and stormy Magellan Strait. The strait was discovered by the Portuguese explorer Ferdinand Magellan, who thought it might be possible to reach the "spice islands" (modern Indonesia) by sailing westwards instead of eastwards. He left Spain in September 1519 and in October discovered the eastern entrance to the strait. He named the land on his left hand Tierra del Fuego, meaning "land of fire", because of the many fires seen burning ashore. It took 38 days to go through the strait to the ocean which, because of its gentle and steady winds, Magellan named the Pacific (peaceful).

Magellan was later killed in a fight with the natives in the Philippine Islands, but one of the five ships of his fleet completed the first voyage round the world and got back to Spain in September 1522.

The Magellan Strait can be divided into two parts. Coming from the Atlantic, the first part runs roughly southwest between flat, peaty shores on which large flocks of sheep are kept. Many of the sheep farms belong to British companies and are managed by Scottish shepherds. Huge quantities of wool and mutton are sent from the port of Punta Arenas (also called Magallanes), which is the only large town in the region. Soon after passing Punta Arenas the strait bends sharply to the right and runs northwest to the Pacific. This second part, although almost straight, is quite narrow in places and bordered by barren rocky islands with steep high cliffs. The strong currents, narrow channel and fierce gusts of wind make this part of the strait dangerous for sailing vessels. The sailing ships of the 19th century usually preferred to go round Cape Horn rather than through Magellan Strait, which saves only about 200 miles. (See CAPE HORN.)

The whole course of Magellan Strait lies within Chile, on which country there is a separate article. There are a few wandering tribes of American Indians in the region, but they are fast dying out.

MAGGOT.

The larvae, or young stages, of some insects are known as maggots. For example, a housefly, after hatching out of the egg, spends part of its life as a maggot. The maggot itself later turns into a pupa, or chrysalis, and finally the skin of the pupa splits and the full grown fly appears. A maggot is to a housefly, therefore, what a caterpillar is to a butterfly.

Maggots are wriggling, squirming creatures with one end tapering almost to a point. This is the head end, but the head is very small indeed, with no proper jaws. The other end of the body is broad and has two tiny black spots like eyes on it. In fact these are tiny holes through which the creature breathes.

The maggots of houseflies are usually found in manure and similar decaying matter. Bluebottles and greenbottles (which are also known as blowflies) prefer dead meat and so it is very important to keep all fish and meat in a larder covered up, so that the females of these flies cannot lay their eggs on it. Their maggots and those of houseflies are really what are known as scavengers; that is, creatures that clear away rubbish. As they have no jaws, they have to turn their food into a liquid before they can absorb it, and so they pour out what is known as a ferment from their mouths. The ferment turns the solid stuff into a kind of broth, which the maggot is then able to suck up.

Some maggots, like that of the celery-fly, are hatched from eggs that have been laid in living plants. When they hatch they begin to feed on the plants, softening the tissues by a ferment as the others do. Maggots of one kind or another spoil many plants and fruits, both by feeding on them and by making them unfit to eat because of the mess they make.

MAGI, THE.

Five or six centuries before the birth of Jesus there arose a group of priests in Persia and other parts of the East called the Magi. They were skilled in astrology (see ASTROLOGY) and in discovering the meaning of dreams.

Magi are said to have visited the baby Jesus just after He was born, having followed a star until it came to rest over the place where He lay. They brought Him gifts which were signs of what He was to become. The gold they brought was the sign that He was to be a king, the incense showed that He was the Son of God, who must be worshipped, and the myrrh foretold a life and death of suffering.

The coming of the three Magi to worship Jesus is celebrated by the Feast of the Epiphany (which means "the showing forth") on January 6. The prophet Isaiah, who lived more than 700 years before Jesus was born, had prophesied that Gentiles (non-Jews) would come to His light and that kings would approach at the time of His birth. For this reason the three Magi are often thought of as kings. They have been given the names Caspar, Melchior and Balthasar.

MAGIC

is the art by which people try to make things happen by saying certain words and making certain actions which may have no real connection with what they want done. It has been practised since very early times, and even today there are magicians and witch-doctors among primitive, or backward, peoples who make magic to bring rain or a good harvest.

The word comes from the Persian word Magus, meaning a wise man or soothsayer. We know this word in its plural form Magi, the Three Wise Men from the East who came to worship the infant Jesus.

It was by magic that man first tried to control nature. He thought this was possible because for a long time he did not know how natural events, such as storms, happen, and gave the wrong reasons for them. He might hear a bird cry in the forest just before a storm and think that the storm came because of the bird's cry so if he made a noise like a bird it would rain. Men believed that because two things looked alike there was a direct connection between them, as in the old European belief that gold will cure jaundice, because the skin of a person with jaundice is yellow, like gold.

Certain spells, which were sentences or separate words, may be recited to bring about magic. They are handed down from generation to generation with directions to repeat them absolutely correctly; failure in magic may often be explained by saying that a mistake has been made in the spell. An example of the importance of the words used in a spell occurs in the story of "Ali Baba and the Forty Thieves", when Ali Baba's brother could not get out of the thieves' cave because he had forgotten the magic words "Open Sesame!" which made the cave door open. The best-known magic word is probably *abracadabra,* which was originally Latin and was thought to cure illnesses such as fevers.

At the same time as reciting the spell the person making magic often has to perform some action. In rain-making, water is often sprinkled on the ground and drums are beaten to imitate thunder.

In many old stories, such as "Snow White and the Seven Dwarfs", "Aladdin", the fairy tales of the brothers Grimm and the stories of King Arthur and his knights, there is a witch or a wizard who has power over other people, sometimes for evil and sometimes for good. They have much in common with the witch-doctors of primitive tribes, who are usually the only ones to know the spells and rites and are much feared by the rest of the tribe. (See WITCHCRAFT.)

The spells cast by these witch-doctors often work, not because there is really such a thing as magic but because people fear the witch-doctor.

Some charms can be cast by ordinary people as well as by magicians. In many parts of the world it is believed that anyone can harm an enemy by making a model of him and burning or otherwise ill-treating it. A case has been known in which a man made a little wax model of someone he hated and, while pronouncing his name, melted the model in the fire. The enemy

wasted away and died because he was so frightened by the magic. An old Scots spell to be said when sticking pins into such a model begins, "As you waste away, may she waste away; as this wounds you, may it wound her".

Closely connected with this idea is the belief in the "evil eye". It is sometimes thought that people and animals can be injured by being looked at by someone who wishes them evil.

Some substances are said to be connected with magic. The most powerful of these is iron, which is why it is said to be lucky to have a horseshoe on the door. Amber is also considered lucky. Both iron and amber were used as charms to ward off the harmful kind of magic often called black magic, while the kind merely used to bring about help is called white magic. (See SPELLS AND CHARMS.)

Another use of magic is to make people fall in love. A Zulu will chew a piece of wood because he thinks this will soften the heart of the girl he loves. Witches and wizards had recipes to make people fall in love.

Nowadays in civilized countries the word magic is used to describe the tricks practised by conjurors and magicians to amuse people. (See CONJURING.) Belief in black and white magic tends to die out as men find out more about how the world works.

MAGISTRATE. There are two main kinds of magistrates in England. Most of them are men and women who have never studied law and are made magistrates mainly because they have done very well in some other profession or are highly thought of by the people of their town. They are helped on questions of law by their clerk, who is almost always a solicitor. They are not paid a salary for this work. There are, however, a few magistrates who are professional lawyers, chiefly barristers. When they sit as magistrates they have, generally speaking, the same powers as two or more of the other magistrates, or justices of the peace.

These professional, trained magistrates devote the whole of their working time to these duties. In the metropolitan (London) police district they are called metropolitan magistrates, and in the other large towns where such magistrates are appointed they are known as stipendiaries, from the word "stipend", meaning salary, because they are paid.

A magistrate's work mostly consists of hearing and deciding cases brought before him for decision and in committing for trial in the Crown Court (see COURTS) those people who are charged with more serious offences than the magistrate has power to deal with. But magistrates always sit with a judge of the Crown Court to hear appeals from magistrates' courts and frequently to hear other types of case.

MAGNA CARTA, or the Great Charter,
was granted by King John in June 1215, at the demand of some of his barons and bishops.

John became king in 1199, and straightway had to fight an expensive war to defend the lands in France which then belonged to the English crown. By 1204 he had lost most of these lands, but for the rest of his reign he tried, without success, to win them back. Also, from 1207 to 1213 John had a great quarrel with Pope Innocent III, which made him very unpopular with many of his subjects. This, together with the great sums of money he demanded for his wars and the cruel way he treated many English people, determined some of the great barons from the north of England to get rid of him altogether.

They took the lead because John's misbehaviour injured them particularly. They, like all the other great barons, held their lands from the King in return for various payments and services. (See FEUDALISM.) By John's time these payments and services had long been fixed by custom; in some cases they were written down in documents like royal charters (see CHARTER), but often they were unwritten, although in these cases they were carefully remembered from generation to generation. John had regularly demanded from his barons far more than he was entitled to. He did this both in matters of money and of service. He kept bishoprics and abbeys vacant so that he might receive the income of their estates for himself. When a baron died and his heir was not yet of age, John (who was by feudal custom the guardian of lands without an adult heir), ruined such lands by cutting down the trees, selling the seed corn, cattle and farm implements as well as by oppressing the peasants.

It was grievances of this sort which drove the barons to revolt, and made them determined to force John to restore what they called "their ancient and accustomed liberties". The final crisis began early in May 1215 when John told Robert Fitzwalter, who was Lord of Dunmow (Essex) and the leader of the barons, that he was prepared to grant all they asked. At this point, however, other great men, notably Stephen Langton the Archbishop of Canterbury, William Marshall the Earl of Pembroke, and Hubert de Burgh, one of John's most able and devoted servants, stepped in to reason with the barons. They persuaded the barons to make

King John met the barons at Runnymede and there had his seal attached to the Articles to show that he accepted them.

their demands less selfish by asking that the grievances of the lesser feudal lords, the towns-people and even the peasants should be dealt with as well. The result of several weeks of discussion was a document called the Articles of the Barons, which was presented to John on June 15, 1215, when he met the barons at Runnymede, a meadow on the banks of the Thames between Staines and Windsor. The King accepted the Articles and had his seal (see SEAL) attached to them to show his agreement. Then he ordered his clerks to convert the Articles into a royal charter, which we call Magna Carta. It took until June 19 to prepare the charter and write enough copies so that one could be sent to the sheriff of every county. (Four of these copies still exist. They are in the British Museum and in Lincoln and Salisbury cathedrals.)

Like the Articles, of which it is a close copy, Magna Carta itself is a very practical document, but composed in rather a hurry and not arranged in a very orderly way. Nearly half its clauses deal with the complaints of the barons, stating exactly what the King is entitled by custom to do, how much money and how much service he may demand, how he should deal with estates temporarily in his keeping, and how his judges should administer the Common Law. The rest protect the rights of the church, of townspeople and of merchants, lay down standard weights and measures for the whole kingdom, and lessen the severity of the special laws which applied to large areas called royal forests reserved for the King's hunting. Finally a committee of barons was allowed, by force if need be, to compel the King to obey the charter.

John did not keep his promises, and Magna Carta failed to achieve its purpose at the time because the barons quarrelled among themselves. Afterwards, however, it had an immense influence on English history. This was because it stated clearly that an English king could not govern as he liked. He must govern according to the law. If he broke the law then his people had a remedy: they could use force to make him behave properly. It was Magna Carta which inspired Englishmen to struggle successfully for what is called constitutional government; that is, government according to law.

MAGNESIUM. The silvery white metal called magnesium is generally used as an alloy; that is, mixed with other metals. It is important because it weighs so little, being one of the lightest of all metals. Steel is more than four times as heavy as magnesium. In the form of shavings or powder, magnesium catches fire easily and burns with a brilliant flame.

The English chemist Sir Humphry Davy, on whom there is a separate article, discovered something about magnesium as long ago as 1808, but the metal was not obtained in a pure state until 1828. Only in the 20th century, when the Germans began making it, was magnesium produced in any quantity.

Magnesium is quite common, forming about one-fiftieth of the earth's crust, but is never found in a pure state because it combines so readily with other substances. Several kinds of mineral rocks contain magnesium, among them dolomite (of which whole mountain ranges exist), magnesite and carnallite. Magnesium is also obtained from natural brine (very salt water) and can be extracted from sea water.

The extraction of magnesium is a complicated process. Magnesium chloride is obtained in the form of carnallite or by dissolving dolomite in

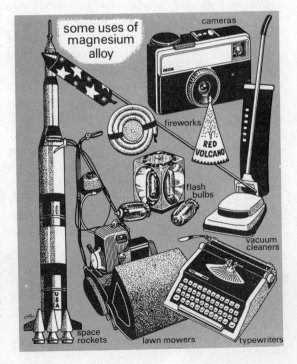

some uses of magnesium alloy

cameras

fireworks

RED VOLCANO

flash bulbs

vacuum cleaners

space rockets

lawn mowers

typewriters

acid. The molten magnesium chloride is then split up by passing a powerful electric current through it (see ELECTROLYSIS) and the magnesium is run off into moulds.

Magnesium is too soft and weak to be used by itself for making things. It is generally alloyed (mixed) with up to one-tenth its weight of aluminium to make it hard and tough, and with a small proportion of zinc or manganese which helps to protect it against being corroded, or eaten away, by sea water or salty air. Such alloys are, weight for weight, as strong as steel. Because of their lightness, magnesium alloys are much used in aircraft, guided missiles, spacecraft, computers, high-speed machinery and in the frames and bodies of buses and lorries; also in vacuum cleaners, cameras and many other goods. They are also used for making bobbins, spools and other parts of high-speed textile machinery. The flash bulbs that are used for taking photographs indoors contain magnesium and aluminium foil. Magnesium powder is used in fireworks and signalling flares.

Magnesium salts, or chemical mixtures of magnesium and other substances, are often used in medicines. One of these is "Epsom salts", a form of magnesium sulphate which has been used to overcome constipation for about 400 years. Another is "milk of magnesia" which contains magnesium hydroxide. A paste of magnesium oxide and chloride sets to a hard white mass and is used as a stopping for teeth. Magnesium oxide is commonly used in industry for lining furnaces and for lagging (coating) steam and hot water pipes to prevent loss of heat.

MAGNETIC POLES.

The two points on the Earth to which the needle of a magnetic compass turns are called the magnetic poles. As they are not in the same places as the North and South Poles, it follows that the needle of a compass does not point truly north and south. Actually the north magnetic pole is in Viscount Melville Sound between Bathurst and Prince of Wales islands in the Arctic Archipelago. The south magnetic pole lies not far from the coast of Antarctica in the Australian Antarctic Territory. The magnetic poles change their positions slowly.

As long ago as 1600 the English doctor and scientist William Gilbert (1544–1603) showed that the Earth must be a magnet with one pole in the Arctic region and the other in the Antarctic. The north magnetic pole was reached in 1831 by the British explorer James Clark Ross (1800–1862). At that time it was in the Boothia Peninsula of the Canadian mainland. Ross later tried to reach the south magnetic pole during his Antarctic expedition of 1839–1843. He failed to reach it but his observations gave its position fairly closely. In Ernest Shackleton's British Antarctic Expedition the south magnetic pole was reached in 1909 after a sledge journey by T. W. Edgeworth David and Douglas Mawson.

The angle between the direction in which the

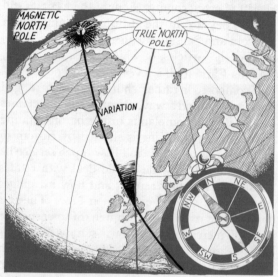

A compass needle points to the north magnetic pole.

magnetic compass needle points and true north is called the variation and differs from place to place. In Great Britain the variation (which is marked on all charts) is roughly 7 degrees west of true north.

MAGNETISM

is the word used to describe magnets and their working. The word magnet comes from Magnesia, the name of a place near Aydin in Turkey where the mineral lodestone is found as a natural magnet. Most magnets are not natural but have to be made. The ancient Greeks knew that a lump of lodestone would pick up and support pieces of iron, but every magnet has other important properties as well. If a piece of iron or steel is stroked with a magnet it becomes a magnet itself. (The stroking must, however, be in one direction only.) Another fact is that every magnet has what are called *poles*, which are points where the magnetism is strongest. If a straight bar magnet is dipped into iron filings (powdered iron) they will cling thickly

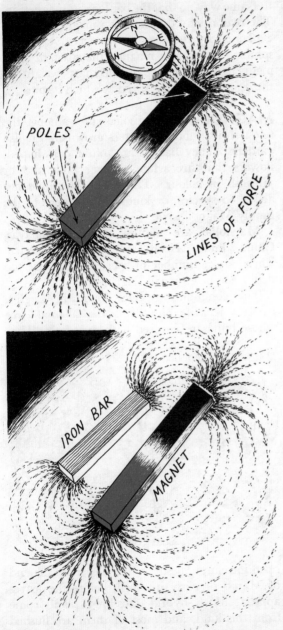

POLES

LINES OF FORCE

IRON BAR

MAGNET

near the ends but not at all in the middle. Next, a magnet has the important property of pointing north and south when hung up or floated so as to be free to turn. (See COMPASS.)

If two magnets hung so that they can turn freely are brought close together, the two north-pointing poles (usually called simply "north poles") swing away from each other, but the north pole of one swings towards the south pole of the other. This can be expressed shortly by saying that "unlike poles attract each other but like poles push each other apart". A final property of a magnet is that if it is cut into pieces, each piece becomes a little magnet with its own north and south poles.

In 1600 William Gilbert, court physician to Queen Elizabeth I, wrote a book in which he concluded that the earth itself was a huge magnet, with its poles at the north and south ends. He was almost right, except that the earth's magnetic poles are not at the true North and South Poles. (See MAGNETIC POLES.)

If a sheet of paper is laid down on a bar magnet and sprinkled with iron filings, the filings will arrange themselves in a pattern of lines called "lines of force". These lines do not cross each other anywhere and their direction at any point shows the direction in which the magnetic force is acting. If a small magnetic compass is put down on the paper, its needle will point in the direction of the line of force beneath it. The spacing of the lines of force indicates the strength of the magnetic force, which is strongest where they are closely crowded together. The whole region covered by the lines of force is called the "magnetic field". If a piece of soft iron is put down on the paper the lines of force near it crowd together so as to pass through it, as it forms an easier path for them than the surrounding air. For this reason, soft iron can be used to screen an instrument from magnetic effects.

All the effects of magnetism described above could be shown with a piece of lodestone, but lodestone is never used for magnets nowadays. For centuries they were made by stroking a piece of iron or steel with a lodestone, until in 1820 Hans Christian Oersted, a Dane, discovered by chance that a freely hung magnetic needle was disturbed when brought near a wire carrying an

Iron filings sprinkled near a magnet arrange themselves in a pattern of lines of force. The pictures show experiments to make with the help of a compass and a soft iron bar.

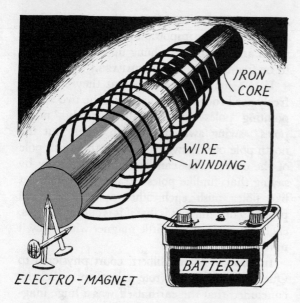

ELECTRO - MAGNET

Magnetizing an iron bar by means of an electric current.

electric current. This discovery that magnetism had something to do with electricity paved the way for the electro-magnet, on which there is a separate article. An electro-magnet can be made by winding wire in a coil round a bar or rod of iron or steel and sending an electric current from a battery through the wire. The strength of the magnet increases with the number of turns in the coil and with the amount of electric current.

A hard steel rod used as the core of an electro-magnet keeps its magnetism after the electric current has been switched off, but a soft iron core loses its magnetism as soon as the current stops. Permanent magnets, which have no wires attached, are therefore made either of hard steel or of alloys (mixtures) of metals that hold magnetism well; among these is alnico, an alloy of cobalt, nickel, aluminium and copper. Permanent magnets are used in magnetos, small machines which when turned produce a high-voltage electric current for making a spark. (Magnetos are used instead of induction coils for providing the ignition, or spark, in some petrol engines; see INTERNAL COMBUSTION ENGINE.)

Magnetism has been explained by saying that every molecule, or particle, of a steel bar is itself a magnet, but that ordinarily these tiny magnets are lying about in all directions and cancel out each other's magnetism. When, however, the

bar is magnetized, the molecular magnets face the same way like soldiers at drill, with the north pole of one towards the south pole of the next. When all the molecules are lined up, the steel bar is magnetized as strongly as is possible. If the bar is hammered or vibrated or made very hot, its molecules are disturbed and no longer face the same way, so that the bar loses its magnetism. The reason why the earth is a magnet has been explained by the theory that every very large spinning object is a magnet, the strength of its magnetism depending on the mass (weight) of the object and on the speed at which it spins.

MAGNOLIA. Magnolias are among the finest shrubs and small trees grown in English gardens. They have large, often cup-shaped, flowers that are white, cream, pink, red or purplish in colour. The genus *Magnolia* has about 80 species, or kinds, and belongs to the family Magnoliaceae.

Magnolias are natives of the Himalayas, China, Japan, North and Central America. There are a number of species which are too delicate to be grown in England.

The commonest species found in English gardens is *Magnolia denudata*, a small tree whose buds are covered with grey hair. They

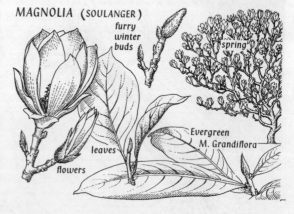

MAGNOLIA (SOULANGER)

furry winter buds

spring

Evergreen M. Grandiflora

leaves

flowers

open into large, fleshy, white flowers at the end of March or early in April, before the leaves appear. Many hybrid (crossbred) plants come from this kind, and most of them are flushed with purple at the base of the petals.

Magnolia campbellii from the Himalayas takes many years to flower. The blossoms are from 15 to 25 centimetres across, pale pink outside and deep red within. *Magnolia stellata* from Japan is a shrub with sweet-smelling white flowers that later turn pink. *Magnolia grandiflora* has fine evergreen leaves and large white flowers.

MAGPIE.

MAGPIE. A handsome and graceful member of the crow family is the magpie. Its head, neck, back, long wedge-shaped tail and part of the wings are glossy black and the rest of the wings and underparts are white. The length is about 45 centimetres.

The magpie is a noisy bird with a loud, chattering call. It feeds on the ground, usually on insects, but it also takes the eggs and young of other birds in spring. It flies rather slowly. When it alights it raises its tail to balance itself.

The magpie nests in trees or bushes. The nest is large and bulky, made of sticks and lined with earth and fine roots. There is a dome of sticks over the top and an entrance hole at the side. The hen lays five to eight eggs, greenish in colour with brown markings. When fledged, the young birds are less glossy than their parents and have short tails. Young magpies are easily tamed and make amusing pets.

The magpie is common in most parts of the

The magpie uses its long tail to balance itself.

British Isles, on the continent of Europe and in western North America. There are several different kinds in India, the handsomest being the green magpie, or hunting crow.

Superstitious people think it unlucky to see a single magpie, from the old rhyme :

> One for sorrow, two for joy,
> Three for a girl, four for a boy,
> Five for silver, six for gold,
> And seven for a secret that's never been told.

MAHOGANY.

MAHOGANY. Many fine pieces of furniture are made of mahogany, a glossy, reddish-brown wood. Mahogany trees were discovered on the islands of the West Indies by early Spanish explorers. The Spaniards used the wood to repair their ships, and so did Sir Walter Raleigh in 1595, but its value for furniture-making was not realized until the early 18th

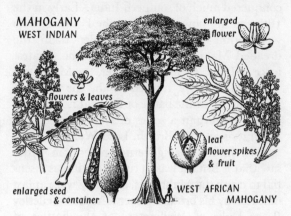

MAHOGANY WEST INDIAN

enlarged flower

flowers & leaves

leaf flower spikes & fruit

enlarged seed & container

WEST AFRICAN MAHOGANY

century. Then Dr. Gibbons of Covent Garden in London had a candle box made from the wood, and by 1750 Thomas Chippendale was using mahogany to make some of the most beautiful and elegant furniture ever produced. Besides its beauty, mahogany is strong and does not warp (lose its shape).

The mahogany tree (*Swietenia* is its Latin name) is tall, with large pinnate (feather-shaped) leaves and small flowers. The fruits are woody and split open to release winged seeds.

In the second half of the 19th century so many of the mahogany trees of the West Indies were cut down that attention was turned to the mahogany trees growing in Central America. (These trees are a different kind but belong to the same family.) Then large quantities of wood from trees of the mahogany family were brought to Great Britain from Nigeria, the Gold Coast (now Ghana) and other West African countries.

The African trees are often well over 30 metres high, with trunks measuring up to 2·5 metres across. At the bases of the trunks a series of flattened supports grow out which help to support the weight of the tree. The timber used from these trees is called African mahogany.

MAHRATTAS.

MAHRATTAS. The Mahrattas (or Mara-thas) are a people of central India found be-tween Gwalior in the north and Goa in the south. They are Hindus and have their own language, and although most of them are simple peasants they have a warlike past. Their great leader was Sivaji Bhonsla (1627–1680) who united the Mahratta chiefs and with their help conquered much of southern India. Early in the 18th century power passed to the Peshwas, who were prime ministers, and under them the dreaded Mahratta horsemen were the greatest force in India. In 1761, however, the Mahrattas were defeated by Ahmed Shah, the ruler of Afghanistan, at the battle of Panipat near Delhi.

In 1779 began a series of wars between the Mahrattas and the British. Lord Wellesley, who arrived in India as governor-general in 1798, saw that if Britain was to rule there it was essen-tial to crush the Mahrattas, and they were at last defeated by his brother General Arthur Wellesley (later Duke of Wellington) at the battles of Assaye and Argaum in 1803. As a result of these victories and others by General Gerard Lake in the same year, much of the Mahratta lands was taken by the British. The former Mahratta states, all of which were under British control by the middle of the 19th century, were Indore, Nagpur, Gwalior and Baroda. They are now part of the states of Madhya Pradesh, Gujarat and Maharashtra.

MAIDENHAIR FERN.

MAIDENHAIR FERN. The common maidenhair is one of the ferns, a large family of plants with no flowers (see FERN). Raindrops run off the leaves of the maidenhair and this is why the genus, or group, to which it belongs has been given the name *Adiantum*, which comes

Maidenhair fern has spreading, hair-like branches.

from a rare Greek word meaning "dry". The name of common maidenhair is *Capillus Veneris,* or "hair of Venus". (Venus was the Roman goddess of beauty.) Common maiden-hair can be grown outside in warm parts of Eng-land, but is usually grown under glass. It is much used in bouquets and wreaths.

There are many other kinds of maidenhair, mostly from warm countries such as Brazil, Peru, Mexico, Australia and New Zealand. Some have rosy leaves and there are a few rare gold and silvery ones.

MAIDENHAIR TREE.

MAIDENHAIR TREE. The ginkgo, or maidenhair tree, is the one living member of a great family of trees that grew all over the world

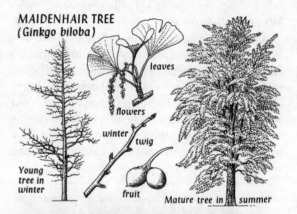

MAIDENHAIR TREE
(*Ginkgo biloba*)
leaves
flowers
winter
twig
Young tree in winter
fruit
Mature tree in summer

in the far-off days of the dinosaurs (see PRE-HISTORIC ANIMALS). The trees in a small grove in China are the only wild maidenhair trees known. In Japan they are grown in temple gardens, and they are cultivated as ornamental trees in Europe and North America.

The living tree, like the ancient ones, has fan-shaped leaves like those of the maidenhair fern. (Ginkgo is the Chinese name.) Far from being a fern, however, it is related to pines and spruces, although it sheds its leaves in winter. There is only one species, or kind, but there are several varieties of it. Some maidenhair trees are narrow and spire-like in shape, some have spreading branches and some droop like willows. They sometimes grow 30 metres tall.

Each maidenhair tree has either male or female flowers. The yellow fruit, which looks like a small plum, has a kernel that is edible.

MAIZE. In America maize is called corn, and in South Africa it is known as mealies. Maize was first cultivated by the American Indians and formed their main cereal food.

Maize plants grow very tall, sometimes as much as 3 metres high. Large grains, generally yellow in colour when ripe, are set closely round a swollen stem known as the cob. A sheath, called the husk, covers the cob and grains. Some kinds of maize have grains that are especially sweet when not fully grown. These are known as

A ripe cob of maize.

sweet corn and are cooked and eaten "on the cob" with butter.

About half of the world's crop of maize grain is grown on the fertile soils of the midwestern states of North America, where there is plenty of sunshine as well as frequent summer rains and warm nights. Most of this crop is fed to farm animals. In Italy, parts of eastern Europe, India, China, Egypt and South Africa, many people live mainly on maize, and the same applies to Central America and Brazil.

Maize grains are made into cornflakes, corn starch for custards and blancmanges, gum for postage stamps and envelopes, alcohol and some chemicals. Paper can be made from the long plant stems, and the cobs can be used as fuel or made into cheap tobacco pipes.

MALAGASY REPUBLIC. Situated in the Indian Ocean south of the equator about 400 kilometres east of southern Africa, the Malagasy Republic occupies the island of Madagascar. (See MADAGASCAR.) The island, one of the largest in the world, is nearly 1,600 kilometres long from north to south. It is sometimes called the "Red Island" because of its red clay soil.

A mountain range runs parallel to the east coast and the larger rivers flow westwards to a wide, grassy coastal plain. The climate is hot and steamy near the coast but cooler in the central highlands. Rainfall is heaviest in the east, where very dense tropical forests grow. The island is the chief home of the lemurs (see MONKEY). Other wild animals include civet cats, crocodiles, many kinds of birds and more than 800 kinds of butterflies.

The people, known as the Malagasy, are a mixture of Africans and Indonesians who came by sea long ago. They have their own language, a soft and musical one called Merina. About half of them are Christians, though there are some Moslems in the northwest; the rest are pagans.

Most of the people are peasants who grow crops and raise cattle. The chief crops are rice, millet, vegetables, fruit and a root called manioc. Coffee, vanilla, cloves, tobacco, sugar and bananas are exported Most of the cattle are humped oxen called zebus which are used both for ploughing and as meat. The women spin and weave silk and cotton and make beautiful mats, baskets and hats from palm leaves and fibre. The chief minerals are graphite and mica, and there are factories making sugar and canning meat.

Paul Popper
Old eggs of giant ostriches are still found on Madagascar, though these birds have been extinct for centuries.

MALARIA

Locator map of Malagasy Republic.

The republic has motor roads linking the principal centres. Diégo-Suarez in the north is one of the best natural harbours in the world but is too far from the centre to be much use, and most shipping uses the port of Tamatave on the east coast. It is connected by rail with the capital, Antananarivo, a city built on a ridge rising from the rice plains. Airlines link Antananarivo with Paris and there are several local air services.

In the years around 1700 Madagascar was the haunt of pirates, including Captain William Kidd. At the beginning of the 19th century the Hova tribe founded the kingdom of Madagascar, but the French took possession of the island in 1895. In 1960 it became the independent Malagasy Republic, remaining a member of the French Community.

FACTS ABOUT THE MALAGASY REPUBLIC

AREA: 586,486 square kilometres.
POPULATION: 7,424,000.
KIND OF COUNTRY: Independent republic. A member of the French Community.
CAPITAL: Antananarivo.
GEOGRAPHICAL FEATURES: A central plateau with mountains up to 2,885 metres high is surrounded by central plains.
CHIEF PRODUCTS: Coffee, rice, sugar, tobacco, vanilla, meat, hides, graphite, mica.
IMPORTANT TOWNS: Antananarivo, Tamatave, Majunga, Fianarantsoa, Diégo-Suarez, Tulear.
EDUCATION: Children must attend school between the ages of 6 and 14.

MALARIA is one of the commonest of all diseases, especially near tropical rivers and coasts. During an attack the patient becomes extremely cold and shivers violently, then grows hot and feverish and develops pains, and then sweats a great deal, after which he begins to get better. The worst thing about malaria is that it keeps coming back.

Once it was thought that malaria was caused by bad air from marshes, and the name malaria is from the Italian words *mal aria*, meaning "bad air". In fact, however, it is caused by a germ carried by an insect, the *Anopheles* mosquito, which spreads the illness by biting people.

When the *Anopheles* bites a person ill with malaria, at a certain stage some forms of the germ go into its stomach, along with the person's blood. In the body of the mosquito, mainly in its stomach, the germ goes through a cycle (the period taken to complete its development) and it cannot go through the cycle anywhere else. If the mosquito later bites another person, the germ is injected into that person's blood and he gets malaria. While a person has malaria he is often bitten by another mosquito, and the whole cycle starts all over again.

The germ was discovered in the blood of malaria patients by Alphonse Laveran, a Frenchman, in 1880. Ronald Ross, an English doctor, noticed that people did not seem to catch malaria from each other, and he suspected that the *Anopheles* carried the germ. To prove this he made experiments in the Roman Campagna (the plains surrounding Rome) where *Anopheles* was common. Healthy people spent the day among malaria patients, and at night they re-

Planet News

Spraying D.D.T. in a breeding-place of mosquitoes.

tired to screened houses. None caught malaria. Then two men in England allowed themselves to be bitten by *Anopheles* brought from the Campagna, after they had bitten malaria patients. The men developed malaria.

The best way of getting rid of malaria is by waging war on the *Anopheles* mosquito. The swamps, stagnant pools, rain barrels, water-filled cans and other places in which the female mosquitoes lay their eggs are drained whenever possible. Another way of killing the insect is to pour oil on the pools where it breeds, for the larvae (young) rise to the surface for air and they cannot breathe through the oil. D.D.T. and similar chemicals have proved very valuable in keeping down the number of mosquitoes and scientists are now experimenting with biological methods of control, that is, sterilizing the mosquitoes so that they do not breed.

The best medicine for curing an attack of malaria used to be quinine (see QUININE). In World War II Japan captured nearly all the world's sources of quinine and chemists in Britain and the United States had to produce substitutes such as Atabrin. Nowadays doctors are able to treat cases with modern drugs, although there are still many thousands of deaths from malaria each year.

MALAWI is a landlocked republic in south-east Africa. It is bounded south and east by Mozambique, west by Zambia and north by Tanzania. It is a narrow country, about 900 kilometres long and 160 kilometres wide. Most of Malawi lies in the Great Rift Valley, which runs from north to south and contains Lake Malawi (formerly Lake Nyasa), the third largest lake in Africa. The Shire River flows from the southern end of the lake and joins the Zambezi River in Mozambique. In the north Nyika plateau rises to 2,400 metres and in the south is Mount Mlanje (3,013 metres), the highest point.

Malawi lies within the tropics but on the Nyika plateau frost is not uncommon in July. There is a rainy season from November to April and it is driest and coolest from May to August. The higher areas are largely scattered and open woodland, but where rainfall is heavy grow forests of cedars and hardwood trees. Animals include elephants, lions, cheetahs, leopards, jackals and deer; and hippopotamuses in Lake Malawi. Reptiles, fish, birds and insects abound.

The people are mostly Bantu (see RACES AND PEOPLES) with a few Europeans and Asians. Most of the population live in the south and are farmers. More than enough food is produced for the country's needs. The chief crops are tea and tobacco, grown on plantations. Groundnuts, maize, rice and cotton are also grown, and exports include coffee, vanilla and sugar. Cattle, sheep, pigs and goats are kept. There are also fishing and timber industries and Malawi contains a variety of minerals, although few are mined. Malawi's light industries include the production of cement, bricks, cigarettes, soap, clothing and furniture. Because the country is still under-developed many people seek work in neighbouring countries. For economic reasons Malawi has friendly relations with South Africa, unlike most independent African states.

The chief towns are Zomba, the capital; Lilongwe (planned to become the capital); and Blantyre City, which is much the largest. More than 600,000 children attend primary schools. The University of Malawi is at Limbe.

Malawi is linked by road with Zambia and by road and rail with Mozambique and Rhodesia. A steamer service on Lake Malawi crosses to Tanzania and there are airports at Blantyre-Limbe, Lilongwe and other towns.

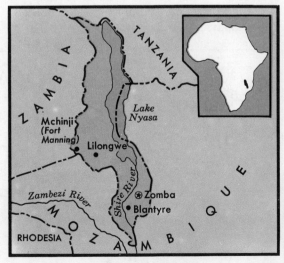

Locator map of Malawi.

MALAYSIA

FACTS ABOUT MALAWI

AREA: 118,484 square kilometres.
POPULATION: 4,552,000.
KIND OF COUNTRY: Independent republic. Member of the Commonwealth of Nations.
GEOGRAPHICAL FEATURES: A plateau country lying to the west of Lake Malawi in the Great Rift Valley.
CHIEF PRODUCTS: Tea, tobacco, groundnuts, cotton, coffee, sugar, rice.
IMPORTANT TOWNS: Zomba, Lilongwe, Blantyre City.
EDUCATION: School attendance is not compulsory.

History

In 1859 the Scottish missionary doctor David Livingstone (see LIVINGSTONE) reached Lake Nyasa. He was followed by other missionaries and by traders, hunters and farmers, mostly from Britain. In 1891 Britain established a protectorate, which in 1907 was named Nyasaland. In 1953 the country was joined with Northern and Southern Rhodesia to form the Federation of Rhodesia and Nyasaland, but because of African opposition the Federation was dissolved in 1963. In 1964 Britain granted Nyasaland independence under the name of Malawi. In 1966 Malawi became a republic, remaining a member of the Commonwealth.

MALAYSIA is an independent federation of states in southeast Asia and a member of the Commonwealth of Nations. It consists of West Malaysia on the Malay Peninsula (the southernmost part of mainland Asia) and East Malaysia in the northern part of the island of Borneo. West Malaysia consists of the states of Pahang, Trengganu, Kedah, Johore, Negri Sembilan, Kelantan, Selangor, Perak, Perlis, Penang and Malacca. East Malaysia consists of the states of Sabah and Sarawak.

A backbone of mountains zigzags down the Malay Peninsula with streams and rivers running to the sea on either side. The east coast has beaches of silvery sand backed by palm trees, and a number of lovely islands off shore. On the west coast, rivers flow sluggishly to the Straits of Malacca through mangrove swamps. Sarawak, on the northwest coast of Borneo, consists of a swampy coastal plain, with rolling hills and many rivers, backed by mountains to the south. Sabah, to the north, is also mountainous, and contains the highest peak in southeast Asia, Mount Kinabalu (4,100 metres). The eastern coastline is swampy but on the west is a fertile plain. Several deep bays provide good harbours. Malaysia's climate is tropical.

More than half of West Malaysia is covered by rain forest, in which grow many kinds of evergreen trees, bamboos, creepers and tropical plants, including about 800 kinds of orchid. (See RAIN FOREST.) Wild animals include elephants, rhinoceroses, tigers, leopards, apes and monkeys. In the forests live the giant bats called flying foxes, as well as flying squirrels, lemurs and lizards which can glide from tree to tree. Crocodiles infest the mangrove swamps and in the jungle live snakes such as the python and king cobra. In Sabah and Sarawak there are more than 150 kinds of snake, as well as lizards, crocodiles and many brilliantly coloured birds. There

MALAYSIA

Left and right: Paul Popper. Centre: Malaysia House

Peoples of Malaysia. Left: Malay fisher lad. Centre: Chinese farmer. Right: Dayak hunter.

are also vast numbers of insects and fish.

In West Malaysia about half the people are Malay, one-third are Chinese and about one-tenth are Indians or Pakistanis. In East Malaysia, Dayaks and Chinese form the largest groups, followed by Malays. The national language is Malay, but Chinese and Indian dialects are common, as is English. All Malays are Moslems, but there is freedom of worship in all religions. Malaysia spends one-fifth of its annual budget on education and more than 2,000,000 children attend school. Primary education is given in four languages: Malay, English, Chinese and Tamil. The University of Malaysia is at Kuala Lumpur, the federal capital. A Malay national university is to be set up, as well as a university college at Penang.

Kuala Lumpur is a pleasant city of modern buildings, about 48 kilometres from Klang (formerly Port Swettenham). The next largest city is Penang (formerly George Town). The chief ports are Penang, Klang and Malacca.

Malaysia's economy is based mainly on the production of rubber, timber and tin, its chief exports. More than one-third of the world's natural rubber comes from West Malaysia. This is the chief crop, employing about 300,000 people, mainly Indians and Chinese, in vast plantations. Much rubber is also produced by smallholders.

About one-third of the world's tin also comes from West Malaysia, the richest field being in the Kinta Valley in Perak State. Most of the mines are worked by Chinese. Other minerals include bauxite (see BAUXITE) and iron ore.

Second in importance to rubber as a crop is rice, and in recent years farmers have been able greatly to increase their harvest by using better methods of cultivation and new varieties of seed. Yet Malaysia still produces less food than it needs and has to import supplies. Coconuts are grown both as food and for their oil, and other crops are sweet potatoes, sago, tobacco, hemp, cocoa, pepper and sugar cane. There are pineapple plantations and citrus fruits are also grown. Chinese market gardeners produce vegetables for local communities and dairy cattle, buffaloes, pigs and poultry are kept. The rivers and sea provide a good supply of fish, and timber from the rain forests is a valuable export, especially from Sarawak and Sabah.

Malaysia is connected by rail with Singapore and Thailand and there is an excellent internal transport system. East Malaysia has good roads connecting the large cities and towns, and river transport is important. There are a number of airports, the chief being the international airport of Kuala Lumpur at Subang.

History

Before European expansion into southeast Asia, what is now West Malaysia was composed of small tribal states which were at first subject to Thailand but later independent. In the 14th century the Malays founded a kingdom centred in Malacca. The Portuguese were the first Europeans to reach the area and in 1511 they conquered Malacca and drove the Malays south.

Courtesy, Malaysian High Commission

West Malaysia produces more than one-third of the world's supply of tin. Here a giant dredger digs tin-bearing soil from the bed of a river.

The English and Dutch were eager to share in the enormous profits made by the Portuguese from the spice trade, and in 1641 the Dutch captured Malacca from the Portuguese.

By the middle of the 18th century the British in India had developed an important trade with China, especially in tea. British ships sailing to China through the Strait of Malacca needed a base in the Malay Peninsula where they could go for repair and take on supplies. In 1786, therefore, Francis Light of the East India Company leased the island of Penang from the Sultan of Kedah. Penang became a thriving port and a serious rival to Dutch trade. After Napoleon Bonaparte had seized the Dutch homeland British influence in southeast Asia increased as that of the Dutch waned. In 1819 the British began to take over Singapore. In 1824 they signed a treaty of friendship with their Dutch rivals, in which Britain kept Malacca in exchange for Sumatra. For some years the British government showed little interest in the Malay Peninsula, beyond keeping out other European nations. But gradually the Malay states were brought under British control and their rulers given British residents to advise them. In this way the states of Perak, Selangor, Negri Sembilan, Pahang, Johore, Kedah, Perlis, Kelantan and Trengganu came under British protection,

although they were never claimed as British territory. Thus all of what is now West Malaysia came under British control, as well as Singapore.

During the 17th century, northern Borneo (present-day Sabah) belonged to the Sultan of Brunei. In return for services to him this region was later given to the Sultan of Sulu in the Philippines. When the British captured Manila in 1762, they released the Sultan of Sulu, who had become a prisoner of the Spanish. In gratitude, the Sultan transferred his rights in North Borneo to the British East India Company.

In 1840 an Englishman, James Brooke, assisted the Sultan of Brunei in crushing a revolt. As a reward, Brooke was made rajah, or ruler, of Sarawak in 1841. By 1888 both North Borneo and Sarawak were British protectorates. In 1946 they became British Crown colonies.

During World War II Malaya, North Borneo and Sarawak were conquered by the Japanese. When the British returned to Malaya after the war their first proposals for self-government were turned down by the people. In 1948 new proposals were accepted and the Malay states became the Federation of Malaya. Britain retained control over defence and foreign affairs. By 1960 the British, with the help of Commonwealth and Malayan troops and police, succeeded in crushing a Communist rising.

In 1957 Malaya became independent. Singapore, North Borneo and Sarawak remained still under British control, but then the people

FACTS ABOUT MALAYSIA

AREA: 329,736 square kilometres.

POPULATION: 10,452,000.

KIND OF COUNTRY: Independent federation consisting of the 11 states on the Malay Peninsula (West Malaysia) and the states of Sarawak and Sabah in northern Borneo (East Malaysia). Member of the Commonwealth of Nations.

CAPITAL: Kuala Lumpur.

GEOGRAPHICAL FEATURES: A backbone mountain range runs through West Malaysia with coastal plains on each side. In East Malaysia, Sabah is mountainous with fertile uplands and Sarawak has a mountainous interior.

CHIEF PRODUCTS: Rubber, rice, coconut oil, copra, pineapples, sago, tapioca, tin, iron ore, timber, pepper.

IMPORTANT TOWNS: Kuala Lumpar, Penang, Port Klang, Ipoh, Malacca, Sandakan, Kota Kinabalu, Kuching.

EDUCATION: Children must attend school between the ages of 6 and 15.

Water transport plays an important part in Malaysia.

states of Malaya, Singapore, Sarawak and Sabah, was founded. In 1965 Singapore left the Federation. After the overthrow of President Sukarno of Indonesia peaceful relations were restored between Malaysia and Indonesia.

MALDIVE ISLANDS. In the Indian Ocean southwest of Ceylon are the 2,000 coral islands which make up the Maldive Republic, the smallest member state of the United Nations. The people are Moslems and their chief occupation is fishing. The islands were under British protection from 1887 to 1965 and Britain still maintains an R.A.F. airfield on Gan, which is also a Commonwealth military communications centre and a ground station for Britain's Skynet satellite communications system. The capital of the republic is Male and the population is 114,469.

wished to join Malaya. In 1963, after much opposition from the Philippines and Indonesia, the Federation of Malaysia, consisting of the 11

MALI. The inland Republic of Mali in west Africa is nearly four times the size of the British Isles. The northern part merges into the Sahara

The design of the huts built by the Dogon people of Mali has probably remained unchanged for centuries.

Desert. Mali is bordered to the north by Algeria, to the west by Mauritania, Senegal and Guinea, to the south by the Ivory Coast and Upper Volta and to the east by Niger. It is a mainly flat country, with the vast plains of the Tanezrouft and Taoudenni to the north and those of Meriyé and Azaouak to the south. The only hilly region lies in the east, where the Adrar des Iforas rises 885 metres above the plains. This is a moister region with pastures suitable for cattle rearing. The climate of Mali is tropical and there is no real winter. The hot, dusty wind called the harmattan blows during the dry season (November to April). Wildlife includes lions, hippopotamuses and antelopes.

Most of the settlements in the south are on or near the Niger River. The people are mostly Negroes and live by farming and by rearing sheep and cattle. In the north are nomadic (wandering) tribes of Tuareg and Moors, who keep herds of cattle and camels. Most of the people are Moslems.

The main food crops are millet, rice, sorghum and corn, but groundnuts and cotton are also grown and sold abroad. Meat and fish are exported to neighbouring countries. Leather and hides are sent abroad, mainly to France.

The capital is Bamako, the main trading centre, which is linked by rail with the port of Dakar in Senegal. Other towns are Timbuktu, Kayes, Mopti, Segou, Sikassu and Gao. The Niger and other rivers are important as means of communication although the road system is being improved.

Mali was the name of the Moslem empire which in the middle ages covered much of West Africa. In the 19th century most of this territory came under French rule. The Mali Federation was formed in 1959 between the former French territories of Senegal and Sudan. Senegal left the federation in 1960 and Sudan became the Republic of Mali.

The population of Mali is 5,031,500.

MALLOW.

Along roadsides and in most waste places in Great Britain the common mallow, with its pale reddish-mauve flowers, and the dwarf mallow, with its pale bluish flowers, are found in the summer. The common

The common mallow has pale reddish-mauve flowers.

mallow grows about two feet high while the dwarf one creeps along the ground. The flowers of the common mallow have five heart-shaped petals; they grow in clusters and are cross-pollinated. The petals of the dwarf mallow are notched and the flower is self-pollinated.

Both plants have long-stalked leaves. Their fruits are round. Both mallows make honey in little pockets covered with hairs.

Another kind is the musk mallow, which has deeply divided leaves and large rose-coloured or white flowers crowded together at the tops of the stems. It grows in dry meadows and hedgerows in central and southern Europe. The tree mallow with its pale purple flowers and the rose mallow, or hibiscus, which has large and splendid flowers, are often grown in gardens.

MALT

is the main substance used for brewing beer and is usually made from barley. The barley is first soaked in water for about two days to make it ready to germinate, or sprout. Then it is spread out on the malting floor. Rootlets appear at one end of the grain and the beginnings of the young plant can be seen growing along the grain under the husk. After 10 or 12 days on the floor, and before the tip of the new plant emerges from the husk, the barley is converted into malt by being put into a kiln and dried with hot air to prevent it from growing any more. When the grain begins to sprout, chemical changes take place inside it which produce sugar and other substances needed by the young plant. These are used in beer and whisky. Growth is stopped as soon as the chemical changes have taken place and before the young plant has a chance to use up the substances they produce.

The barley remains in the kiln for about four days, the temperature of the kiln varying according to the type of malt required. Then the rootlets are removed and the malt is stored for use.

Other methods of malting are called drum and box malting, when the grains are grown in large drums or in long boxes. The buildings in which malt is made are called maltings. Malt is used mainly in making beer, for the malt extract familiar to children and for malted milk drinks.

MALTA is an island in the middle of the Mediterranean Sea, about 96 kilometres south of Sicily. Together with the other Maltese islands of Gozo and Comino it is somewhat smaller than the Isle of Wight. Seen from the air Malta is yellow, for it is composed of soft honey-coloured rock and has little soil. The north and east coasts have a number of bays and natural harbours, including the bay where St. Paul is said to have been shipwrecked. There are hills in the southwest but they are not high. Malta has a pleasant warm climate but little rain falls and there are no rivers and few trees. Instead of hedges there are stone walls and the square, flat-roofed houses are built of the yellow limestone which is so soft that it can easily be pared with a knife or sawn.

The Maltese are a people of mixed blood (mostly Italian), of middle height and sturdily built, with dark hair and eyes. Their skins are

FACTS ABOUT MALTA

AREA: Malta 246 square kilometres, Gozo 67 square kilometres, Comino 3 square kilometres.
POPULATION: 322,000.
KIND OF COUNTRY: Independent member country of the Commonwealth of Nations.
CAPITAL: Valletta.
GEOGRAPHICAL FEATURES: Malta consists of a plateau which descends by gentle steps to a plain in the southeast. The coast is rocky with many inlets.
CHIEF PRODUCTS: Wheat, barley, potatoes, vegetables.
CHIEF EXPORTS: Clothing, manufactured goods, potatoes, textiles.
IMPORTANT TOWNS: Valletta, Sliema, Pawla (with Tarxien), Hamrun, Birkirkara.
EDUCATION: Children must attend school between the ages of 6 and 14.

somewhat fairer than those of southern Italians. They are thrifty, hard working and good-natured although quick of temper. They have large families and are devoted to their children. Nearly all of them are Roman Catholics. Although the Maltese wear modern European

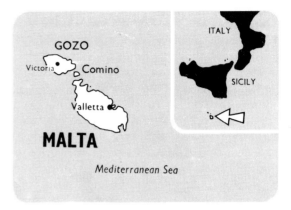

clothes, a few of the country women still wear the national head-dress called the faldetta, like a nun's veil made of black silk stiffened with whalebone. The Maltese language is Arabic in origin but it has many Sicilian words. Many of the people speak English as well as Maltese. Children must attend school between the ages of 6 and 14. There are a number of secondary and private schools and Malta has its own university.

The capital of Malta is Valletta, built on a steep peninsula which divides in two the magnificent Grand Harbour. On the southeast side of the harbour the three crowded cities of Vittoriosa, Cospicua and Senglea are clustered round the dockyard and on the northwest side is the modern suburb of Sliema. The old capital of Notabile (in Maltese, Mdina) in the southwest hills contains the Cathedral Church of Malta and some picturesque early 15th-century palaces. The chief town in Gozo, which is a hillier and greener island than Malta, is Victoria (in Maltese, Rabat). Malta has some very interesting ancient tombs and temples built of huge stone blocks at Hal Tarxien and elsewhere, probably dating from about 4000 B.C.

Malta is very thickly populated and it has for some years been difficult to find work for so many people in such a small country with so few natural riches. About one-eighth of the people depend on farming. The fields are often very small and great care is taken not to waste a scrap of soil. The chief crops are wheat, barley, potatoes, tomatoes, onions and green vegetables. Grapes, olives, oranges, figs and other fruits are also grown, and much honey is produced in Gozo. Goats, pigs, sheep and cattle are kept, although pasture land is meagre. Malta produces less than a quarter of its food needs, and has to import the rest.

The island is famous for its fine lace and silver work. Until 1959 the economy depended heavily on the docks used by the Royal Navy, but when the British decided to leave the base new work had to be found for the unemployed. The dockyard was converted into a commercial one for repairing merchant ships, and factories were built to manufacture plastics, metalwork, textiles, paints, light engineering and other goods. The discovery of oil in Libya, only 220 miles away, raised hopes that tanker traffic might rely increasingly on Valletta's docks.

Malta has a good bus system, and there are regular air services from Luqa and ferries from Valletta. The Malta railway closed in 1931.

History

The builders of the ancient temples are the first known inhabitants of Malta. Pieces of ancient pottery and their ornamentation have led archaeologists to believe that these people may have come from Sicily or Crete. In about 1000 B.C. Malta may have been a colony of the Phoenicians, a great seafaring people who once dwelt on the eastern shores of the Mediterranean Sea. Centuries later, Malta formed part of the Roman Empire and the Maltese enjoyed the same privileges as the Romans. In A.D. 60 St. Paul was shipwrecked on the island and converted its people to Christianity. After the fall of the Roman Empire Malta was conquered by the Arabs, but in 1091 it was freed by Count Roger the Norman who gave back to the islanders their religious liberty.

In 1530 Malta was given to the Knights of St. John, a religious order originally founded to look after pilgrims to Jerusalem but later engaged mainly in fighting the Turks (see KNIGHT). The Knights promised to protect the rights and free-

Courtesy, Malta Government Tourist Office

The Silver Gate of St. John's Co-Cathedral in Valletta.

dom of the Maltese and under their Grand Master, Jean Parisot de la Valette, they drove off the Turks after a siege lasting four months in 1565. Later de la Valette began to build the magnificent fortified capital of Valletta, which is named after him.

In 1798 Malta was captured by Napoleon Bonaparte and the French army on their way to Egypt. The French tried to sell the property of the church and the Maltese, being devout Roman Catholics, rebelled against them. The Maltese asked for British help and Admiral Lord Nelson sent the fleet to blockade Malta; that is, to prevent soldiers or supplies from being brought in to help the French. After a siege of two years the French surrendered. The Maltese did not want the rule of the Knights to be restored as they feared this would bring back French influence, so they became British subjects by their own choice in 1813. From then on, Malta became an important centre of British naval and military strength in the Mediterranean and many of the people obtained work in the great naval dockyard.

In World War II Malta underwent a siege that lasted for three years. Food ran short as ships bringing supplies were sunk one after another, and bombing attacks by German and Italian aircraft did tremendous damage and killed about 1,500 civilians. For the heroic behaviour of its people Malta was on April 15, 1942, awarded the George Cross. After the war

Courtesy, Malta Government Tourist Office

Top: The foreshore of Valletta marina on Malta's Grand Harbour, the main port of the islands. Below: Fishing in Malta is carried on from small inshore boats mostly during the summer. Many of Malta's fishing boats are based at Marsax-lokk harbour where these boats are drawn up.

57

the British government paid large sums to Malta for repairing war damage.

In 1958 the Maltese government resigned because of disagreement on the amount of financial help offered by the British government. In 1961 Malta was given a new constitution under which Britain continued to be responsible for Malta's defence and relations with foreign countries. Agreement was reached on a new constitution, on defence and on financial aid from Britain. On September 21, 1964, Malta became an independent state within the Commonwealth. A new agreement signed in 1972 allowed Malta to be used as a military base by Britain and other members of the Nato alliance until 1979.

MALTHUS, Thomas Robert (1766–1834).
Malthus is famous for his ideas about the growth of population. He was born near Guildford, Surrey, on February 17, 1766, and while studying at Cambridge University became a brilliant mathematician.

His most famous book, *An Essay on Population*, set out his idea that the population of the world was increasing much more quickly than the food supplies of the world. To prove that this was true he gathered facts and figures about many countries and about many different periods of history. These led him to the conclusion that a time would come when there would be so many people in the world that they would not have enough to eat. It was Malthus whose ideas suggested the theory of evolution to Charles Darwin and A. R. Wallace. (See EVOLUTION.)

Although later scholars have proved that some of Malthus' ideas were wrong, there is no doubt that many people still do not have enough to eat, and this is a problem which men are still trying to solve. (See also FOOD SUPPLIES; POPULATION.)

Malthus died on December 23, 1834, and was buried in the Abbey Church at Bath, Somerset.

MAMBA
is the name given to a group of slender, active snakes some of which live in trees. They are closely related to the cobras and are often called tree-cobras. Because of the strength of their poison, mambas are among the most dangerous of poisonous snakes. They are found in tropical and southern Africa.

There are several species of mambas. Some are a bright leaf-green colour which makes them very difficult to see when they are coiled among the leaves of a tree. These are called green

Mambas are among the most dangerous of poisonous snakes. They are closely related to the cobras.

mambas. Others are a dark, gun-metal grey and are commonly known as black mambas. These live on the ground. They have been known to reach as much as 13 feet in length.

Many exciting but exaggerated tales have been told of the fierceness and speed of mambas when attacking, but they, like all snakes, will try to escape whenever they can.

Mambas live on small birds and rodents, such as rats. Their eggs are left to hatch on their own.

MAMMAL.
Human beings are mammals, and so are many of the farm animals and pets they keep. Mammals have warm blood and backbones and the females all feed their newly born young with milk produced in special glands called *mammae*. Mammals also have hair, but the quantity of this varies considerably. Some mammals are covered with hair all over while others have hardly any at all.

Mammals are divided into three main groups. The first of these, called the egg-laying mammals, contains only two kinds, the duck-billed platypus and the echidna. These strange animals hatch out their young from eggs as birds do and then feed them on milk.

The second group is made up of the marsupials, or pouched mammals. Their young are born in a very undeveloped state and are generally less than an inch long. Among marsupials are the kangaroo, Tasmanian devil, flying phalanger and opossum.

The third and largest group is known as the

placental mammals. The placenta is an organ which develops inside the mother and from which the growing baby gets its nourishment. After birth, the placenta also comes away and is therefore also known as the afterbirth.

The placental mammals are further divided into ten main groups :

Insectivores (insect-eaters) are mostly found in the eastern half of the northern hemisphere and in Africa, though there are some in North America. The best known are the moles, shrews and hedgehogs.

Chiroptera (hand-winged) are the bats. Nearly all the large ones eat fruit and most of the smaller ones catch insects.

Primates (first) are the lemurs, monkeys, apes and man. They are best described as animals with hands and feet.

Edentates (without teeth) include some animals without any teeth at all and others with just a few. The best known kinds are sloths, armadillos and ant-eaters.

Rodents (gnawing animals) are the most numerous of all. There are more than 15,000 kinds of mammals and more than 6,000 of them are rodents. Porcupines, guinea pigs and beavers are rodents, and so are rats and mice.

Carnivores (flesh-eaters). Well-known land carnivores are lions, tigers, hyenas, bears and domestic cats and dogs. Carnivores that live in the sea include seals, sea-lions and walruses.

Cetacea (whales) are fish-shaped mammals almost without hair and so adapted to water life that they are helpless and die if stranded on land. Besides the true whales, this group includes dolphins and porpoises. The blue whale is the largest living animal.

Proboscidea (with a trunk). Today the Indian and African elephants are the only members of this group still living.

Sirenia (mermaids) are the manatees and dugongs, a group of plant-eating animals which live in water all their lives.

Hoofed mammals are divided into two groups, the odd-toed and even-toed. The odd-toed ones include horses and zebras (one toe) and the rhinoceroses (three toes). The even-toed hoofed mammals include the ruminants, or animals which chew the cud—the camels, deer, giraffes, antelopes and cattle. They also include the pigs and hippopotami, which have two toes but do not chew the cud.

There are separate articles in this encyclopaedia on most of the mammals mentioned here.

The three main groups of mammals. Left: Egg-laying mammals—duck-billed platypus and echidna. Centre: Marsupials, or pouched mammals—kangaroo, flying phalanger, opossum. Right: Examples from the ten groups of placental mammals.

Courtesy, Australian News and Information Bureau

The echidna or spiny anteater, which comes from Australia, Tasmania and New Guinea, belongs to the most primitive order of mammals, known to scientists as monotremes. Its only relative is the duck-billed platypus. These curious creatures are in fact only distantly related to other known mammals. Unlike all other mammals they lay eggs and in other ways are more like reptiles. The female echidna lays a single egg which is incubated inside a pouch on her stomach. The egg hatches inside the pouch and the young echidna stays there for some time, feeding on its mother's milk. The echidna shown in the photograph is scratching its snout and the strong claws, used for digging, can be clearly seen. The echidna uses its long, sensitive snout and tubular, sticky tongue to catch the insects on which it feeds.

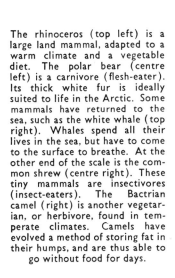

Photographs: (top left, centre left, right), Edward Van Baerle; (top right) Alexander—FPG; (centre right) John Markham

The rhinoceros (top left) is a large land mammal, adapted to a warm climate and a vegetable diet. The polar bear (centre left) is a carnivore (flesh-eater). Its thick white fur is ideally suited to life in the Arctic. Some mammals have returned to the sea, such as the white whale (top right). Whales spend all their lives in the sea, but have to come to the surface to breathe. At the other end of the scale is the common shrew (centre right). These tiny mammals are insectivores (insect-eaters). The Bactrian camel (right) is another vegetarian, or herbivore, found in temperate climates. Camels have evolved a method of storing fat in their humps, and are thus able to go without food for days.

MAN belongs to the group of mammals known as primates which is divided into two main stocks. One includes the lemurs, lorises, bush-babies and tarsiers which are mainly small, nocturnal tree dwellers found in the Old World tropics. The other includes the smaller long-tailed monkeys of South America, the larger short-tailed monkeys and the apes, all of the Old World tropics, and man himself.

Many characteristic features of the primate group developed as they adapted to living in trees. There the sense of smell is of little use and so the snout became shorter. To help in judging distance when swinging or jumping, the eyes have come to point forwards so that their fields of vision overlap. The thumb and big toe are offset so that branches can be grasped between them and the other digits. Primates in trees cling and leap in an upright position and so they usually walk upright when on the ground. As a result, when the ancestors of modern man began to live on the ground, they soon walked permanently upright. This left the hands, with their grasping thumbs, free to use tools or weapons. The tail was lost, though the tiny bone called the coccyx, at the base of the spine, remains as a relic of this. A combination of all these primate features led to the evolution of the upright, tailless, short-faced, tool-using creature we call man.

Like the other primates, man is also unusual in his intelligence and social organization. The two features are probably linked. Intelligence is based on the ability to learn during life. Many animals do not learn but behave in each situation according to instincts inherited from their parents. Learning takes time and so primates have a long period of growing up. For this they need to live in a safe social group. In turn, this fact led to greater communication with each other by means of facial expressions or by varied sounds. Chimpanzees have at least 35 noises in their vocabulary. In man, speech developed and information or beliefs could be passed on from one generation to the next. The development of different language and beliefs in different social groups helped to make the various cultures which exist today.

Man, or *Homo*, belongs to the hominid group

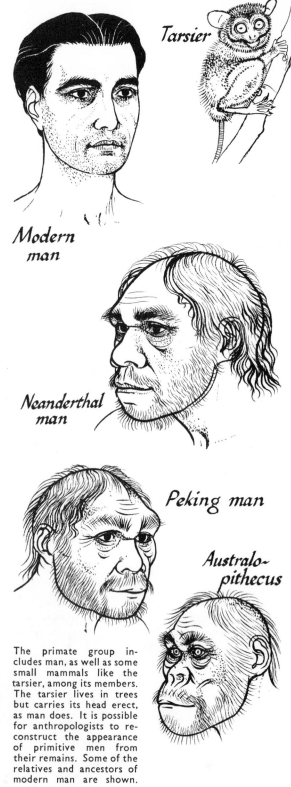

Tarsier

Modern man

Neanderthal man

Peking man

Australo-pithecus

The primate group includes man, as well as some small mammals like the tarsier, among its members. The tarsier lives in trees but carries its head erect, as man does. It is possible for anthropologists to reconstruct the appearance of primitive men from their remains. Some of the relatives and ancestors of modern man are shown.

of primates, those most closely related to the apes. This does not mean that man evolved from an ape, only that man and apes evolved from a common ancestor which had no specializations of either group. Fossils of animals known as dryopithecines, which had developed some of the special characteristics of apes, have been found in deposits about 28,000,000 years old. Probably the hominid line had already branched off by that time and was developing its own characteristics.

The earliest fossil hominids known, however, are only between 8,000,000 and 14,000,000 years old. These belong to a form from India known as *Ramapithecus*, and a closely related creature is known from Africa. Unfortunately only the jaws and teeth of *Ramapithecus* have so far been identified. It is not until about 3,000,000 years ago that man's early history is represented by more complete remains. These belong to a form known as *Australopithecus*.

Australopithecus was about 1·4 metres high and his remains were first found in 1924 in Botswana. Other remains have since been found in other parts of South and East Africa, especially in Olduvai Gorge, Kenya, by Dr. L. B. Leakey. The cheek and jaws of *Australopithecus* were heavily built and his brain was only about a third of the size of modern man's. However, he walked upright like a man, not like an ape, and there is good evidence that he used tools. There seem to have been two different species of *Australopithecus*, one slightly larger and with stronger jaws and teeth than the other. This more robust species became extinct about 700,000 years ago. The other more lightly built species was probably an ancestor of man himself.

Though man appeared about 1,000,000 years ago, he was not the same as modern man, *Homo sapiens*. Early man was once called *Pithecanthropus* but is now known as *Homo erectus*. First found in Java, this species has also been found in China (Peking man), in Europe and in Africa. About 30 centimetres taller than *Australopithecus* and with a brain nearly twice as large, this earliest type of man had a longer, thicker, lower skull and still had deep ridges in his brow. He had begun to use a greater variety of tools, in-

cluding the hand "axe", probably used for digging and scraping, and to use fire.

Homo erectus became extinct about 400,000 to 500,000 years ago and was replaced by the first representatives of our own species, *Homo sapiens*. From this time onwards, man endured the effects of a series of five Ice Ages. During each of these the world's climate became colder and wetter. First known about 400,000 years ago, the early forms of *Homo sapiens* had a larger brain than *Homo erectus* but the shape of his skull had changed little. This is particularly well shown in Neanderthal man. Although formerly classed as a separate species, *Homo neanderthalensis*, Neanderthal man is now thought of as a form of *Homo sapiens*. Neanderthal man was first found in western Europe where he lived between 70,000 and 50,000 years ago. This was during the early part of the last Ice Age and some discovered skeletons of Neanderthal man have shown signs of arthritis.

At about the same time as Neanderthal man appeared, the ancestors of modern man are also found, with a higher, shorter skull and without brow ridges. Fully modern types are known from about 50,000 years ago and gradually replaced Neanderthal man. There is more about early man in the article STONE AGE.

MAN, ISLE OF. In the middle of the Irish Sea and lying at equal distances from England, Ireland, Scotland and Wales is the Isle of Man. Its area is 588 square kilometres. Although it belongs to the English crown it is not part of the United Kingdom but forms what is called a crown dependency. It has its own parliament, the Court of Tynwald, which is of Viking origin. The name Man is believed to come from the Celtic word *mon*, meaning "mountain". The natives of the island are known as Manx.

In shape the island is oblong. The length from the Point of Ayre in the north to Spanish Head in the south is about 55 kilometres and the greatest width about 20 kilometres. To the south a small island, the Calf of Man, is separated by a swift tidal channel called The Sound. South of this again is the Chicken Rock lighthouse.

The Isle of Man has a large central upland whose highest point, Snaefell Mountain, rises to

2,034 feet. The upland, mostly covered with heather and moorland, is split by a deep central valley. Other tree-lined glens in the slaty mountains carry the chief rivers: the Sulby, Dhoo, Glass, Neb and Silverburn. Douglas, the capital, takes its name from the junction of the Dhoo and Glass.

The climate is mild and snow and frost are rare, though in winter fierce gales may blow from the southwest. Many plants that will not grow outdoors in most parts of Britain flourish in the Isle of Man. Fuchsias, hydrangeas and dragon palms are common. The best-known animal, the Manx cat, is a rather heavily built cat with no tail. It is not native to the island and may have originated in Malaysia. Grey seals breed on the southwest coast and Calf of Man and rare sea birds are found in the bird sanctuaries on the Calf of Man and Langness Peninsula. There are no moles, foxes, snakes, toads or newts.

The parliament buildings and government

Courtesy, Isle of Man Tourist Board

A Manx cat. Tail-less cats are also found in the Far East.

offices are at Douglas on the east coast. An unusual survival is a horse-drawn tramway along the Douglas promenade. An electric tramway from Douglas runs north to Ramsey with a branch to the top of Snaefell, and a narrow-gauge railway using steam locomotives runs to Port Erin in the south during the summer.

The Court of Tynwald, or parliament, is presided over by a lieutenant governor appointed by the sovereign. He represents the Queen and is appointed by her as Lord of Man. There are two Houses—the Lower House (House of Keys) has 24 members elected from the six "sheadings", or ship districts into which the island was divided by the Vikings, and from the chief towns and villages. The Upper House (Legislative Council) corresponds to the House of Lords at Westminster. It includes high officials such as the bishop and the deemster (high court judge).

Each year on July 5 the Tynwald assembles on Tynwald Hill at St. John's in the centre of the island for a ceremony that dates back more than 900 years. All the acts passed in the previous 12 months are read aloud in Manx and English so that no-one can plead ignorance of the law. Every Manx citizen with a grievance has the right of direct appeal to the sovereign's representative. The Isle of Man has its own taxation (see TAXES).

Until 1869 the capital was Castletown in the south, with the seat of government at Castle Rushen, a mediaeval stronghold which is still preserved. Peel, on the west coast, is one of the principal fishing ports, and every summer quanti-

Courtesy, Isle of Man Tourist Board

The assembly of the ancient Court of Tynwald.

ties of herring are landed, many being smoked to become Manx kippers. Just offshore from Peel is the islet of St. Patrick, with a wall built all round it. Within are the ruins of Peel Castle and of the Cathedral of St. Germain. Because of its connection with the Cathedral, Peel claims the rights of a city. Ramsey in the north and Port Erin and Port St. Mary in the south are popular tourist resorts.

The chief industry is the tourist trade, as more than 500,000 visitors come to the Isle of Man each year. The island is famous for the International Tourist Trophy (T.T.) motor-cycle races held each June over the 37-mile T.T. mountain circuit.

The second most important industry is farming. The chief crops are oats, wheat and barley, and large numbers of sheep and cattle are reared. Because the island is usually free from cattle diseases the export of breeding stock is an important part of the farming industry. Besides herring, the fishing industry yields scallops (shellfish) known as Manx tanrogans for export.

Passengers to the Isle of Man may travel by sea from Liverpool to Douglas, a voyage of some 75 miles. The airport at Ronaldsway links the island with several cities in Britain.

Manx History

The Romans do not seem to have occupied the Isle of Man, but from the 8th century onwards Viking raids were frequent. (See VIKINGS.) In the 11th century the Norwegian kingdom of the Sudreys and Man was created, the Sudreys being the southern Hebrides. During that period the bishopric of Sodor and Man was established and the present bishops still bear the same title.

The Norwegians were in 1263 defeated at the Battle of Largs (Ayrshire) by the Scots, and three years later the Isle of Man came under the kings of Scotland until it passed to the English in 1405. Henry IV gave it to the Stanley family, who were later earls of Derby. They ruled the island as "Lords of Mann", but always refused to call themselves kings. Later, the Isle of Man became a haunt of smugglers, and to stop goods being smuggled to Britain the British government bought the lordship in 1765.

The badge of the Isle of Man, three golden legs on a red ground, has the motto *Quocunque jeceris stabit*—"Wherever you throw it, it will stand". The population is about 50,000.

MANATEE. The manatee and its close relative the dugong are thought to be the animals that give rise to many of the stories about mermaids. They float along upright in the water and from a distance they could perhaps be mistaken for human beings. They are, however, by no means as beautiful as mermaids are reported to be, and they may weigh nearly a ton.

Manatees and dugongs are large mammals, not fishes, though they always live in the water. They have streamlined bodies, blunt heads, paddle-shaped forelimbs and no hindlimbs. The manatee has a broad, flat, shovel-like tail and three tiny nails on each forelimb. The dugong is larger and has a forked tail and no nails. The male dugong also differs from the manatee in having tusks up to ten inches long, like those of a walrus. Dugongs can live only in the sea, but some manatees are found in lakes and rivers as well as in estuaries.

American manatee, a species found on the coast of Florida.

There are three kinds of manatees. One kind is found in West Africa, one along the coast of Florida and in the West Indies and one along the eastern and northern coasts of South America. The dugong is found off Australia and in the Red Sea and the Indian Ocean.

Manatees and dugongs are often referred to as sea-cows, for they browse on seaweed and river plants. The true sea-cows, Steller's sea-cows, lived in the Bering Strait but became extinct in the 18th century.

MANCHESTER is one of the largest and most important cities in Britain, second in importance only to London. Formerly in Lancashire, in the reorganization of local government Manchester becomes the centre of the separate metropolitan county called Greater Manchester. The city lies on the rivers Irwell, Irk and Mersey. Excellent links by land, sea and air make Manchester a great industrial and trading city. Coalfields lie in surrounding districts and in the nearby manufacturing towns engineering of all kinds takes place. Atomic machinery, chemicals, refined oil, textiles and foodstuffs are made. About 542,000 people live in Manchester itself and nearly 2,459,000 in the city and surrounding areas.

Although it stands inland, Manchester is a great seaport, connected to the sea by the Manchester Ship Canal. This is almost 60 kilo-metres long and was opened in 1894. Ships of 15,000 tons can reach Manchester from Merseyside and at Eastham there is the largest oil dock in Britain. Manchester airport is one of Britain's largest and busiest international airports.

Manchester today is more important as a business centre than as a manufacturing town. People travel to the city to work in large shops, banks, insurance offices, shipping agencies and other commercial and distribution firms.

Manchester is renowned for its libraries. The John Rylands Library, named after a Manchester merchant, is one of the most notable English libraries and contains rare books and manuscripts. Chetham's Library, attached to the school called Chetham's Hospital, was the first free library in England. Manchester is also noted for its music. Musicians can study for a professional career at its Royal College of Music, and the city's Hallé orchestra is world famous. The City Art Gallery has fine paintings, sculpture and pottery.

Manchester University began as a college founded in 1846. Ernest Rutherford did much of the early work that led to the splitting of the atom here (see RUTHERFORD). At Jodrell Bank, near Manchester, the University's department of astrophysics has a radio astronomy observatory where two great radio telescopes, one weighing several thousand tonnes, have been built. (See the article RADIO ASTRONOMY.) Manchester Grammar School, founded in 1515 by Hugh Oldham, Bishop of Exeter, is one of the most famous schools in England.

Manchester is the largest centre of newspapers and broadcasting outside London. *The Guardian*, formerly called the *Manchester Guardian*, which is one of Great Britain's most respected daily papers, was first published there. The British Broadcasting Corporation has its North Regional Headquarters in Manchester, and a television studio. There are commercial television studios and a transmitting station in the area. Manchester also has its own local radio station.

Test matches are played at Old Trafford, the Lancashire County Cricket Ground, and important tennis tournaments at the Northern Lawn Tennis Club. The two Association foot-

Courtesy, City of Manchester

This curving building, nicknamed the "Lazy S", leads to Piccadilly railway station in Manchester.

ball clubs Manchester United and Manchester City are enthusiastically supported. At Belle Vue in West Gorton there are exhibition halls, a zoo and an amusement park.

The Romans built a fort at Manchester on one of their chief roads and called the place Mancunium. This name is still remembered in the word "Mancunian", a resident of Manchester. In the 13th century Flemings from Europe settled there and taught the people the art of making textiles, or woven materials. With the coming of powered machinery in the Industrial Revolution, Manchester developed into a great manufacturing and commercial city.

The city became a borough largely through the efforts of Richard Cobden in the 19th century. Later, Cobden and John Bright helped to change the harmful Corn Laws. (See BRIGHT, JOHN; COBDEN, RICHARD.)

MANCHURIA is the northeastern part of China. It is made up of the three provinces of Heilungkiang, Kirin and Liaoning together with the northeastern part of the self-governing region of Inner Mongolia. In the south, Manchuria has a coastline on the Yellow Sea jutting out into the Liaotung peninsula, but in other directions it is shut in by mountains. Within the mountains, the central Manchurian plain is drained by the Nonni and Sungari rivers flowing into the Amur River along the northern boundary, and by the Liao River in the south.

The highlands of Manchuria provide much of China's timber and many rare beasts and birds live in the forests, including the Manchurian tiger. Except on the coast, the climate ranges from intense heat to extreme cold, with a severe dry winter. Most of the rain falls in the short summer when the crops need it. The people are mostly Chinese, but there are a number of Manchus, whose ancestors have lived in the region for more than 2,000 years, and also some Koreans. Farming is the chief occupation. The most important crops are kaoliang (a grain like millet), soya beans, maize and wheat, with some rice and cotton in the south. Sheep and cattle are kept in the drier districts in the east.

Manchuria is China's greatest industrial region. Huge supplies of coal are mined from open pits at Fushun near Shenyang (formerly Mukden), and in the same region iron, manganese and bauxite (aluminium ore) are plentiful. There are also big deposits of oil shale, a kind of slaty rock from which oil is obtained. Great quantities of iron and steel are made at the Anshan works southwest of Shenyang. Electricity is obtained from hydro-electric power stations on the Yalu, Sungari, Mu-tan and Nonni rivers. Machinery of all kinds, chemicals and other goods are made at Shenyang and Harbin and there are shipbuilding and heavy industries at Liu-ta (formerly Dairen and Port Arthur). The chief cities of Manchuria are Harbin in the north, Kirin and Ch'ang-Ch'un in the centre, and Shenyang in the south. Manchuria is much better provided with railways than the rest of China and the deep-water harbour of Liu-ta is one of the chief Chinese ports.

History

Manchuria lies outside the Great Wall of China, which the Chinese built more than 2,000 years ago to keep out the Manchus and other tribes (see GREAT WALL OF CHINA). Nevertheless, the Manchus conquered China in 1644 and set up an empire that lasted until 1911, when China became a republic (see CHINA).

Russia and Japan wanted the riches of Manchuria, and competed for the southern part of the Liaotung peninsula with its valuable harbours. This rivalry led to the Russo-Japanese War of 1904–1905, which Japan won. Thus Russia controlled the north of Manchuria and Japan the south. Japan's influence grew steadily and in 1931 Japanese troops drove out the Chinese and took over the country, renaming it Manchukuo.

When Japan surrendered at the end of World War II in 1945, Russian troops occupied Manchuria but later allowed the Chinese to take control. After the Communist revolution in China in 1949, Manchuria became part of the Chinese People's Republic.

MANDALAY is the second largest city in Burma. It lies in the middle of that country on the east bank of the Irrawaddy River. The kings of Burma often began their reign by building a new capital, and Mandalay was founded in this way by King Mindon in 1856.

The royal city once contained a splendid palace of carved teak wood, but this was destroyed during World War II. To the northeast lies Mandalay Hill, where there are pagodas and shrines visited by Buddhist pilgrims.

The population of Mandalay is over 360,000.

MANDOLIN.

Mandolin.

The mandolin is a small musical instrument which came from Italy and which belongs to the lute family. It usually has four pairs of strings tuned to the notes G, D, A, E. Notes are plucked on the strings with a plectrum, a small piece of material made of tortoiseshell or whalebone. Plucking across a pair of strings gives the mandolin's characteristic tremolo effect. The sound box of the mandolin is curved outwards at the back giving the instrument a pear shape. Its tone is more delicate than that of the banjo, and less loud than the tone of the guitar. Music has been written for the mandolin by Handel, Mozart and Beethoven, and also by modern composers, but it is an instrument which is more often heard in popular folk music.

MANDRAKE.

Many legends are told about the mandrake plant, the best known being that it screams when it is pulled up. Such stories arose because of the plant's strange shape, for it usually has a forked root that makes it look rather like a man. From this root, which is short and fleshy, a short stem rises up. The large stalked leaves and a tuft of purplish, bell-shaped flowers come out in a bunch at the top, and the fruit is an orange berry.

The mandrake is a poisonous relation of the potato. It grows in the Mediterranean region and as far south as the Himalayas.

Mandragora is the genus, or group, name of the mandrake, and the same name is also given to a drug that is made from the mandrake.

MANET, Edouard (1832–1883).

To paint as clearly and truly as possible exactly what he saw in front of him was the aim of the French painter Edouard Manet. To do this he experimented with new ways of using light and colour as he tried to catch all the light and movement of the everyday life around him and put it down on the canvas.

Manet's paintings inspired a group of artists who became his friends and shared some of his ideas. They were later given the name of "Impressionists". (See IMPRESSIONISTS.)

Edouard Manet was born in Paris on January 23, 1832. When he was 19 years old, he became a pupil of a well-known artist of the day named Thomas Couture, but already he was far too independent to copy other people's ways of painting and used often to annoy his master. On several occasions, too, he left Paris to travel in Austria, Germany, Italy and Holland and study painting on his own. He was charming and witty and it was not long before a group of friends and fellow painters gathered round him.

In 1863, Manet sent a painting of a picnic on the grass called "Déjeuner sur l'Herbe", to be shown in the Salon, the official art exhibition in France, but the men who were responsible for choosing the pictures refused to show it. This decided Manet and his friends to defy the Salon and have their own exhibition. Two years later the picture which is now one of the most famous of all Manet's works, "Olympia", was shown in the Salon, but even then it was attacked by many critics who disagreed with Manet's idea of beauty and thought the picture was ugly and disgusting. With tremendous energy and determination, however, Manet went on painting and showing his pictures and eventually opinion about them began to change. People at last recognized his greatness, and two years before his death he was

Courtauld Institute of Art

"A Bar at the Folies-Bergère", painted in 1882, was one of Edouard Manet's last and greatest works.

awarded the Cross of the Legion of Honour.

Some of Manet's fine pictures can be seen in the National Gallery in London.

MANGANESE is a metal seldom used in its pure state, but very important in the making of steel. Pure manganese is a greyish metal rather like iron, and manganese and iron are often found together. Manganese ores are mined in many countries, the largest producers being the U.S.S.R., India, South Africa and Ghana.

The three forms in which manganese is used for steel making are ferromanganese, spiegeleisen and silicomanganese. All are alloys (mixtures) of iron and manganese, obtained by smelting (melting down) ores containing iron and manganese with coke and limestone in blast furnaces like those used for making iron (see the article IRON AND STEEL). Most of the manganese used in the world is put into steel to improve it. When added in small quantities, manganese combines with the oxygen in the steel, which would otherwise be porous, or full of holes caused by the oxygen gas. The manganese also gets rid of sulphur, which would make the steel brittle when hot. When added in larger quantities, manganese makes steel very strong and tough and it can then be used for heavy-duty tools, such as the teeth of mechanical shovels. Safes for keeping money and valuables, armour plate and the "points" of railway lines may also be made of manganese steel.

Manganese bronze, consisting of copper, zinc, tin and manganese, is used for making the propellers of ships because it is not eaten away by sea water. Copper wire containing manganese offers a high resistance to an electric current and therefore gets very hot when a current is sent through it. Wire of this kind is used in electric fires and toasters.

Among other substances containing manganese are manganese dioxide, used in making the batteries of electric torches, and sodium permanganate ("Condy's fluid") and potassium permanganate, both of which are disinfectants. Manganese dioxide is also mixed into paints and varnishes to help them dry quickly.

MANGO.

The most important fruit growing wild in India is the mango, which has probably been cultivated there for about 4,000 years. It is now also grown in all the other tropical countries except in the wettest parts.

The mango tree is evergreen, reaching 40 to 60 feet in height, and its branches spread as widely. Although the wood is soft and of little value as timber, the trees are long-lived. Some planted by Akbar, the Mogul Emperor who reigned in India from 1556 to 1605, were still alive and vigorous 300 years later.

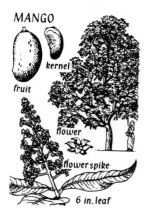

MANGO

fruit

kernel

flower

flower spike

6 in. leaf

The mango fruit looks rather like a large, kidney-shaped plum. It is used unripe to make chutneys and preserves. When ripe, the thick skin is green, yellow or orange, sometimes with a red flush. Inside is a single seed, encased in a shell, and fibres spread outwards from the shell into the yellow or orange flesh of the fruit, which is very juicy. The best varieties have a sweet and distinctive flavour and are very popular for eating.

MANGOLD.

The mangold, or mangelwurzel, is a root crop belonging to the same family of plants as sugar beet. It is not a kind of turnip. Early in the 19th century it was brought to England to feed to cattle during the late winter and early spring. The German name mangel-wurzel, which means "root of scarcity", was given to it largely because it was available at the time of year when other feeding-stuffs were scarce.

Mangolds are like sugar beets in many ways, but most varieties have bigger, fleshier and more regularly shaped roots. These are mainly above ground and are therefore easier to pull than those of sugar beet. In these roots food is stored up during the first summer's growth and is used the following year to produce stems, leaves, flowers and seeds. Mangolds are lifted (pulled up) in the first year, as the farmer uses only the roots. Crops of mangolds are costly to produce as they need well fertilized ground and careful thinning and weeding. The roots contain much water, but 45 tons an acre may be produced. Like turnips, cabbage and kale, mangolds leave the ground in good condition.

Mangold.

MANGROVE.

Mangrove forests grow along the shores of many tropical countries. Some of the roots of mangrove trees grow out from the trunk and with the branches they form a tangle that catches floating mud and driftwood. In this way natural banks are formed.

As well as from the roots, new trees grow from the seeds, which sprout while they are still on the trees. When the new little root has grown some length it becomes long and dart-shaped. It then breaks off the tree and falls with the rest of the seed, sinking into the soft mud below and so planting itself.

Exclusive News Agency
A mangrove forest on the coast of Malaya at low tide.

Although mangrove wood polishes well, the trees are usually too small to be used as timber. The wood of some of the largest trees, however, is sometimes used to build docks and piers because it is not attacked by wood-boring waterworms. The bark contains tannin.

MANILA

MANILA is the largest city and chief port of the Philippines, on which there is a separate article. The city lies at the mouth of the Pasig River on the western side of the island of Luzon, and looks out over a wide bay. The sunsets over Manila Bay are famous for their splendour.

The city was founded south of the river by the Spanish conqueror Miguel Lopez de Legazpi in 1571, but most of the old Spanish walled city (called Intramuros) was destroyed in World War II. To seaward of Intramuros is the dock area, built largely on ground dredged (scooped out) from the bay. This area is protected from the heavy surf that sometimes runs in the bay by a large breakwater, forming a basin where large ships can lie.

North of the river is the modern commercial city built by the Americans, with some fine business buildings and shops. Most of the people are Tagalogs, one of the groups of brown-skinned Malay peoples in the Philippines, but there are large numbers of Chinese traders and shopkeepers. The houses vary from big blocks of flats and handsome dwellings built in Spanish style, to shacks of wood and bamboo in the slum districts.

Except for a short period of British rule (1762–1764), Manila was governed by Spain from its founding until 1898. In that year, during the Spanish-American War, an American fleet defeated the Spaniards in Manila Bay. Under United States rule, Manila was the capital of the Philippines. It was occupied by the Japanese from 1942 until 1945, when it was recaptured by the United States.

After World War II, when the Philippines became independent, the capital was moved to Quezon City, which is situated on higher ground northeast of Manila. Most of the government buildings, however, are in Manila.

The population of Manila is about 1,400,000 and of Quezon City about 755,000.

MANITOBA

MANITOBA in central Canada is the eastern-most of the three prairie provinces. (Prairies are grassy, treeless plains.) It is about twice the size of the British Isles and is bordered by the Northwest Territories on the north, Hudson Bay and Ontario on the east, Saskatchewan on the west and the United States on the south.

Manitoba is a land of many lakes and rivers. In the south are the huge Lake Winnipeg, itself larger than Wales, and its neighbours Cedar Lake, Winnipegosis and Lake Manitoba. All around these southern lakes, which are very shallow, there was once an even more enormous sheet of water called Lake Saskatchewan which slowly drained away to leave wide stretches of treeless prairie under which is fertile soil of great depth. There are countless lakes in the northern part of the province, much of which is thickly wooded. Underneath there are rocks which are rich in minerals. The Saskatchewan and Assiniboine Rivers from the west and the Red River from the south drain into Lake Winnipeg, which itself drains into Hudson Bay through the Nelson River. Other rivers flowing into Hudson Bay are the Beaver, Severn, Churchill and Hayes.

On the whole, Manitoba is flat, and the Porcupine, Riding and Duck mountains in the southwest are little more than 2,500 feet. The agricultural land lies mainly in the southwest part of the province and the best wheat comes from an area south of a line drawn through Winnipeg and Brandon. Manitoba, like most places far inland, has a continental climate, which is a climate of extremes. There is a long, bitter winter with snow lying from December to March, but by May the temperature is as high as in England and in July and August it becomes really hot. The rainfall is not heavy but fortunately most rain in the south falls at a time when it is most needed to bring on the crops. The chief trees in the northern forests are spruce and pine, with some birch and poplar, but much of the forest land is covered with scrub or is "muskeg" country growing only mossy plants. This scrub, muskeg and other waste and rocky land make up about two-fifths of the province. In the north live caribou (American reindeer) and the large deer known as moose and wapiti, as well as black bears and wolves. The fox, lynx, beaver, otter, muskrat, mink and squirrel are hunted or trapped for their fur.

Most of the people of Manitoba live in the southern part. The earlier settlers were of British and French-Canadian stock, but they were later joined by people from other countries. North of Winnipeg, near the lake, are several Icelandic villages, many of whose inhabitants speak Icelandic as well as English. South and west of Winnipeg many farmers are Mennonites, members of a strict religious sect which was driven out of Europe in the 17th century. The largest groups of other nationalities are the French, Ukrainian, Polish and German. Some thousands of American Indians in Manitoba live in reservations, which are areas set apart for them by the government. The capital of the province is Winnipeg (see WINNIPEG). Other cities are St. Boniface, across the Red River from Winnipeg, Brandon on the Assiniboine River, and Portage la Prairie a few miles south of Lake Manitoba.

Primary schooling in Manitoba is free and there are many secondary schools. The large University of Manitoba near Winnipeg has one of the best medical schools in Canada.

Farming, once the most important occupation, has declined somewhat since the 1930s. Agriculture is concentrated in southern Manitoba, and there have been attempts to make some of the land in the north fit for farming. Crops grown include wheat, oats, barley, sugar beet, flax, potatoes and rye. In the Red River valley sunflowers are grown for their oilseed. Mixed farming (crops and animals) is carried out extensively. Cattle are bred for meat and milk, and pigs, sheep and poultry are also kept. There are large areas of pasture, and maize, clover and roots such as mangolds are grown for feeding the animals in winter. Manitoba honey is extremely good and many farmers keep bees.

Plenty of timber is obtainable from the forests in the northern part of the province for building and for making pulp and paper. Large quantities of valuable furs are sent abroad, some being

Courtesy, Manitoba Government Public Information Branch

Ships docked in harbour at Churchill, Manitoba (left), waiting to be loaded with grain for export. Right: The central legislative building in Manitoba. From here, the province is governed by elected representatives.

got by trappers but even more from farms where the fur-bearing animals are bred in captivity. The many lakes and rivers abound in fish, Lake Winnipeg providing about half the annual catch, most of which is exported to the United States.

Manitoba is rich in mineral resources. Copper, zinc, gold, silver, cadmium, selenium and tellurium are produced at Flin Flon, the principal mining and smelting centre, on the Saskatchewan border, and copper and nickel are mined at Lynn Lake. Gold is mined at Bissett and around Herb and Snow lakes and nickel is mined and refined in the Mystery-Moak lake area. Petroleum is produced near Virden in the southwest of the province. Hydro-electric power is abundant.

The most important occupation is manufacturing, which between 1947 and 1957 almost doubled in capacity. Industries employ almost 50,000 people and include food and drinks, iron and steel, petroleum and coal; railway wagons and buses. Motor-car and aircraft parts are made and there is large clothing industry, including fur, textile and leather products.

Both the great Canadian railways and the Trans Canada Highway pass through Winnipeg. There are more than 100,000 miles of roads in Manitoba.

The shortest sea route from the Canadian prairies to Europe is from Churchill on Hudson Bay, which is connected by rail to the junction at Le Pas (now usually called The Pas) in western Manitoba. The Hudson Strait is free from ice from about mid-July to mid-November so that wheat from the prairies can be sent to Europe by this route. The international airport at Stevenson near Winnipeg is the centre of the Canadian airlines and a point of departure for the far north. Aircraft are also widely used to reach lonely outposts and mining camps.

History

The name Manitoba is said to be obtained from an Indian word meaning "the god that speaks". In 1739 the French trader Pierre de la Verendrye pushed his way westwards from Lake Superior as far as Lake Manitoba, but apart from trading posts set up by the Hudson's Bay Company and its rival there was no attempt to settle Manitoba until 1812. Then a band of Scottish pioneers under Thomas Douglas, fifth Earl of Selkirk (1771–1820), founded a settlement near what is now Winnipeg. They suffered great hardships as they did not understand the kind of farming that was needed and were too far from the world's markets to sell their produce. However, they persevered, and the town of Selkirk some miles north of Winnipeg is a memorial to them and their leader.

In 1867 the British government arranged for the land owned by the Hudson's Bay Company to be transferred to Canada, the purchase being made by the new Dominion of Canada. Some of the French settlers in Manitoba were afraid that the Canadian government would take their land or interfere with their religion, and they began a rebellion. This was put down and in 1870 Manitoba was made a province, with a total population of about 12,000. The province was originally only a small area on both sides of the Red River, but it was enlarged in 1881 and again in 1912. The completion of the railway connection to Manitoba in 1878 led to a rush of settlers and the building of a railway right across Canada a few years later brought a further increase in population. The railway to Churchill was completed in 1929 and soon afterwards the great mineral wealth in the western part of the province was discovered.

Manitoba sends representatives to the federal Canadian parliament at Ottawa and is governed by an executive council and a legislative assembly which is elected by the people for five years.

MANNA. When the Israelites under Moses were wandering in the wilderness after leaving Egypt they lived on manna, which tasted "like wafers made with honey" and appeared on the ground like hoar frost. The manna mentioned in the Bible is thought to have been a lichen which often grows in quantities in eastern deserts. (See LICHEN.) Another possibility is that the manna came from a shrub called tamarisk. (See TAMARISK.)

Today a sweet juice from a number of plants is called manna, the best known of these plants being the manna ash, a tree that grows wild in southern Europe. Manna is obtained from the sap. It hardens on drying and is pleasant to eat.

MANNERS.

The way in which people behave towards each other is governed by social customs and rules and a person who follows the recognized customs or rules of etiquette is said to have good manners. Customs and social habits change very quickly and people do not usually insist on keeping to such a strict code of manners today as they did in the early part of the 20th century, for example. However, there are still occasions when it is useful to know the correct way to dress and behave.

It is polite for a boy to open the door for a girl.

Like most human habits, manners vary in different countries, so that what is polite for one nation is not always so for another, and they also change from time to time, so that the rules of one century are not the same as those of another. In Stuart times, for instance, it was quite correct for men to wear their hats at meals, whereas today it is generally considered impolite for a man to keep his hat on indoors. Or again, at the beginning of this century no girl ever danced more than two or three times with the same man at a ball, unless she was engaged to him. She would not be allowed to go out in the evening unless accompanied by her mother or by a chaperon, a married or elderly woman whose job was to take charge of her. In most Western countries ideas on these things have changed and customs have changed with them, but in Italy and Spain, for example, young women are still much less free to go out unaccompanied than they are in Great Britain or the United States.

Many social customs are so simple and obvious that they would occur to any thoughtful person without the need of rules. A man would normally open a door for a woman or an aged person. He would not usually sit down when a woman was standing or push into a room in front of her. He would not let her carry a heavy burden if he could do it himself. However, it is not a worldwide custom for men to make special courtesies of this kind to women. Manners develop from a people's whole way of life and religion and therefore differ in various countries. Some personal courtesies are general, however. A well-mannered person would not talk all the time himself, giving others no chance to put their point of view; neither would he interrupt when other people are talking.

Equally, he would try to be punctual for an appointment, since other people's time is quite as valuable as his own, and to be kept waiting is annoying and inconvenient. There is an idea among some people that women can be unpunctual, without impoliteness, when meeting a man, but this is not so. Punctuality has been called the politeness of kings and should be shown by both sexes. To be late for a meal is bad manners, for it may mean that the meal is spoilt for everyone else; and to break an appointment without due notice and apology shows lack of consideration for others.

Courtesies of this sort need no explanation, for they are simply the result of taking thought for others. There are, however, some forms of behaviour whose origin is not so obvious and which are really survivals from an earlier age.

A boy takes off his right glove in order to shake hands.

It is usual for a man to remove his glove when shaking hands and this is not done, as might be supposed, for fear that the glove may be dirty. It is a very ancient habit that goes back to more dangerous and violent times, when the glove was removed to prove that there was no dagger hidden in it. Again, when a man and woman are walking together in the street, he usually takes the outside of the pavement. Some people think that the origin of this custom was to give the man more freedom of movement in case he had to use his sword. Perhaps a better explanation is that, in olden days when roads were narrow and muddy, the person on the outside of the pavement was likely to be in danger from passing vehicles

A boy walks on the kerb side of the pavement.

and be splashed by mud. Today the outside of the pavement is still the more dangerous.

Another survival is that when a man drinks from the loving-cup—a large bowl, often in silver, from which everyone drinks in turn—at any London livery company's banquet, his neighbours on either side rise and remain standing until he has finished. They did so, originally, in case they had to defend him from attack while he was drinking from the heavy cup and unable to defend himself. (See LIVERY COMPANIES.)

Calling and At Home Days

In England when a new family settled in a district, they were not formally accepted into its social life until the people who had lived there for a long time had called upon them and left visiting cards; that is, small white cards with the owner's name printed on them. It was for the old inhabitants to decide whether they wanted to know the new people, and the first move was with them. In France, however, the newcomers called upon their neighbours first.

Before World Wars I and II, which altered many old habits, calling played a great part in social life, and there were rules about the leaving of cards and the time to be spent in each house. Many women had regular At Home days, once a month or oftener, when they were at home between certain hours and ready to entertain any acquaintance who chose to call. The time and day was printed on their visiting cards so

that everyone knew when the At Home day was.

Nowadays, when most people are much busier than formerly, this custom has fallen into disuse and visits (other than those to close friends) are more likely to be the result of a direct invitation. But the old At Home day had many advantages, for the caller was quite certain that his visit was convenient and the hostess was usually sure of seeing all her friends in turn without the trouble of sending out invitations. To be "at home" in the social sense means to be "ready to receive visitors". Therefore, it was quite correct—and not untruthful—to say that a person was "not at home", even though he or she was in the house at the time.

Letters and Invitations

Good manners should be observed in writing and addressing letters. Letters must be suited to the people who are going to receive them, since one that is suitable for a close friend is unsuitable for a slight acquaintance, and a business letter should not be worded in the same friendly manner as a letter to one's aunt. A letter which has a formal beginning should also have a formal ending, such as "Yours faithfully" or "Yours truly". (See LETTER WRITING.)

The address on the envelope is also important and care should be taken to see that it is correct. Most people would take trouble if they were writing to a duke or to an archbishop because these people have definite titles, the first because he has inherited it and the second because it shows his position in the church. Carelessness is often shown, however, over the form of address for people with less obvious titles and over the use of the word "Esquire".

This word comes from the days of chivalry and originally meant "shield-bearer". In later years it was used for a gentleman of established position who had no other title. It is now used far more freely but people do not always realize that it is a title in itself and must never be joined to any other. Thus, when writing to someone called Henry Martin, it is correct to put "Henry Martin, Esq.," on the envelope, whereas "Mr. Henry Martin, Esq.," is too much. If in the course of time Henry Martin becomes a clergyman or a captain, he is no longer ad-

You are invited the Birthday

For some occasions a formally worded card is sent.

dressed as "Esquire" but by the titles appropriate to clergymen and captains. (Some of these are given in ADDRESS, FORMS OF.)

Sending and replying to invitations is also a matter of rule and custom. For a friendly gathering, a pleasant letter or a telephone call is enough, but for ceremonial occasions a formally worded card is sent and a formal reply expected.

Dress

Good manners demand that dress should if possible be suited to the occasions on which it is worn. To wear elaborate clothes when simple ones are called for is as wrong as to appear in everyday clothes at a dinner or dance. It is strictly correct for a man to wear a special kind of tail-coat, trousers and white tie for a formal ball, and a dinner-jacket and black tie for a formal dinner. When he receives an invitation to a daytime function the invitation card may state that "morning dress" is to be worn, and he knows that he must wear another sort of tail-coat with special trousers, waistcoat and tie. There are special rules of dress for the full-dress attire of peers of the realm or Knights of the Garter and the occasions on which it is worn. (The article DRESS describes different types of dress throughout the ages.)

Rank and Precedence

In Great Britain the law treats everybody as equals, but socially there are many differences. The sovereign and the royal family, dukes, marquesses, earls, viscounts and barons, privy councillors, members of the government, ambassadors, dignitaries of the church, baronets, knights, mayors, sheriffs, judges and many others all have their special titles and functions. What are known as the rules of precedence tell

us where their social positions are in relation to each other. Without definite rules it would be very difficult to know how each of the people mentioned earlier should be addressed, either in speech or by letter, or in what order he should sit at table or enter a room at ceremonial dinners or gatherings. The rules provide an orderly way of doing things and are intended to avoid awkwardness.

The rules of precedence do not apply only to occasions when very important guests are being entertained. People should still follow them when, for example, they are arranging a meeting or a dinner at which the mayor of the town, the vicar of the parish and an important visiting speaker are all present together. Even a simple dinner party may need some knowledge of these rules, for the host is expected to take the most important lady guest into the dining room; and when introducing two strangers he should present the less to the more important of the two, if

Introducing a young man to an older one.

they are both of the same sex. A man is always introduced to a lady.

MANOR. Many English villages have a house called Manor House or The Manor, which is often fairly big and, even if all of it is not very old, often has extremely old parts in it. Some of these houses began as the biggest and grandest houses of the manors that once were found in many parts of England. To discover what a manor was we must go back to the middle part of the middle ages, and look at the way in which most people lived and earned their living.

At that time towns were very small and there were not nearly so many of them as there are

H. Schwarz

The farming community of a mediaeval manor was close-knit and largely self-dependent.

today. Most people worked on the land and lived in the country. Very little money was used, and the officials who did the work of government (as local rulers, judges, police and soldiers) as well as the church officials (bishops and priests) were paid not with money but with land. Land was divided into blocks of different sizes so that officials could be "paid" more, or less, according to the type of work they did. The manor was the biggest block into which land was divided, and it corresponded more or less to what we call a village.

We can most easily see how this system worked by looking at what was done by William the Conqueror after he conquered England in 1066 and set himself up as king, with his Norman followers as his local officials. In order to reward them for the fighting they had done, and to pay them for the help they gave him in ruling England, he divided the land among them. The most important received many manors and the less important perhaps only one. The lord of a manor then divided some of its land among its inhabitants in return for services they gave him. (This is explained in the article FEUDALISM.)

About 20 years after he first became king, William ordered a great survey to be made of England. The result of the survey is the Domesday Book (see DOMESDAY BOOK), which is still of great use because it tells us how the manors over most of England were organized. It shows that they varied according to the type of countryside they were in. On the high hills and the moors most of the inhabitants of a manor were occupied in sheep farming. However, the most usual type of manor was concerned with growing crops and was found in the midlands and the south. The people farmed two or sometimes three large fields. Each field was divided into narrow strips about 220 yards (1 furlong) in length. The lord of the manor had his strips and the people of the manor had theirs. Instead of paying rent to the lord for their strips, they cultivated his strips. Only the least important lords had only one manor, so by no means every manor had its own manor house. There might be the home of the lord's steward, or manager, but the most noticeable building—except the church —was usually the great barn or grange in which

the lord's share of the crops was stored. The lord of the manor was much more than a landlord. He was a local ruler and was responsible to the king for law and order in his manor. He therefore held a law court and either presided over it himself or appointed someone to act for him.

The work of the manor was often arranged by the people themselves. Every year part of the arable (cultivated) land was left fallow but it was ploughed twice. Of the rest, one half was sown in autumn with wheat or rye, and the other half was sown in March with barley or oats. Animals —cattle, sheep, pigs, goats and horses—were put on to the stubble after harvest to gather what food they could, and helped to manure the land. Most of the cattle were slaughtered before winter set in because there was nothing to feed them on during the winter months. (It was not until the 18th century that root crops were grown as winter food for cattle.) The animals also grazed on the common land (see COMMONS), on the edge of the manor or in the woods and, after the hay was cut, in the grass meadows. All these things needed careful arrangements which were made at village meetings—although usually in accordance with custom, or what had been done before. The custom of each manor varied and was a matter of pride to its members. In accordance with custom they fixed a period when the ploughing, sowing and harvesting were to be done, and decided who was to do the various jobs. They appointed and gave instructions to the shepherd, cow-herd, and swine-herd. By custom and discussion, arrangements were made for gathering and distributing many other things, such as the honey of the wild bees that was used for sweetening food, and fallen branches for firewood. Trees had to be felled and cut up for building and repairing houses, barns and fences, and fish were netted for food.

This system grew up at a time when there was very little money about. In the later middle ages —when feudalism had brought more security— trade and towns began to grow. More money came into use, at first in the towns and then in the country areas. People began to be paid in money for the work they did for the lord of the manor, and often lost their right to strips. Wealthy men, often from the towns, took as their homes the biggest house in many a village or, as often happened, converted the old grange into a house and called such houses "manor houses", even though the manorial system was ceasing to exist and the new owner was not the lord of the manor.

MANUSCRIPT.

In the days before printing was invented in Europe in the 15th century, all books and all reading matter of any kind had to be written out by hand. Hand-written books and papers of this kind are called manuscripts— the word "manuscript" comes from two Latin words, *manu* meaning "by hand" and *scriptus* meaning "written".

In Europe during the middle ages the main places of learning were the monasteries and it was the monks who chiefly developed the special art of manuscript writing. The scribes, as these writers were called, did not sit at flat-topped tables to work but instead sat, or occasionally stood, at desks that sloped at an angle which seems most inconvenient and uncomfortable today. They wrote with a feather or quill, usually a goose feather, and made their ink by

The Gospels of Lothair, a French manuscript of about 850.
Courtesy, Bibliothéque Nationale

This work on navigation was written in about 1580.

dissolving carbon (or lamp-black, the soot made by a burning lamp) in water. The writing was done on parchment made from specially prepared skins of sheep, goats or calves.

Although most scribes were monks, there were numbers of others who wrote out different kinds of manuscripts, such as documents dealing with law and government. In England by the 14th century there must also have been some scribes employed by private persons to make copies of much less official writings, for there were manuscript copies of the poems of Geoffrey Chaucer, for example, before they were ever put into print. Other popular manuscripts were the "bestiaries". These were illustrated descriptions of the animals of the world. (See BESTIARY.)

Many religious manuscripts and some of the others were ornamented or "illuminated". The art of illuminating manuscripts began with the drawing or painting of a large initial letter to begin a new chapter or section—perhaps to help the reader find his place—and gradually little pictures came to be included in the initial. Later on, each page of a manuscript might be surrounded by elaborate patterns and pictures done in gold paint and with brilliant blues and reds. The Book of Kells (see KELLS, BOOK OF) is one beautiful illuminated manuscript that still exists and there are many others in museums all over the British Isles.

The Lindisfarne Gospels (top left) were written by monks in 8th-century Northumbria. The first words of St. Mark's Gospel (bottom right) completely fill a "carpet page" from the Book of Kells. The Joshua Roll (top right), a 10th-century Byzantine manuscript, has life-like figures. A 15th-century Flemish Book of Hours shows the court dress of the period.

A decorative letter from the beginning of the Psalms in the 12th-century Winchester Bible shows David attacking a bear and rescuing a lamb from a lion.

The usual abbreviation for "manuscript" is MS., and for the plural "manuscripts", MSS. or mss. The word is now used mainly to describe an author's work before it is printed, even though it may be typewritten and not written by hand.

MAORIS.

When Europeans first discovered New Zealand they found a people called the Maoris already living there. The Maoris are a Polynesian people, fairly tall, with rather long heads and faces. Their skins are light brown and their hair is often slightly wavy. They are a very intelligent people. (See POLYNESIANS.)

Maori legends say· that they came to New Zealand from "Hawaiki", which is believed to have been the island of Savaii in Western Samoa, about 1,800 miles to the north. There are thought to have been three chief migrations, or movements. The first was about 1,000 years ago. About 200 years afterwards, the legends say, some canoes from Hawaiki were caught in a storm and drifted across the ocean to New Zealand. They were followed by a search party led by a hero called Toi, and when they reached New Zealand they found people descended from those of the earlier migration and intermarried with them.

The third migration, the largest and most important, was made from Rarotonga in the Cook Islands, probably in about 1350. A fleet of canoes crossed the ocean, and the families of the Maori chiefs today trace their descent back to the leaders of those canoes.

The last people from Rarotonga brought along the sweet potato (a South American plant) and the paper mulberry, from the papery bark of which they made sheets, called tapa cloth. This they used to make clothes, but they were not warm enough, and the plant would grow only in the extreme north. In New Zealand, however, they found a plant rather like flax with large, thick leaves from which fibres could be made,

Keystone Press

Maori sailors of the Royal New Zealand Navy dancing a *Haka* (a traditional war dance) on the deck of their ship.

and they learned to plait and weave it. In order to protect themselves from the rain they made cloaks, sometimes covered with feathers.

The Maoris hunted and killed a big ostrich-like bird called the moa, which is now extinct. They had brought dogs from Rarotonga, but they had no horses, cattle, sheep or goats and therefore no milk or butter. Those that lived around lakes or on the sea-coast caught cray-fish or fishes for food. One of the main supplies of food was the underground stems of tree ferns, and the Maoris also ate berries.

In the Maori community many things were taboo; that is, they were considered too sacred to be touched. (See TABOO.) The ordinary people worshipped gods who looked after such things as trees, birds, the sea and fish, and the priests believed in a god who was above the others.

Maori houses were built of wood, which the men cut with adzes (axe-like instruments). As they had no metal they made adzes of stone, often a green kind something like jade. With these tools they made beautiful carvings around their doors. Their custom was to have one room only in each building, so several houses were necessary, and one family might have a sleeping house, a feeding house and a kitchen house.

It seems probable that at first a few families, all related to each other, lived close together without any special arrangement except a family assembly house. As the population increased, there were conquests and raids, and houses were built closely together inside fortifications. Each group of houses had its own land, which belonged to the whole group. Each household had the right to use some of the land, but it could not sell it.

In the past the Maoris were divided into tribes, and these tribes were further divided into clans, or large families. Although the clans sometimes quarrelled among themselves they always united against a common enemy. Today this organization is disappearing, although it is still remembered. In the years since the first Europeans settled in New Zealand, the Maoris have gradually changed their way of life and are now fully involved in the town and industrial life of the country. More and more mixed marriages between people of Maori and European descent take place. Nearly all New Zealand's Maoris have some European ancestry. Although much of their traditional way of life has disappeared, some Maori traditions, especially their songs and fine carving work, are kept alive. The New Zealand parliament has some Maori members and efforts have been made by the government to improve education for Maoris so that more will be able to compete on equal terms for jobs with other New Zealanders. Changes in the law about Maori land have made it easier for ancestral land to be sold, though many Maoris believe that inherited lands should be kept for their people.

Maori Wars

When the British first arrived in New Zealand in the 19th century, they fought with the Maoris over possession of land. In 1840, British rule was proclaimed in New Zealand and Maoris were promised that their tribal lands would not be taken from them, but the promises were soon broken. The Maori lands were owned in common and many plots were sold to white settlers by individuals. Disputes arose when other Maoris refused to recognize these sales and the arguments flared up into fierce struggles.

A serious rebellion by the Maoris in 1845 was put down by the wise and firm action of Captain George Grey, who was sent over from South Australia to restore order (see GREY, SIR GEORGE). In 1860, however, fighting broke out again over a land deal in Taranaki. The Maoris elected a king and resolved to keep their hold over the King Country in the centre of the North Island. Ten years of war followed, during which British soldiers were sent from the United Kingdom. Their red coats against the evergreen bush made them an easy target, but the Maoris were bad at organizing and were hopelessly outnumbered by white troops and settlers. Nevertheless, they fought with tremendous courage. The storming of their fortified stockades often led to many casualties on both sides. The most famous of the Maori leaders were Rewi and Te Kooti. Some Maori fighters, such as the chiefs Ropata and Kemp, fought for the whites because the other chiefs were their tribal enemies. The British government grew tired of the war and

A Maori girl, wearing her national dress, stands beside one of New Zealand's hot springs or geysers.

withdrew all but one regiment, leaving the colonial troops and friendly Maori tribes to carry on. The war petered out in 1871.

MAO TSE-TUNG (born 1893).

The founder and leader of the People's Republic of China, Mao Tse-tung, was born in Hunan province and in his youth read widely about political systems. In 1921 he helped found the Chinese Communist Party and saw that in China revolution must come from the peasants; not (as European Communists taught) from the towns. He raised a peasant army in Hunan and in 1927 led it against the Nationalists. In 1934 Mao's army had to retreat and made the "Long March" to the northwest. Thereafter Mao controlled the Communist Party.

Communists and Nationalists worked together in World War II but afterwards fought each other. With Russian help, the Communists won control and Mao led the new government in 1949. China underwent profound changes as Mao tried to industrialize it. He resigned as government chairman in 1959 and quarrelled with the U.S.S.R., but remained leader of the Party. In 1965 he encouraged the Red Guard movement in the "Cultural Revolution"—a continuous process of violent change. A small book of Mao's writings became the symbol of the revolution and guided Chinese thought and life.

MAPLE.

The maple family includes the sycamore. Like the sycamore, the field maple has winged seeds which are carried by the wind. The field maple is native to Great Britain.

Maple leaves, which contain sugar, are glossy and are divided round their edges into five parts.

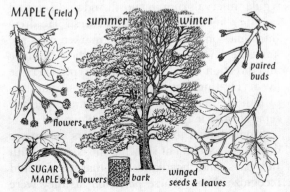

MAPLE (Field) summer winter
paired buds
flowers
SUGAR MAPLE flowers bark winged seeds & leaves

They used to be collected as food for cattle, for cows enjoy them. The yellow-green flowers, which open in May and June, stand up in little clusters. Though the bark of the tree is rough and lined, the wood has a fine grain and is easily polished, so it is used for furniture-making.

The sugar maple grows in Canada and the United States. From it comes maple sugar, which is collected from the trunk. Japanese maples are grown as shrubs in gardens. The maple leaf is the emblem of Canada.

MAP READING.

The intelligent use of maps is called map reading. The map maker squeezes information into a very small space by making use of different colours, symbols (signs), abbreviations such as P for Post Office and even by using different kinds of lettering.

The chief things that can be read from a map are the size, position and shape of features such as bays, mountains and lakes shown on it. A map is bound to be smaller than the district it represents and its *scale* indicates how much smaller it is. The scale may either be given as, for example, "one inch to the mile" or by a fraction such as 1/63,360. This means that a lake shown on the map as 2 inches long is really 2 miles long, or that one inch on the map represents 63,360 inches on the ground.

The direction of one place from another is simply found, as the top is usually north when the map is the right way up for reading. If this is not so, the map carries an arrow pointing north. If parallels of latitude are shown they run east and west. Meridians of longitude run north and south. (See LATITUDE AND LONGITUDE.)

The shape of features such as mountains and valleys is shown by colours or by contour lines. Thus white may represent snowclad peaks and be used for the highest ground, while the lower slopes may be brown. Yellow may be used for ground of moderate height and green for lowlands. Dark blue may be used for deep water and lighter blues for shallower parts. Contour lines join places which are the same height above sea level or the same depth below it. The 500-foot contour line on a mountain is where the water level would be if the country were flooded to a depth of 500 feet.

Contour lines form certain patterns which are easily learned. The contour lines of a river valley are V-shaped with the pointed end of the letter facing upstream; those of the end of a ridge are generally U-shaped. A peak is marked by rings of contour lines.

The various symbols (signs) used on maps include those for airports, towns, canals, roads and railways, and, on large-scale maps, those for such things as churches, post offices and even telephone boxes. These symbols together with the different colours used are usually explained by a "key" printed at the foot of the map.

The National Grid

The national grid provides a method of describing the position of any place in England, Scotland or Wales and of finding it on the map. The map is printed over with a grid, or crisscross pattern, of lines running east and west and north and south. These lines are spaced so that they form squares with a side of 100 kilometres (a kilometre is a distance of 1,000 metres). Each of these large squares is given two letters to distinguish it. Thus London is in square TQ and Edinburgh in square NT. The bottom left-hand corner of the complete grid is a point some distance west and a little south of Land's End in Cornwall.

The large squares are further divided into smaller squares with a side of 10 kilometres. On most maps the smaller squares are again subdivided into squares of 1 kilometre. The grid lines forming the squares are numbered and the position of any place can be described by the use of these numbers, which together with the two letters make up what is called the *grid reference*.

To give the grid reference of a place, the letters of the 100-kilometre square containing it are first written down. Then are added the numbers of the grid lines at the bottom left-hand corner of the 1-kilometre square on the map in which the place lies, *the figures of the north and south line being put before those of the east and west line*. Thus Winchelsea Station in Sussex is in large square TQ. The bottom left-hand corner of the 1-kilometre square in which it lies is where grid line 89 crosses grid line 18, giving grid reference TQ 8918. For greater accuracy, the distance of

the place in tenths of a kilometre from the bottom left-hand corner of the 1-kilometre square may be estimated, again giving the distance from the north and south line first. Winchelsea Station is nine-tenths of a kilometre from grid line 89 and three-tenths of a kilometre from grid line 18, so its six-figure grid reference is TQ 899183.

MAPS AND MAP MAKING.
A map is a drawing of part of the Earth's surface. People turn to maps to learn about countries and districts with which they are not familiar. Travellers, tourists, ships' captains and aircraft pilots all use maps to plan their routes and to keep to them. Maps used by mining engineers show the kinds of rock forming the land and other special maps are made to show such things as the amount of rainfall, the number of people living in each square kilometre and the distribution of crops.

Early maps were made in many ways. The South Pacific islanders made maps of their voyages by tying together reeds and the American Indians painted maps on deerskins. The ancient Assyrians scratched on a slab of clay which they then baked hard.

As knowledge grew about the lands of the world, people needed maps showing larger and larger areas. The map makers were in difficulties. They had nothing to go on but travellers' and sailors' tales—how were they to show that one place was to be reached from another after a five days' march or a three weeks' sail? The answer was given in the 2nd century A.D. by the Greek astronomer Ptolemy. He believed the Earth was a great ball and that he knew its size. He pictured it ruled into sections by lines at regular intervals running north and south crossed by other lines running east and west. He drew these lines on a map sheet and marked on it the lands he knew of, according to their distance and direction from Alexandria (Egypt) where he lived. He thus invented the system of parallels of latitude and meridians of longitude (see the separate article LATITUDE AND LONGITUDE).

From about 1300 onwards, sailors used maps drawn on parchment showing the coastline with the bays and headlands so that they could recognize them. These *portolani*, as they were

☐ Read about MAKING YOUR OWN MAP in the blue pages of volume 17

called, carried a spider's web of lines joining together all the different ports to give the sailors the correct course (direction) to steer by compass. These and other maps used by navigators are properly known as charts. (See CHART.)

In 1585 the famous geographer Gerardus Mercator of Flanders brought out a book of maps whose cover had a picture showing the giant Atlas carrying the world on his shoulders. Since then, a book of maps has been called an atlas (see ATLAS).

The simplest and the most accurate way to represent the whole world is with a map drawn on the surface of a globe. No flat map can be really accurate because the Earth's surface is curved. The skin of an orange cannot be laid out flat. The best that can be done with a flat map is to draw it in such a way that it is accurate in one respect, such as distance or direction or area, and inaccurate in all other respects. Or, if the area to be shown is not too large, the map maker can provide a map that is fairly accurate in most ways but not quite accurate in any.

Any map must be based on the network of criss-cross lines formed by the parallels of latitude and the meridians of longitude. The method used for drawing this network is known as the *projection*. A simple projection first used in 1568 by Mercator and named after him is often found in maps of the world and the charts used by sailors. Suppose the world is drawn on the outside surface of a hollow globe, the land areas being coloured dark and the seas left transparent. If a sheet of paper is now wrapped round the globe in a cylinder which touches the equator, and a bright light placed inside the globe at the exact centre, the arrangement will act like a film-strip projector with the paper serving as the screen. If the outlines of the dark land areas are traced in pencil on the paper it can afterwards be unrolled to form a flat map.

A map on Mercator's projection has the parallels of latitude at right angles to the meridians, as they should be, and therefore it shows the direction of one place from another correctly. On the other hand, it exaggerates the sizes of areas far from the equator and cannot show the polar regions at all. Iceland, for example, appears to be about seven times as large as it would if it were on the equator. Another type of projection often used for world maps represents areas correctly but nothing else. Conic projections, obtained by wrapping the sheet of paper round the globe in a cone instead of a cylinder, are fairly accurate in most respects and are therefore often used in atlas maps. Zenithal projections, sometimes used to show the polar regions, have the North or South Pole in the middle with the

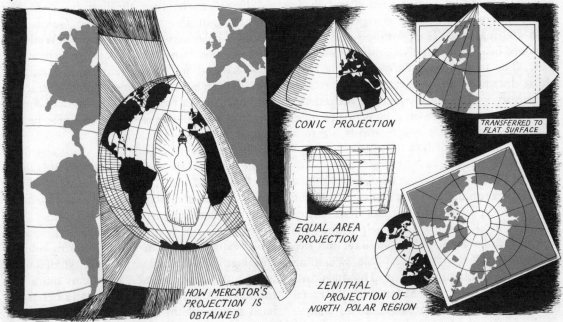

CONIC PROJECTION

TRANSFERRED TO FLAT SURFACE

EQUAL AREA PROJECTION

HOW MERCATOR'S PROJECTION IS OBTAINED

ZENITHAL PROJECTION OF NORTH POLAR REGION

parallels of latitude as circles round them and the meridians arranged like the spokes of a wheel. A special projection for long distance airlines is designed so that the shortest route between two places is shown as a straight line.

Surveying

The information needed by the map maker is collected by surveyors. In most civilized countries maps are prepared by a government department and in the United Kingdom this is done by the Ordnance Survey, which employs both map makers and surveyors. The surveyor measures the distances and directions of mountains, rivers, lakes, roads and other features, using instruments and the branch of mathematics called trigonometry. He must also measure the height of the land from place to place.

Countries where travel is difficult are often mapped by aerial photography, and this method has been used for most of northern Canada and many parts of Australia and Africa. The aircraft flies along a chosen straight line at a fixed height and the camera photographs the ground at regular intervals. When fitted together these photographs form a map of a long strip of country. A series of overlapping strips is arranged so as to cover the whole area.

Once the outlines of the map have been drawn the details are filled in using special symbols, or signs, to represent such things as woods, railways, roads and marshes. These symbols are usually explained in a key, or small diagram, on the map itself. The map always carries a scale from which distances can be measured. The Ordnance Survey maps mostly used by walkers are to a scale of $2\frac{1}{2}$ inches or 1 inch to the mile. Those used by cyclists and motorists are to a scale of $\frac{1}{2}$ inch or $\frac{1}{4}$ inch to the mile.

MARATHON is a place in Greece which gave its name to a running race. In 490 B.C. the Greek soldier Pheidippides ran 150 miles from Athens to Sparta in 48 hours to fetch help against the Persian invader Darius. For two days and two nights he travelled over hill and dale, swimming rivers and climbing mountains. He afterwards fought in the Battle of Marathon and raced back to Athens—a distance of about 24 miles—with the news of victory. This last effort was too much for him, and he fell dead as he reached the city, gasping "Rejoice, we conquer!"

When in 1896 the first of the modern Olympic Games was held at Athens (see OLYMPIC GAMES), a race from Marathon to Athens was included in honour of Pheidippides. It was won by a Greek peasant called Loues, to the delight of his countrymen. Women threw their jewellery at his feet, a hotel keeper offered him free meals for a year and a boy promised to black his boots free for the rest of his life.

When the Olympic Games were held in London in 1908, the distance for the marathon race was 26 miles 385 yards, which was the distance from Windsor Park to the royal box in the White City stadium. It was a very hot day, and the British runners set off so fast that many of the 75 competitors collapsed on the way and the leaders finished in a state of utter exhaustion. The first to reach the stadium was a young Italian, Dorando Pietri, who collapsed at the entrance to the track. He was helped up, but fell again and again and was almost carried past the winning post. Naturally, second and third protested, as Pietri could never have reached the tape without help, and he was disqualified. However, Queen Alexandra gave him a special gold cup for his plucky effort.

There was another thrilling finish to the marathon in the 1948 Olympic Games. E. Gailly of Belgium was the first to reach Wembley Stadium after 26 miles run in sweltering heat, but he was dazed and almost fainting with exhaustion. Before he could stagger round the track to the finish, he was passed by D. Cabrera of Argentina and T. Richards of Great Britain, so he was placed third in the result.

The distance of 26 miles 385 yards was fixed as the length of the marathon race in the Olympic Games of 1924. This distance, however, applies only to the Olympic Games and for other meetings there is no fixed length of course. The marathon is run mainly on roads and is much more exhausting than track or cross-country running. A man may lose as much as half a stone in weight during the race, and many marathon runners pickle their feet to withstand better the hard surface of the road. A marathon runner

When the battle had been won, Pheidippides set out to run from Marathon to Athens with the news of the victory.

needs powerful legs, plenty of heart and lung power and should be small and light. The race is one in which the older runners have a good chance of victory.

There is no official world record for the Marathon since the severity of the courses varies. The best time over the distance is 2 hours 8 minutes and 33·6 seconds by Derek Clayton of Australia.

MARATHON, BATTLE OF.

The Battle of Marathon, fought in a plain about 50 kilometres northeast of Athens (Greece) in the year 490 B.C., is one of the most important events of ancient history.

For some time before 490, the Persians had been conquering territory in Ionia (the western, coastal part of Asia Minor) and islands in the Aegean Sea. In about 500 B.C. the main Ionian cities rebelled against Persian rule and were helped to do so by Athens and Eretria, city states on the mainland of Greece. The Persian King, Darius, therefore decided that he must punish Athens and Eretria. He sent a large expedition which began by laying waste Eretria and capturing its inhabitants. Athens was the next target for his wrath. The Athenians sent a famous runner, Pheidippides, to ask help from the people of Sparta. The Spartans said they could not send help until a religious festival was finished. Rather than wait for the Persians to reach Athens, the Athenians marched to Marathon, where the Persians were encamped. The Athenians had about 9,000 men and were joined by about 1,000 gallant men from Plataea, a city near Thebes.

The Persians, with about 20,000 men, were encamped on the level ground at Marathon, close to the sea shore. The Athenians took up their position on higher ground, with their backs to the passes leading to Athens and with the flanks (sides) of their army protected by the mountains. The Persians were thus trapped between the Athenians and the sea. The Athenian commander-in-chief was Callimachus but the famous statesman Miltiades took the leading part in the Athenian councils of war. He decided that their troops should charge down the sloping ground at great speed straight into the Persian ranks. They did this, and after putting the Persian flanks to flight they then turned on the centre of their army and completed the victory. The Persians lost more than 6,000 men and the Athenians 192; among them, however, was Callimachus.

The Athenians made desperate attempts to seize the Persian ships that were anchored in the bay, but all except seven escaped and sailed to Athens. Miltiades then marched his troops at great speed back to Athens. When the Persians saw them drawn up on the shore near Athens they gave up the enterprise and sailed away.

MARBLE

usually means a decorative rock which may owe its fine appearance when polished to the changes which have taken place in the original limestone. The word marble is used by builders and craftsmen for any rather fine soft decorative rock, even though it may not have been altered. Such, for example, is the Purbeck marble so common in the interiors of churches in Britain. Purbeck marble is an ordinary freshwater limestone full of the shells of small snails which live in fresh water. Other marbles may not have the composition of limestone at all.

Scientists, on the other hand, use the word marble to describe limestone, the form of which has been altered by heat or (more usually) by intense pressures and movements which have taken place deep in the Earth's crust when the rocks have been buried beneath later rocks and squeezed with tremendous force. Both limestone and marble in this sense have the same composition, namely that of calcium carbonate. The commonest mineral of this composition—which is by far the most important mineral in marbles—is calcite.

The ancient Greeks carved some of their most beautiful statues out of a pure marble which they

British Museum

Marble sculptures from the north frieze of the Parthenon. They are part of the Elgin Marbles in the British Museum.

obtained from the island of Paros in the Aegean Sea. This Parian marble, as it is called, takes on a fine waxy appearance when it is polished. The Greeks also used a marble from Mount Pendelikon, northeast of Athens, and from this material built the great temple of the Parthenon at Athens, the pillars of which are still standing. (See PARTHENON.) Modern sculptors often use marble that comes from the district round Carrara in northwestern Italy. Stone from this district was also used by the ancient Romans and then, much later, in the 16th century A.D., by the great sculptor Michelangelo (see MICHELANGELO). Other modern sources of marble are Belgium, Ireland, Sweden, Switzerland, the

United States and India.

Marble is not often used for buildings in the damp climate of Britain because dampness and the smoky, acid atmosphere of big cities make it crumble, but in dry climates it is a hard-wearing stone. However, both white and coloured marbles were often used for the rooms of the great country houses that were built in Britain in the 18th century.

MARBLES is a game something like a miniature form of bowls (see BOWLS). It is a very ancient game and is played by grown-ups as well as children. The Roman Emperor Augustus (63 B.C.–A.D. 14) used to play marbles. Originally, fruit-stones, nuts and round pebbles were used for the game, but in the 18th century the little balls were made from chips of marble and the game got its present name.

Marbles range from the home-baked clay "maradiddles" to beautiful rare ones made of agate (see AGATE). Some schoolboys fix different values for the different kinds of marbles when exchanging. Thus a clay "commoney" is worth one and is called a one-er. "Taws" and "stoneys" of brown marble are three-ers. "Alleys" made from coloured glass (but so called because they were once made of alabaster) range from four-ers to six-ers. A "blood alley", which is an "alley" streaked with red, may be anything from a twelve-er to a forty-eight-er, according to its size and beauty. Although maradiddles have died out, the newer kinds of marbles include the glass stoppers out of lemonade bottles—called "glasseys"—and the big, bright steel ball-bearings called "steelies".

The idea of most marble games is to roll one marble so that it hits another. The marble is shot by being laid on the inside of the forefinger and flicked with the thumb-nail. When shooting, the player must "knuckle down", or have the knuckle of the forefinger touching the ground.

Some of the more popular marbles games are:

Boss Out (or *Hit and Span*). One player rolls his marble as a mark. The other shoots at it, and if he hits it or comes within a hand-span of it, he takes it. If he fails, his marble becomes the mark for the first player to aim at.

Ring Taw. Each player puts a few marbles inside a ring drawn on the ground. The players then

Fox Photos

A school marbles championship at Castleford, Yorkshire.

young Marconi also began to experiment.

He did not invent the instruments he used, although he improved on those of others. He was probably the first to realize that with the aid of a Morse key the waves could be used to send messages. At first Marconi, like the other experimenters, could not receive signals at distances more than 100 yards from the transmitter, but then he had the idea of attaching an elevated wire and an earth connection to both transmitter and receiver. Immediately the range of his signals increased to a mile.

By this, Marconi transformed wireless waves from a scientific curiosity to an entirely new form of communication. He offered his ideas to the Italian government but without success, so he brought his apparatus to England. At that time, Britain was the greatest seafaring nation and therefore likely to be interested in equipment which, by keeping vessels in touch with each other and with the shore, could save lives.

In 1896, at the age of 22, Marconi took out the world's first patent for wireless telegraphy and in the following year founded his own company (now the Marconi Company). A tireless worker, he gathered a small band of engineers around him and continued experimenting, continually improving the range of his apparatus. In 1900 he patented the tuned circuit, which enabled several stations to transmit at the same time without interfering with each other's signals. In 1901 he astonished the world by sending wireless signals over the Atlantic from Poldhu, Cornwall, to St. John's, Newfoundland.

In the years that followed, wireless communication came into world-wide use on land, at sea, and later in the air. It was a great satisfaction to Marconi to know that wireless had been the means of saving innumerable lives at sea; one notable instance of this was in 1912 when the great liner "Titanic", on its maiden voyage, struck an iceberg in the North Atlantic and sank. Its distress signals saved many lives.

Marconi did much to develop the short-wave beam system and microwave communications. He received honours and decorations from many countries and was also awarded the Nobel Peace Prize. He was experimenting successfully up to the time of his death in 1937.

shoot in turn at the marbles, taking those that they knock out of the ring.

Pit. The marbles are aimed at a small hole in the ground. Several holes can be dug at a distance from each other and a game of miniature golf played.

Bridge Board (or *Nine Holes*). The marbles are aimed to roll through numbered arches in a wooden board.

Bounce Eye (or *Bombers*). A few marbles are put inside a ring drawn on the ground. In turn, each player stands over the ring, holds a marble to his eye and drops it. He keeps all the marbles he knocks out but adds his marble to those in the circle if he misses.

MARCONI, Guglielmo (1874–1937). The father of radio communications, Guglielmo Marconi was born at Bologna, Italy. His father was an Italian landowner and his mother was Irish. He was educated at Florence and Leghorn. He studied under Professor Rosa and attended lectures by Professor Righi, both of whom were experimenting with Hertzian waves (as radio waves were then called, after Heinrich Hertz, the first man to generate them). The

Radio Times Hulton Picture Library

With simple equipment like this, Marconi pioneered the way towards world-wide radio communication.

The Italian government gave him a state funeral and wireless stations all over the world fell silent for two minutes in his honour. He was buried at his native Bologna.

Further examples of Marconi's work are given in the articles RADIO and WIRELESS TELE-GRAPHY.

MARGARINE is a mixture of oils, fats and pasteurized milk, to which vitamins A and D and various sorts of flavouring have been added. In appearance and food value it is similar to butter. Margarine was first made in France in the late 1860s by the chemist H. Mège-Mouriès. Soon large quantities were being made in the Netherlands but it was not until the 20th century that Great Britain had many margarine factories. Margarine is now made in most countries, including the butter-producing countries. Vitamins began to be added during the 1920s because margarine lacked vitamins.

Most of the oils used in margarine are obtained from vegetable products such as groundnuts, coconuts, palm kernels, soya beans and sunflowers. Some animal fat and oil is used—mostly beef-fat and whale oil. The nuts, beans and seeds are crushed to extract the oils, which have to go through many processes before they are pure enough to use. When pure they are mixed with pasteurized milk. Then vitamins A and D and various flavourings are added. The mixture is churned to a creamy emulsion (see EMULSION) which, when it is passed over cooling drums, is turned from a liquid into solid flakes.

After various other processes, machines shape and wrap the margarine ready for the shops.

MARIE ANTOINETTE (1755–1793) was the wife of the King of France when the French Revolution broke out in 1789. (See FRENCH REVOLUTION.) She was hated by the people because of her extravagance and helped to bring about the downfall of the King and the execution of them both.

She was the 15th child of the Holy Roman Emperor Francis I and his wife Maria Theresa,

Mansell Collection

Marie Antoinette, wife of King Louis XVI of France.

who ruled over Austria, Hungary and Bohemia. At 15 she was married to Louis, who became King Louis XVI in 1774. She soon became unpopular both at the French court and in France generally. Because of her un-French manners she was known as "the Austrian" and because of her extravagance as "Madame Déficit". (This word means a shortage of money.) She had a strong influence over the King, who was rather weak, and over the government, but she often behaved without much sense of tact. She loved luxury and had no understanding of the terrible conditions in which most people lived. The people hated her extravagance and her Austrian origin.

When revolution broke out in Paris in 1789 and the mob stormed the Bastille (see BASTILLE), the King and Queen were at their palace of Versailles, in the country southwest of Paris. The mob therefore went to Versailles and forced them to return to Paris. In June 1791 the royal party secretly escaped from Paris and made for the eastern frontier of France. When they had almost reached it a village postman recognized the King and galloped ahead to warn the guards. They stopped the coach at Varennes and the royal family were forced to return to Paris as prisoners. The King did not seem to care what happened, and it was Marie Antoinette who tried to save his throne. However, when she called on the rulers of Europe—especially her brother Leopold II of Austria—for help, the mob broke into the Palace of the Tuileries in Paris where they were living. For their own safety the royal family were imprisoned in a fortress-like building known as the Temple. Their end was now near. The King was executed in January 1793 and in October the Queen was found guilty of encouraging civil war and betraying her country. On October 16 she was executed, after being driven to the guillotine (see GUILLOTINE) in a cart through streets filled with jeering people.

MARIGOLD.
The marigold is a hardy garden plant whose golden-orange, daisy-like flowers bloom all year round.

The marigold belongs to the Compositae family, and therefore its head is made up of many tiny flowers, or florets. The ray, or outer,

The golden marigold blooms all the year round.

florets are female and the disc, or inner, florets are male. In one kind of marigold, called the hen and chickens, there is one flower-head surrounded by other, smaller heads. Each flower-head of the marigold bears a number of fruits when the petals have fallen.

The home of marigolds is the Mediterranean region, where there are about 14 different kinds. They have been cultivated for at least 300 years. There are other garden plants called marigolds which belong to different groups in the same family, such as the African or French marigold (*Tagetes*) and the corn marigold (*Chrysanthemum*), from the flowers of which a yellow dye used to be made in Germany. The marsh marigold belongs to the buttercup family and is another name for the kingcup. (See KINGCUP.)

MARINE ENGINES.
The engines driving a ship are called marine engines and may be of several kinds. The chief kinds are: steam reciprocating, steam turbine, turbo-electric, diesel and diesel-electric.

The steam for driving a steam engine of any kind has to be made in a boiler. A ship's boilers are usually carried low down underneath the funnel or funnels through which the smoke from the furnace escapes. The fuel burnt is either coal or oil. When oil is used, it is pumped through a heater to warm it and then sprayed into the furnace. Air for burning the fuel is usually blown into the furnace under pressure by fans or blowers. The use of nuclear energy for heating the boiler is a development which results in ships being able to travel for a long time without refuelling, as a few kilograms of uranium will drive the ship for a long voyage. Such ships include the American "Savannah", the Russian icebreaker "Lenin" and the German freighter "Otto Hahn". (See the article NUCLEAR ENERGY.)

The boilers are of two main kinds. A few older and slower ships have cylindrical fire-tube boilers in which the flames and hot gases from the furnace are led through tubes which are surrounded by water in the boiler. Boilers of this kind (sometimes called Scotch boilers) supply steam at a pressure of about 13 bars. The other kind of boiler, called the water-tube boiler, is smaller and lighter and works on the reverse principle, the water being inside the tubes and the flames outside. Water-tube boilers supply steam pressure of 41 bars or more.

In the earliest steamships, which were built in the last quarter of the 18th century, reciprocating engines were used to turn paddle wheels on each side of the ship. In a paddle steamer, the lower parts of the paddle wheels dip into the water so that when the wheels are turned they drive the ship along. About the middle of the 19th century, the screw propeller took the place of paddle wheels, and paddle steamers are now commonly used only on rivers and in sheltered waters. The propeller is fixed to a shaft that goes through the stern, or rear end, of the ship. The propeller has blades which work in the same way as those of an electric fan. When the shaft is turned the propeller blades thrust the water backwards and so push the ship forwards.

Steam Engines

The word "reciprocate" means to move to and fro. The reciprocating engine uses the steam to push a close-fitting piston up and down inside a cylinder. When the piston reaches the bottom of the cylinder, a valve worked by the engine shaft shuts off steam from the top of the cylinder and admits steam to the lower part, thus pushing the piston up again. After the steam has done its work in one cylinder it is still at quite a high pressure and so is led to a second cylinder, and after that to a third and sometimes even to a fourth. The piston of each cylinder is made to turn the shaft of the engine in much the same fashion as the legs of a cyclist move up and down to turn the pedals of his bicycle. The shaft of the

Courtesy, Harland and Wolff Ltd.

Left: A four-crank triple-expansion steam engine. This kind of marine engine is still found in many ships. Right: A turbine set with the covers lifted. The high-pressure turbine is in the foreground, the low-pressure one at the back. The double-reduction gearing on the right enables the ship's propellers to turn at a comparatively slow speed.

Courtesy, Harland and Wolff (left); Cunard

Left: A three-bladed propeller of a passenger liner. Above: The engine room of the "Queen Elizabeth 2", which is powered by two turbines driving six-bladed propellers.

engine is connected to the propeller shaft. To make the ship go astern (backwards), reversing gear is worked so that the valves admit steam to the cylinders in the opposite direction.

When the steam has finished its work in the engine it is led to a condenser, where it passes through tubes surrounded by water pumped in from the sea. The cold sea water keeps the tubes cool so that the steam immediately condenses, or turns to water, inside them. The condensed water is pumped into a hot well or feed tank from which it is pumped back to the boilers and used again. The condenser was first used in steamships in about 1838. Before that, sea water had to be used in the boilers, which had to be shut down every few days in order to clean out the deposits of salt inside.

Many large fast ships are driven by steam turbines. The turbine works rather like a windmill, using the steam to push against blades fixed to the outside of a drum supported on a shaft, thus forcing the drum (called the rotor because it goes round) and the shaft to turn. There are several rows of blades on the rotor and after the steam has done its work on one row it is led to the next. The rotor is enclosed in a casing so that no moving parts can be seen, and in fact a steam turbine runs so smoothly and quietly that it is difficult to tell if it is working or not. After the steam has passed through one turbine it may be led

through a second and third which are arranged to drive the same propeller shaft. As a turbine cannot be made to run backwards by sending steam through it the reverse way, separate astern turbines are provided which are used only for driving the ship backwards.

A turbine runs best when turning fast but propellers do not work well unless they turn slowly. There are two ways out of this difficulty. In some ships the turbine shafts are connected to the propeller shafts through gearing so that the propellers turn at only about one-thirtieth the speed of the turbine rotors. (See GEARS.) Other ships use turbo-electric drive, in which the turbines drive alternators (dynamos) which supply alternating current to fairly slow-running electric motors connected to the propeller shafts. (See DYNAMO.)

Steam turbines were first used for driving a ship in 1894, when Sir Charles Parsons created a sensation at the naval review at Spithead by making his "Turbinia" race between the lines of anchored warships at $34\frac{1}{2}$ knots (nearly 65 kilometres an hour). Large turbine-driven ships were not built until 1905 but are now common.

Diesels and Gas Turbines

Diesel engines, which work in the same way as those of motor buses and heavy lorries, came rapidly into use for driving ships after World

War I. Those used in big ships are generally large, heavy engines with anything up to eight cylinders. Smaller ships may use high-speed diesels connected to the propeller shafts either by mechanical gearing or, in diesel-electric ships, by using alternators and electric motors like those described for turbo-electric drive. Diesel engines are economical, giving more power for each ton of fuel burnt than any other kind. They have the further advantage that they burn their fuel oil inside the cylinders and therefore need no boilers, thus saving weight and space.

Gas turbines have been tried as marine engines in small fast ships such as motor gunboats in the navy. The kind of gas turbine used is that described as a "propeller turbine" in the article INTERNAL COMBUSTION ENGINE.

The separate articles BOILER; DIESEL ENGINE; STEAM ENGINE; TURBINE will help you to understand marine engines more fully.

MARINE LIFE.

The word "marine" comes from *mare*, the Latin word for "sea", and marine life means the tremendous number of plants and animals that live in the waters of the sea. For a long time marine life was a great mystery, and the men who sailed the seas imagined that various kinds of monsters lived in their depths.

It was not until about 100 years ago that real exploration of the sea bottom began. Edward Forbes (1815–1854) collected animals from the sea bed with a dredge. At first he worked in the seas off the British Isles and later he went to the Mediterranean. Gradually he let his dredge down deeper and deeper until he was fishing animals up from 200 fathoms (a fathom is six feet). Yet even Forbes thought that there could be no life in the depths below 300 fathoms (1,800 feet).

Soon after Forbes had started his dredging work, British and Norwegian scientists joined in. The nets were let down deeper and deeper, but they always came up filled with crabs, starfishes, worms, fishes and other animals. About this time the telegraph was invented, and plans were made to lay a telegraph cable below the sea to link Great Britain with America. Before long the governments of both Britain and the United States were sending out ships to take soundings of the bed of the Atlantic.

Interest in the sea bed was growing, and in 1872 the steamship H.M.S. "Challenger", with scientists on board, set out from Britain to explore the oceans of the world and discover if life could be found in the depths of the sea. The expedition lasted for nearly four years, and from it came the first real knowledge of the ocean bed.

Since the days of the "Challenger" expedition, many other ships have been sent out from many countries and much has been learnt about the ocean and its life, though much still remains to be learnt. Among the discoveries so far made is the fact that Forbes was wrong and life can exist well below 300 fathoms. Even in the greatest depths animals, though not plants, live.

Geography of the Sea Bed

The geography of the sea bed is not unlike that of the land, for there are ranges of hills, high mountains, deep valleys, rolling plains and plateaux (tablelands) just as on dry land.

On the edge of the sea is the part known as the seashore, where each day as the tide goes out a strip of rock, sand or shingle is left uncovered. This is known to scientists as the littoral zone. The types of marine life found there are described in the article SEASHORE.

Below the low tide mark (where the tide goes back farthest), the bottom of the sea slopes gently downwards to a depth of about 100 fathoms in the form of a shelf, known as the continental shelf. In some parts of the world this shelf extends for a distance of four or five miles, but off some parts of the British Isles it extends for more than 100 miles. The waters of the continental shelf are particularly rich in fish, for animals find it easier to live there than in the very deep waters. The shelf, like the littoral zone, is covered with sand and rock or with mud brought down by rivers.

The continental shelf ends with a steep slope, reaching to a depth of 1,000 fathoms or more. This steep slope is known as the continental slope and it forms the sides of the great basins that hold the oceans.

At about 1,500 fathoms the slope levels out and becomes a plain, the bed of the ocean, known as the abyssal plain. Here there are deep valleys and great mountain peaks jutting up

through the water. At depths greater than 100 fathoms the ocean bed is covered with various fine muds, made up partly of substances from volcanoes and partly of the remains of tiny, long-dead plants and animals.

Seaweeds are not found at greater depths than 50 fathoms, for they need fairly strong light to build up their food. At 350 fathoms there is just enough light to be seen by the human eye, and at 500 fathoms scientists who exposed photographic plates for two hours have found on them faint traces of the action of light.

Animals at Different Depths

The animals that live around the edge of the sea are not very different from the ones found on the continental shelf, except they are generally larger in the deeper waters. From the littoral zone to 100 fathoms deep live sponges, sea anemones, crabs, lobsters, shrimps, molluscs (shellfish) of all kinds, fishes, octopuses and squid. Beyond the continental shelf, in the truly deep seas, different forms of these creatures are found.

Sunlight cannot reach far below the surface of the sea, and so the depths, besides being dark, are also very cold. Another way in which the deep seas are different from the shallow waters is in pressure. The deeper the sea, the stronger the pressure of water, until on the abyssal plain it is up to four tons to the square inch. The creatures that live at great depths are specially adapted to withstand the pressures, and if taken out into the air they are likely to explode.

Marine animals are divided into three kinds. On the bed of the sea the creatures are known as *benthos*. Some move about, like the crawling starfishes, and others are fixed, like corals, or move very slowly, like sea anemones.

On the surface of the sea, drifting with the currents, is the *plankton*. This includes many tiny floating plants and animals, the eggs and young of larger animals and jellyfishes. Plank-

(1) Jellyfish. (2) Seaweed. (3) Sea anemone. (4) Blue crab. (5) Keyhole limpets. (6) Seaweed limpets. (7) Starfish. (8) Lobster. (9) Grass sponge. (10) Single-rayed sponge. (11) Mussels. (12) Octopus. (13) Sea louse. (14) Branching coral. (15) Squid. (16) Plaice. (17) Mackerel. (18) Skate. (19) Haddock. (20) John Dory. (21) Blue shark. (22) Blue whale. (23) Lantern fish. (24) Angler-fish.

ton is very important, for a great many animals feed on it. It is often known as the pastures of the sea. (See PLANKTON.)

Finally there is the *nekton,* animals able to swim freely, even against the current. Among them are fishes, whales and squid.

Some animals change from one kind to another at different times of their lives. For example, the larvae (young) of starfishes are planktonic, but the full-grown starfish is benthic.

In the cold, dark depths of the sea the nektonic animals, particularly the fishes, squid and prawns, are much more fragile and delicate in appearance than those from parts of the sea where the pressure is less. They are usually the same colour all over their bodies (either black or red), though some are colourless or almost transparent. Most of them have spots on their bodies which glow faintly in the dark. Some have large eyes and can see, but others are completely blind, and it is thought that they feel their way about in the darkness with the help of a bunch of sensitive tentacles on the head.

Deep-sea fishes generally have wide, gaping jaws with long, sharp-pointed teeth, and with these they can prey on other fishes and squids. Many can swallow creatures larger than themselves, their stomachs being able to stretch enormously. Any animals living below 50 fathoms have to feed either on living animals which they catch or on dead creatures which sink down from the upper layers of the sea. (See DEEP-SEA FISH.)

The largest animal found in the sea is the blue whale of the Antarctic, which is also the largest animal in the world. It may measure 100 feet in length and weigh 150 tons. Giant squid, measuring up to 60 feet from the hind-end of the body to the tip of the tentacles, have occasionally been cast up on the shore. There is reason to suppose that even larger squid, measuring up to 100 feet, may be living in the ocean depths, but none has so far been caught.

Many tales have been told of sea serpents, and even nowadays there is sometimes a report that one has been seen. They are probably either giant squid or very large eels.

For years mermaids were believed to exist, and possibly the idea of them was suggested by sailors seeing the dugong and manatee, marine mammals generally known as sea cows, which float upright in the water. They live in the sea all their lives, unlike seals and sea lions, which go to land to breed.

The United States and the U.S.S.R. spend huge sums of money on marine research, largely for military purposes, but also for other reasons. Men look to the seas as possible sources of new food for the starving; fishing industries need to know the locations of fish they are trying to catch, and how many may be caught without killing off whole species.

MARK, Saint. St. Mark is thought to be the writer of the second Gospel. He was not one of the disciples who regularly accompanied Jesus while He was on Earth, but it is thought that after the Resurrection Mark played a part in proclaiming the good news. The evidence for this belief comes from the Acts of the Apostles, which, based on St. Paul's epistles, tells how Mark accompanied Paul on his missionary journeys. His mother's home in Jerusalem was one of the places where the apostles used to meet and it was probably there that the young Mark came to know them all. Later in his life he joined St. Peter and went with him to Rome.

It is not known for certain that St. Mark did, in fact, write the second Gospel, nor are its date or place of origin known. Some scholars believe that it was written in Rome, probably about 30 years after Jesus' death. However, it is possible that it was written as late as 50 years after His death, and some hold the view that its place of origin was somewhere in the Greek-speaking church in the east, possibly Syria or Asia Minor, since it is known to have been first written in Greek. The Gospel record was made to preserve the events of Jesus' life for times when all who had known Him personally would be dead.

If Mark was the author, his record was not based on personal knowledge, because he had not been one of the little band who had gone everywhere with Jesus. Peter supplied this personal knowledge and Mark used it to produce what is really a biography of Jesus. It is clear that it is based on the account of an eye-witness of Jesus' life. For example, it does not hesitate to point out the faults of the disciples, showing how slow they were to grasp what Jesus was trying to teach them, and how often they failed Him. Peter would naturally remember such things and was not the kind of man to pretend that they had never happened. Mark's Gospel is really a collection of stories that tell what Jesus did in His life-time and what His enemies did to Him. It contains very little of His teaching: it has no detailed account of the Sermon on the Mount and contains fewer of the parables than the Gospels of St. Luke and St. Matthew.

St. Mark's Day is celebrated on April 25.

MARKET GARDENING.
A market gardener is a person who grows fruit, vegetables or flowers for sale. Nowadays an area larger than a garden is generally used for this purpose, but the first market gardeners began by growing their produce in the gardens surrounding their cottages. After using as much as they and their families needed they drove the rest to the local markets in their carts.

This way of selling still goes on at some markets in country towns. Generally, however, market gardening has now become a section of the farming industry and is known as commercial growing.

Practically all the fruit, flowers and vegetables now grown for market is graded and packed, either at the farm packhouse or at a central station used by several growers. It then goes by train or lorry to the big horticultural markets, either in London or the provinces. Covent Garden, in London, is one of the biggest of these markets and often acts as a centre for redirecting produce to other markets where supplies are less plentiful (see COVENT GARDEN). Greengrocers and florists come into these markets and buy the supplies to take back to their shops.

There are two other methods of selling market garden produce. The growers themselves often have a kiosk or small shop facing the main road, as well as frequently having a stall at the local Wednesday or Saturday market. Then there is prepackaging, which means putting the fruit and vegetables into small plastic bags instead of into market boxes. These packages are ready to be taken straight home and, because there is no dirt, they are popular with grocers, many of whom now sell market produce.

Many market garden crops grown nowadays never find their way to market at all. They are grown for canning and quick-freezing. The food processing companies collect the produce direct from the farm and take it straight to their factories.

Some market growers still have quite small plots of ground for their crops, although generally they are much larger than in the old days. However they all use modern mechanical tools and the latest methods available for producing the best and largest crops. Large sprinklers and irrigation lines supply regular water so that, even in a dry summer, crops keep growing.

S. W. Burrage, Wye College

Growing chrysanthemums at Wye College, Kent.

Dutch lights, which are box-like structures with glass tops, are sometimes used to grow the crops as early as possible. Long tunnels made of plastic film have replaced many of these, however. Some of the tunnels are large enough to walk through. Throughout their life, from the time they are tiny seedlings until they are ready for harvesting, the plants have to be sprayed and dusted with chemicals to kill the pests which attack them and to keep away disease. Exact amounts of fertilizers have to be applied to give the different crops the various foods they need for growth.

Greenhouses, often movable from site to site

and pulled along on wheels by powerful winches, are used to grow tomatoes, cucumbers and flowers like carnations, chrysanthemums and roses. In winter they are used to grow lettuces when it is too cold to produce them out-of-doors.

Most of the early flower crops, anemones, daffodils and violets, come from the warmer parts of Great Britain including the Channel Isles, the Scilly Isles, Cornwall and Devon. There are also famous bulbfields in the Spalding area of Lincolnshire, where tulips are a speciality.

The Vale of Evesham, in Worcestershire, is a famous district for vegetables and soft fruit, which includes strawberries, raspberries, currants, gooseberries, loganberries and blackberries. These are also grown in large quantities in Cambridgeshire, Kent and Scotland. Apples and pears are called top fruits and come chiefly from Kent, Essex, Norfolk, the Isle of Ely around Wisbech, and Worcestershire. Kent is the leading cherry county and Evesham has a name for its plums.

The famous glasshouse areas are Guernsey in the Channel Isles and the Lea Valley near London. These, with the western parts of Lancashire and the Clyde Valley area of Scotland, produce most of the British tomatoes.

However, there are few areas which do not grow some market crops. Because they have to concentrate so hard on actually growing the crops, market gardeners often join growers' associations which deal with the marketing for them and send the crops to market under a recognized trade name. These associations also buy manures, seeds and machinery in large quantities and sell them to members.

MARKETS are places where people gather for the buying and selling of goods. They are sometimes held in the open air and sometimes in special buildings. Nowadays, too, there are shops called supermarkets where the housewife can select the goods she wants to buy, placing them in a wire basket provided by the shop and paying for them on her way out.

There have been markets since the earliest times. In England there are towns where the market dates back at least as far as Saxon days.

Chipping Campden (Gloucestershire) and Chipping Norton (Oxfordshire) are good examples and they got their names from the Anglo-Saxon word "cepinge", which meant market. After the Norman Conquest all market rights were granted by the sovereign and the right to levy tolls (taxes) on goods sold at markets was given to

Henry Grant
Farmers in the cattle market at Bury St. Edmunds, Suffolk.

a town or to a private person. Sometimes these rights were bought by a town from a private person. In more modern times the towns stopped claiming tolls on the goods sold at the markets and instead a charge was made for the stalls.

The markets in country towns are usually held once a week, on a day chosen so as not to clash with the markets of neighbouring towns. Farmers go to market to buy and sell livestock and produce. If they have corn to sell they very often take a sample so that those who are thinking of buying can judge its quality. If the farmer wishes to sell bigger things, such as potatoes and root crops, the merchant has to take his word for their quality.

Also attending the market are the agents of firms who sell farm machinery like tractors and ploughs. Sometimes there is a small exhibition of new farm machinery.

Very often there is a market for chickens, turkeys, ducks and geese. In the spring and early summer the farmers—or more often their wives —buy the young birds and then, just before

Christmas, sell the adult birds fattened and ready for the table. Pigs which have been fattened— also bullocks—are sold by auction in the markets and in Great Britain the average prices obtained for these are guaranteed by the government. For example, if the average auction price falls below a certain level the government adds a sum of money known as a subsidy.

The parts of the market where crops and cattle are sold is entirely a man's world. The farmers' wives often accompany their menfolk into the town but once they have arrived they part company. The women go off to do their shopping— either in the ordinary shops of the town or at the stalls that are often set up on market day, at which a wide variety of different kinds of goods may be bought.

In the days before motor cars, when travelling was not easy, country people made few journeys apart from their weekly journey to the market. Some villagers went on foot, carrying baskets of eggs, butter, fruit or dressed poultry, covered with snowy white cloths. Sometimes they travelled by the carrier's horse-drawn waggon, exchanging local gossip as they jogged up and down. The farmers and their wives went in their own vehicles and as they usually had spirited horses sped along at a spanking pace.

In the market itself there was interest in other things besides prices. News came in from outlying parts and people could always be sure of meeting one another. Almost as important as

the market was the favourite inn of the town, where the men had plentiful helpings of good food, washed down with tankards of ale.

In the market towns all over England there may still be seen an ancient cross (sometimes it is a pointed stone, but is still called a cross), a fountain, pump or some other monument put up hundreds of years ago in the place where the market was held. Sometimes there are old buildings in which certain types of goods were sold; at Dunster in Somerset there is the Yarn Market —an eight-sided building with a sloping roof— and at Wymondham in Norfolk there is a similar building that stands on posts.

The articles BILLINGSGATE MARKET, COVENT GARDEN, LEADENHALL MARKET, and SMITH-FIELD MARKET describe some of the great covered markets that are still held in London. Besides these there are many street markets where almost anything, old or new, can be bought. The most famous are the Caledonian Market, opposite the Tower of London on the south side of the River Thames, one in Middlesex Street (often known as Petticoat Lane) near Liverpool Street Station, and the Portobello Road Market in Notting Hill, west London.

MARLBOROUGH, JOHN CHURCHILL, 1ST DUKE OF (1650–1722). The Duke of Marlborough was one of the greatest of all English soldiers and his skill broke the power of Louis XIV of France. (See LOUIS XIV.) He was the son of Sir Winston Churchill, a Dorsetshire landowner, and was born on May 26, 1650, at Ashe, in the parish of Musbury in Devon. He went to St. Paul's School in London and at 15 became page to the Duke of York (the heir to the throne). He became an officer in the foot guards in 1667 and served abroad with great distinction.

When the Duke of York became King James II in 1685 Churchill was very popular at court. In July he helped to win the Battle of Sedgemoor against the Duke of Monmouth's supporters. (See MONMOUTH'S REBELLION.) About this time, however, he declared that if James, who was a Roman Catholic, should attempt to make England a Catholic country he would leave his service. When it became clear that this was what James was trying to do, Churchill was one of those who in 1688 invited William of Orange and Mary to come to England from the Netherlands. James had to flee and William and Mary became king and queen. (See ENGLISH HISTORY.) William made Churchill Earl of Marlborough, a privy councillor and commander-in-chief of the army in England.

However, Marlborough continued to write to James II, who was in exile in France, and William became suspicious of him and had him imprisoned in the Tower of London on a charge of treason. The evidence against him was proved false so he was released. There is no doubt, however, that he was in close touch with James. During the last years of William's reign he was restored to royal favour.

When Queen Anne came to the throne in 1702 Marlborough was given even greater honours, partly because his wife Sarah was a great friend of the Queen. He became a duke, a Knight of the Garter and commander-in-chief of all British troops at home and abroad. Soon afterwards, when Britain, the Netherlands and Austria went to war against France, he was made commander-in-chief of the British and Dutch forces. He showed great skill in planning and fighting battles and his patience with difficult and unwilling allies was remarkable. He was keenly interested in the welfare of his men, who named him Corporal John.

Marlborough's greatest triumph came in 1704

when the French king Louis XIV and the Elector (ruler) of Bavaria were threatening Vienna, the capital of Austria. The allied governments wanted the army to stay in the Netherlands, but Marlborough realized that if Vienna were lost the alliance would break up. Therefore he risked all by marching to southern Germany where he was joined by Prince Eugène, one of the Austrian generals. On August 13 near the Bavarian village of Blenheim (Blindheim in German) was fought the great battle in which Marlborough's leadership brought victory. Vienna was saved and the French had to leave Germany. Marlborough entered London in a triumphal procession and the Queen gave him

Courtesy, Trustees of the National Portrait Gallery
Marlborough was one of England's greatest generals.

the manor of Woodstock (Oxfordshire). A great palace was built for him at Woodstock, paid for by public money. He called it Blenheim after his victory.

Victories at Ramillies, Oudenarde and Malplaquet followed between 1706 and 1709, but all was not well, for the Queen quarrelled with Sarah, and Marlborough was accused of using public money for himself. He was dismissed on January 31, 1711, and the next year left England to live in Europe.

When Queen Anne died in 1714 he returned and again took up his military posts, but played little part in public affairs. He died on June 16, 1722, and was buried in Westminster Abbey. His body was later moved to the chapel of Blenheim Palace.

The most famous of Marlborough's descendants was Sir Winston Churchill, about whom there is a separate article.

MARLBOROUGH.
Marlborough is a region in the northeast of the South Island of New Zealand and is about half the size of Wales. Most of it is mountainous or hilly, the highest mountain being Tapuaenuku (2,885 metres) in the beautiful Kaikoura Ranges parallel to the east coast. The chief rivers are the Clarence, Wairau and Awatere. On the northern coastline are long, deep, winding inlets of the sea between high frowning cliffs. Captain James Cook, who first explored New Zealand, often used Queen Charlotte Sound as an anchorage.

The land in Marlborough is chiefly used for sheep-farming, but in the sunny sheltered valleys apples, pears, hops, grain and some tobacco are grown. Other industries are dairying and beekeeping.

The chief town and business centre of Marlborough is Blenheim on the Wairau River. Its port is Picton about 32 kilometres farther north at the end of the railway. Blenheim is also connected with other towns by air services.

The population of Marlborough is about 30,000.

MARMOSET.
Marmosets are tiny monkeys which live in the tropical forests of Central and South America. They are very dainty and attractive in appearance, being about the size of small squirrels and generally having long fur on their heads and necks. Many also have tufted ears. Their tails are rather furry and often have ring-like markings on them.

Marmosets differ from all other monkeys in their teeth and in having pointed claws, instead of flat nails, on all their fingers and toes except

their big toes. With the help of these claws they are able to climb nimbly up tree trunks. They live in small groups among the trees.

The food of marmosets is fruit and insects, and

the insects in particular seem to be very important to them. Although they make pretty and interesting pets, marmosets do not keep really healthy unless they get plenty of insects and sunshine.

S. C. Bisserot—Bruce Coleman
A white-fronted marmoset.

The common marmoset is the one most often kept as a pet. It comes from Brazil and its silky fur is mottled grey and blackish. Its body is about 9 inches long and its tail measures 11 inches. The lion marmoset is very handsome, with a bright golden body and tail. It is much larger than the common marmoset.

Another group of marmosets is the tamarins, which are without either ear tufts or rings on their tails. One of the most striking of these is the red-handed tamarin, which has orange hands and feet and a dark body.

MARMOT.
Marmots are rodents—that is, animals with strong teeth for gnawing—and are related to squirrels. There are several different species, or kinds, and they are found in North America, central Asia and Europe. Marmots are plump, brownish animals, generally between 12 inches and 24 inches long, with short bushy tails and short legs.

Marmots live among mountains or on plains. They make burrows close together and live in families each family having its own home. During the day one or more members of the family sit at the entrance to each burrow and keep an eye on what is going on, while others scamper about near the burrows, sometimes playfully boxing each other.

Leonard Lee Rue IV—Bruce Coleman

Yellow-bellied marmots ready for hibernation.

Marmots hibernate, or sleep during the winter. They take quantities of hay into their burrows to make nests for themselves and sleep soundly until the following spring, but the length of hibernation depends on the climate and local conditions. They eat grass, roots, leaves and sometimes insects. The female marmot has between two and nine young at a time.

The two European marmots are the Alpine marmot of the Alps and the bobac, which lives farther east on the Russian steppes. In central Asia live many marmots, including the red marmot, which is larger than the others and has a tail half the length of its body.

Marmots found in North America include the yellow-bellied marmot, the woodchuck and the whistling marmot.

A relative of the marmots is the prairie dog, also known as the prairie marmot.

MARRIAGE. A man and woman marry when they wish to live in a home together and bring up a family of children (see FAMILY). In Great Britain and other Western countries men and women are usually free to choose the people they want to marry. However, marriage is seldom allowed between close relations in any part of the world. Many primitive, or backward, peoples do not let anyone marry a person outside his or her own tribe.

Religion always has a good deal to do with marriage and in the Christian Church it is regarded as a Sacrament. (See SACRAMENTS.) In Moslem countries it used to be very general for a man to have as many as four wives at once, although nowadays this is not so frequent in countries such as Morocco, Tunisia and Pakistan. In Turkey and Persia the wives used to live in a separate part of the house, sometimes called a harem.

Much rarer than polygamy (having more than one wife) is polyandry, which means that one woman has several husbands at the same time. In Tibet a girl may marry several brothers and they all live in the same home.

Hindus believe a man will need his wife after death, and they used to burn the widow on the funeral pyre with the dead man. This custom, which was called *suttee*, was stopped by the British when they ruled India.

Customs and Ceremonies

In many countries marriages are arranged by parents, who choose who is to marry their son or daughter. The bride and bridegroom are often not allowed to meet before the wedding. Sometimes the arrangements include gifts between the two families. In parts of Africa the family of the bridegroom gives the bride's father a bridewealth (a certain number of cattle or tools). This makes sure that any children born of the marriage will be legally accepted as those of the husband, and also makes up for the fact that the bride no longer works for her father.

In the middle ages in England marriages were often arranged by families who owned land. Often, too, in the case of noble families, the bride and groom were married when they were children. Today, however, no one under 16 can marry, and marriage is considered as a partnership in which the husband and wife share things equally.

Many rites, or customs, which are practised at a wedding ceremony today date from very early times. The custom of carrying the bride over the doorstep of the new house marks the beginning of a new life. The joining of hands in the Christian marriage service is also found among primitive peoples.

Some old rites were intended to ward off evil. The bride's veil was originally worn to protect her from the evil eye; that is, from anyone who could do her harm by looking at her. Others were to make sure the bride would have children. Corn thrown over her was supposed to do this, and the confetti now thrown at weddings is a reminder of that belief.

MARS. Next to Jupiter the great sky-god, Mars was the most important god of the Romans and the other peoples of ancient Italy. The Romans came to think of him as the god of war, and this is how he is remembered today.

At first, however, as well as being the war-god he was one of the mightiest gods of nature. People prayed to him to bless their farmwork and protect their crops and animals from harm. The first month of the old Roman year (March) was dedicated to him as it was the beginning of spring.

It was natural that the Romans should think more and more about the warlike side of Mars, because wars happened often in Roman history. After a time the Romans told stories about him which were really stories about the Greek god of war named Ares. One story was that he fell in love with the goddess of love and beauty,

Mars, god of war and of crops, with Venus and Cupid.

whose Greek name was Aphrodite and whom the Romans called Venus, and that Eros, or Cupid, the boy god of love, was their son.

Mars the war-god was worshipped especially in cities, and in Rome there were special priests who looked after ceremonies in his honour. The place where the Romans held warlike competitions was called the Field of Mars. The emperor Augustus had two great temples built

and dedicated to Mars Ultor, which means Mars the Avenger. Augustus did this after he himself had avenged Julius Caesar by defeating and killing the men who had murdered him.

One of the planets is named after Mars, and it is the same one the Greeks called the star of Ares, after their god of war. Tuesday was his day, and although the English word is different because it comes from the name of another pagan god, the French word for Tuesday, *mardi*, still shows that it is "Mars' day".

MARS, the fourth planet from the Sun, and next beyond the Earth, is named after the Roman god of war. Mars has been known to men since prehistoric times, and, after the Earth itself, is the best known of all the planets (see PLANET and SOLAR SYSTEM).

Mars looks reddish, even to the naked eye. When, in its passage round the Sun, it comes closest to the Earth it is three times as bright as Sirius, the brightest star. When it is farthest away, it is no brighter than the Pole Star.

Mars is quite like the Earth in many ways. It rotates on its axis in 24 hours 37 minutes 22·6 seconds, so the Martian day is only slightly longer than the Earth day. However, it takes 687 days for its journey round the Sun, so the Martian year is nearly two Earth years.

Although its diameter is more than half the diameter of the Earth, Mars weighs only one-tenth as much as the Earth. As a result, the pull of gravity (see GRAVITATION) is much less on the surface of Mars than on the Earth's surface.

Mars is about one-and-a-half times as far away from the Sun as the Earth is, and so does not get as much heat as the Earth. This makes the surface temperature lower than the Earth's. However, Mars has seasons in just the same way as the Earth. The white north and south polar caps of Mars, once thought to be of ice, are more probably made of frozen carbon dioxide. They spread in winter and shrink in summer, just as on Earth, and may be a few metres in depth.

The atmosphere of Mars is very thin. By comparison, Venus is completely covered with thick clouds, and the Earth is partly cloud-covered but Mars has only occasional clouds. On the surface of Mars the pressure of the atmosphere is

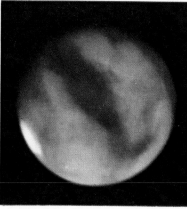

Courtesy, NASA; Jet Propulsion Laboratory, California Institute of Technology

Mars is sometimes called the "red planet". Its surface was photographed in detail by the Mariner 9 spacecraft. Large areas of Mars are covered with channels and craters.

less than one-hundredth of that on the surface of the Earth (see ATMOSPHERE.)

The Martian atmosphere contains carbon dioxide, but there is a little water vapour and nitrogen and argon may also be present. These gases, which are explained in the article AIR, are also found in the Earth's atmosphere, but this contains far more oxygen than the atmosphere of Mars. Animal and human life as it is known on Earth could not survive on Mars, but simple plant life might be able to.

The surface of Mars can be seen quite easily through a small telescope. Except for the ice caps, most of the surface is red-brown, with bluish markings whose appearance changes from time to time. Occasionally yellow clouds can be seen. In addition most astronomers see on Mars long dark streaks called canals. (These were first reported by two Italian astronomers in the 19th century and called *canali*, which is Italian for "channels" or "grooves".) It was once thought that these were artificial waterways built by some Martian civilization. However, it is almost certain that each canal really consists of isolated dark spots that cannot be seen separately except through the best telescopes.

Several unmanned spacecraft have taken detailed close-up pictures of Mars. These show that large parts of its surface are covered with craters, as is the Moon. The largest are several hundred kilometres across. Some areas of Mars are quite featureless and others are crossed by

numerous ridges. In 1971, when much of the planet was covered under a dense dust cloud, three spacecraft were put into orbit around Mars and the Russian Mars 3 probe soft-landed a capsule.

Mars has two very small natural satellites, or moons, which were discovered by the American astronomer Asaph Hall in 1877. They are called Phobos and Deimos, and are both too faint to be seen with the naked eye. Photographs taken from orbiting spacecraft show that they have an irregular shape and a cratered surface. Phobos is 24 kilometres long and 21 kilometres broad, almost twice the size of Deimos.

MARSDEN, Samuel (1764–1838).

Samuel Marsden was the first person to bring Christianity to the Maoris of New Zealand. He was born at Farsley in Yorkshire and went to Hull Grammar School. In 1793 he was ordained as a clergyman and went out to New South Wales (Australia) as chaplain to the convicts who in those days were transported there.

After he met a Maori interpreter he longed to convert and help other Maoris and in 1814 he was able to start a mission in New Zealand. This was in the Bay of Islands where on Christmas Day he preached from the beach to the Maoris from the text, "Behold, I bring you good tidings of great joy".

Marsden won the respect and trust of the Maoris and made five more voyages there from Australia. His success was praiseworthy, because the Maoris, who had been cannibals, gave up their pagan ways to please him and the other missionaries who followed him.

MARSEILLES

is the second largest city and the greatest seaport of France. It lies on the Mediterranean coast on a bay looking westwards across the Gulf of Lions. It may have been founded by the Phoenicians (a people from the country that is now called Lebanon) before it was settled by Greeks from Asia Minor in about 600 B.C.

South of the old harbour is a steep hill of white limestone on top of which the Church of Notre-Dame de la Garde forms a very bold landmark for sailors. The old harbour is now used only by fishing vessels and small craft. The Rue Canne-bière leading inland from the head of the basin is the centre of the life of the city. Just north of the old harbour, new dwellings stand on the site of the old town, which was a maze of steep, narrow, dark streets and was blown up by the German army in 1943. From here northwards the waterfront is taken up by the docks and basins of the port.

The port is connected with the Rhône River by a canal that goes through the Etang de Berre, which is a big lagoon, or land-locked piece of water connected with the sea. Most of the tankers bringing oil from the Middle East un-load their cargo at Lavéra, the oil port of Mar-seilles at the mouth of the Rhône. Other im-portant cargoes brought in are grain, coal, fruit, sugar, groundnuts, fertilizers and vegetable oils. The chief industry is the manufacture of petrol from oil in the refineries around the Étang de Berre. Other important manufactures are soap, sugar, cement, chemicals, metals and machin-ery. Marseilles sends ships to the eastern Medi-terranean, Africa, the West Indies and India, while it is a chief port of call for big ocean liners. Just off the harbour lies the islet called Château d'If, about which Alexandre Dumas wrote in his book *The Count of Monte Cristo*. The French national anthem is called the "Marseillaise" be-cause it was first sung in 1792 by revolutionary troops from Marseilles.

Marseilles has a population of about 778,000.

MARSUPIAL. The group of mammals whose females carry their young in pouches on their bodies are called marsupials. The best known marsupial is the kangaroo, of which the largest is the great grey kangaroo. Its newborn young is only an inch long, and, like all baby mar-supials, completely helpless. This is why they have to live in their mothers' pouches. Most marsupials live in Australia and the islands near by, but the opossum is found in North and South America.

Besides the kangaroo, Australian marsupials include the koala, a rather heavily built tree-living animal sometimes called the native bear; the wombat, which looks a little like a beaver; the Tasmanian wolf (now very rare), which lives only on the island of Tasmania; and tiny mouse-like and mole-like creatures.

The tree kangaroo of New Guinea is one of the marsupials that lives in trees. Others are flying phalangers, which have membranes be-tween their front and back limbs on each side. With these they can glide from tree to tree. The opossums also live in trees, although one species, or kind, spends much of its time in water.

The bandicoots are marsupials which live in New Guinea and Australia. They look a little like kangaroos, the smallest being the size of rats while others are as large as rabbits. There are many different kinds of bandicoots and they have been divided into three groups—the rat bandicoots, the rabbit bandicoots, which are

Four kinds of marsupial: phalanger (which is often called "opossum" in Australia), kangaroo, Tasmanian Devil, koala.

Baby kangaroos stay in the pouch for about six months.

MARTIAL LAW.

MARTIAL LAW. Martial is a word meaning "warlike", and the term martial law is used to describe two rather different things.

First, martial law means the special law which may be brought into force during a state of emergency, such as war, to control British subjects and anyone else who is entitled to protection by the British government. When war or disorder is going on, officers of the armed forces may use force to restore order, but afterwards they may be brought before the courts to answer for their actions.

Secondly, martial law means the law by which military authorities control enemy subjects in wartime. When British forces are occupying enemy land, the martial law is settled by the orders of the general in command.

great burrowers, and the pig-footed bandicoot. Except for the rare pig-footed bandicoot, which is a vegetarian, these animals are especially fond of large worms and beetle grubs, which they smell in the ground and then dig out.

Rabbit bandicoots are much hunted for food, but they can dig burrows almost as fast as a man can dig after them, so when the natives want to catch one they listen to find where it is lying in its burrow and then dig straight down to it.

There are separate articles in this encyclopaedia on the following marsupials: KANGAROO; KOALA; OPOSSUM; TASMANIAN DEVIL; WALLABY and WOMBAT.

MARTELLO TOWERS.

MARTELLO TOWERS. Along the southern and eastern coasts of England and of the Channel Islands some of the short, stout, rounded towers known as Martello towers still stand. They are reminders of the days at the beginning of the 19th century when England waited in fear for the Emperor Napoleon to cross the English Channel with an invading army. The invasion never came, so we do not know whether Martello towers would have been a good defence or not.

Martello towers are built of brick with thick walls. At the top is a platform for two or three guns and inside are vaulted rooms for soldiers to live in. Some Martello towers are surrounded by a wide, deep moat, or ditch filled with water.

MARTIN.

MARTIN. The martins are smaller birds than the swallows, with shorter wings and tails that are not so sharply forked. Like swallows, they spend much of their time in the air, gliding and fluttering about the sky as they catch insects on the wing. They perch on buildings, boughs and telegraph wires, and come to the ground only for nesting material. In summer, two kinds of martins visit the British Isles to nest, the house martin and the sand martin.

The house martin is about five inches long and has a noticeable white rump, or hinder part, showing up against the rest of the back, wings and tail, which are bluish black. The underparts are white. House martins start to arrive in April and build their nests in May or June, sometimes on cliffs but usually under bridges and the eaves of houses, where there may be several nests in a row. The nest is shaped like half a cup and built of pellets of wet mud, held together with grasses and lined with straw and feathers. The mud becomes dry and hard enough to bear the weight of the mother and her four or five white eggs and, in due course, two or three broods of youngsters. By the end of July some of the birds begin to gather and twitter on wires and house-tops, and by the end of October most of them have already gone off to South Africa for the winter.

The smaller sand martin is brown above and white below, with a broad line of brown on its breast. It starts to arrive in Britain in March and later nests in colonies, or groups, in places like sandy banks and gravel pits. Each pair makes its own tunnel, two or three feet long, and the white eggs are laid in a nest of straw and feathers at the end. Like house martins, sand martins breed in most parts of Europe and Asia, but are also found in North America, where they are called bank swallows. The larger

John Markham

A sand martin feeding its young at the nest.

purple martin of North America builds in hollow trees and often in nesting boxes.

MARTINIQUE is a French island in the West Indies. It lies between the islands of Dominica and St. Lucia and is a little smaller than the English county of Bedfordshire. Martinique is mountainous and beautiful, its thickly wooded heights broken by steep cliffs and gorges. The highest mountain, Mont Pelée, is a volcano which in 1902 erupted and destroyed St. Pierre (then the largest town), killing about 30,000 people. On several occasions hurricanes, or tremendous gales, have done great damage to the sugar plantations.

The hot, moist climate of Martinique makes tropical crops grow well. The chief crop is sugar-cane, but bananas and coffee are also grown. The island is famous for its rum, a strong spirit drink made from sugar.

Martinique was probably discovered by Christopher Columbus in 1502. It has been French since 1635, except for brief occupations by the British during their wars with France. Most of the people are Negroes, although there are a few whites and some of mixed blood. Martinique is an overseas *département*, or district, of France and sends members to the French parliament in Paris. The capital is Fort-de-France on the west coast and the population is about 326,000.

MARTYR. The word martyr, which comes from the Greek word *martys* or "witness", means a person who has preferred to be killed rather than give up his faith. There have been martyrs in every age. The great Athenian philosopher Socrates refused to change his beliefs when tried for impiety in 399 B.C. and willingly chose death instead. Among the early Christian martyrs put to death by those whom they tried to convert two of the best known were Stephen and Sebastian. (See STEPHEN; SEBASTIAN.) One of the victims of the Inquisition (see INQUISITION) was Joan of Arc, who was burned at the stake as a heretic in 1431 and made a saint in 1920 by the same church which had condemned her. (See JOAN OF ARC.) In 1535 Sir Thomas More was beheaded for refusing to accept Henry VIII as supreme head of the church. (See MORE.)

During World War II many ordinary people died rather than accept Nazism. In the early 1960s in South Vietnam Buddhist monks burned themselves to death in protest against the government. In 1968, Dr. Martin Luther King, a leader in the American Negroes' struggle for equal rights, was shot dead, having survived earlier attacks.

Martyrs have died for many religious and political beliefs, but they share in common the courage to which their deaths bear witness.

MARX, Karl (1818–1883). Karl Marx was one of the chief founders of the political belief known as Communism and thus has had a very great influence on the ideas and events of the last 100 years.

His full name was Karl Heinrich Marx and he was born at Trier in western Germany on May 5, 1818. His parents were originally Jewish but they became Christians in 1824. After attending school at Trier, Marx studied law, history and philosophy at the universities of Bonn and Berlin. By this time he was already a

Karl Marx lived the later part of his life in London.

ing classes must soon come and must be successful. It appeals to workers in all countries to unite in overthrowing the governments of the time. After he arrived in London, Marx went on to develop his ideas about economics (see ECONOMICS) and set them out in his chief work, which is often known by its German title *Das Kapital* (in English "Capital"). Besides this, Marx wrote much about the revolutionary struggles that took place in Europe from 1848 to 1850. In 1864 he took a leading part in founding the International Working Men's Association, which is known as the First International.

Marx thought that any government was really the result of the economic conditions of a country; therefore in order to understand what was going on in politics it was necessary to examine what was happening in the economic life of a country. Marx claimed that the economic struggle, or the struggle to make a living, had divided people into social classes and that throughout history these classes had been struggling against one another, each trying to get the upper hand. He considered that, at certain times when economic conditions were in their favour, the oppressed classes had revolted against their masters and had become masters themselves. At the time when he was writing he said it was time for the working classes to revolt and make themselves masters of society. He said that if they did this they would set up the "dictatorship of the proletariat". In simpler words this means the rule by the working classes. Marx thought that this would be the beginning of a society that had no social classes.

Communist countries all over the world claim that they are carrying out Marx's ideas. In the U.S.S.R. his ideas are unquestioned and its founder, Lenin, was a firm disciple of Marx. (See LENIN, VLADIMIR ILYICH.)

Marx died in London on March 14, 1883, and was buried in Highgate cemetery.

socialist so he started to work for a socialist newspaper. In 1843 he went to Paris, where the socialist movement was at its height, and met Friedrich Engels. Engels was a German socialist too, and the two men remained friends for life and wrote some of their political books together. In 1845 Marx was expelled from France because of his political views and went to live in Brussels, where Engels soon joined him. In 1848 revolutions broke out in several European countries and when one broke out in Germany, Marx and Engels returned there to take part in it. However, it failed and Marx was expelled—this time from his own country. He came to London and lived the rest of his life there, spending much of his time in the reading room of the British Museum.

The most famous of his early writings is *The Communist Manifesto*, which he and Engels wrote together in Brussels and published early in 1848. It sets out their ideas about how the social classes of European countries grew up, and uses these ideas to argue that a revolution of the work-

MARY, QUEEN OF SCOTS (1542–1587)

was queen of Scotland by birth, queen of France by marriage and was regarded by Roman Catholics as the rightful queen of England.

She was the daughter of James V of Scotland and his French wife Mary of Guise, and was

Dear Member,

I trust this finds you safe and well as we look forward to warmer days and more freedom in

mber
r her
n of
ed to
and
with
ed to
the

y re-
usin
the
th I
d no
the
and-
enry

any
ox,
her
ere
rust
her
was
in
oon
and
ver,
was
of
der
y it
in

re-
in-
nd
4,
ur
er
e-
In
y
ar
to
le
a

prisoner and half as a guest. Plots were made to restore her to the throne of Scotland and even to place her on the throne of England. The English Catholics did not consider that Elizabeth was their rightful queen because they believed that Catherine of Aragon was Henry's true wife

For nearly 19 years Mary was moved from castle to castle.

and did not recognize his marriage to Anne Boleyn, who was Elizabeth's mother. Protestants were anxious to get rid of Mary in order to remove the danger to Elizabeth herself and to prevent the possibility of a Catholic coming to the throne. However, Elizabeth could not bring herself to have Mary executed without definite proof that Mary was plotting against her. In 1585 Mary was suspected of taking part in a plot by which Anthony Babington was to murder Queen Elizabeth so that Mary could take her throne. She was arrested, tried and found guilty. Elizabeth still delayed her execution but finally signed the death warrant. Mary was executed at Fotheringay Castle in Northamptonshire on February 8, 1587, meeting her end with great courage and dignity. Her body was buried in Peterborough Cathedral and in 1612 was removed to Westminster Abbey.

MARY, THE MOTHER OF JESUS.

For centuries in Christian countries the name of Mary has been a favourite name for girls. This is because parents see in the character of Mary, the mother of Jesus, the character they would like their own daughters to have. The New Testament shows Mary as the perfect woman—obedient to God, pure in heart, making a happy home for her family and, at the time of the Crucifixion of her Son, wonderfully courageous.

St. Luke describes some of the events in Mary's life from the time of the Annunciation (announcement) onwards. In the first chapter of his Gospel he tells how the angel Gabriel was sent to announce to Mary that she had been chosen to be the mother of Jesus. This news surprised her greatly, for although she was engaged to Joseph she was not yet married to him. Gabriel therefore explained to her that the seed of the baby would be planted in her womb not by Joseph but by the Holy Ghost. (This is why, in the Apostolic Creed, Christians speak of "Jesus Christ, conceived by the Holy Ghost, born of the Virgin Mary".) Mary did not question Gabriel any more: she just said, "Behold the handmaid of the Lord; be it unto me according to Thy word".

Shortly after this Mary went to see her cousin Elisabeth who also was awaiting the birth of a baby. (This baby grew up to become John the Baptist, about whom there is a separate article.) Elisabeth was overjoyed to see Mary and greeted her with the words, "Blessed art thou among women, and blessed is the fruit of thy womb." To this Mary replied with the song of praise and thanksgiving known as the Magnificat.

After staying three months with her cousin, Mary returned home to Nazareth. Soon after this the Romans (who ruled Palestine at this time through King Herod; see HEROD) decided to hold a census, or have the people counted, and ordered all the citizens to go to certain towns to be registered. Mary and Joseph had to go to Bethlehem and it was there that Jesus was born.

The Holy Family did not remain long in their own country. In the second chapter of his Gospel St. Matthew explains why. When King Herod heard from the Wise Men that the newly born baby would one day set up His own kingdom in Israel, Herod thought this meant that he would be overthrown. He therefore ordered all babies under the age of two to be killed. Joseph was warned of this by an angel and immediately fled with Mary and Jesus to Egypt. They did not return to Nazareth until they heard that Herod was dead.

Very little is known of Mary's life between her return to Nazareth and the beginning of Jesus' teaching. St. Luke tells us that the family visited Jerusalem every year for the Passover (see PASSOVER), and he tells how, on one of these visits, the 12-year-old Jesus remained behind talking with the learned men in the Temple. Mary and Joseph had to search three days for Him.

In the accounts of Jesus' life after He began His teaching, Mary is mentioned from time to time. We read that she was present at the wedding in Cana of Galilee and, again, of her unsuccessful attempt to talk to Jesus when He was busy teaching. She appears again at the Crucifixion and was one of the few followers who did not run away in fear when Jesus' work seemed to be ending in total failure. She stood by Him to the bitter end. St. John tells how Jesus spoke to Mary and to him from the Cross, bidding them look after each other, saying to Mary, "Woman, behold thy son!" and to John, "Behold thy mother!" We hear no more of Mary except that she was one of those who, according to the Acts, gave themselves up to prayer after Jesus had ascended into heaven.

The main church festivals held in honour of Mary are the Conception, known to Roman Catholics as the Immaculate Conception (December 8), her Nativity or birth (September 8), the Annunciation (March 25), the Purification (February 2), the Visitation (July 2) and the Assumption or Falling Asleep, when she was received into heaven (August 15). The article LADY DAY explains how four of these feasts used to be called Our Lady Days or Lady Days. Now only the Annunciation is called Lady Day.

MARY CELESTE.

The story of the "Mary Celeste" is one of the mysteries of the sea. The American brigantine "Mary Celeste" left New York on November 7, 1872, bound for Genoa, Italy, with a cargo of crude alcohol. There were ten people on board. On December 5 the British

Painting by Gordon Johnson

The crew of the "Dei Gratia" look for signs of life as they approach the drifting "Mary Celeste".

ship "Dei Gratia" sighted the "Mary Celeste" about 650 kilometres east of the Azores. The ship was drifting and there was no sign of life on board. Nothing more was ever heard of the passengers and crew of the "Mary Celeste".

Many theories have been put forward to try and explain what happened. Mutiny, murder and piracy seem unlikely and there was no evidence of an explosion. The ship was perfectly seaworthy. The last entry in the log was made at 8 a.m. on November 25 and there was also a hastily-written and unfinished message from the mate to his wife. The ship's boat and its papers were missing. Some food had been taken yet clothes, boots and even pipes had been left scattered about.

One possible explanation is that the "Mary Celeste" was abandoned when a mistaken reading of the sounding rod used to measure water in the hull caused the captain, Benjamin Briggs, to think the ship was taking water and about to sink. The metal sounding rod was found beside its cover, suggesting that it had been used just before the ship was abandoned. With his wife and baby daughter on board and knowing land was not far off, Captain Briggs may have failed to check the sounding himself and hurriedly ordered the crew to abandon ship. From meteorological records it is known that there was a sudden storm on the afternoon of November 25 and this may have swamped the ship's boat.

The "Mary Celeste" was sailed into Gibraltar by men from the "Dei Gratia" and went on trading until 1885, when it was wrecked off the coast of Haiti.

MARYLEBONE CRICKET CLUB.

The governing body of cricket is the Marylebone Cricket Club, usually called the M.C.C. It was founded in 1788 when the White Conduit Club —the leading club in London—moved to Lord's Cricket Ground at Marylebone and changed its name. (See LORD'S CRICKET GROUND.)

A committee formed from members of the club revised the laws of cricket and reissued them. Ever since then the M.C.C. has been accepted as the authority on the laws.

With the coming of Test matches the M.C.C. formed a board of control to run all the Tests played in England, and itself took the responsibility for sending English teams overseas. As well as being accepted by the world as the chief authority on the laws of cricket, the M.C.C. arranges many matches for its members and staff and chooses sides to play against the leading cricket schools and clubs.

MASEFIELD, John (1878–1967).

The poem "Cargoes" by John Masefield begins

> Quinquireme of Nineveh from distant Ophir
> Rowing home to haven in sunny Palestine,
> With a cargo of ivory,
> And apes and peacocks,
> Sandalwood, cedarwood, and sweet white wine.

It is one of many beautiful and exciting poems written by John Masefield, who from being a runaway sailor lad at the age of 13 became one of the best known of English writers, and in 1930 was honoured by being made the Poet Laureate, the national poet of England. Besides poems he wrote plays, novels and books for children, including *The Box of Delights.*

John Masefield ran away to sea, and was then trained as a sailor on board the "Conway" in the River Mersey—he described this part of his life in a book called *New Chum.* At 15 he sailed round Cape Horn, the southernmost tip of South America, in one of the great sailing ships known as windjammers. As he wrote later, he saw many "strange lands from under the Arched White Sails of Ships", and many of his fine poems sprang from these experiences.

Eventually he settled in London and after some hard work made his name with a book of sea-poems, *Salt-Water Ballads.* Here is a verse from one of them, "Sea Fever" :

> I must down to the seas again, to the lonely sea and
>   the sky,
> And all I ask is a tall ship and a star to steer her by,
> And the wheel's kick and the wind's song and the
>   white sail's shaking,
> And a grey mist on the sea's face and a grey dawn
>   breaking.

He went on to write other poems, not all of them about the sea. One of the best known is *Reynard the Fox,* which Masefield described as "an attempt to understand the mind of a shy wild animal when sorely beset". In it a fox hunt is described, with the fox running for his life.

As a boy, Masefield knew the sea and sailing ships.

MASK. Today, masks are usually put on for amusement or sometimes for disguise, but they were once used a good deal in religion, and primitive, or backward, peoples still put them to many curious uses.

An old belief was that people's souls can enter into other beings and that they themselves can be possessed by strange spirits. Another belief is that if a person puts on a mask representing an animal or an evil spirit he can by some mysterious power become the animal or evil spirit he is imitating.

Primitive tribes often look on particular animals as sacred. They hold religious dances at which they wear masks like their animal, in order to be given the magic powers this animal (or totem, as it is called among Red Indian tribes) is supposed to possess.

Masks are frequently carved to look terrifying, and in many parts of Africa they are worn by the medicine-men, or witch-doctors, to chase away evil spirits. They are made of wood, cloth or straw and usually painted in bright colours, as it is believed that the more hideous a mask is the more power it has to frighten the demons away. (See PRIMITIVE ART.)

Masks may be used to cure illnesses. Some peoples believe that when one of them is ill his soul has been stolen by the dead, so the medicine-man puts on a magic mask and goes to the graveyard in search of the lost soul, the mask giving him the power to seize back the soul from the dead. In Ceylon masks are made to represent various diseases and worn by dancers to get rid of the spirits who cause the diseases.

Sometimes the mask itself is believed to be a demon or spirit. This is the case in a tribe in New Guinea, where they treat the masks with respect, talk to them as if they were alive and refuse to part with them. Certain of the masks they even regard as guardian spirits and appeal to them for fine weather, help in hunting and in war and so forth.

Masks are often used in connection with dead people. When the graves of Mycenae, the great city of early Greece, were opened in the 19th century, masks of gold were found on the faces of the dead. They were also placed on the faces of Egyptian mummies. (See MUMMY.) In some parts of the world the skull of a dead chief or notable warrior is preserved and painted and then worn by members of the tribe in the belief that the courage of the dead man will pass on to the wearer. The Aztecs of Mexico did this.

Frequently death masks are made of dead people by taking an impression of their face in wax. It is like a portrait and shows exactly how the person looks.

Masks have been used on the stage since ancient times. Greek theatres were so large that

Top: An eagle mask made by the Kwakiutl Indians of North America. By pulling strings through the eyes the wearer could move the wing-like side pieces to frighten his audience. Left: This fearsome-looking Balinese mask from the East Indies represents a witch. It was used in a dance-play. Above: A mosaic mask worn by the Aztecs of Mexico. Made of cedar wood inlaid with turquoise and shell, it may represent the Aztec god Quetzalcoatl. Masks like these were used in ritual magic, dance and drama by peoples throughout the world.

the people sitting farthest from the stage could not see or hear the actors clearly, and so the actors wore great masks which often covered the whole of their heads, as well as their faces. They were usually made of painted canvas, with openings for the eyes and mouth, and sometimes tubes were put in to make the voices louder. They were painted to show the kind of character that the actor was playing. Comic masks had features twisted out of shape and tragic masks were painted to show noble suffering. Today pictures of masks, one with the mouth turned up at the corners (comedy) and one with the mouth turned down (tragedy) are seen on some posters or programmes of plays. Masks are still used in the sacred and historical plays of the East.

MASQUE. In the 16th and 17th centuries people delighted in splendid festivities, and one of these was the masque or mask. A masque was a kind of play acted in masks, and as well as dialogue it contained music, dancing and pageantry. Masques were often performed at court and presented by the noble ladies and gentlemen of the court itself. The costumes and scenery were very elaborate, and complicated machinery was often used to achieve stage "effects" such as the descent of a chariot from the sky.

Masques spread to France and England from Italy. One writer described how in 1512, on Twelfth Night (January 6), King Henry VIII and 11 of his courtiers disguised themselves with masks (which had not been seen before in England) and surprised the ladies by asking them to dance with them. Masques were most popular in the time of James I and Charles I. Many were written by the poet Ben Jonson, with Inigo Jones, a famous architect of the day, designing the machinery. One of the most famous of all masques, *Comus*, was written by John Milton.

MASSAGE. True massage is a special kind of rubbing with the hands, and it should be done only by people who have been trained to do it and know all about the structure of the body and how the different parts work. Massage is used for many purposes, including soothing

pain and getting rid of swellings, improving the circulation of the blood and strengthening muscles and other parts of the body which have been injured by accident or disease.

Three main kinds of movements are used in massage : stroking, kneading (or squeezing) and tapping. Stroking may be gentle movements on the skin, or firmer movements which are to affect organs inside the body and improve the flow of blood. Kneading consists of squeezing movements with the fingers or knuckles or with the thumb. Tapping is done with the points of the fingers.

A man who is trained to perform massage is called a *masseur* and a woman a *masseuse*.

MASTER OF THE QUEEN'S MUSIC is a musician appointed by the Queen to be in charge of musical affairs at court. Musicians have been employed by the kings and queens of England since very early times, both to amuse them and to provide the music and singing at religious services in their private chapels.

In the days of Queen Elizabeth I some of the most famous composers and musicians of the time were Gentlemen of the Chapel—Thomas Tallis, William Byrd (see BYRD, WILLIAM), Orlando Gibbons and Thomas Morley. They wrote and played beautiful madrigals (see MADRIGAL) and church music for her, much of it still heard today. In 1626 Charles I appointed one man to be in charge of all the court musicians. This was Nicholas Lanier and he was known as the Master of the King's Musick. In Charles II's time the "King's 24 Violins" played to him while he ate, and performed on state occasions, sometimes accompanying birthday odes (a form of poem).

By Queen Victoria's reign the orchestra consisted of wind instruments only, but in 1840 it was expanded. From then on the Master of the Queen's Music was always a highly respected musician who provided music for court functions such as coronations and royal weddings. Sir Edward Elgar (see ELGAR, SIR EDWARD) and Sir Walford Davies were the Masters during the reign of George V, followed by Sir Arnold Bax during the reign of George VI. The present Master is Sir Arthur Bliss.

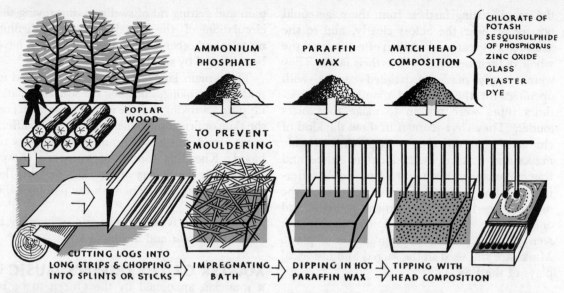

AMMONIUM PHOSPHATE

PARAFFIN WAX

MATCH HEAD COMPOSITION

CHLORATE OF POTASH
SESQUISULPHIDE OF PHOSPHORUS
ZINC OXIDE
GLASS
PLASTER
DYE

POPLAR WOOD

TO PREVENT SMOULDERING

CUTTING LOGS INTO LONG STRIPS & CHOPPING INTO SPLINTS OR STICKS

IMPREGNATING BATH

DIPPING IN HOT PARAFFIN WAX

TIPPING WITH HEAD COMPOSITION

MATCH. Nowadays matches are so common that it is difficult to imagine a time when, in order to light a fire, men had to rub pieces of wood together, or strike flint against steel and catch the spark on "tinder". (There were many kinds of tinder—plant-down, small pieces of rotten wood, charred cotton rags, dried fungi soaked in saltpetre and many other substances that would readily ignite.)

The first usable matches to light by friction were invented by an Englishman in 1827, when John Walker, a druggist of Stockton-on-Tees, in the County of Durham, tipped pieces of wood with a mixture of gum arabic, antimony sulphide and chlorate of potash. These matches were lit with some difficulty by drawing them through a piece of sandpaper. A few years later a German chemist substituted phosphorus for antimony sulphide, which made the matches easier to strike. That, with many refinements, including the substitution of a compound of phosphorus for phosphorus, is how matches are made today.

Matches may be divided into two kinds: safety, which strike only on a specially prepared surface; and "strike anywhere", which will strike on any rough surface.

Safety matches were invented by Johan and Carl Lundström in Sweden in 1852, although the first safety matches were not actually produced until 1855. The match head contains chlorate of potash and sulphur, which will not

readily ignite until brought into contact with red phosphorus on the side of the box.

"Strike anywhere" matches combine chlorate of potash and sesquisulphide of phosphorus in the match head. These two chemicals will burst into flame when rubbed against a rough surface.

The wood for matches comes from the aspen group of trees, which is the variety of poplar that has quivering leaves. Long strips of the thickness of a match are peeled off the logs and then placed under a chopping machine to be cut into splints, or sticks, of the correct length. The splints are then dipped into ammonium phosphate. This prevents the wood from glowing after the match has been struck and blown out, and thus lessens the risk of fires being started by matches carelessly thrown away after use.

After they have been dipped in ammonium phosphate the splints are inserted about one-eighth of an inch into holes in metal plates which are arranged in an endless belt on the match machine. As the machine moves, the matches go through a bath of hot molten paraffin wax. Then their tips are lowered on to a rotating table which is covered with the match composition. When they are raised, they have received their heads and then pass on to dry for about 60 minutes before being automatically placed in their boxes. The boxes are then wrapped by machine into dozens, grosses (144) and, finally, cases before being delivered to the shops.

MATHEMATICS.

Gardeners and builders use special tools to help them in their tasks. If we want to work with numbers, solve a problem or send a rocket into space we too shall need special tools for the job.

Long ago men invented these special tools and called them arithmetic, geometry, algebra and trigonometry. Together, these four tools are usually called by the single word mathematics.

Consider a few of man's achievements from having learnt to use these tools. Explorers marched or sailed into the unknown and made their maps and charts as they went. Other men built fine cities and bridges and again others designed powerful engines and machinery of all kinds. Today we can talk to, and often see, people many miles away. Coloured pictures are sent through space; computers have been invented to make difficult calculations; and men have travelled round the Moon. You can probably think of many other things that make our lives easier and more pleasant, or which increase man's control of his surroundings. To achieve them, men had to think out the problems and find the answers.

For example, the problem of sending men round the Moon could not be solved by guesswork. It would be no use saying to the astronauts: "We are going to send you round the Moon, and with a bit of luck you should be able to return to Earth." What happened was that mathematicians worked out the gravitational pull of the Earth and the Moon, so that the forces acting on the spacecraft—and thus the thrust needed to launch it—could be calculated. Later, mathematicians calculated the directions in which the spacecraft must travel so as to meet the moving Moon at the correct place without

crashing into it. Into computers they fed questions in the form of numbers which asked: "What happens if the astronauts are sent round the far side of the Moon? Will they be on the right course to come back to Earth?" The computer answered "Yes", and when the attempt was made the astronauts did return and the mathematicians were happy.

Are you happy when you have to check your change in a shop, build a rabbit hutch or make a model? Can you find your way across country by day or night, or could you find the position of a ship at sea? Can you make pleasing Christmas decorations, find the height of a tree or the width of a river, measure speeds or draw a house that looks like a house?

You can do all these things and more once you have learnt how to use the tools of mathematics. The great inventors, scientists and engineers started as you have started, although many

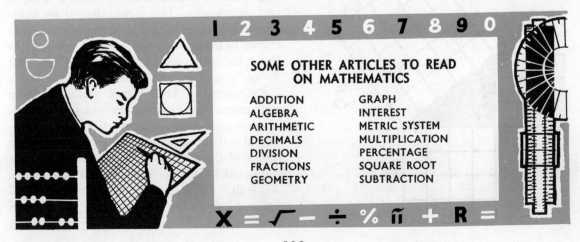

SOME OTHER ARTICLES TO READ ON MATHEMATICS

ADDITION	GRAPH
ALGEBRA	INTEREST
ARITHMETIC	METRIC SYSTEM
DECIMALS	MULTIPLICATION
DIVISION	PERCENTAGE
FRACTIONS	SQUARE ROOT
GEOMETRY	SUBTRACTION

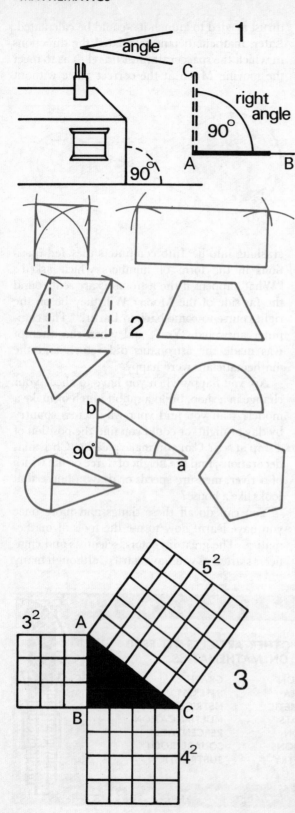

of them had far fewer aids to learning when they began using mathematics. Some of them were not even good at sums when they were at school.

Here are a few simple things you need to know.

Angles and Shapes

Angles. The space between two meeting lines is called an angle. Doors and windows may be opened so that they make various angles with the wall. The hands of a clock revolve at different speeds so that there is usually an angle between them. In diagram 1, if AB is a closed door and AC the same door open, the door has been opened through what is called a right angle. Angles are measured in degrees and the right angle is 90 degrees—usually written 90°.

You can easily recognize right angles. The corner of a book forms a right angle and the walls of a house are at 90° to the ground. When drawing or building we must be able to construct right angles. The builder uses a large set-square. In geometry we can use a protractor, which enables us to construct angles of any size.

Triangles and other shapes. Once we can construct angles we can start constructing shapes. Shown in the illustration are a few you can draw for yourself, using the straight edge of a ruler, a protractor and a pair of compasses. See how many of these shapes you can recognize in everyday things.

One of these shapes is a right-angled triangle. A fact worth knowing about every triangle—whether right-angled or not—is that its three angles always add up to 180°, which is equal to two right angles. This means that, if we know the angle a in the right-angled triangle shown in colour in diagram 2, we can find the angle b from the sum $b = 180° - (90° + a)$, so that $b = 90° - a$. This is often useful.

Pythagoras. The Greek mathematician Pythagoras (see PYTHAGORAS) discovered that, in every right-angled triangle, the square of one side plus the square of the other side equals the square of the hypotenuse (the side opposite the right angle). We shorten this to the rule $AC^2 = AB^2 + BC^2$ (AC^2 is the way of writing "AC squared", or $AC \times AC$.) The rule is proved in diagram 3. The square on AB contains 9 small squares. Adding 16 small squares in the square on BC makes a total of 25. In the square on AC (the hypotenuse) there are also 25 small squares.

You may notice at this point that Pythagoras' rule can be used to make a builder's set square. All you have to do is to form a triangle by joining together lengths of wood 5 feet, 4 feet and 3 feet long. The rule is also valuable when solving several kinds of problem, such as finding the height of a mast or tree, or the width of a river.

The Circle. The circumference of a circle is the length of the line forming it. The other parts of a circle are named in diagram 4. Suppose we need to calculate the circumference of a coin, a tin, a bicycle wheel or even of the Earth. We can do so by multiplying the diameter by 3·1416, or—near enough—by $\frac{22}{7}$.

The reason is that no matter how big a circle is, its circumference is *always* slightly more than three times the diameter. For "slightly more than three" we use the Greek letter π (pi), which stands for 3·1416.

Prove this by winding a tape measure round a tin. Find the diameter by measuring with a ruler and divide the measured circumference by the diameter. The answer will be just over 3.

The circle is useful for constructing a great many shapes such as the square, regular hexagon and equilateral triangle (one with equal sides) and also for constructing cylinders and stars. Try to copy the shapes based on the circle which are shown. If you place the point of your compasses at 1 in each case and, following the arc so made, go on to 2, you will soon find how to construct the various shapes.

Making a magnetic compass. Once we know something about the circle we can consider making a magnetic compass to show direction. Draw a circle on white card and put in two diameters at right angles to each other. The four main points of the compass (called cardinal points) are then marked N, S, E and W. Call the centre of the card X. If the right angle NXW is halved (each half being 45°) and this line continued through the centre to the circumference, you can mark off two more points, NW and SE. Continue the bisecting (halving) of angles until 16 points have been marked.

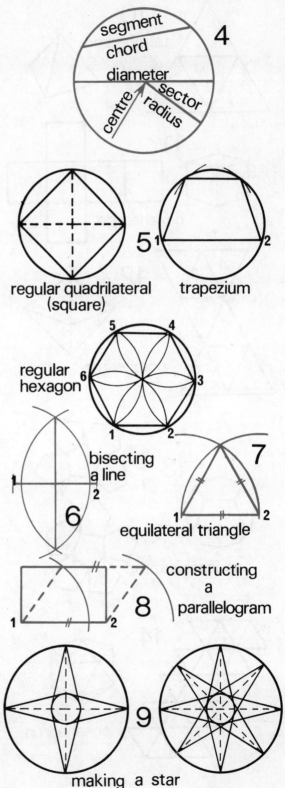

4 segment chord diameter centre radius sector

5 regular quadrilateral (square)   trapezium

regular hexagon

bisecting a line

6

7 equilateral triangle

8 constructing a parallelogram

9 making a star

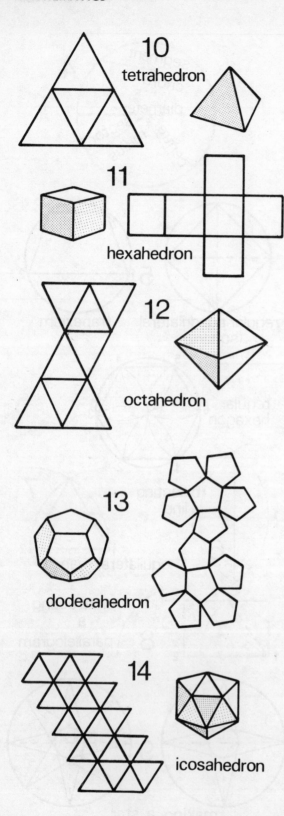

10 tetrahedron

11

hexahedron

12

octahedron

13

dodecahedron

14

icosahedron

If you take a strip of thin steel—a razor blade will do—and stroke it repeatedly in one direction only with the end of a bar magnet, this will make the strip into a magnetic needle. The strip can be fixed to a cork with cement or with a drawing pin. Float the assembly in water and mark the north-pointing end with N. Then cut away the centre of the compass card so that the cork can turn freely in the hole, and place the card over a shallow bowl of water. Float the cork in the water.

Solid Shapes

If we look around us we can find interesting shapes in nature which man has copied for his own use, such as the cells of a honeycomb, snowflakes or the crystals of salt or sugar. All these have different shapes and are given names according to the number of sides or faces they have.

Some flat shapes can be built up to form patterns. The shapes are often used as tiles, pieces of glass or slabs of concrete, but you can cut them from coloured paper and fit them together. These flat shapes are in a single plane. They have no depth, or thickness, as crystals or other solids do.

There are only five regular solids. If many solids of the same shape are put together, the result has the same form as a lump of sugar, a honeycomb or a diamond. The names of the regular solids tell us how many faces each has. For example, a hexahedron is a solid with six faces—a cube, in fact. The regular solids are :

Tetrahedron	4 faces	made of triangles meeting at each corner
Hexahedron	6 faces	made of squares, three meeting at each corner
Octahedron	8 faces	made of triangles, four at each corner
Dodecahedron	12 faces	made of pentagons (five-sided figures), three to a corner
Icosahedron	20 faces	made of triangles, five at each corner.

For any solid with flat faces, if you add the

number of corners to the number of faces, the total is the number of edges of that solid plus 2.

These solids also make interesting decorations. To make them, you need some card and a roll of sticky tape. For any of the five regular solids you need first to draw and cut out one basic shape— an equilateral triangle, a square or a regular pentagon. By using this as a pattern and tracing round it, you can produce the number of faces required for the solid you have chosen. By folding carefully along the lines the solid takes shape, and can be taped as you go along. Because of its 12 faces, the dodecahedron when painted can be made to serve as an unusual and colourful calendar.

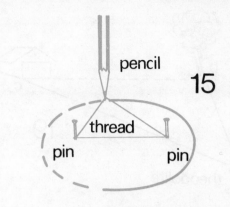

Ellipses

The great astronomer Johann Kepler in the 16th century tried to find some connection between the five regular solids and the spacing of the planets Mercury, Venus, Earth, Mars, Jupiter and Saturn. He believed that the spacing had something to do with the shapes of the solids, but failed to prove it.

Nevertheless, Kepler did prove that every planet travels along an orbit, or path, around the Sun in a special shape known as an ellipse. The ellipse is another shape found in nature and copied by man. If you half fill a mug with water and tilt it, the shape of the surface is an ellipse.

The illustration shows how to draw an ellipse using a thread stretched around two pins. Each pin is known as a focus of the ellipse (plural foci). Kepler stated that every planet travels in an elliptical orbit with the Sun at one of the foci. If you experiment, you will find that as you move the pins closer together the ellipse becomes rounder, until when the pins are touching it becomes a circle.

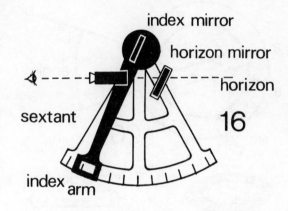

Navigation

In order to work out the course that must be steered by a ship or an aircraft, or to find its position, the navigator uses a number of aids. His compass, once it has been adjusted for certain errors, tells him the direction of north and enables him to steer any chosen course.

He sets about finding his position by measuring the altitude, or angle above the horizon, of

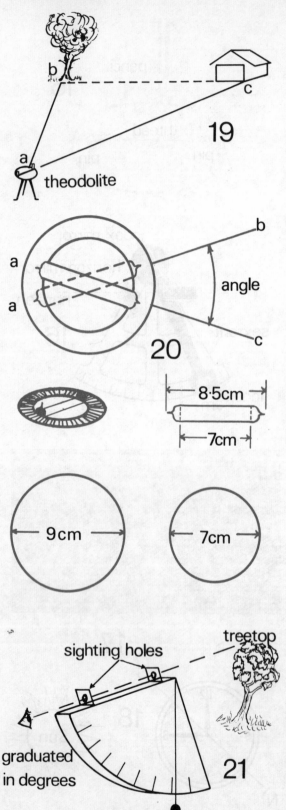

theodolite

19

b

angle

a

a

c

20

8·5cm

7cm

9cm

7cm

sighting holes

treetop

graduated
in degrees

21

the Sun or one of the bright stars. An early instrument used for measuring altitudes was the astrolabe, although the sextant is the instrument used nowadays. If he knows the exact time, the navigator can work out his exact position by using tables. The calculations for position-finding are somewhat complicated and you can read more about the principle in NAVIGATION.

It is worth remembering that the altitude of the Pole Star is almost the same as the latitude of the place from which it is observed. (See LATITUDE AND LONGITUDE.) This was known in ancient times, and Christopher Columbus and other early navigators relied on Pole Star altitudes for finding their latitude.

If you know where to look for the Pole Star you can tell the true direction of north. You can find this star by lining up two of the stars in the constellation called the Great Bear, as shown in the diagram.

You can also find the direction of north by using a watch. Hold the watch horizontal and turn it so that the hour hand points in the direction of the Sun. Next, note the line joining the figure 12 with the centre of the watch. This line makes an angle with the hour hand. Then imagine a line which divides this angle in half. This imaginary line points roughly south, so true north is roughly in the opposite direction.

In air navigation the wind affects the aircraft because the plane is flying through a body of air which is itself moving. This motion caused by wind is called drift. If the wind is blowing from right ahead it reduces the speed of the aircraft over the ground, so that the flight will take longer and use more fuel. This affects what the pilot calls his flight plan, and he must make an allowance for drift. He knows what course he must steer over the ground to reach one place from another. If he knows the speed and direction of the wind he can calculate the course he must steer by compass to allow for drift.

A long-distance flight may be affected by the route the aircraft follows. The shortest distance between two points on a flat surface is the straight line joining them. Such a course cannot be followed when travelling over the surface of the Earth, because the Earth is not flat. To find the shortest distance between two places on a globe, stretch a thread over the surface so that it joins them and measure it. This distance, called the "great circle" distance, is the shortest path. Except on northerly or southerly courses or along the equator, it is somewhat shorter than the distance covered by drawing a straight line between the two places on a chart and steering along it on a steady compass course. An airliner flying from London to New York saves about 100 miles by following a great circle course.

For surveying, or fixing positions on land, an instrument called a theodolite is used. You can often see surveyors working with theodolites when housing estates or roads are being planned. The theodolite is mainly used for measuring angles in the horizontal plane. (See SURVEYING.)

In diagram 19, the distances from the tree and from the house to the theodolite can be found by measurement. Using the theodolite, the surveyor measures the angle between tree and house. He then plots the angle and distances on paper and in this way can find the distance between tree and house.

You can quite easily make your own theodolite. Cut out the two discs and the sighting bar shown in diagram 20. The ends of this bar, bent vertical and cut to a point, are used for sighting. The larger disc must be marked out in degrees from 0 to 360 and the smaller disc fixed to the underside of the sighting bar. With this simple instrument you can survey your own garden so as to make a map of it. The other thing you need is a measure of distance. Get this by pacing out the distances and counting your steps. By measuring a distance with a tape measure along the ground and pacing it out, you can find the average length of your pace. If, for example, you take 40 steps to cover a measured distance of 100 feet, the average length of your pace is $\frac{100}{40} \times 12 = 30$ inches.

Another useful instrument you can easily make is the quadrant, which measures altitudes, or angles in the vertical plane. It does the same job as a sextant, but is much simpler. Kepler, when mapping the stars, used enormous quadrants—one of them was 19 feet high—so as to get accurate results. Anyone handy with tools can make a quadrant from the details shown in diagram 21, but it need not be 19 feet high—

1 foot is enough. In use, altitude in degrees is read off the scale at the point where it is cut by the arm of the plumb bob, which can be a length of wire or string with a weight at the end.

After pacing out the distance from the foot of a tree or tall building, you can measure the altitude by bringing the two sighting holes in line with the top. Plot the observations on squared paper to obtain the height of the tree or building. Never try to measure the Sun's altitude with this instrument; you can injure your eyes.

Diagram 22 shows how a sextant or quadrant could be used to find the distance between the Earth and the Moon. Two observers situated at P and Q, on opposite sides of the Earth, take sextant altitudes of the Moon at the same instant. This gives the angles a and c. Angles b and d can be calculated from the latitude and longitude of P and Q. Angle $y = a + b$ and angle $z = c + d$. So we can find the angle x, which is $180° - (y + z)$, or $180° - y - z$.

We now know the three angles of the triangle. We can also find the length of one of the sides of the triangles—the distance between the two observers, which is the chord of a circle. This allows us to calculate the long sides of the triangle. It will be seen that this is a somewhat inaccurate method, as the angle x is so tiny. A small error in observing the altitudes therefore leads to a large error in the answer. Therefore astronomers used to find the distances of planets and stars by making observations from each end of the Earth's orbit, at intervals of six months.

Radar, however, allows more accurate measurements to be made. (See RADAR). Electromagnetic waves travel through space at the speed of light, which is about 186,000 miles a second, or 300,000 kilometres a second. By noting the time interval between sending a radar pulse to a planet and the instant of its return to Earth, the distance to the planet in miles can be easily calculated as half the interval (in seconds) multiplied by 186,000. The distances to the stars, however, are so vast that they are expressed not in miles but in light years. A light year is the distance travelled by light in a year—roughly 6 million million miles. Distances to the stars are found by measuring the colour and other characteristics of the light they send out.

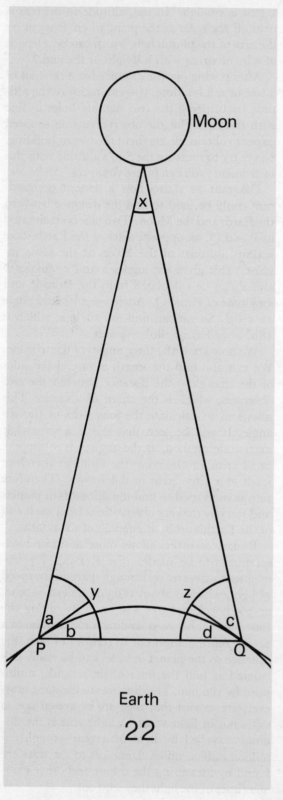

Moon

x

y   z

a
 b   d   c
P   Q

Earth

22

Space Travel

With the increase of space exploration, scientists are more and more concerned with speeds. To understand speeds we need to know some mathematics. Speeds are easily calculated when the moving object travels at a steady pace. For example, an aircraft that travels 1200 miles in 4 hours does so at an average speed of $\frac{1200}{4}$ or 300 miles an hour. But what happens if the speed is not steady? An example of this is found with falling objects.

If a stone drops from a cliff top and its fall is timed, we find that in the first second it drops 16 feet but that at the end of the next second it has fallen 64 feet. In fact, the distance fallen after any given time is 16 feet multiplied by the square of the time in seconds. Thus after 4 seconds the stone will have fallen $16 \times 4^2 = 256$ feet. The speed reached by the stone in feet a second is 32 times the time in seconds for which it has been falling, so after 4 seconds it is falling at $32 \times 4 = 128$ feet a second.

These facts are important. Although they can be obtained by measurement, they can also be calculated by a more advanced branch of mathematics called differential calculus.

The ability to use this kind of mathematics helps in space exploration. We need to know the correct angle at which the spacecraft must leave the Earth, and how much fuel is needed to yield a thrust that will give enough speed to escape from the Earth's gravity. We need to get the astronauts back safely, and mathematics helps to find the right spot in the atmosphere for re-entry and also the angle and speed of re-entry, for if they are too great the craft will burn up.

The speed, orbit and the position in space where the spacecraft must meet the Moon or a planet can all be calculated by various branches of mathematics. The size of the rocket used for launching depends on the total weight it has to lift off the ground. The larger space rockets are built in two or more sections called stages. Each stage is dropped as soon as its fuel has been exhausted, so that useless dead weight need not be carried. In order to escape from the pull of the Earth's gravity a speed of 25,000 miles an hour must be reached, this speed being known as the escape velocity from Earth. With manned space-craft this may mean burning fuel at the rate of about 5,000 tons a minute. The bigger and heavier the craft, the more powerful the rocket must be, and the bigger the rocket is, the harder it is to get it off the ground.

The mathematical problems of space travel are at least as difficult as the engineering work needed to design and make the spacecraft.

Areas and Volumes

Another kind of mathematical problem comes much nearer home than calculations about spacecraft. How much room do we take up if we mark out a football pitch? How much water will it take to fill an aquarium? This kind of question arises every day.

In diagram 23, the *rectangle* represents a post-card. How big is it? By that we mean how much space does it take up, or what is its area? There is a simple formula, or rule, for this. The area of the rectangle is found by multiplying the base by the height. That is, if the base is 14 centimetres long and the height 8 centimetres, the area of the postcard is $14 \times 8 = 112$ square centimetres. (When doing sums of this kind, the word centimetre is usually written cm and square centimetres as cm².)

To prove this formula, draw a rectangle of this size on squared paper. You will find that the area contains 112 small squares each of 1 cm².

The area of any *triangle* is found by multiplying the base length by the vertical height divided by two. The area of a *parallelogram* is the product obtained by multiplying one of the parallel sides by the perpendicular distance between them, which is the same as the product of base and height. In a *trapezium*, which is a four-sided figure having two parallel sides of unequal length, the area is obtained by multiplying the average length of the two parallel sides by the perpendicular distance between them. If one of the parallel sides is 8 cm long and the other 12 cm, the average is 10 cm. (See AVERAGES.) If the distance between those sides is 7 cm the area is $10 \times 7 = 70$ cm².

By using the relationship of π already mentioned we can find the area of a circle or of a ring, and also the surface area of a cone or of a

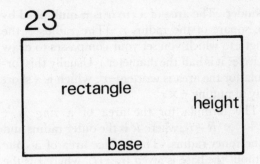

23

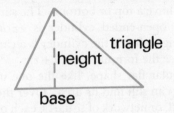

24

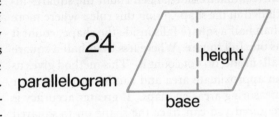

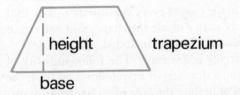

25

cylinder. The area of a *circle* is π multiplied by the square of the radius r. (The radius is the length to which you set your compasses to draw a circle; it is half the diameter.) Usually this formula for the area is written πr^2, which is a short way of putting $\pi \times r^2$.

The formula for the area of a *ring* is $\pi (R + r) \times (R - r)$, where R is the outer radius and r the inner radius. The surface area of a *cone* without the base is given by $\pi r L$, where r is the radius of the circle forming the base and L the slant height—not the vertical height. A *cylinder* may or may not have a top or bottom. The surface area of an open-ended cylinder is $2\pi rh$, where h is the height. But if the cylinder is a can with two ends, use the formula $2\pi r (h + r)$.

With an irregular flat shape, like the one in diagram 25, you can still find its area. Over the shape draw a grid, or network of squares, each of one centimetre side. Then count the squares included in the shape, using this rule: where more than half a square falls inside the shape, count it as one full square. Where less than half a square falls inside, do not count it. This method gives us an approximate area and can be very useful for measuring areas on maps. If greater accuracy is required you can trace the shape on to squared paper divided into centimetres and millimetres. Then, in the case of every centimetre square that falls only partly inside the shape, you can count the square millimetres included.

Enlarging a drawing. The following way of enlarging a drawing or map follows on from the method of finding the area of an irregular shape.

To enlarge a drawing to three times the size of the original, cover the original with a grid of small squares—for example, each of 1 centimetre side. (To avoid spoiling the original, you can draw the grid on tracing paper and lay it over the drawing, securing it with drawing pins.) Then rule up your paper with a lightly pencilled grid of squares each of 3 cm side. Next number the squares on each grid from 1 onwards, as this helps to avoid confusion. Then proceed to copy the drawing in relation to the small squares, but do so on the large squares.

Clearly the same method can be used for making a reduced copy. In this case, the grid of large squares is laid over the original and the reproduction is made by copying into the smaller squares.

Volumes. If we have a room and wish to find its volume we simply use the formula:

$$\text{volume} = \text{length} \times \text{breadth} \times \text{height}.$$

Denoting the three measurements, *l, b* and *h,* this can be written $\text{volume} = lbh$. Therefore a room 5 metres long, 4 metres wide and 3 metres high has a volume of $5 \times 4 \times 3 = 60$ cubic metres. This is often written 60 m^3.

The same formula is used for rectangular solid objects such as blocks and bricks. The standard metric size for bricks, for example, is 225 by $112\frac{1}{2}$ by 75 millimetres, and the volume of a brick can be calculated by the same method.

It need not be thought that this is just calculating for the sake of calculation. The weight of an object is directly proportional to its volume, and the cost of things is usually based on their weight.

A few other formulas for volumes are these: For a cylinder, $\text{volume} = \pi r^2 h$, where r is the radius of the base, and h the vertical height. It is useful to remember that the volume of a cone is always one-third of that of a cylinder having the same base area and vertical height, or $\frac{1}{3}\pi r^2 h$. The volume of a sphere is $\frac{4}{3}\pi r^3$, where r is the radius.

When calculating the volume of a rectangular case or box, treat it as a solid block and then subtract the volume of the block of air inside. Suppose we design a steel box used for storing valuables and wish to know how much it will weigh. Its outside measurements are to be 10 by 9 by 6 centimetres; the steel is to be 1 centimetre thick; and we are told that a cubic centimetre of steel weighs 8 grammes.

External volume $= 10 \times 9 \times 6 = 540$ cm^3

Internal volume $=$

$(10 - 1 - 1) \times (9 - 1 - 1) \times (6 - 1 - 1)$ cm^3

$= 8 \times 7 \times 4 = 224$ cm^3

So volume of steel is $540 - 224$, or 316 cm^3

Weight of box $= 316$ cm$^3 \times 8 \frac{\text{grammes}}{\text{cm}^3}$

$= 2,528$ grammes or 2·528 kilogrammes.

To find the weight of a hollow cylinder or hollow ball, follow the same method—that is,

☐ See MATHEMATICAL PUZZLES in the blue pages of this volume

subtract the internal volume from the external volume. But if the cylinder or ball has a very thin wall (for example, a tin can), simply multiply the surface area by the thickness. For a sphere, the surface area is given by the formula $4\pi r^2$, where r is the radius.

Using Algebra

Sometimes problems arise which are most easily solved by the use of algebra. As a simple example consider the question: "What must be added to 3 to make 8?" In algebra, this is written $3 + x = 8$, x being the unknown number that has to be added. This method of setting out the problem is called in algebra an equation, because 3 plus x equals 8. The only number that gives a true answer, or "satisfies the equation", is 5. Many difficult problems are solved by algebra because it is often impossible to reach the solution by the use of numbers alone.

Here is a simple problem showing the use of algebra:

In a right-angled triangle, the lengths of the sides enclosing the right angle are 3 cm and 4 cm. What is the length of the hypotenuse?

From Pythagoras' rule we know that the square of the hypotenuse is equal to the sum of the squares of the two shorter sides. So if we call the hypotenuse x, we can write:

$$x^2 = 3^2 + 4^2$$
$$= 9 + 16$$
$$\text{so } x^2 = 25$$

Now take the square root of both sides of the equation. This gives:

$x = 5$, so the hypotenuse is 5 cm long.

A different sort of problem whose treatment is sometimes classed as a branch of algebra is this: In how many ways can the letters of the word ORANGE be arranged?

We can try this by writing ORANGE, ORENGA, ORGANE, ORNAGE and so forth, but we shall soon find that this is going to take ages. The mathematician sets out the problem as:

$$_6P_6$$

This means that the 6 letters in the word have to be permuted, or exchanged, six times. This is

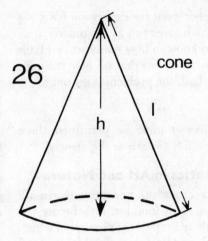

26   cone

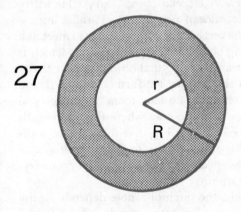

27

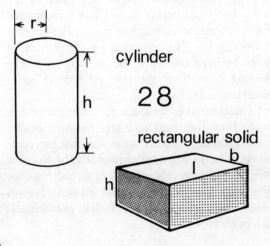

cylinder

28

rectangular solid

done by multiplying out the expression $6 \times 5 \times 4 \times 3 \times 2 \times 1$, which gives 720 as the answer.

If we wish to know in how many ways 3 balls can be put into 7 holes so that no hole contains more than one ball, the problem is set out:

$$_3P_7$$

Now the number 7 must be permuted three times, giving $7 \times 6 \times 5 = 210$ as the answer.

Mathematics in Art and Nature

Mathematics crops up unexpectedly in all sorts of subjects. It is found in art. Before the 15th century, all artists painted pictures in which the background, middle distance and foreground appeared to be in the same plane, conveying no impression of depth or distance.

Geometry was introduced by the Florentine painter Paolo Uccello (1397–1495). He introduced the rules of perspective. Parallel lines—such as the verges of a road—appear to meet at a "vanishing point" in the far distance—which is another way of saying that objects appear to decrease in size as they get farther away. If you stand at one end of a long room or passage you will notice that the lines where floor and walls meet appear to rise, but that those where walls and ceiling meet appear to fall. These simple rules of perspective are no more than geometry. (See DRAWING.)

In music, the pitch of a note depends on the number of sound vibrations produced in a second by the voice or instrument. Thus the note middle C is fixed at 264 vibrations a second. The more rapid the vibration, the higher the pitch of the note. The C an octave higher has a frequency of 528 vibrations a second, or exactly double that of middle C. The intervals, or differences in pitch, between one note and another that give pleasing harmonies are also related by strict mathematical rules.

In nature, the intervals at which branches spring from the trunk of a tree become shorter towards the top. In the same way, the intervals between leaves get smaller towards the tip of a twig. These intervals are related to one another by a mathematical law called a Fibonacci series which was discovered by an Italian mathematician in about 1200.

A Problem to Work Out!

This article is concluded with an example that you can work out for yourself. Diagram 29 shows a hutch suitable for two or three guinea-pigs. The front is open and covered with wire netting; the opening at one end allows the pets out into an exercise run, and also permits the hutch to be cleaned out.

The problem is to calculate the area of wood that would be needed to make the hutch. The diagram shows all the measurements in centimetres.

The best way to approach the problem is to draw an "exploded", or opened-out, view of the floor and the three walls, as shown in the lower diagram. This does not include the roof, which must overlap the ends and sides by 1 centimetre all round.

Calculation will give the total area of wood re-

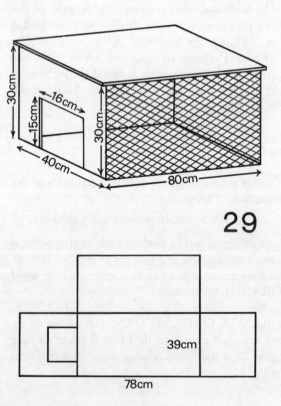

29

quired in square centimetres. Remember that to find the area you must multiply the length of each section by its width. Then add up the individual areas to find the total area.

MATILDA (1102–1167).

King Henry I of England had two children: a son called William, who was the heir to the throne, and a daughter called Matilda. However, in 1120 William was drowned off the coast of northern France when his ship, the "White Ship", hit a rock and sank. King Henry was therefore left without a son to succeed him.

By this time Matilda was already married to the Holy Roman Emperor Henry V (see HOLY ROMAN EMPIRE), but he died in 1125 and soon after this King Henry made the English barons swear that they would accept Matilda as queen after he himself died. They did not want to have a ruling queen (see QUEEN) and were particularly against Matilda after she married her second husband, Geoffrey Plantagenet, a great French noble, in 1128. However, they did swear to support her.

King Henry died in 1135 at a time when Matilda was out of England. His nephew Stephen hurried across the Channel from France and had himself crowned king, although he also had sworn homage to Matilda. However, he was of a weak character and by 1139 both the barons and the bishops were rebelling against him. That same year Matilda landed in England and was strongly supported by Robert, Earl of Gloucester. Stephen was defeated and captured at Lincoln in 1141 and Matilda was elected "Lady of the English". She would no doubt have become queen soon after this if she had not been so haughty that she made enemies of people who might have supported her. In 1142 King Stephen was released in return for the Earl of Gloucester, who had been captured by the King's side. For the next few years there was fighting and great confusion in England. In 1147 things began to look brighter for Stephen because Robert of Gloucester died and Matilda left England to live in Normandy. However, her son Henry continued the struggle and in 1154 was crowned King of England. Matilda continued to advise him until her death.

MATISSE, Henri Emile Benoit (1869–1954).

Henri Matisse is thought by many people to be the most important French painter of the 20th century. He was born at Le Cateau in France on December 31, 1869. He studied law and took up painting at the age of 20 while recovering from an illness.

At first the young Matisse copied the Old Masters in the Louvre in Paris, but his whole attitude to painting changed after he saw the work of the Impressionist painters. (See IMPRESSIONISTS.) The Impressionists, and particularly the work of Camille Pissaro, inspired Matisse to try out new ideas. In 1905 a portrait of his wife called "Woman with the Hat" caused a public outcry when it was put on show. Matisse and other painters who shared his ideas used colour so wildly that some people who saw their pictures called them the *Fauves* or "wild beasts" and jeered at their work.

However, Matisse continued his work and painted a series of great masterpieces, some influenced by visits to Morocco and to Italy, and by his studies of Eastern art. His canvases were rich in invention and bold colour. He went to live in Nice in the south of France and there he continued to paint until past his 80th birthday.

Courtesy, French Government Tourist Office

The chapel at Vence, near Nice, designed by Matisse.

"The Inattentive Reader", oil on canvas, painted by Matisse in 1919.

While living in Nice he designed a beautiful Dominican chapel, including stained glass, furniture, vestments and mural paintings on white tiles. He described this chapel as his masterpiece. Matisse also produced sculptures, etchings and lithographs and he illustrated several books.

MATTER is the word given to the substances of which things are made. The three main "states of matter", or forms in which matter can exist, are solid, liquid and gas.

We can tell whether a substance is solid, liquid or gas quite easily. A solid, such as a brick, has a fixed shape and a fixed size. It cannot be changed in shape, or made to occupy more space or less space, without applying a good deal of force to it. Also, a solid "coheres", or sticks together, for the whole brick can be lifted by picking up one end of it. A liquid behaves differently, for it has no fixed shape but takes the shape of the vessel it is poured into, whether a saucer or a bottle. Like solids, liquids have a fixed size—a quart cannot be squeezed into a pint pot. Liquids do not cohere like solids. As for gases, they have neither a fixed shape nor a fixed size and cohere even less than liquids. A gas expands, or spreads out, to the boundaries of any space enclosing it. For instance, an escape of gas can soon be detected all over the room. On the other hand, a large quantity of gas can be squeezed into a small container.

All substances can exist in all three states of matter, but in the ordinary way most of the substances that we know exist in one state only. The chief and most familiar exception is water, which exists as a solid when frozen to ice, as a liquid at normal temperatures and as a gas when boiled off as steam. By altering the temperature and pressure a substance can be made to change from one state to another. This is because the activity and movement of the molecules of a substance ("molecules" are the tiny particles of which the substance is made) increase when it is heated. In a solid, the molecules, although held in fixed patterns, try to move when heated but succeed only in vibrating, and it is this rapid vibration that makes a heated solid feel hot when touched. When more heat is applied it frees the molecules from each other and the solid loses its shape as it melts to a liquid. If the heating is increased still more, the molecules move faster until the liquid boils. Then the molecules are set quite free. (See HEAT).

Although substances are changed from one state to another by heating or cooling, the temperature at which the change takes place depends on the atmospheric pressure. The boiling point of a liquid is increased by raising the pressure. As an example, although water in an open saucepan cannot be heated to more than $100°C$ it can be made much hotter inside a pressure cooker. At increasing heights above sea level the atmospheric pressure is reduced, so that on a high mountain water boils well below $100°C$.

The melting point of most solids and the freezing point of most liquids is raised by compressing them, although ice and water are important exceptions to this (see ICE). To make a gas into a liquid, which is often done so that it can be carried about more easily, it must be compressed as well as being cooled. Cooling to very low temperatures is difficult, but if the gas is first compressed it turns to liquid with much less cooling. (See LIQUID AIR.) There is, however, for each gas a "critical temperature" above which it cannot be compressed into a liquid.

To change a solid into a gas it is usually necessary first to melt it into a liquid. But in some conditions "sublimation" may take place, the substance changing from solid to gas direct.

When a substance consists of particles larger than molecules but too small to be seen by the naked eye, it is known as a colloid. Paint, milk, foam, dust and mist are colloids, and living things also consist mostly of colloidal matter.

MATTERHORN. Although the steep tooth-like peak of the Matterhorn is not the highest mountain in the Alps it is one of the most famous because of the sport it offers to climbers. It lies on the Swiss-Italian border about 9 kilometres southwest of Zermatt and is 4,478 metres high. The top is a narrow crest with one summit in Switzerland and one in Italy. Four ridges and four faces, like those of a pyramid but much steeper, lead to the top and all these have been climbed, some of them at great risk to life.

Until 1865 the Matterhorn had never been climbed and there was great rivalry between the Swiss and Italian mountaineers as to which should reach the top first. In that year Edward Whymper, an English climber already famous at the age of 25, decided to make an attempt from Zermatt by the northeast ridge, in spite of the difficult obstacle called the Shoulder which juts out about 250 metres from the top. With three English companions and three local guides, Whymper reached the summit on July 14. On the way down, one of Whymper's party, who was inexperienced and did not have very good climbing boots, slipped and fell to his death, dragging with him three others. Whymper and two of the guides escaped through the breaking of the rope linking them to the others. Three days later the top was reached by climbers from the Italian side.

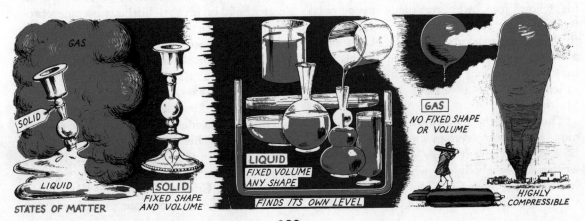

GAS

SOLID

LIQUID

SOLID
FIXED SHAPE
AND VOLUME

STATES OF MATTER

LIQUID
FIXED VOLUME
ANY SHAPE

FINDS ITS OWN LEVEL

GAS
NO FIXED SHAPE
OR VOLUME

HIGHLY
COMPRESSIBLE

Paul Popper
The Matterhorn has taken the lives of many mountaineers.

The other ridges of the Matterhorn were conquered one by one. The four faces gave mountaineers a harder task because of their very steep walls, which are swept by avalanches of stones and rock (see AVALANCHE). The last to be climbed was the ice-sheathed north face in 1931.

MATTHEW, Saint.

Saint Matthew was one of the Twelve Apostles, or chief disciples, of Jesus Christ. Before he became an apostle he was employed by the Romans (who were in occupation of Judaea at the time of Jesus' life) as a tax collector. This made him very unpopular amongst his fellow Jews, who regarded anyone who worked for the Romans as a traitor. He gave up this job when Jesus called him and, like the other apostles, spent all his time helping his new master. In the New Testament he is sometimes called Levi, but is always known now as Matthew.

The first of the four Gospels is named after him, but nobody is certain whether he wrote the book as we know it today or whether it was written by somebody else who used notes that Matthew had made. It is almost certain that it was written after the Gospels of St. Mark and St.

Luke—and it is likely that Matthew was dead by that time. So perhaps he started it and somebody else finished it.

It is clear that it was written especially for Jews—both for those who had become Christians and those who had kept to their own faith. The writer sets out to show how Jesus fulfilled all the hopes and expectations that the Jewish people had held for so long. Their prophets had always taught that one day there would come a Messiah to save and deliver them (see MESSIAH). Many Jews did not believe that Jesus was the Messiah, and the writer of St. Matthew's Gospel was trying to convince them that they were wrong. He carefully points out that Jesus was descended from David, exactly as the prophets had said the Messiah would be descended.

St. Matthew's Gospel has much to say about the Kingdom of heaven—there are 32 occasions when the phrase "Kingdom of heaven" is used. Moreover, there are ten parables about the Kingdom which are not to be found in the other Gospels; these ten include such well known ones as the Labourers in the Vineyard and the Ten Virgins.

St. Matthew's Gospel also devotes three whole chapters to the Sermon on the Mount, which contains all the special instructions given to the disciples about the kind of life that God expects His followers to live.

St. Matthew's Day is on September 21.

MATTHEWS, Sir Stanley

(born 1915). The great English footballer Stanley Matthews was born and educated at Hanley, Staffordshire. At the age of 15 he was signed by Stoke City as an amateur and on his 17th birthday became a professional. In 1933 he played 16 times in the league side and Stoke City won promotion to the first division. He obtained his first England cap against Wales at Cardiff in the following year. When World War II began he had become a regular player for England and was regarded as a brilliant outside right and one of the greatest dribblers in the history of football. During the war he served in the Royal Air Force. In 1947 he was transferred to Blackpool and in 1953 they won the F.A. Cup at Wembley against Bolton Wanderers, two of their four goals being due

Sport and General
Matthews beating an opponent on the run for the ball.

of the time when Christ washed the feet of His disciples on the Thursday before He was crucified on the first Good Friday. In mediaeval England the king washed the feet of as many poor men as there were years in his life and also gave them meat, money and clothes.

When Queen Elizabeth I came to the throne she had the paupers' feet washed by somebody else before she washed them. James II, who reigned from 1685 to 1688, was the last English sovereign to perform the foot-washing ceremony, although it continued to be performed on behalf of the sovereign until 1754. The ceremony now consists of the giving of Maundy Money—specially minted silver coins.

entirely to Matthews' great skill. In all he played for England 56 times. In 1957 he was made a C.B.E. and in 1965 he was knighted.

MAUNDY MONEY is money which the British sovereign distributes to poor people at a service, often held in Westminster Abbey, on Maundy Thursday, the day before Good Friday.

The idea dates back to the early middle ages when European sovereigns, nobles and priests used to wash the feet of poor people in memory

MAURITANIA is a republic, over four times the size of Great Britain, in West Africa. The country, apart from the low coastal region and the Senegal valley in the south, forms part of the Sahara Desert. The climate is hot and, in the desert, very dry. The people are mostly Moors. Some are nomads breeding hump-backed cattle, sheep and goats, or camels; others have settled in the oases where they grow crops for their own use. In the south there are many Negroes, most of whom, like the Moors, are Moslems. Nouakchott, the capital, is one of the country's few towns. Valuable deposits of iron ore and copper are mined and make up the chief exports. Other products include dates, livestock, salt, and gum from acacia trees.

French traders visited the coast of Mauritania in the 17th century. In the 19th century French influence extended inland and in 1904 Mauritania was made part of French West Africa. In 1960 the Islamic Republic of Mauritania became independent and remained in the French Community. The population is about 1,171,000.

MAURITIUS. The island of Mauritius is an independent member of the Commonwealth. It is named after a Dutch prince, Maurice of Nassau. Most Mauritians are of Indian stock.

Mauritius is in the Indian Ocean about 885 kilometres east of Madagascar. It is an egg-shaped island and is surrounded by coral reefs. The climate is very hot from November to April but cool and fairly dry for the rest of the year.

Courtesy, Royal Mint
Maundy Pennies. The Queen's head is shown on the back.

135

Hurricanes sometimes do great damage—there was a disastrous one in 1960. Mauritius was once thickly forested with ebony and ironwood trees but most of the land has been cleared for crops. There are few wild animals. The dodo, a large flightless bird, was killed off in 1681.

The capital and chief port of Mauritius is Port Louis on the west coast. Behind it rises a picturesque range of hills, one of three bordering the central plateau (tableland). The coastal plain around the plateau is narrow except in the north.

The fertile red clay soil suits nearly all tropical crops but most of the plains form a vast sugar-cane plantation. Some tea and aloes (plants whose juice is used for medicine) are also grown. Much of the money earned from the sugar crop is used to bring in food for the people, chiefly rice. There are light industries round Port Louis.

Mauritius is among the most thickly populated countries in the world and there is much overcrowding. About two-thirds of the people are Indians. Apart from some Chinese, the rest are of French, British, African or mixed blood. French is spoken more than English, and the language used by the non-white Mauritians is a dialect called "creole" with mostly French words.

Most of the Indians in Mauritius are Hindus and most of the Europeans are Roman Catholics. The schools are free and about 75% of the children attend them. Mauritius is linked by regular sea and air services with France, Britain and South Africa, and by sea with Japan and by air from Plaisance Airport with Australia.

Although Mauritius was known to the Portuguese they made no settlement there and the

Dutch took possession of the island in 1598. There were never more than a few hundred Dutch settlers and they abandoned the island in 1710. Soon afterwards it was taken by the French, who re-named it "Île de France" and brought in African slaves to tend their large plantations of sugar, rice and indigo (a plant from which a blue dye is obtained). During the Napoleonic Wars, French warships used Mauritius as a base from which to attack British vessels in the Indian Ocean. To put a stop to this a British force captured the island in 1810. It was agreed that the inhabitants should keep their own laws, customs and religion. When the slaves in British lands were set free in the 1830s most of the Africans on the plantations were replaced by hired workers from India. Many of the Indians chose to remain in Mauritius and thus the country obtained a large Indian population.

Mauritius remained a British colony until 1968, when it became independent. It also administers the island of Rodrigues about 560 kilometres to the east, where a population of 24,000 lives mainly by growing maize.

FACTS ABOUT MAURITIUS

AREA: 1,865 square kilometres.
POPULATION: 844,000.
KIND OF COUNTRY: Independent parliamentary state; member of the Commonwealth of Nations.
CAPITAL: Port Louis.
GEOGRAPHICAL FEATURES: Mauritius consists of a central plateau bordered by hills (up to 826 metres high) which fall away to a coastal plain.
CHIEF PRODUCTS: Sugar cane, aloes, tea, tobacco.
IMPORTANT TOWNS: Port Louis, Beau Bassin-Rose Hill, Curepipe, Mathurin (Rodrigues).
EDUCATION: School attendance is not compulsory.

MAXWELL, James Clerk (1831–1879).

The great scientist James Clerk Maxwell was born in Edinburgh. He studied at the University of Edinburgh and then at Cambridge University, where he took a brilliant degree in mathematics. After being a science professor at Aberdeen for four years he taught physics at

King's College, London, but in 1865 his health failed and he retired to his family home in Kirkcudbrightshire. In 1871, however, he was persuaded to go as a professor to Cambridge and there to arrange and take charge of the new physical laboratory, now famous as the Cavendish Laboratory. He was 48 when he died.

Maxwell had original ideas and also the great mathematical knowledge without which he believed science could never progress. He did important work on colour and colour-blindness and also on the properties and behaviour of gases. By far his greatest achievement, however, was his work on light and other electro-magnetic waves. His book *Electricity and Magnetism,* which was published in 1873, proved that light was a form of radiation moving out in waves like the ripples from a stone thrown in a pond. The difference between one kind of radiation and another, he said, lay only in the wave-length, or the distance between the crest of one ripple and the next. This led Maxwell to say that there must exist waves longer than the longest light-waves and shorter than the shortest ones, but that they would travel at the speed of light and would obey some of the same laws, such as that of reflection. Not until after Maxwell's death were the longer waves actually discovered by the German scientist Heinrich Hertz and used in radio signals. The radiations with wave-lengths shorter than those of light, such as X-rays and gamma rays, were also discovered later.

MAY DAY is May 1, which used to be celebrated with great merriment and revelry. Although such celebrations are less important than they used to be, they are still held in country towns and villages and the people still regard the beginning of May as a turning point on the road to summer. In a number of places it is still the custom for a young girl to be crowned May Queen and for dancing to be held round the maypole on the village green.

The celebration of the beginning of summer goes back thousands of years to pagan times (see PAGANS), and pagan ceremonial continued to be used long after people became Christians. Naturally, different peoples celebrated it in different ways. In southern Sweden a mock battle

was staged between summer and winter and a similar ceremony took place in the Isle of Man, which was probably introduced by the Viking invaders (see VIKINGS).

The various Celtic peoples of Europe welcomed in the day with a feast called *Beltane.* All

The Bedfordshire Times
At Elstow, near Bedford, the maypole is set up in front of the old Moot Hall. John Bunyan was born in this village.

the fires in a village were put out and a special fire was lit—probably to represent worship of the sun god—and from this fire people took pieces to rekindle their own house fires. A cake was baked in the fire and everyone ate bits of it.

Some people in northern England prepared a *sillabub* for their May feast; this was made of milk, still warm from the cow, mixed with wine and cake. A wedding ring was dropped in the middle of it and the young people fished for it to see who would be married first.

In medieval and Tudor England, May Day was a great public holiday. Everyone got up with the dawn and went "a-maying". Branches of trees and flowers were brought back to towns and villages and the centre of the procession was occupied by a maypole dressed with wreaths and ribbons. In country districts maypoles were usually made of birch and were set up for the one day only. In London and other large towns they were made of harder wood and were left standing all the year round.

The Puritans, with their serious ideas, hated people to dance and enjoy themselves, and when they obtained political power during and after the Civil War of the 17th century they forbade

May Day celebrations. However, when Charles II was restored to the throne maypoles and dancing came back into favour—in 1661 a maypole 134 feet high was erected in the Strand, in London—and May Day festivities continued to be a regular feature of English life until the end of the 18th century.

The best known of such ceremonies today is tne one which takes place at Magdalen College in Oxford University. At six o'clock in the morning the choir boys of the college chapel sing a May morning hymn at the top of the chapel tower. How this custom started is not certain but it may originally have been a merry concert, having nothing to do with a religious ceremony. Immediately after the singing of this hymn the Morris-men, wearing white clothes with fluttering ribbons and bells on their legs, dance through the streets. (See MORRIS DANCING.)

In Southampton (Hampshire) a rather similar event takes place on May Day, when the mayor and civic officials attend a service of psalms and hymns on top of the ancient Bar Gate. Minehead in Somerset and Padstow in Cornwall celebrate the day by parading a hobby-horse (a man

Brian Shuel

The Padstow 'Oss dances through the streets on May Day.

wearing an enormous hoop covered with flowing material) through the streets. At Padstow the young men start out very early in the morning with their hobby-horses. They prance and bow outside the houses and every so often pretend to die—only to spring up again when water is sprinkled on them.

At the end of the 19th century socialist parties in various European countries gave the name Labour Day to May 1. In Britain Labour Day is celebrated on the first Sunday after May Day.

MAYFLY. In the early part of the summer swarms of mayflies can often be seen performing their dancing flight near lakes and streams. The mayflies seem to rise and fall, fluttering straight up into the air for a little while and then floating quickly down again.

Mayfly nymph at the surface and adult in flight.

The mayfly is a fragile insect with two pairs of transparent wings, the front pair being much larger than the hind pair. From the end of the body there hang, like tails, three long threads or bristles.

Mayfly grubs are called nymphs and feed mostly on water plants. Most kinds crawl about at the bottom of the stream, though some can swim. When the nymph is fully grown, which may take as long as three years, it comes to the surface of the water and its skin splits along the back. It then crawls out in its adult form, though it is not yet the glossy-winged mayfly. Another change takes place. It sheds its skin again and this time creeps forth with brighter colours and shinier wings.

Some kinds of mayflies lay their eggs on the surface of the water, but others actually enter the water and lay their eggs under stones. As a rule mayflies do not live long, sometimes not more than a few hours. Fish are very fond of these insects and they eat large numbers of them.

MAYO is a large county in the province of Connaught in the Republic of Ireland. It is the place where the last invasion of Ireland from the continent of Europe took place. There is more about Mayo in the article CONNAUGHT.

MAYOR is the title given to the head of a borough council. On formal occasions he wears a red robe and a gold chain of office. Although many boroughs lost their administrative powers when local government was reorganized, some titles, including the office of mayor, were retained. (See LOCAL GOVERNMENT.)

A mayor is elected each year by council members, and although he may serve for more than one year he may not do so without being re-elected. He is usually a member of the council before being elected but need not be; he must, however, be on the register of voters (see ELECTIONS) for the area. A mayor usually appoints his wife—or if he is a bachelor, another lady—to be the mayoress. If a woman is mayor she often appoints another woman to be mayoress.

The mayors of certain big cities—for example London, York and Birmingham—have the title lord mayor, but this does not give them extra powers. In Scotland the title provost is used instead of mayor.

Lincolnshire Echo
The Mayor of Lincoln showing schoolboys his ring, chain and robes of office—and proclaiming a school holiday.

MEAD is one of the oldest alcoholic drinks and is made by the fermentation of honey mixed with water and herbs. (The process of fermentation is explained in the article FERMENTATION.) In ancient times the Egyptians, the Romans and the Greeks all made mead of one kind or another. In the Greek legends nectar, which is a form of mead, was the drink of the gods.

Mead was being brewed in Britain as early as the 4th century B.C. The Anglo-Saxons who came to Britain in the 5th and 6th centuries A.D. also made it, and from those far-off days comes the tradition of the wassail bowl. Before drinking the mead, people wished each other *wes hal,* or "good health". Later these words changed to *waes hail* and then to wassail. At feasts the mead was passed round in a great bowl, known as the wassail bowl, from which each person drank in turn. The custom still survives in the loving cup—a large bowl often made of silver—that is passed round at the banquets of the London livery companies. (See LIVERY COMPANIES.)

Until the 16th century a great amount of mead was made in England—particularly in the west—and in Wales. However, as sugar from the West Indies became available and people no longer had to rely on honey for sweetening, they stopped keeping so many bees and had much less honey. By the 17th century hardly any mead was made except in private houses. In recent years there has been a new interest in mead and small quantities are being made once more.

When spices are added to mead it is known as metheglin. The spices used are cloves, cinnamon, ginger, rosemary, nutmeg, maize and orange peel. They can be used separately or together.

MEALS. The number of meals people eat each day, the times at which they eat them and the kind of food they like vary greatly from country to country. Many British boys and girls expect a breakfast, followed possibly by a mid-morning drink, a substantial lunch, a large tea and then some supper before bed.

The eating habits of grown-up people in Britain are not so alike. Some people have a big meal at midday (which they call dinner), a cooked tea sometimes known as high tea and supper just before they go to bed. Others have a fairly small meal at midday (which they call lunch), perhaps only tea to drink in the afternoon and a big meal about seven o'clock in the evening, which they call dinner. However, most British people eat two or three meals every day, whereas in the Middle East and Far East many people eat only one meal a day. Millions of people in poorer countries are fortunate to have even one meal a day and often go hungry.

The times at which meals are eaten also vary. In Britain and North America the last main meal of the day is usually eaten not later than eight o'clock. In Spain, however, dinner may not even begin until ten o'clock—and children are allowed to stay up and eat with their parents. Again, among the Arabs meals do not take place at any regular hour. The big meal of the day is eaten when the sun is beginning to go down, because it is cooler then.

When it comes to the kind of food people like there is an even greater variety of taste and habit. The traditional British breakfast of porridge or cereal, bacon and egg, toast, marmalade and tea or coffee seems much too heavy to the Frenchman who is accustomed simply to rolls, jam and coffee, or to the Indian with his fruit and tea, or to the Norwegian with his coffee, bread and goat's cheese. The Englishman, on the other hand, is surprised at the breakfasts of his American friends, who have sausages together with pancakes and sweet maple syrup as one dish.

Most countries have their own special dishes which are often called national dishes because each one is so closely connected with the country of its origin. In England the national dish is roast beef and Yorkshire pudding, whereas for Italy one thinks of spaghetti, and for India and China, rice accompanied by a variety of other dishes, some of them highly spiced. In the Scandinavian countries many different types of pickled fish, meats and salads are eaten accompanied by several different kinds of bread. The Swedes call this *smørgåsbord* (pronounced smergawsboor) and the Danes and Norwegians call it *koldt bord*. Somewhat similar is the Polish *zakaski* (pronounced zakonski). Among some African people there is no such thing as different courses to a meal, and the food is served in three bowls—one for the men, one for the women and one for the children.

Perhaps even stranger are the national delicacies. In Spain, "pulpo" stew is thought of as a great delicacy; this is a very rich stew made from a variety of red octopus cooked in its own ink (see Octopus). The finished dish looks like hot black Indian ink with little bits of red rubber tubing floating about in it. In China a rare delicacy is soup made from sea slugs or from the nests of a bird called the swiftlet. This bird builds its nest on the walls of caves and does so simply by secreting a substance from glands in its mouth, which it attaches to the cave wall; no twigs or other materials are used. The nests are gathered, cleaned and made into soup. Dried shark's fin is another Chinese dish that is much sought after. In Norway a kind of raw, pickled fish, looking like jelly, is eaten hot with mustard, and is a traditional Christmas dish.

In Australia and South Africa the times and kinds of meals are not very different from those of Great Britain. In both countries a good deal of tea is drunk and meat is very popular. In South Africa many dishes include rice as one of the ingredients, and in addition to the usual fruits and vegetables pumpkin is often served. Large numbers of Europeans went to live in Australia after World War II, and as a result the food there, particularly in the cities, has become more continental in character. However, steak, eggs and tomatoes is still a favourite Australian dish (often for breakfast). The people eat more salads and fresh fruit than they used to, but kangaroo-tail soup, which is considered a great delicacy, is not so often eaten.

Nowadays many of the great cities of the world have foreign restaurants which serve the dishes of many different countries. Many British towns have Chinese and Indian restaurants and holidays and travel abroad have made many people more aware of the variety of different foods eaten in other countries.

MEALWORM. In spite of its name, the mealworm is the larva, or grub, of a beetle and not a worm at all. It is found in granaries and other places where dried food is stored, sometimes even in bread-bins, and is often a serious nuisance. Mealworms are, however, useful for feeding to certain pets, especially reptiles.

The full grown mealworm is about 2 centimetres long, very shiny and light brown in colour. It has three pairs of legs and moves surprisingly fast. The full grown beetle is rather narrow and dull black in colour.

MEASLES.
Nearly every child in Great Britain used to catch measles, for it is a very infectious disease and if one child caught it everyone in his class at school might get it. Now children can be vaccinated against measles, and given immunity which will last for several years at least.

The disease is caused by a filtrable virus; that is, the smallest kind of germ known. Measles starts about two weeks after the child has come in contact with a measles patient. It starts in the nose and throat and at first seems like a heavy cold and a headache, cough and temperature. It is not until between three and five days later that spots appear. They are red and usually in groups. They spread all over the body, and may even be inside the mouth, where they are whitish in colour. The fever, cough, sniffles and headache continue for a time, and the temperature may become very high. The spots remain for about four days.

Measles is infectious for about seven to nine days altogether. One reason why it spreads so quickly is that it is some time before the spots appear, and so parents often let their children go to school and play with their friends, thinking they have only a cold. In fact, measles is infectious even before the first symptoms appear. Children who have been in contact with a case of measles are often kept away from school for two weeks afterwards so that they do not spread the disease. Grown-ups seldom get measles, as they have generally had it in childhood.

A much milder disease is German measles, which is also very infectious. A pink rash appears on the face and body, remaining for about a week, and the glands of the neck become swollen. Grown-ups catch German measles as often as children do. The only danger is when a woman gets it six or seven months before she has a baby, for the baby may then be born blind or deaf or with heart disease.

MEASUREMENT.
Supposing you farmed one end of a lonely island where you could grow crops but had no animals, and at the other end was a farmer who kept cows and pigs but could grow no crops. The need for weights and measures would soon arise between you and him. You would have to settle how much potatoes or grain would be a fair exchange for his meat and milk. You might agree to exchange, let us say, 20 potatoes for a jugful of milk, but when it came to exchanging wheat or barley you could hardly start counting the grains. You might agree on four handfuls of grain for a jugful of milk. If you had no jug, you would have to use something like an empty coconut or big sea shell. If you wanted to exchange some of your land for some of his, you would have to measure the plots by pacing them out or by using a stick of a fixed length. In each case, the jugful or coconut-shellful or handful, or length of foot-pace or stick, would be a *unit* of measurement.

In early times people used parts of the body for measuring lengths. The cubit used by the ancient Egyptians was the length of the forearm from the elbow to finger-tips (about 50 centimetres) and the digit the breadth of the forefinger. The width of the hand was called the hand, and is the unit equal to about 10 centimetres still used for measuring horses. The

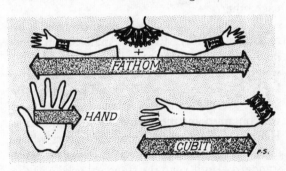

fathom (1·8 metres) began as the length of the outstretched arms between the finger-tips, and was used for measuring depths in the sea.

Although a man's foot is about 30 centimetres long, the measurement called the foot (about 30 centimetres) seems to have come from a unit used by the Babylonians for measuring bricks. Their unit was two-thirds of a cubit, or about 33 centimetres. With many variations in size, this foot came into use all over Europe. The Romans used the word *uncia* to mean a one-twelfth part, and this gave our word "inch". It also gave our word "ounce", which was once the twelfth part of a pound. Lengths shorter than an inch were measured in England by barleycorns, and only a century ago children learnt tables with the line "three barleycorns—one inch".

A length of one mile was divided into eight furlongs each of 220 yards. A furlong, or "furrow long", was the length of furrow that could be ploughed without the oxen having to rest.

Areas of land could be measured by seeing how much seed was needed to sow them or the time taken to plough them. The English acre began as the amount of land that could be ploughed in one day. Small quantities of material could be measured by balancing them against grains of wheat or barley. This led to a unit called the grain; 700 grains made one pound. Measures of capacity, or volume, began as rather vague units such as the basketful or boat-load.

There were two main objections to these early units. First, if a unit were based on the size of a part of the body, it would be different when measured by different people. Secondly, the various units such as digit, hand, cubit and fathom would have no simple connection with each other.

The first difficulty was soon overcome by making *standards*. Even in Anglo-Saxon England there were fixed standards of length and weight, such as the standard yard—an iron bar kept at Winchester—which could be copied for use all over the country. A later standard yard was obtained by measuring the arm of King Henry I, but of course it did not matter whose arm was used so long as everyone had the same standard. Until 1959 the standard yard was the distance between two lines marked on a bronze bar kept at Westminster by a government department called the Board of Trade. Then the yard was fixed as 0·9144 of a metre, which is a length explained later in this article. At the same time, the standard pound (hitherto the mass of a particular cylinder of platinum) was fixed as 0·45359237 of a kilogram. There did not have to be an actual standard measure of

volume, or capacity, because the gallon was defined as the volume of ten pounds of pure water at 62 degrees Fahrenheit.

There are government inspectors of weights and measures who check the scales, rulers, tapes and measures used by merchants and traders.

The second difficulty with the ancient units—that there was no simple relationship between a digit based on the forefinger and the cubit obtained from the forearm—was removed by choosing the cubit as the standard and ordering that other lengths must be fractions or multiples of it. Thus in Egypt the digit became one-twenty-eighth of a cubit and the fathom four cubits, and so on.

In the French Revolution, at the end of the 18th century, the new government chose a new unit of length called the metre. It was originally meant to be one-ten-millionth of the distance along the Earth's surface between Pole and equator and was about the same as a yard. From the metre were obtained a unit of volume called the litre and a unit of weight called the gram. A bar of platinum and a cylinder of the same metal were made as standards of the metre and kilogram. A kilogram is 1,000 grams—about 2 pounds. In 1875, in order to encourage the spreading of the metric system to other countries, an International Bureau of Weights and Measures was set up at Sèvres, a suburb of Paris. New standards of the metre and kilogram were made and sent to the various countries. Later, the International Bureau took part in standardizing other kinds of measurement, such as temperature, the brightness of light, atmospheric pressure and electric current. This work resulted in the International System of Units (SI). (See WEIGHTS AND MEASURES.)

Until the 1950s the standard metre was a bar known as "M", made of a mixture of platinum and iridium and kept at Sèvres. It was then decided to have a standard that could not change or be lost, and one that scientists could reproduce anywhere. The length of the metre was fixed as 1,650,763·73 times the wave-length of the orange light given off by a gas called krypton 86. (Wave-length is explained in the article LIGHT.)

In 1968 the British government decided to adopt the metric system of units by the end of

Using a laser interferometer to measure a scale of length. The caged laser is behind the machine to the left.

1975 and a Metrication Board was set up to help the public as they began to use the metre and the kilogram instead of the yard and the pound. (See METRIC SYSTEM.)

The kilogram is a unit of *mass*, that is, the amount of matter in an object. In everyday speech the word "weight" is used, as here, to mean mass. But for a scientist *weight* has a different meaning (see GRAVITATION).

The other important quantity that has to be measured is time. The article CALENDAR explains about years, months and days. Short intervals of time were at first measured by noting the time taken for a candle to burn or by sand-glasses (see HOUR-GLASS). Then in 1581 the Italian Galileo discovered that a pendulum of a fixed length makes the same number of swings in a particular time, no matter how violently it is swung or how heavy it is. This paved the way for clocks that kept good time. Time measurers in laboratories are controlled by quartz crystals which, when electricity is applied to them, vibrate at an absolutely constant speed. The second is now defined in terms of the frequency of one of the radiations from caesium 133 atoms. (See TIME.)

MEAT is a food that people have eaten since the earliest times. Early men had to go out and hunt wild and often dangerous animals, but as people became more civilized they began to tame animals and keep them in captivity so that they could obtain meat more easily. Nowadays animals are specially bred to give the greatest amount of meat that people will like best. As the really choice meat, such as chops and sirloin steaks, comes only from certain parts of an animal those parts must be well developed. Also the animals must be young and not have too much fat on them.

The main kinds of meat used in Great Britain are beef and veal from cattle; bacon, ham and pork from pigs; and mutton and lamb from sheep. (See CATTLE; PIG; SHEEP; BACON; HAM.) The flesh of poultry birds—chicken, turkey, goose and duck—is also classed as meat and so is that of game, or wild birds—pheasant, partridge, grouse and wild duck.

Meat is an important food because it contains proteins and vitamins in an easily digestible form. (See DIET; VITAMIN.) Some countries like Ireland, Australia and New Zealand produce far more meat than their people need because they specialize in producing meat. Others, like Britain, Italy and the German Federal Republic, cannot produce nearly enough for their needs because their people specialize in producing industrial goods. Therefore the industrialized countries buy large amounts of meat from the meat-producing countries. Britain is one of the biggest buyers of foreign meat.

This meat does not come in the form of live cattle and sheep, and therefore has to be preserved to prevent it going bad. There are two ways of preserving meat while it is being transported, and both are forms of refrigeration. One method is to freeze it hard and the other to chill it, or keep it at a temperature just about freezing point. The second method is usually preferred because it does not destroy the flavour of the meat as much as freezing does. When meat has been frozen or chilled it has to be kept frozen or

Courtesy, National Film Board of Canada
Butchers cut and prepare joints at a packing plant.

four sections, each of which consists of a leg and part of the body. These sections are known as quarters—those from the front of the animal as the forequarters and those from the back as the hindquarters. Carcasses of sheep and lambs and calves are usually left whole but pigs are sometimes cut in half down the back. Some carcasses and quarters are reduced to smaller pieces known as "cuts". The cuts are sold to butchers as they are or sealed in plastic bags. No air is allowed into the bag and after the meat is put in the seal prevents air getting in. This method of preserving meat is known as "vacuum" packing and it helps to keep meat fresh for long periods. The butcher often cuts the meat into much smaller pieces that are suitable for the table. These joints and steaks, as they are called, and the best ways of cooking them, are listed in the article COOKING.

Butchers often find it suits them best to buy meat in the big wholesale markets which are found in cities such as Birmingham, Manchester, London and Glasgow. The biggest of these is in London at Smithfield. Many butchers go to the abattoir and personally select the meat which best suits their customers. Some even buy animals at the market, send them to the abattoir and collect the carcasses when they are ready.

chilled until it is sold for eating. It therefore has to be transported and stored in ships and storage depots that have enormous cold rooms.

However, although Britain buys so much meat abroad, over half is produced at home. The cattle are often bred in one area and fattened ready for the table in another. The farmers of the Republic of Ireland send some of their young cattle to England to be fattened. The English farmers buy these "store" cattle and fatten them on high quality cattle food. The highlands of Scotland and places like the county of Cumberland also produce young cattle that are fattened in other parts of the country. When the animals are ready or "finished" the farmers can send them to market where they are sold by auction. Many animals are sold direct by the farmer to a meat company.

After the animals have been sold, they go to a place known as a slaughterhouse, or abattoir. Here they are stunned, killed and then dressed. Dressing means removing the hide or skin and taking away those parts that cannot be eaten, which leaves the carcass. There are inspectors to make sure the meat is fit for food.

After the animals have been slaughtered the carcasses are made ready for delivery to the butchers. The carcasses of cattle are cut into

MEATH is a county in Leinster, a province of the Republic of Ireland. Once there was a province of Meath, and at Tara the high king, the greatest of Ireland's kings, was crowned. There is more about Meath in the article LEINSTER.

MECCA. In a barren hollow in the hills, about 80 kilometres inland from the Red Sea port of Jedda, lies the largest Arabian city, Mecca. To Moslems it is the holiest city in the world and a great place of pilgrimage. (See ISLAM.)

Even before the time of the Prophet Mohammed, Mecca was an important centre of trade, as it lay on the caravan route by which incense, gold and spices were carried from southern Arabia to the eastern Mediterranean. It was a place of pilgrimage, too, for in the city stood the Ka'aba, a square temple said to have been built by Adam. Later Abraham and Ishmael were supposed to have rebuilt the temple and to have put in one of its corners the Black Stone given them by the Archangel Gabriel. Near by is the well of Zamzam from which Hagar drew water to save her son Ishmael's life after Abraham had cast them out to die in the wilderness.

In about A.D. 570, Mohammed was born at Mecca. He lived there for many years and founded the Moslem religion, but only after overcoming much opposition were he and his followers able to get rid of the idols in the Ka'aba and establish Mecca as the holy city of Islam (see MOHAMMED).

Since then, Mecca has been the centre of the Moslem faith. When they pray Moslems must turn towards Mecca and they must be buried facing Mecca. If they can do so, they are bound to make a pilgrimage thither once in their lives. Year after year, thousands of Moslems from all over the world have made their way to Mecca to worship in the way laid down by Mohammed.

For some miles round the Ka'aba the soil is sacred and may be trodden only by Moslems. Once in this area, the pilgrims must wear sandals and a special garment made of two white cotton cloths. Some of the ceremonies of the pilgrimage are held outside Mecca, but in the city the pilgrims must pray at the Ka'aba and walk round it seven times, then kissing the Black Stone. Moslems who have made the pilgrimage

may call themselves *hajji* and wear a green band round their headdress.

The chief building in Mecca is the great mosque, or Moslem temple. Inside the mosque are the well of Zamzam and a stone which is said to show Abraham's footprints. The Ka'aba stands in the courtyard. Good roads connect Mecca with Jedda and the holy city of Medina, where Mohammed was buried, and also with Riyadh, the capital of Saudi Arabia. The city is an important market town and the capital of the coastal province of the Hejaz. Most Meccans earn their living by letting rooms to pilgrims or acting as guides in the pilgrimage ceremonies.

The population of Mecca is about 200,000.

MECHANICS is the study of how objects behave when acted on by forces such as pushing and pulling. It is a practical subject which has to be used daily by engineers of all kinds, whether they design bridges, aircraft or nuclear power stations. Mechanics is divided into two main branches. The first branch, called *statics*, has to do with objects at rest. The second branch, *dynamics*, deals with moving objects.

Force is one of the most important ideas in mechanics. The force that everyone can feel is that of gravity, which is the pull exerted on every

Paul Popper

The Ka'aba at Mecca. The black cloth that covers the temple is embroidered in gold with sayings from the Koran.

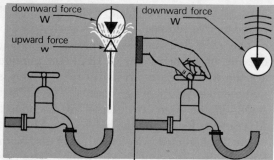

The downward force W (the weight of the ball) is balanced by the upward force w of the water, until the tap is turned off.

object by the Earth's attraction. The greater the mass of an object (the more stuff there is in it) the greater the pull it feels. What we call "weight" is simply the force of gravity felt by any object. The unit of force is the newton and an object of mass 1 kilogram has a weight of approximately 10 newtons. (See FORCE.)

In statics, the forces acting on the object are balanced. If they were not balanced the object would move. This can be shown by resting a table tennis ball on a jet of water. The weight of the ball is a downwards force and this is balanced by the upwards force which the water applies to the ball. (If you put your hand in a water jet, you can feel the push of the water against your hand.) When the water is turned off, the ball falls because its weight is no longer balanced. When engineers are deciding how thick and strong they must make the parts of a bridge, they have to think about balancing the forces that the parts will feel. Those forces may be caused by a lorry or a train pushing down on

the bridge or by a high wind pushing it sideways, as well as by the weight of the material of the bridge itself.

Another part of statics deals with forces tending to turn an object about a pivot. If a heavy man sits at one end of a seesaw and a small boy at the other, the plank will balance only if the man sits much nearer the middle than the boy does. The rule is that, if the plank is to balance, the man's weight multiplied by his distance from the pivot in the middle must be equal to the boy's weight multiplied by the boy's distance from the middle. If the man moves a very small distance towards the middle, his end of the seesaw will go up—he will be lifted. This is the principle of the lever, by means of which a small force can be made to lift a load of greater weight. (See MACHINE.)

When a force moves an object it does work, and the amount of work done depends on the size of the force and the distance through which it moves the object. Work is measured in joules. If a man whose weight is 750 newtons goes up a flight of stairs 4 metres high he does $750 \times 4 = 3,000$ joules of work. Power is the *rate* of doing work. If work is done at the rate of 60 joules every second, the power is said to be 60 watts. So that if the man ran up the same stairs in 3 seconds, he would for that short time have been exerting

$$\frac{3000}{3} = 1000 \text{ watts.}$$

When work is done, energy must be used; energy is therefore measured in work units. It

The man's weight W is greater than the boy's weight w. So the boy's distance D from the middle of the seesaw must be greater than the man's distance d in order to balance it.

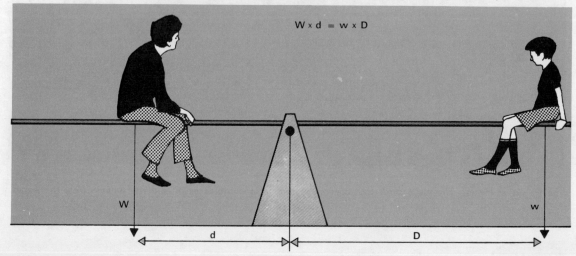

$W \times d = w \times D$

takes 1 joule of energy to do 1 joule of work. The man running upstairs obtains energy from the food he eats (products from the digestion of food give out energy when they combine with the oxygen in the air he breathes). Most engines obtain energy in a similar way from the fuel they burn. (See ENERGY; FUEL.)

In dynamics, where force is connected with movement, three of the most important laws were stated in 1687 by the great English scientist Sir Isaac Newton. You can read about them in the article FORCE. Using these laws, space scientists can, with the aid of a computer, work out the path that a rocket must take in order to reach the Moon or Mars.

When a force acts on an object free to move, the object moves faster and faster, or is said to *accelerate*. The acceleration, or rate at which it gains speed, depends on the size of the force and the mass of the object. If two lorries have the same mass, the one with the more powerful engine, capable of exerting a greater force, accelerates more rapidly. On the other hand, a loaded lorry has less acceleration than when it is empty.

When an object is moved by a force it is given *momentum*. Momentum is described as the mass of the object multiplied by its speed. If two objects collide, their total momentum is unchanged. Thus if a trolley moving at 10 metres

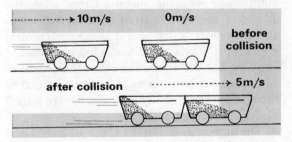

per second collides with a stopped trolley of the same mass, and if the trolleys become locked together at the collision, the two will move together at 5 metres per second.

MEDALS AND DECORATIONS. For

centuries most countries have honoured their citizens for bravery and for good services, both in war and peace, by giving them medals or decorations. Usually these honours are given by the king or queen, the president, the grand duke, or whoever is the head of state.

In the United Kingdom the sovereign may make a person a member of one of the orders of chivalry for outstanding services, while decorations are usually awarded for gallantry or distinguished service. Medals are also given for lesser acts of bravery or devotion, for participation in campaigns, or for long service in the armed forces, the police, and other official organizations.

The highest British orders of chivalry are the Orders of the Garter and the Thistle, the latter being particularly associated with Scotland; the Order of St. Patrick, formerly associated with Ireland, is no longer awarded. These, the "Great Orders", are very highly prized and only rarely bestowed.

Other British orders (awarded in several classes, of which the two highest confer knighthood on the recipient) are those of the Bath, of St. Michael and St. George, and of the British Empire, while the Royal Victorian Order is given for services to the Royal Family.

On important occasions the knights of these orders make a magnificent sight as they walk in procession wearing their mantles, collars, stars, and badges. Knights-Companions of the Order of the Garter wear on the left leg a dark blue velvet garter, lettered in gold *Honi soit qui mal y pense*, meaning "dishonoured be he who thinks ill of it".

Two interesting awards which confer neither knighthood nor precedence, yet are most highly regarded, are the Order of Merit (O.M.) and the Order of the Companions of Honour (C.H.). They are sparingly awarded to those who have won the highest fame in literature, science, art, or in other service to the country.

The method of wearing the badges of orders varies according to the class. The highest class, usually Knight (or Dame) Grand Cross, has the badge worn from a sash over one shoulder to the opposite hip, except on important occasions, when it is worn from the collar of the order. Badges of second and third classes are usually worn at the neck, while those of the fourth and fifth classes of five-class orders, are worn on the left breast with other decorations and medals.

The Distinguished Service Order (D.S.O.), founded in 1886, is classed as an order, not of chivalry, but of distinction; it is given to senior officers of the armed forces for outstanding leadership or bravery in war.

Decorations normally rank below orders, except the Victoria Cross and the George Cross (on which there are separate articles); these are worn on the left breast before any other awards. The Royal Red Cross is a decoration given only to women of the nursing services.

The three fighting services each have their own decorations for gallantry, ranking below the D.S.O. The Distinguished Service Cross is awarded to officers of the Royal Navy and Royal Marines, while ratings and other ranks can receive the Conspicuous Gallantry Medal or the Distinguished Service Medal. The equivalent Army awards are the Military Cross for officers and the Distinguished Conduct Medal and the Military Medal for other ranks. Officers of the Royal Air Force can receive the Distinguished Flying Cross, while other ranks are awarded the Conspicuous Gallantry Medal (Air) or the Distinguished Flying Medal, all for gallantry in action. The Air Force Cross and the Air Force Medal may be awarded for brave acts while flying but not in action against the enemy.

For a second and each subsequent award of the same decoration, a bar is added to the ribbon, and when ribbon strips only are worn a small rosette on the ribbon indicates each bar. In the case of the V.C. and G.C., however, the ribbon strip automatically carries a miniature of the cross, so a second award would be indicated by the addition of a second miniature cross on the ribbon.

Life-saving medals are usually worn on the right breast, but surviving recipients of the Albert Medal, given for saving life at sea or on land, or the Edward Medal, awarded for heroic acts in mines and factories, wear their medals on the left side. Since 1949, however, these two medals have been awarded only posthumously.

Campaign medals were first given in Great Britain for the Battle of Waterloo, but were later dated back to 1793. Since then they have been given for actions in all parts of the world, sometimes with bars to indicate specific battles or service in a particular region. In World War II such services were marked by the Atlantic Star, Africa Star, Burma Star, and several others.

Foreign Decorations

Many foreign decorations have existed for centuries, although with changes in government, such as the replacement of a monarchy by a republic, the old orders of chivalry have often been replaced by fresh awards.

Among the best known is the French Legion of Honour, founded by Napoleon Bonaparte in 1802, as even republican France recognized the need to have a decoration to take the place of those swept away in the revolution. The Legion of Honour is given for outstanding services to the state, both in peace and in war, and one often sees Frenchmen wearing a tiny red rosette or a narrow red ribbon at the buttonhole of the coat or jacket.

Another well known decoration is the Prussian Iron Cross. This was at first a temporary award, instituted three times, in 1813, 1870, and 1914, and discontinued after each war, but in 1939 it was revived as a German order. Several million were awarded to German troops and their allies in World Wars I and II.

In the United States the highest decoration is the Medal of Honor, dating from 1861–2 and comparable with the Victoria Cross, while the Medal of Freedom is given for contributions to the national interest, world peace, or cultural endeavour. The United States has no orders of chivalry, but the decoration called the Legion of Merit was instituted in 1942, and is awarded to members of the United States and foreign armed forces.

The highest award in the U.S.S.R. is the Gold Star Medal, associated with the title, "Hero of the Soviet Union". Although the U.S.S.R. has abolished all the Tsarist decorations it still keeps for the modern Order of Glory the orange ribbon with three black stripes of the old Order of St. George.

Many foreign decorations have been awarded to British subjects. Permission has to be obtained from the sovereign to accept and wear them, and they are worn after British awards.

VICTORIA CROSS   GEORGE CROSS   DISTINGUISHED SERVICE ORDER

DISTINGUISHED SERVICE CROSS   MILITARY CROSS   DISTINGUISHED FLYING CROSS   AIR FORCE CROSS

DISTINGUISHED CONDUCT MEDAL   CONSPICUOUS GALLANTRY MEDAL   DISTINGUISHED SERVICE MEDAL

MILITARY MEDAL   DISTINGUISHED FLYING MEDAL   AIR FORCE MEDAL   GEORGE MEDAL

These are medals and decorations awarded within the Commonwealth in World War II.

MEDICI FAMILY.

The Medicis were a noble family who lived in Florence, Italy (see FLORENCE). They were rich and powerful, and were well known for some 400 years. They became rich through trading and business in Italy and also in the rest of Europe. One of the reasons for their great power was that they were extremely clever in politics, and were always able to hold important positions in the state.

Today, people in Florence and throughout the world remember the Medici family best for the wonderful works of art on which they spent a good deal of their money. During the time when the most successful members of the family lived, they made Florence one of the most beautiful cities in Italy, by building magnificent churches and palaces. They had these fine buildings decorated by the great artists of the day with statues and paintings which are now famous all over the world. The Medicis were very generous patrons of the arts; that is, they encouraged artists to do their work by paying them to paint pictures, or build chapels, or carve tombs and statues for them.

Not all that the Medici family did, however, was noble, for although they loved beautiful things they also loved to rule and be powerful. Often they were cruel and scheming in their attempts to defeat their rivals, and would murder them if it suited them to do so.

The first well-known Medici, who built up the wealth and greatness of the family, was Giovanni (1360–1429), who made his fortune in trade. His son Cosimo (1389–1464) showed the good and evil sides of the family character. He did not set himself up as a ruler, and the city of Florence still governed itself as a republic; but in spite of this he managed to gain complete control of the republic and he was able to banish his enemies. (A republic is a country which has an elected head of state rather than a king.) That was the evil side of Cosimo's character. Yet he also encouraged painting and sculpture, he started an academy for the study of the Greek philosopher Plato; he opened the first public library at his own expense; and he spent huge sums of money on fine buildings, such as churches and palaces. It was largely due to Cosimo that Florence was the most famous of the European cities for art and learning during the period called the Renaissance. (You may read more about this period in the article RENAISSANCE.)

The next great Medici was Lorenzo the Magnificent (1449–1492), who was Cosimo's grandson. He was not as skilled in politics and business as his grandfather had been, but he succeeded in becoming practically a dictator by violent and cunning methods. He kept many spies and he often meddled in the most private affairs of the citizens; yet he was a poet, too, and a learned man. Like Cosimo, he was a patron of artists, among them the sculptor Michelangelo, and one of the most important things he did was to persuade writers to use their native language, Italian, instead of Latin, which was the usual language for literature at this time, even though it was no longer spoken. Lorenzo's great palace was full of books, paintings and sculpture from all over the world. Though he was a tyrant, and evil in many ways, he deserved his title of "the Magnificent".

For a time the Medici family lost its power because Piero, Lorenzo's son, surrendered to the king of France when he invaded Italy in 1494. All the family were sent into exile, but they managed to return 18 years later, and grew stronger than ever. One of Piero's brothers, Giovanni, became Pope Leo X and in 1523 another member of the family was elected Pope Clement VII. Then in 1533 Catherine de Medici, who was a great-granddaughter of Lorenzo the Magnificent, married Henry II, King of France, which meant that members of the Medici family had become powerful in the most important countries of Europe. Catherine, too, encouraged the arts, but in politics she was dishonest and ruthless. It was she who was largely responsible for the terrible Massacre of St. Bartholomew's Day when thousands of French protestants were murdered.

After the 16th century, the Medici family gradually became less important, even though they continued to be rulers. They ruled harshly, however, and forced their subjects to pay high taxes, which meant that the city of Florence became poorer and poorer, and lost the greatness it had enjoyed when Cosimo and Lorenzo were

SOME OTHER ARTICLES ON MEDICAL SUBJECTS

ABSCESS
AMBULANCE
ANAESTHETIC
ANATOMY
ANTIBIOTICS
ANTISEPTIC
APPENDIX
ASTHMA
ATHLETE'S FOOT
BABY
BANDAGE
BLINDNESS
BLOOD
BOILS
BONE
BRAIN
BREATHING
CHICKENPOX
CHILBLAINS
CHOLERA
COD-LIVER OIL
COLD, COMMON
CRAMP
DEAF AND DUMB
DENTIST
DIABETES
DIAPHRAGM
DIET
DIGESTION
DIPHTHERIA
DISINFECTANT
DOCTOR
DRUGS
EAR
ECZEMA
EPIDEMIC
EYE
EYESIGHT
FIRST AID
FROSTBITE
FUNNY BONE

GERMS
GIDDINESS
HAY FEVER
HEADACHE
HEALTH RULES
HEART
HICCUP
HOSPITAL
INFLUENZA
IODINE
IRON LUNG
JOINTS AND LIGAMENTS
KIDNEY
LARYNX
LIVER
MALARIA
MASSAGE
MEASLES
MUMPS
MUSCLE
NATIONAL HEALTH SERVICE
NERVOUS SYSTEM
NETTLERASH
NOSE
NURSING
PENICILLIN
PHYSIOLOGY
PINS AND NEEDLES
PNEUMONIA
POISONS
POLIOMYELITIS
PUBLIC HEALTH
PULSE
QUARANTINE
QUININE
RHEUMATISM
RICKETS
RINGWORM
SCARLET FEVER
SCURVY
SINUS

SKELETON
SKIN
STINGS AND BITES
SURGERY
TEETH
TUBERCULOSIS
TYPHOID FEVER
VACCINATION AND
  INOCULATION
WARTS
WHOOPING COUGH

alive. Gaston, who was the last of the Medicis, had no children and so when he died in 1737 the power of the family came to an end after nearly 400 years.

MEDICINE, HISTORY OF. People have

suffered from diseases from the very earliest times, and they have always searched for medicines to cure them. It was a long time, however, before man learned to apply the right medical treatment for diseases because his knowledge of how the parts of the body work increased very slowly. Some of the early kinds of treatment can be guessed at from those of primitive, or backward, peoples living today.

It seems certain that prehistoric men sometimes went further than making medicines from herbs and berries. Skulls have been found with little round pieces cut out of them, and these must have been removed with flint knives. Now this is very like the modern operation of trephining which is done to remove tumours (growths) on the brain and to treat bleeding inside the skull. Prehistoric men, however, knew nothing about such things, and it seems likely that they did this operation, which must have been very painful, in order to relieve severe headaches, or perhaps to let out evil spirits which they thought were in the head. Sometimes the patients died, either from the disease or from the operation, but sometimes they recovered.

Hundreds of trephined skulls have been found in prehistoric burial places in such widely scattered parts of the world as France, Bohemia in Czechoslovakia, Portugal, Peru and Japan, and the same operation is still done for headache today by savage tribes in Bolivia in South America and in some of the South Sea Islands. The little pieces of bone removed by the prehistoric operators seem to have been worn round the neck as charms to keep away evil, for they often had a hole bored through the middle so that they could be threaded on a string.

Early medicine, in fact, was mixed up a good deal with magic, and among primitive peoples the witch-doctor who cures illness is much more like a magician than a doctor. Even people like the ancient Egyptians, who studied medicine seriously and knew much about the uses of drugs and herbs, believed in magic at the same time.

The Egyptian doctors were also priests and were only allowed to treat people according to the rules of their sacred books. These were supposed to have been written by Thoth, the god of wisdom and learning, but in fact they were the work of some of the earlier priests of his temples. If a priest-doctor broke the rules of treatment set out in the books he was liable to be punished and if the patient died he was put to death. This naturally did not encourage people to look for new methods of treatment, and medicine soon became a matter of charms and superstitions.

Herodotus, the Greek historian who lived in the 5th century B.C., says that the Egyptian priest-doctors each looked after one part of the body only. Some looked after the eyes, some the head, some the stomach—which sounds as though they were like modern specialists in one way at least.

According to Herodotus, the Babylonians had no doctors at all. Sick people were laid in the market-place, and anyone who knew about the disease was expected to stop and give advice.

This must have led to some quarrels across the sick-bed!

The study of drugs (pharmacology) began with the Egyptians, and they were also careful about diet and cleanliness. It was, however, the Jews who paid most attention to health in general, and their laws for making sure that people ate safe food, kept themselves clean and lived healthy lives can be read in several books of the Old Testament.

Meanwhile, nearly 3,000 years ago in India, a high standard was reached in surgery, or the art of performing operations. The Hindu surgeons of those days used instruments very much like those of today, among them scissors, saws, needles and forceps. They did many of the same operations, such as the amputation (cutting off) of limbs, the removal of cataracts from the eyes and even skin grafting and plastic surgery. They also made new noses for people who had lost them in battle or had had them cut off by an irritated rajah.

The ancient Chinese, on the other hand, knew little about surgery and had all kinds of peculiar ideas about the organs of the body, which they believed were related, friendly, or at war with each other. The heart, for instance, was supposed to be the son of the liver, the father of the stomach, the friend of the spleen and the enemy of the kidney.

Medicine in Greece and Rome

The Greeks called Aesculapius, who was one of their earliest physicians, a god and built temples in his honour. The last words of the philosopher Socrates, spoken to a friend, were "We owe a cock to Aesculapius; pay it therefore, and do not neglect it."

The greatest physician of ancient Greece was Hippocrates, who left writings about his teachings. He taught that the first duty of a doctor is to do nothing to harm his patients. When the pupils of Hippocrates became doctors themselves they had to swear an oath (make a solemn promise) that they would help the sick according to their ability and judgment, never give poisons, not tell other people what their patients had told them and keep both themselves and their professions pure. The Hippocratic oath, as this was

All aspects of the doctor's profession have been drawn by artists and the developments in medicine can be seen in works of art. However, many techniques remained unchanged for centuries. The doctor examining his patient's liver (top left) is from a 2nd-century B.C. Roman sculpture. Right: Preparing a cough mixture, shown in a 13th-century Mesopotamian manuscript.

Bottom left: A woodcut from Mondino's *Anathomia*, 1493, shows Mondino giving instructions for a dissection. Right: A Chinese doctor tends his patient's wound.

called, became the standard of conduct for doctors all through the ages. (See HIPPOCRATES.)

Aristotle was another great teacher and, besides medicine, he also studied natural history and believed in making experiments to find out the causes of things. Aristotle produced the idea that everything is made up of the four elements (earth, air, fire and water), which in their turn are made up of hot, cold, wet and dry. Fire, for example, is hot and dry, water is wet and cold. (See ARISTOTLE.)

The Romans looked down on doctors and thought that the medical profession was only fit for slaves. Many of them kept a slave trained in medicine to look after their families, and when Greek doctors came to Italy they were often received with contempt.

Nevertheless, the greatest doctor of the ancient world after Hippocrates was one of those despised Greeks, called Galen, who lived in the 2nd century A.D. He studied at Alexandria in Egypt, at the best medical school of those times, and then came to Rome where he was physician to the Emperor Marcus Aurelius.

Galen did much dissection (cutting open of dead bodies to study their parts), and found out a good deal about muscles and the arteries. Unfortunately he got hold of a mistaken belief from the days of Hippocrates that the body is composed of four humours, or liquids: blood, phlegm, black bile and yellow bile. When one increased or lessened in quantity, the balance of the body was upset and the person became ill.

Galen added the idea that there are also three kinds of spirits in the body, and he called them natural, vital and animal spirits. According to him, they too had to be blended in just the right quantities. The beliefs in the four elements, the four humours and the three spirits were widely held by doctors and other learned men throughout the middle ages.

The Middle Ages

In the 4th century A.D. the Roman emperors moved to Byzantium, which later became Constantinople and is now Istanbul. Constantine, who was then ruler of the empire, was the first Roman emperor to make Christianity the state religion. Christianity taught that it was people's duty to help sick persons, but nevertheless an old Jewish belief that diseases are sent as a punishment, or that they are due to devils, began to be generally held. Also, the thoughts of good Christians were so much on Heaven that they began to despise their bodies and to feel that it

Radio Times Hulton Picture Library
Illustration from a 13th-century book on surgery.

was sinful to take care of them, even to the extent of keeping them clean.

The science of medicine did not flourish in these circumstances, but in Persia the caliphs, or rulers, welcomed learned men from all over the world, and among them were many doctors. They were known as the Arabian physicians, though among them were Christians, Jews and Persians. The caliphs built beautiful hospitals for the poor, with fountains playing in the courts and music and storytellers to amuse the patients. Each patient was given five gold pieces so that he did not have to start work again at once.

Meanwhile, European doctors were becoming ignorant and superstitious, although monks and nuns opened hospitals for the sick poor and always nursed them devotedly. The leaders of the church sometimes spoke against using treatments, saying that they were sinful, and forbade even the simplest surgery. However, things improved a little in the 11th and 12th centuries, when there was a great medical school at Salerno in Italy, which trained women doctors as well as men.

In the 15th and 16th centuries a great change came over Europe. (See RENAISSANCE.) All branches of learning, particularly art and literature, improved greatly, but medicine did not profit as much as some because the doctors of those days were very slow to accept new ideas.

One sign of the change was a fresh interest in surgery and the founding, under Henry VIII, of the Barber-Surgeon Company. The Guild of Surgeons was united with the barbers and both agreed to act together for the good of the patient. The company lasted until 1745, by which time the barbers had decided to concentrate on hairdressing and to leave surgery to the surgeons. The physicians were luckier. Their Royal College in London, also founded by a charter granted by Henry VIII in 1518, has existed ever since. It has always shown great interest in medical education and in professional standards.

Modern Medicine

Real advances in treatment of patients could not take place until there was a better understanding of the body's anatomy (structure) and physiology (function).

The renewed study of anatomy was brought about by Vesalius (1514–1564) who performed most of his work in his famous medical school at Padua in Italy. (See the articles ANATOMY and BIOLOGY.) Later, the invention of the microscope in 1590 by a Dutchman, Zacharias Janssen, greatly helped in the study of both anatomy and physiology. A full knowledge of anatomy is vital for surgeons operating on the body. John Hunter (1728–1793), by his studies and teaching of anatomy and physiology, and by his collection of anatomical specimens, laid the foundations for a more scientific approach to surgery.

Better knowledge of anatomy led to an increased understanding of physiology. In describing the way in which the blood is pumped round the body by the heart, William Harvey (1578–1657) made a major discovery. Over the next

Radio Times Hulton Picture Library

Vaccinating children and grown-ups against smallpox—a 19th-century scene in the East End of London.

three centuries every system of the body was studied. The Frenchman Claude Bernard (1813–1878) examined the processes of digestion and discovered some of the functions of the liver, showing how it can store sugar or release it when necessary.

A systematic classification of diseases was the main work of the English physician Thomas Sydenham (1624–89). Later, the abnormalities of the body which are responsible for disease were studied. This study, called pathology, began seriously during the 19th century and was led by a German, Rudolph Virchow (1821–1902), who showed that the cells of the body which could be seen only with the microscope

might be the most important in understanding diseases. The discovery of bacteria (see BACTERIA) completely changed people's ideas about disease and made its treatment and prevention possible. Louis Pasteur (1822–1895) showed that bacteria can cause many diseases and also demonstrated how some minute organisms could be destroyed. (See the article PASTEUR.) Another bacteriologist, Robert Koch (1843–1910), discovered the bacteria causing tuberculosis. Viruses, even smaller than bacteria, were discovered in the 20th century and were shown to cause many diseases, including influenza and the common cold. (See GERMS.)

Methodical examination of the patient by his doctor began early in the 19th century. The method of percussion, or tapping the chest with the finger, was discovered by Leopold Auenbrugger (1722–1809), a Viennese physician whose father, an innkeeper, used to tap the wine casks to discover the level of wine inside. Auenbrugger applied this method to examining the chest for fluid. The development of the stethoscope by René Théophile Hyacinthe Laënnec (1781–1826) was a very important advance. He found that he could hear the sound in a patient's lungs and heart much more distinctly by listening through a rolled-up paper tube. The earliest stethoscopes were simple wooden tubes.

Progress in physics and biochemistry during the 19th and 20th centuries also resulted in better techniques of investigation and treatment. X-rays were discovered in 1895 by the German, Wilhelm Conrad Röntgen (1845–1923), and now help doctors to find out what is wrong with their patients. (See the article X-RAYS.) The study of biochemistry has also helped in the treatment of diabetes and kidney diseases among others. Blood tests examine both the biochemistry and also the cells of the blood (see BLOOD).

The development of bacteriology (the study of bacteria) has led to important methods of treatment. The Scottish surgeon Joseph Lister (1827–1912) read Pasteur's work and realized that chemicals could kill the bacteria which attacked patients during and after surgical operations, leading to sepsis (infection) of wounds and often the death of the patient. He devised the system of "antisepsis" by using a carbolic spray

operating room   patient's room   laboratory

nursery   X-ray room   blood bank

medical supply room   laundry   kitchen

outpatient clinic   emergency room   emergency generator

The modern hospital requires a wide range of skills, from surgeon to cook.

in the operating theatre and showed that there was less spread of bacteria if the surgeons wore masks and gowns. (See LISTER, JOSEPH.) Bacteria are also destroyed by antiseptic solutions or by heating. Surgical instruments are now sterilized by heating in high temperature ovens (autoclaves) before use.

The discovery of antibacterial substances for the treatment of disease was first made by Paul Ehrlich (1854–1915). Gerhard Domagk (1895–1964) developed sulphonamides, some of which are still used for treating bacterial diseases. Most important of all has been the discovery and development of antibiotics—which are prepared from other living organisms. Sir Alexander Fleming (1881–1955) observed that bacteria did not grow around the mould *Penicillium*. In 1939, Howard Florey (1898–1968) began a survey of antibacterial substances and produced the first antibiotic, penicillin. Penicillin is now used to treat many types of infections. Another important antibiotic is streptomycin, discovered in 1944 and used to treat tuberculosis.

Immunization is an important part of prevention against disease. If foreign proteins are injected into the body, it reacts by producing antibodies to fight them. These, in turn, react with the original protein if it ever re-enters the body.

Edward Jenner was the first to take advantage of the process of immunity. He inoculated people to give protection against the fatal disease of smallpox by vaccinating them with cowpox. (See the articles JENNER, EDWARD and VACCINATION AND INOCULATION.) Whooping cough, tetanus, diptheria and polio can also be prevented by immunization.

Discoveries of many useful drugs for the treatment of disease have been made during the 20th century. Among the few effective drugs known at the beginning of the century were digitalis for heart disease, quinine for malaria and morphia for pain. Insulin for the treatment of diabetes, and antibiotics for the treatment of infections have been amongst the most dramatic later discoveries. The number of drugs now available is enormous and many specialists are concerned with testing them for safety and effectiveness (see DRUGS). The use of radioactive materials in

diagnosis and treatment has been another important feature. The discovery of radium in 1898 by Pierre Curie (1859–1906) and his wife, Marie Curie (1867–1934), paved the way for the use of radioactive irradiation in the treatment of cancer and some blood diseases. Every large hospital now has a department for "radiotherapy".

Very major technical advances have been made in surgery during the 20th century, especially in making it possible to transplant organs from a dead person to another with seriously diseased organs. Transplants of the kidney have been particularly successful, but the heart and lungs have also been attempted.

This progress has depended on advances in other fields. Antisepsis, as shown by Lister, antibiotics, blood transfusion and the administering of fluids into the veins have all been vital to progress in surgery. Perhaps the most important of all has been the development of anaesthetics. (See ANAESTHETIC.)

Collaboration with engineers has also helped medical science. For instance, there are now machines which can take over the function of breathing and others which can take over that of the kidneys when they no longer work. These inventions have saved many lives. The role of the nursing profession in modern medicine has also been of great importance. During the 20th century the importance of community health has been emphasized, with the need for good water supplies and sewage. Poisonous fumes and smoke are seen as a danger in cities and factories. General inoculation and legal controls prevent the spread of epidemics. In Britain, the care of health in the welfare state was ensured by the National Health Service, established in 1948, which provides free treatment for all.

MEDITERRANEAN SEA. The Mediterranean Sea is almost landlocked, being joined with the open ocean only by the narrow Strait of Gibraltar. It lies between Europe and Africa and takes its name from the Latin words *medius* (meaning "middle") and *terra* (meaning "land"). It fills a deep trench which millions of years ago stretched half way round the world. It is even now more than 3,220 kilometres long and covers an area about ten times the size of the United Kingdom.

The African coast of the Mediterranean is fairly regular, with no big peninsulas or gulfs. The only large river on this coast is the Nile, most of whose waters are taken for irrigating (watering) the soil of Egypt so that little reaches the sea. The north side of the Mediterranean is broken up by the Adriatic and the Aegean Seas, by many smaller inlets and by the peninsulas of Italy and Greece. Most of the islands are in the northern part of the sea. The Mediterranean is divided into two basins by Italy and Sicily. These basins are connected only by the narrow Straits of Messina and by the Sicilian Channel less than 160 kilometres wide. Compared with other oceans and seas, the Mediterranean has been fairly recently formed and the land is still shaking down into place. This is shown by the frequent earthquakes which take place beneath the sea itself and in the lands around its northern coast, and by volcanoes such as Etna and Stromboli.

The Mediterranean lands have a hot, dry summer and a mild, rainy winter. The summer sun evaporates, or draws off as vapour, far more water from the sea than is received from rivers or from rainfall. Therefore the Mediterranean grows slowly more salty. The saltier water sinks because it is heavier but cannot escape through the Strait of Gibraltar as there is a "sill" there only about 305 metres below the surface. Most of the water lost by evaporation is made up by a strong surface current coming in through the Strait of Gibraltar, but some water also enters from the Black Sea through the Bosporus and the Dardanelles. Without these inflowing currents the Mediterranean would have become a shrinking inland sea like the Caspian Sea. Over most of the Mediterranean the rise and fall of tide is less than 30 centimetres between high and low water, although it is greater at the head of the Adriatic, being between 60 and 150 centimetres at Venice.

Most of the Mediterranean is ringed by high mountains except along the Egyptian and Libyan coasts. Many of the coastal plains are quite small, being the deltas (see DELTA) of short rivers and separated from one another by rocky peninsulas. The deltas have formed chiefly because there are no tides to carry away the mud brought down by the rivers. When drained, the deltas make good farm land, but in the past they were swampy and unhealthy. A great deal of Mediterranean farming has to be done by cultivating the hill slopes. In many places the slopes have been made into terraces like steps for growing vines, olives and fruit trees. Although some of the coastal plains are fertile, Mediterranean agriculture in most places does not give rich crops. In the same way, the sea is less rich than most in fish. Tunny and sardines are the chief fish. Sponges are gathered in many places.

Some of the earliest known civilizations began among people who learned to till the soil and build settled homes and towns in the lands east of the Mediterranean. When these people reached the sea they soon made voyages on it because, especially in summer, it was calm and had clear skies and steady winds. More than 1,000 years before the time of Christ, the Phoenicians—a people from the countries now called Syria and Lebanon—were trading in their ships to Egypt, North Africa, Greece, Spain and possibly as far as England. In places where great rivers emptied or there were gaps in the mountains, the ancient trading posts have grown into great ports such as Alexandria, Marseilles and Genoa. By the time of Christ most of the lands around the Mediterranean belonged to Rome. When the Roman Empire fell, trade in the Mediterranean was reduced by piracy and did not recover until about A.D. 1200, when Venice and Genoa grew to power.

By about 1500, however, the spread of Turkish power in the eastern Mediterranean and the Portuguese discovery of a way to the east round South Africa caused another decline. The riches of India and the "spice islands" (Indonesia) and later of America drew the ships of western Europe away from the Mediterranean. The Industrial Revolution in the 19th century had little effect on the Mediterranean as coal and iron were scarce around its shores.

In 1869 the Suez Canal was opened, thus making the Mediterranean the shortest sea route between Europe and the East.

Great Britain and the other countries of western Europe depend for their oil almost entirely on supplies from the Middle East countries—Iraq, Saudi Arabia, Persia and the Persian Gulf states. Some of this oil flows through the pipelines from the oil-fields to ports on the coast of the eastern Mediterranean, where it is loaded into tankers.

MEDUSA.

The ancient Greeks told stories of a terrible monster called Medusa, one of three sisters known as the Gorgons. Snakes grew out of Medusa's head and wings from her scaly body. According to some descriptions she had a round ugly face with her tongue always hanging from her mouth, but according to others her face was terrible in beauty and sadness. Anyone who looked at it was turned to stone.

Medusa was finally killed by the hero Perseus. The goddess Athene lent him a shining shield and, holding it so that he could see the monster reflected in the shield, he crept up while she slept and stabbed her. From her blood sprang the winged horse Pegasus.

MEDWAY RIVER.

The chief river of Kent is the Medway, which is about 110 kilometres long. It rises in Ashdown Forest in Sussex and flows east, forming the county boundary between Sussex and Kent. It enters Kent near the town of Ashurst and flows north, past Tonbridge, and through Maidstone. It then passes through a narrow gap in the North Downs.

As far as Maidstone, the Medway is little more than a pleasant country stream. A few kilometres north of the town it broadens and the waters rise and fall with the tides. Past Rochester the Medway opens out to form a wide estuary, or mouth, with several islands, and it finally joins the Thames estuary.

Much shipping travels down the Medway to the Thames estuary. The towns of Chatham and Gillingham at the mouth of the Medway are important to Kent, though the docks are not used as much as they were when Chatham was an important naval base.

Since very early days Rochester has guarded the crossing of the Medway, and for this reason a castle was built in Norman times to overlook the river. One of the curious sights of the Medway is the Rochester Court of Admiralty, which

Chatham News

The Rochester Court of Admiralty is held once a year to give judgement on fishing rights and similar matters.

is held once a year on a barge moored at the end of Rochester pier. The mayor of Rochester (who is permitted by ancient charter to entitle himself Admiral of the Medway) presides over the court and is attended by a mace-bearer and other officials in old-fashioned costume. The Rochester Court of Admiralty does not hear cases, but is concerned with fishing rights and similar matters.

MEE, Arthur (1875–1943).

One of the most successful journalists of the early part of the 20th century was Arthur Mee. He had the gift of being able to make dull, dead facts come alive and whatever he wrote was always interesting.

Radio Times Hulton Picture Library

Arthur Mee.

As a young man of 20 he became editor of a Nottingham evening newspaper. Later, when he came to London, he worked on the staff of a magazine all day and at home at night wrote long articles for the evening papers. He could write on almost any subject under the sun without going out of his house. He did it by means of his collection of press cuttings, items of news of all kinds cut out of the papers. This collection was so huge—there were hundreds of thousands of cuttings—that he had to have a special cabinet made to hold it. The cuttings were arranged in specially designed envelopes.

Journalists are not often remembered after they are dead, but Arthur Mee is remembered because of two achievements, the *Children's Encyclopaedia* and the *Children's Newspaper,* both of which he founded and edited. The encyclopaedia was started in 1907 for his daughter Marjorie. Into it he put all that he thought a child should know, in a way that it could understand. It was very successful and was translated into many languages. He started the *Children's Newspaper* soon after World War I. From then until 1965 the newspaper brought the world's news to many boys and girls.

Like all good journalists, Arthur Mee was full of curiosity. He was also kind and trustful and had the highest ideals.

MEKONG RIVER. One of the great rivers of the world is the Mekong, which is about 4,000 kilometres long. It rises in the high, snow-clad ranges of Tibet in southwest China and flows south through rugged valleys with bare rocky walls at the speed of a mountain torrent. Little is known about the upper course of the river.

After entering Laos, the Mekong forms for a long distance the boundary between that country and Thailand. Lower down it winds for some 640 kilometres through Cambodia and southern Vietnam, countries which owe much of their fertility to the river. In Cambodia the Mekong is connected to the great lake called the Tonlé Sap. The river brings down with it huge quantities of mud which has formed an enormous delta at its mouth (see DELTA). Rice scattered on the flooded delta land sinks on to the mud, sprouts there and grows up through the water. The heavy summer rains along the lower part of the river bring it to its highest level in October, but after that the flow is much less until May. Seagoing ships can go up the river as far as Phnom Penh, the capital of Cambodia.

MELBOURNE, WILLIAM LAMB, 2ND VISCOUNT (1779–1848). From 1834 until 1841, with only two short breaks, Lord Melbourne was Prime Minister of Great Britain.

Born on March 15, 1779, he was the second son of Peniston Lamb, the first Lord Melbourne, and was educated at Eton College and Cambridge University. In politics he was a Whig (see LIBERAL PARTY) and he became a member of parliament for the first time in 1806. For many years he sat in the House of Commons, but when his father died in 1829 he inherited the title (his elder brother also having died) and therefore took his seat in the House of Lords. In 1830 he became Home Secretary and four years later made the working classes very indignant by his support for the harsh treatment of six agricultural labourers who were punished for taking part in trade union activities. They belonged to the village of Tolpuddle, Dorset, and became known as the Tolpuddle Martyrs (see TOLPUDDLE MARTYRS).

In 1834 Melbourne became Prime Minister for a few months and then held that office again from 1835 to 1841, with only a very short break in 1839. While he was Prime Minister his party never had a big majority in the House of Commons and therefore could not introduce measures that were likely to upset the Opposition too much. However, his government carried through important measures which gave the people of the Canadian colonies more control over their affairs, and set them on the road to becoming united and fully independent.

Melbourne always gave the impression of being very idle and when any change was suggested he always asked, "Why not leave it alone?" The amusing writer Sydney Smith realized that Melbourne's laziness was really only a pretence and teased him by saying, "I accuse our Minister of honesty and diligence."

Queen Victoria was always devoted to Lord Melbourne. She came to the throne in 1837 as a young girl of 18 who knew little of politics, and her Prime Minister—who was 58—became a very understanding and fatherly adviser, teaching her about the way in which Britain was governed.

The Australian city of Melbourne was named after Viscount Melbourne.

MELBOURNE is the capital of Victoria and is in the southeastern corner of Australia. In 1835 a settler from Tasmania named John Batman

The twin tower of Princes Gate Building, seen across the Yarra River, dominates the southern entrance to Melbourne.

rowed from the bay of Port Phillip some way up the Yarra River and said "this will be the place for a village". Now Greater Melbourne covers over 1,810 square kilometres and Melbourne is Australia's second largest city.

Melbourne is a spacious city and more than a quarter of its area is taken up by parks and gardens. The streets are wide, regularly planned and lined with trees. St. Kilda Road, nearly 90 metres wide, consists of a series of roads and footpaths separated by plantations and ornamental palms and is Australia's finest boulevard. There are many handsome buildings, including the two cathedrals, the State Parliament House, the university, the Victorian Arts Centre and the Shrine of Remembrance (the war memorial).

Melbourne became a centre of banking and commerce and grew very rapidly when in 1851 gold was discovered at Ballarat and Bendigo and other places in Victoria. It is also a busy industrial city. The city is about 60 kilometres from the open sea and ocean-going ships use the docks of Port Melbourne on the Yarra River. Most of Victoria's roads and railways fan out from Melbourne, which has an international airport. On the racecourse at Flemington is run the race for the Melbourne Cup and there is also a famous cricket ground. The 1956 Olympic Games were held in Melbourne.

The population is about 2,389,000.

MELODY is the tune of a piece of music. People generally remember music by the tune of it, which is the top part and can easily be sung or whistled. For a long time music consisted only of these simple melodies, sung by one person or played on one instrument. There was no other music beneath these tunes as there came to be later, when harmony was introduced beneath the tune. (See Harmony.)

Probably the first melodies were simply imitations of the high and low pitches (called inflections) in people's ordinary speaking voices. When people say, "How nice to see you" or "I did have a lovely time at the party" there is almost a tune in the inflections of the words. Melody was also an imitation in music of the different emphasis, or strength, given to spoken words. If you think of the emphasis given to the word "nice" in the first sentence and to "did" in the second, you begin to feel that there is a rhythm, or lilt, in the sentences. Thus speech gave the idea both of tune and rhythm.

Melodies of a rather different kind came about through imitations of the rhythms of folk dances. It was natural for people to sing while they danced, and as different peoples had different dances, with quite different rhythms, so melodies grew up in one country that were quite different from those in another. These differences still exist in melodies today. A

161

Russian melody, like "The Volga Boatmen", rather slow-moving and heavily emphasized, and a French melody like "Frère Jacques", short and sharp, are unlike each other and both are different from any of the English folk melodies.

It is not only in folk melodies that these national differences occur—they are found also in the works of the great composers. The melodies of the German composers Schubert and Schumann have much in common with the tune, or inflections, of the German language. The melodies of the English composer Vaughan Williams—for example, in his *Serenade to Music*—are often like the rhythm and tune of the English language.

All good melodies are simple, which explains why we easily remember them. However, they are not easy to write. No one can really say how a melody is written and nobody can teach a composer how to write one. He must be born with the gift of expressing the simple, true things of life in the notes of a melody, just as a poet is born with the gift of making words into a poem.

MELON. The melons are related to cucumbers and marrows, and the fruit, which is generally oval and may be quite small or weigh up to 66 pounds, is usually eaten raw. The flesh is very juicy and the fruit varies in colour between pale greenish yellow and salmon pink. The plant is a trailing one with hairy leaves and stems, and lives for only one season. In most European varieties separate male and female flowers grow on the same plant.

The home of the melon is said to be Asia, although it has never been found growing wild.

Some kinds were probably grown by the ancient Egyptians and Greeks, and it was introduced into Europe before the time of Christ. Now it is cultivated in all hot, dry regions where water can be brought to the plants. Three main types are grown.

The netted melon is much grown in fields in America, and has a rather soft, pale yellowish skin with a netlike pattern and green or salmon-coloured flesh. The cantaloup melon has a warty, rough greenish skin and the winter melon has a smooth skin and is without the musky

flavour of the others. It can be kept for several months after being harvested.

In England the netted melon can only be grown in greenhouses or frames with artificial heat, but cantaloups may be planted in ordinary frames. The plants need well-drained soil in

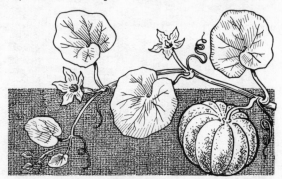

Flowers, leaves and fruit of the cantaloup melon.

which to grow, and should not be given a lot of rich compost or they will merely grow very large and leafy and not bear much fruit.

The watermelon, which is the kind usually seen in English shops, is a cousin of the others. The leaves of the plant are more divided and the fruit, which is very large, may be oval or long. The most popular varieties have bright red flesh and black seeds.

MELVILLE, Herman (1819–1891). On a summer afternoon in 1842 a boat from an Australian ship was pulling into the harbour of the island of Nukuhiva, in the South Seas, when suddenly the crew saw a white youth dash across the beach and jump into the ocean. As they helped him aboard, the spears of a party of natives showered into the water. That was how Herman Melville, later to become famous as the author of *Moby Dick,* escaped from the tribe of the Taipis, who were said to be cannibals.

Herman Melville, who was born in New York, went to sea when he was 19. In 1841 he sailed round Cape Horn, the southernmost tip of South America, on a whaling ship bound for the South Pacific, but after a year and a half he deserted the ship and was captured by the Taipis.

Soon after he returned to New York after more voyages, Melville wrote two books describing his life among the native peoples. In 1851 his most famous book, *Moby Dick*, was published. It is a strange and gripping story of the long battle carried on over the great oceans of the world, between an old whaling captain—the terrifying Captain Ahab—and a savage white whale.

Melville's story *Billy Budd* has been made into an opera by Benjamin Britten.

MEMBER OF PARLIAMENT. Members of both the House of Lords and the House of Commons are members of parliament though the term "Member of parliament" or "M.P." always means a member of the House of Commons. Any British subject who is not a lunatic, a peer, a criminal or a bankrupt can, if properly elected, be a member of parliament. However, he cannot at the same time be a civil servant, a full-time judge, a serving member of the armed forces, or a clergyman of certain churches. Nor may he hold certain offices of profit that are paid for by the community as a whole. (If he wishes to resign his seat he has to disqualify himself by taking an office of profit from the crown—either the stewardship of the Chiltern Hundreds or the stewardship of the Manor of Northstead. There are no duties to be done by the holders of these ancient offices.)

After he has been elected (see ELECTIONS), the M.P. must affirm or swear an oath of allegiance to the British sovereign, after which he can take his place in the House of Commons. Although he represents his constituents (the people living in the part of the country for which he was elected), he is not bound to do what they tell him or to vote as they would like him to vote. Naturally he has to help them, and if one of them tells him of a grievance against a government department, the M.P. is expected to take it up with the minister in charge or ask him a question in the House of Commons itself. Or, the M.P. may take up the matter with the Parliamentary Commissioner. (See OMBUDSMAN.)

Members of parliament receive hundreds of letters every year and a lot of their time is taken up in answering them and asking government departments to give information or take action on the problems raised in the letters. This help is given to constituents of any political party,

not just to the M.P.s' supporters. Some of the people they represent come and visit their M.P. in the House of Commons. Members visit their constituency (district) to see the people there.

The members of the House of Commons begin their main work at 2.30 p.m., although smaller numbers of them work in the mornings also. Question Time comes first, when M.P.s are then able to question the various ministers. Then there follow the main debates on subjects which the government or the opposition want to have discussed, such as bills the government wants passed into law and other matters such as Great Britain's relations with other countries. Sometimes individual members are able to debate a subject of their own choice or even to bring in a bill to change the law.

M.P.s called whips ensure that as many members as possible attend debates, which may cease if fewer than 40 are present. Normally when a debate finishes members are asked whether they are in favour of what is proposed or against it. If they do not all agree to the proposal a "division" takes place, which means the M.P.s leave the Chamber of the House and walk through the doors marked "Ayes" (in favour) and "Noes" (against), into what are known as the division lobbies. Here votes are counted by officials of the House. If the result is a tie, the member in charge of the debate, who is called the Speaker (see SPEAKER), can decide the matter by casting his vote in favour of one side or the other. If the government is defeated on some important question it usually resigns so that a general election may take place.

Members who wish to speak in the debate have to "catch the Speaker's eye", since he acts as chairman. Members may not read their speeches, unless speaking for their party from the front bench, but in the House they can say whatever they like without fear of being brought before the courts for what they say. This freedom of speech is one of the most important privileges of M.P.s.

MEMORY means the ability to keep what we have learnt in our minds so that we can call it up again for use later on. What we remember in this way may be words, figures, dates, poetry, events in our own lives, and even skilled actions such as playing the piano or riding a bicycle.

The amount that is remembered differs a good deal with different persons. Try calling out sets of figures, like telephone numbers, to a friend—2764, then 35018, and so on—and see how many he can repeat after hearing them once only. A child of 5 should be able to repeat four figures, a child of 6 or 7 five figures and grown-ups can usually repeat as many as seven or eight. If you try them with something that has a meaning, like a poem or a hymn, they will probably remember much more. This is because the words join up into sentences and, as we hear them, they make connections within the brain, like linking up telephone wires.

Therefore, if you find it hard to remember something, it will help you if you think of possible connections or links. For instance, Mr. Adam's telephone number is 2810, and you may remember it by thinking of Adam and Eve and the apple—"Two ate one o". It is sometimes thought that people can improve the power of memory by daily practice, much as they strengthen their muscles by exercise with dumb-bells. This is quite wrong, but anyone can discover how to make the best use of what memory he has, no matter how poor it is.

Just as human beings have five different senses, so it may be said that they have five different kinds of memory. Some people find it easiest to remember things by picturing them in their mind's eye, and making as it were a mental photograph. Others have good memories for sounds; tunes, rhymes and jingles, such as "Thirty days hath September, April, June and November", tend to go on ringing in their ears. Others again find it best to say things silently to themselves in actual words. Everyone should try to discover and use the strongest kind of memory he possesses.

However weak your memory may be, you can make up for it by attending closely to what you want to remember, and repeating it over and over again. Then, after a short spell of hard learning, you should rest for a minute or two before taking up the next piece of work. You will recollect a thing best if you spread the repetitions out : it is better to spend quarter of an

hour on four different days than to keep working at it for one whole hour all at once. This is because people's memories fade most quickly at the beginning, so that nearly half of what has been learnt is forgotten during the first 12 hours. Yet nothing that has been learnt is ever *completely* forgotten. It is always lurking somewhere in the mind ; and, even if you cannot recall it just when you want to, it will often pop up again of itself when you are not worrying any more about it.

MENDELSSOHN, Felix (1809–1847).

Unlike many musicians Mendelssohn was brought up in a wealthy home and lacked nothing. He was born on February 3, 1809, at Hamburg (Germany) where his father was a banker. Although he is always known as Felix Mendelssohn, his full name was Jakob Ludwig Felix Mendelssohn-Bartholdy. His mother was a fine amateur musician and gave him his first lessons.

At the age of nine he gave his first public concert and at 11 was already composing music. His brothers and sisters all loved music—he and

Fanny (who also composed) played their own or each other's music on the piano, Rebecka sang and Paul played the violoncello. When he was only 17 Mendelssohn composed some of his finest music —the overture (see OVERTURE) to Shakespeare's play *A Mid-summer Night's Dream*.

Radio Times Hulton Library
Felix Mendelssohn.

Many years later he added much more to the *Midsummer Night's Dream* music, including the Wedding March.

Mendelssohn filled some of the most important musical posts in Germany and travelled widely in other countries. On a visit to Italy he wrote the *Italian Symphony* (see SYMPHONY) and a visit to Scotland inspired the *Scottish Symphony* and an overture called *The Hebrides,* after the islands on the west coast of Scotland. He often came to England, where he played to Queen Victoria and Prince Albert at Buckingham Palace. His last oratorio (see ORATORIO),

Elijah, was produced at the Birmingham Festival shortly before his death. He is best known today for his *Violin Concerto* and the *Midsummer Night's Dream* music.

Although Mendelssohn wrote oratorios, symphonies and chamber music, the style does not vary very much; it is elegant and light-hearted with long flowing melodies. Besides being a composer, conductor and pianist, he was also good at drawing and painting, wrote poetry and played billiards and chess very well. He died at Leipzig (Germany) on November 4, 1847, at the early age of 38.

MERCHANT ADVENTURERS.

During the middle ages great amounts of English wool were sold abroad, but towards the end of this period sales dropped considerably. Englishmen began to make their wool into cloth in England, and did so very successfully. Some of them shipped the cloth abroad and these men were said to go "adventuring". Similarly, when merchants grouped together to strengthen their position the groups they formed were called Merchant Adventurers. Such groups were formed in various towns—at Newcastle upon Tyne, York, Hull (where the group was called the Gild of St. George) and London, among others. By the end of the middle ages the most powerful group was that in London, whose members called themselves the Merchant Adventurers of England.

Although it was mostly cloth that the Merchant Adventurers sent abroad from England, they dealt in many other goods as well, because they bought foreign goods—especially wines, silks and spices—to sell in England. Many members of the London company were also members of other great companies, such as the Grocers', Drapers', Skinners', Haberdashers', Tailors' and Fishmongers' companies. (These are explained in the article LIVERY COMPANIES.)

In those days foreign trade was often a dangerous affair, so the companies made rules to guide and help their members. Each member was allowed to handle only a certain amount of trade so that everybody could be certain of having *some* trade. Ships had to sail at fixed times so that nobody arrived before anybody else.

The companies also asked foreign rulers to grant them charters (see CHARTER) to protect them and their goods. As early as 1296 the Duke of Brabant (a state in what is now Belgium) granted a charter to the Adventurers trading in his territory. In time the Adventurers came to have complete control of the trade in English cloth throughout western and northern Europe, and those who were not members found themselves unable to take any part in the trade. Many famous men of the day, like Sir Thomas Gresham, financial adviser to Queen Elizabeth I, and the great explorer Sebastian Cabot, were Merchant Adventurers. (See CABOT, JOHN AND SEBASTIAN.) They lent money to the government and had great influence on kings, queens and ministers.

The Merchant Adventurers made their headquarters in the countries now called Belgium and the Netherlands because their main trade was centred there. However, terrible wars were fought there during the second half of the 16th century which made things difficult for them, so they moved to northern Germany. This did not solve all their problems, however, because other English traders began to trade very successfully in northern Europe during the 17th century. Perhaps they were more adventurous than the Adventurers—and it certainly did seem that the Adventurers were more interested in keeping trade to themselves than in increasing the amount of trade so that the whole nation would benefit. Their numbers and importance began to dwindle and by the end of the 17th century they were of no importance. Their place was taken by new companies like those which grew up to trade with Russia, the Middle East, Hudson Bay (Canada) and India. (See EAST INDIA COMPANY; HUDSON'S BAY COMPANY.)

These new companies were organized in a different way. The Adventurers had grouped together and obeyed the same rules, but they had traded as *separate individuals*, each man for himself. The members of the new companies clubbed together and pooled their money, which was used by and for the companies *as a whole*. It was these new companies that brought about the increase in trade which made Britain so powerful from the 18th century onwards.

MERCHANT NAVY.

MERCHANT NAVY. The merchant fleet of the United Kingdom became known as the Merchant Navy after World War I, when the title was granted by King George V in recognition of the part played in the war. In 1928 the Prince of Wales was created Master of the Merchant Navy and the Fishing Fleet by the king. The earlier names for the Merchant Navy were mercantile marine and merchant service.

The Merchant Navy is the whole fleet of British ships used for carrying cargoes and passengers. The cargoes may be raw materials such as grain, minerals or oil, or they may be manufactured goods.

The Merchant Navy includes a number of people, such as the managers and office staffs, whose work is done ashore, but this article is mainly about the seagoing side. The article SHIPPING describes the different kinds of merchant ships and the work they do, and it is clear that shipboard life must vary as between the several kinds of ships and trades. Life in a small coasting vessel is very different from that in a great passenger liner like the "Queen Elizabeth 2", or in an oil-tanker trading between the Persian Gulf and Great Britain.

All the main duties are the same in every merchant ship. They are to take the ship from port to port in safety, avoiding shipwreck, fire, collision and all other dangers. The ship must be kept clean for reasons of health and comfort. The cargo must be taken on board without damaging it, carried across the sea without spoiling it and landed in good order at the distant ports. To do all these duties properly much knowledge and experience are needed. Besides the captain, most merchant ships have navigating officers, engineer officers and radio officers. The crew includes seamen, engine room men, cooks, stewards, and stewardesses if women passengers are carried. A large passenger liner also has doctors, pursers (who look after the money, stores and office work), musicians, barbers, butchers, bakers and even lift attendants and shop assistants. All the officers and crew members (ratings) sign a paper called "the articles of agreement" (generally known as the Ship's Articles) which outlines their duties as well as their rate of pay and the food to which they are entitled. At the beginning of a voyage the Ship's Articles are signed in the presence of a government official called the shipping master and at the end of a voyage the crew "sign off" in the same way.

The head of the ship is the master, usually known as the captain. He wears four bands of gold lace on the sleeves of his jacket and his uniform cap has a row of gold oak leaves on the peak. The captain is responsible for everyone and everything on board and therefore is given great powers. He leads a rather lonely life, keeping no regular watch (a "watch" is a spell of duty, usually of four hours) but taking charge when entering or leaving harbour or whenever he is called in an emergency. According to its size and length of voyage, a ship may have two, three, four or even as many as eight navigating officers. The senior of them is called the chief officer and is in general charge of the deck department. The navigating officers are responsible to the master for the navigation and safety of the ship. (See the article NAVIGATION.)

The chief engineer, like the master, keeps no regular watch. Under him is a staff of engineers who look after all the machinery in the ship. This includes the main engines driving the ship (see MARINE ENGINES), the dynamos, electric machinery, winches, pumps and fans, and the special machinery for refrigeration (cooling) needed for chilled meat and other perishable cargoes. Radio equipment is worked and looked after by radio officers who send and receive messages, and must also listen for distress calls sent by other ships or by aircraft. In most ships they also look after the radar sets which are used by the navigating officers. (See the article RADAR.)

At sea there is always at least one navigating officer on the bridge of the ship and an engineer officer in the engine room or central room. These officers are said to be "on watch". Crew members are on watch as helmsmen, lookouts and messengers and also as mechanics, greasers and firemen. The helmsmen—or, in big ships, senior seamen called quartermasters—steer the ship, though in open waters steering may be done by an automatic helmsman linked to the gyro com-

Courtesy, British India Steam Navigation Company

This merchant seaman on the bridge is controlling the pitch of the screws on a twin screw vessel. A change in the ship's speed is made by changing the pitch of its blades.

pass. Mechanics and greasers help the engineer officer on watch. Firemen keep up the steam in the boilers of steamships.

The chief officer is particularly responsible for the upkeep and good order of the ship, and gives the necessary orders to the boatswain (pronounced "bosun") who acts as the foreman of the sailors. The chief officer also looks after the stowage and unloading of the cargo. With a general, or mixed, cargo, care must be taken that the heavy articles are stowed low down in the holds in order to prevent the ship from becoming unsteady. On the other hand if there is too much heavy cargo near the bottom of the ship she may be made uncomfortable or even dangerous by rolling jerkily in bad weather at sea. Also, the cargo must if possible be stowed so that articles can be unloaded without disturbing pieces of cargoes that are to be discharged at a later port of call. Care also has to be taken that cargoes like pepper and tea are not spoiled by stowing

them too near each other. All this demands great skill and experience. The second officer is particularly responsible for seeing that navigational equipment such as compasses, charts and echo-sounders (for finding the depth of water) is kept in good order.

Many shipping companies carry navigating and engineer cadets. These are trainee officers who usually join their first ship between the ages of 16 and 21. The training period is three to four years. During this time they are taught the work of their department and attend courses at nautical colleges to obtain nationally recognized and professional qualifications. The British Shipping Federation in London has a department for selecting and recruiting cadets and gives advice on the subject.

At sea the cadets assist the officers and help with the practical work of the ship. They continue their studies by means of correspondence courses (lessons sent by post) provided by the colleges. When they have sufficient experience at sea they sit their first official examination. This is the second mate's or second engineer's examination which is a stage towards master's or chief engineer's certificate. A still higher qualification, which is not a certificate of competency, can be taken. This is the extra master or extra chief engineer certificate.

It used to be said that the fool of the family was sent to sea, but nowadays the fool or the misfit stands little chance and it is not possible to "run away to sea" any longer. Even boy seamen and catering boys are expected to have had training at a seamanship school.

A boy seaman starts work in a ship as deck boy and next becomes an ordinary seaman. After three years, having obtained an Efficient Deck Hand's Certificate, he can become an A.B., which means able seaman. Later he can become quartermaster or boatswain. However, a seaman who has served the necessary time at sea and who passes the examination for second mate can become an officer without having been a cadet.

The United Kingdom could not exist without a large and efficient Merchant Navy to bring food and raw materials from abroad in exchange for manufactured goods. Although life at sea is no longer one of hardships such as overwork, cramped quarters and a diet of salt pork and mouldy biscuits, it is still a life calling for men of character and courage. A young man who has been to different parts of the world quickly develops confidence in himself and a knowledge of men and of the world. He learns to take responsibility and leads an active life.

For many years past there has been a Royal Naval Reserve of officers and ratings who in peacetime have served in the Merchant Navy, but who have voluntarily trained in the Royal Navy. This provides a necessary link between the services in wartime. There has also been a Royal Naval Volunteer Reserve, which has been made up of people who are not professional seamen, but have trained as Royal Naval volunteers. In November 1958 the former Royal Naval Reserve, together with the Royal Naval Volunteer Reserve, were combined and reorganized into the Royal Naval Reserve.

MERCURY was the Roman name for the god whom the Greeks called Hermes, the messenger of the gods. He is described in the article HERMES. The planet Mercury is described in the article SOLAR SYSTEM.

MERCURY. Sometimes called quicksilver, mercury is a silvery-white metal and a very unusual one because it is a liquid at ordinary temperatures. It does not become solid until frozen to $-39°C$ and it boils at $357°C$. It is more than 13 times heavier than water so that a 1 litre bottle of it would weigh about 13 kilograms—more than most people would care to lift. Unlike water or oil, mercury does not wet the walls of glass bottles or tubes, but leaves them perfectly clean as soon as it is emptied out of them, without any film or drops clinging to the surface.

Mercury is usually found combined with sulphur in the red mineral cinnabar, found in Italy, Spain, Mexico and other countries where volcanoes have been active. The cinnabar is heated in a current of air to about $500°C$, so that the mercury in it is turned to vapour, or gas. The vapour is then condensed into little beads of liquid by being passed through a cooler, and the beads are strained through chamois leather in order to separate the mercury from the ashes and dirt.

In ancient times, cinnabar was used for making the red pigment (colour) called vermilion, and as early as 415 B.C. mercury was used for gilding and in medicines. When the alchemists of the middle ages were trying to make gold (see ALCHEMY) they thought mercury was an almost magical material and often used it in their experiments. Mercury dissolves most other metals, forming a bright film or coating on them called amalgam. Because of this, mercury is used for refining, or purifying, the precious metals. However, it does not form an amalgam with iron and is therefore stored in iron flasks. As it swells a good deal when heated, mercury is useful for thermometers, except those for measuring very cold temperatures. It is also used in some barometers. (See BAROMETER.) As mercury forms an easy path for an electric current, it is often used in switches for turning the current on and off. If two metal rods called "contacts" are led into a glass tube with closed ends and half full of mercury, current can flow between the contacts through the mercury. If, however, the tube is tilted so that the contacts are no longer bathed in the mercury, the current can no longer flow.

Although mercury and its vapour are very poisonous, drugs and medicines are often made of its compounds. (A "compound" is a combination of one substance with another.) Fulminate of mercury, made by dissolving mercury in nitric acid and adding alcohol, explodes when heated or struck and is used in detonators for setting off other explosives (see EXPLOSIVE). When electric current is passed through mercury vapour it gives off what are called ultraviolet rays. Lamps of this kind are used in hospital for giving treatment.

MERIONETH was the name of a former county in Wales which after the reorganization of local government in 1974 became part of the new county of Gwynedd. This article describes Merioneth as it was before 1974. A description of Merioneth as a part of Gwynedd can be found in the article GWYNEDD.

Situated opposite Cardigan Bay on the west coast of Wales, nearly all of the former county of Merioneth is included in the Snowdonia national park. Of its mountain peaks the best known is probably Cader Idris—the "chair of Idris"—on the west, which rises to a height of 890 metres. Merioneth is chiefly a farming region. Not many crops are grown, but mountain sheep are kept in the upland areas. Beef and dairy cattle are also kept in large numbers.

Llyn Tegid or Bala Lake, from which flows the Welsh Dee, is the largest natural lake in Wales. The estuaries of the rivers Dovey and Mawddach open on to Cardigan Bay.

Forests have been planted in Merioneth, and quantities of plants grow there, including alpine plants on Cader Idris. The area round about has been made a nature reserve to protect these plants. All kinds of birds can be seen on the estuaries and it is believed that Bird Rock near the Dysynni estuary is the only inland rock in the country where cormorants breed. Geologists

find Merioneth interesting because of the many different kinds of rocks to be found there.

Gold was discovered along the northern bank of the Mawddach in the 1830s, but mining it became increasingly difficult as time went on. Nevertheless, gold from the mines of Merioneth has been used to make royal wedding rings.

Dolgellau (Dolgelly), the old county town, is near the Mawddach estuary, Cader Idris and the ruins of Cymmer Abbey, the only abbey in Merioneth. Dolgellau is a market town and is also popular as a holiday resort because of the wonderful walks through mountain scenery round about. Farther north, the nuclear power station at Trawsfynydd was completed in 1965.

Many people also visit Aberdovey Barmouth and Harlech, which are all on Cardigan Bay. Harlech, once the county town, is a small place but has a fine castle built by Edward I.

Merioneth has no big towns, the largest being Blaenau Ffestiniog in the extreme north of the county. The deepest slate mine in the world is near Blaenau Ffestiniog.

The name "Merioneth" comes from Meirion, a Welsh chieftain of the 5th century, and in Welsh it is Meirionydd. For a time it was a separate kingdom.

Many an English army in the middle ages turned back from Merioneth because of the cruel mountains and bitter weather. It was, however, conquered by Edward I and the king made it into a shire in 1284.

The little town of Bala, near Bala Lake, was the home of Thomas Charles, a Methodist leader. One day he was visited by a young girl called Mary Jones who had walked for 40 kilometres hoping to buy a Bible from him. He had none to sell, but gave her his own. Realizing how few Bibles there were in Wales, Thomas Charles helped to found the British and Foreign Bible Society in 1804. This society has issued Bibles in hundreds of languages throughout the world.

MERLIN.
In the old legends and romances about the deeds of King Arthur and the knights of his Round Table, the wizard and enchanter Merlin was the counsellor of the King. The story of Merlin's life and of his strange powers was told differently by different authors. The 12th-century writer Geoffrey of Monmouth, for example, in a book called *The History of the Kings of Britain*, told how Merlin's mother was a Welsh princess but his father a demon and how even as a boy he was able to see into the future and understand things that were hidden from ordinary men. Merlin became skilled in unearthly wisdom and in magic, and other stories told of how, as King Arthur's trusted counsellor, it was he who conducted his master to his rest in Avalon after his last battle. According to one tale, Merlin in spite of his skill was beguiled by an enchantress named Nimue and shut up in a rock. Another was that Vivien, the Lady of the Lake, entangled him in a thornbush by her spells and there he sleeps till this day.

Strange though the stories are, they may have begun in the first place about a real person, for there was a Welsh bard, or poet, called Myredin and he was supposed to be the author of many prophecies about events to come in history.

MERMAIDS AND MERMEN.
Most peoples who live near the sea or a lake or a great river seem to have believed at some time that there are people living in the water as there are on land. The usual English names for these imaginary people are mermaids and mermen—sea-maids and sea-men. Animals which really live in water, such as seals and manatees, may have something to do with this belief. The sea-people, however, are thought of as either completely human in shape, like the Nereids of Greek stories, or human above the waist with a fish's tail below, like Greek Tritons and the mermaids and mermen in the tales of many countries. There are also stories, for instance in the islands off Scotland, of seals which can take off their skins and then appear as women.

Very like mermaids are those creatures, such as the Sirens in Greek stories and the Lorelei in a German one, who sit on dangerous rocks and sing so delightfully that sailors come close to hear them better, and so are wrecked and drowned. The sea-people are quite often said to sing or make music in some way. Generally, both mermaids and mermen were supposed to be dangerous to human beings. (See MANATEE.)

MERSEY RIVER.
The most important river in the north of England is the Mersey. It flows westwards to the Irish Sea in the area between Lancashire and Cheshire. The Mersey is formed by two Derbyshire rivers, the Goyt and the Etherow, and drains much of the Peak District.

Beyond the town of Warrington in Cheshire the Mersey's estuary, or mouth, begins. For some way it is narrow, then it becomes 3 or 4 kilometres wide before narrowing again. The great port of Liverpool stands on the north bank where the estuary measures just over a kilometre across. On the south bank are the industrial towns of Birkenhead and Port Sunlight. There are two tunnels which carry traffic under the river. One links Liverpool with Birkenhead and the other extends to Wallasey. (See also LIVERPOOL and MERSEYSIDE.)

MERSEYSIDE is the name of a metropolitan county created from parts of Lancashire and Cheshire when local government in England was reorganized in 1974. Merseyside is centred on the estuary of the Mersey River and on the city of Liverpool, the greatest port in the north of England and one of the country's most important industrial areas. (See LIVERPOOL.) The history of the Merseyside region up until 1974 can be found in the separate articles LANCASHIRE and CHESHIRE.

In the past the industries most closely associated with Merseyside have been sugar refining and the cotton trade which grew up because of Liverpool's importance as a port. This also led to a shipbuilding and repairing industry being established at Birkenhead near by. However, as the port-based industries began to decline, new ones, such as the production of motor vehicles and electrical engineering, were encouraged. There are large chemical works in the area around Bebington and Bromborough and light industrial estates at Aintree, Speke and Kirkby. St. Helens, which grew from a group of mining villages, is now a glass-manufacturing town where plate, sheet, fibre and safety glass are made as well as bottles of all sorts. At Bootle near Liverpool there is another large dock system.

Merseyside is also an important farming region and among the many vegetables grown are potatoes and peas. The holiday resorts of Southport, Crosby and Formby are also in Merseyside. Southport is the largest of these and has fine streets and well laid-out gardens. A famous flower show is held there every year. Southport is also the only place where a kind of spider called *Tegenaria larva* is found.

MESON. The atoms of which everything is made are themselves composed of smaller particles, the chief ones being the protons, neutrons and electrons. It was suggested in 1937 that the protons and neutrons were held together in the nucleus, or central body of the atom, by another particle which was called the "meson". It is now known that there are at least four different kinds of meson in the nucleus. When freed from the other particles they quickly break up.

MESOPOTAMIA. The name Mesopotamia comes from Greek words meaning "between the rivers" and was once used for the prosperous valleys of the great rivers Tigris and Euphrates and the lands between them. Mesopotamia forms part of the country now called Iraq.

Mesopotamia was a highly civilized country 6,000 years ago under the Sumerians, whose rule was followed by that of the Assyrians, Babylonians, Persians and Greeks. Then for centuries Mesopotamia was a battleground between the Romans, the Scythians, the Parthians and the Persians. The country was conquered by the Arabs in A.D. 640 and in 1258 was invaded by the Mongols who destroyed irrigation works which watered the land. Mesopotamia was conquered by the Turks in the 16th century, though there was continuous fighting with the Arabs. British troops defeated the Turks in 1918. Later, the oil found in Mesopotamia helped to make Iraq prosperous. (See IRAQ.)

MESSIAH is a word which comes from a Hebrew word meaning "the anointed one". In the Bible it is one of the names given to the person whom the Jews were constantly expecting to come as their great deliverer and ruler. Even when they were suffering at the hands of invaders they never ceased to believe that God would one day send His Messiah to save them from their enemies and to set up His Kingdom on earth.

Christians believe that the New Testament makes it quite clear that Jesus was the Messiah whom the Jews had so long expected. Indeed, the word "Christ" has exactly the same meaning as the word "Messiah"; there are the two words because "Christ" comes from Greek and "Messiah" from Hebrew. (See JESUS CHRIST.) One of the main reasons why the Jews did not accept Jesus as their deliverer and king was that He was so different from the man they had been led to expect. They had always thought that the Messiah would be a warrior king who would conquer their enemies and that the kingdom he would set up would be as strong and mighty as those he would defeat. However, this was not the kind of deliverer that Jesus chose to be. He thought it was more important to deliver people from their sins against God than to deliver them from invaders. Furthermore, He came to set up the Kingdom of God on earth for people of every race, not only for the Jews. These things were so difficult for His fellow countrymen to understand that only a very few of them recognized that Jesus really was the Messiah.

METAL. There are about 100 elements, or different substances from which all chemical compounds are formed, and more than 70 of them are called metals. Of the rest, about 20 are definitely non-metals while five elements are halfway between metals and non-metals. Most metals are solid at ordinary temperatures (mercury is an exception) and when polished or freshly broken have a bright lustre, or sheen, and reflect light well. Most metals are good conductors of heat and electricity. When melted and cooled most metals solidify into a crystalline form, although the crystals are usually too small to be seen by the naked eye. These crystals can be seen at the surface of broken cast-iron.

Metals can be divided into two classes, pure metals (elements) and alloys. Iron and copper are pure metals, but bronze (made by mixing molten copper and tin) and brass (made by mixing molten copper and zinc) are alloys.

Except for gold, platinum and some copper and silver, metals are rarely found on the earth in a pure state. Most metals are found as *ores*, which are rocks or earth in which the metal is chemically combined with other substances such as oxygen, sulphur and carbon. There are two main methods of obtaining the metal from its ore. The most usual method is by smelting (heating in a furnace, usually with carbon) but sometimes the metal is obtained by electrolysis (see ELECTROLYSIS).

The *relative density* of a metal is used to describe its weight as compared with water. Thus iron has a relative density of 7.8, meaning that it is nearly 8 times as heavy as water. The lightest metal is lithium (relative density 0.5) and the heaviest osmium (relative density 22.5). Metals are often chosen for their densities, lead being used for weights and light alloys of aluminium and magnesium for building aircraft.

All metals are silvery or greyish in colour, except gold, which is yellow, and copper, which is reddish. The colour of a metal shows best when seen in a light which has been reflected many times off the surface of the metal. The polished inside of a silver jug or spoon is much richer in colour than the outside.

Each metal has a fixed temperature at which it melts. The metal with the lowest melting point is mercury ($-39\,^{\circ}$C), but the rare metal caesium melts at about the same temperature as butter and bursts into flames if exposed to the air in an ordinary room. Tungsten does not melt until heated to $3,400\,^{\circ}$C, and is therefore used for the filaments, or fine wires, inside electric light bulbs. All metals boil if heated enough. Mercury boils off into a vapour, or gas, at $357\,^{\circ}$C, which is not much hotter than the melting point of lead, but tungsten boils only at $5,930\,^{\circ}$C—about the temperature of the Sun's surface.

Most metals expand (swell) when warmed and contract (shrink) when cooled. An everyday example of this is the mercury thermometer used for measuring temperatures (see THERMOMETER). However, an alloy of iron and nickel, called "invar", hardly alters its size at all with temperature, so the tapes used by surveyors for measuring land are made of it. (See EXPANSION.)

Most metals are good conductors of heat. If an iron rod is held with one end in the fire the other end soon becomes too hot to hold, but an iron rod with a wooden handle can be held in the same manner for a long time because wood is a poor conductor of heat. Some metals conduct electricity better than others, silver being the best. Copper is the metal most used for electric wires. Aluminium, although not nearly such a good electrical conductor as copper, is sometimes used because it is so much lighter and cheaper. When the atoms of a metal such as copper pack together to form a solid structure (see MOLECULE), each atom gives up a fixed number of electrons (two in the case of copper), leaving a positively charged atom, or *ion*. The spare electrons can move freely in the metal and, since they carry electric charge, make the metal a good electrical conductor. These electrons can also transfer mechanical energy from molecule to molecule (from ion to ion) so that the metal is also a good conductor of heat. (See HEAT.)

Few pure metals can be made into magnets.

The only ones with strong magnetic properties are iron, nickel and cobalt. In one of the best magnetic metals, alnico, cobalt and nickel are alloyed with the non-magnetic metals aluminium and copper. Even more remarkable are some combinations of the non-magnetic metals manganese, aluminium and copper, which produce alloys with marked magnetic properties. Magnetism depends on the arrangement of the atoms in a material, as well as their type, so that an alloy may have a favourable structure for magnetism which is lacking in the individual metals.

Metals can be worked into the shape needed by rolling or hammering while hot (see FORGE). When the metal has already been rolled into fairly thin sheets, such as are used for motor car bodies or aluminium saucepans, further heating is unnecessary and shaping is done in a press while cold. Some metals can be made into rods and bars of any shape by what is called "extrusion", the hot metal being squeezed like toothpaste through a hole of the right shape made in a "die" of very hard steel. To make wire, bars of metal are rolled out into rods and then pulled through one die after another, the hole in each die being smaller than that in the one before it. (See EXTRUSION.)

A common method of shaping metals is by casting, the metal being melted and poured into a mould of the required shape (see FOUNDING). In die-casting, the molten metal is forced into a metal die or mould under pressure. Yet another method of shaping is to make the metal (or mixture of metals) into a powder which is pressed whilst cold into the shape required and then sintered, or melted into one piece. Thin coatings of metal, useful for preventing rust on steel articles and for improving appearance, can be made by dipping the object in molten metal. Thus galvanized iron and fencing wire are coated by dipping in molten zinc and "tins" are still sometimes made by dipping cans made of very thin steel into molten tin. Thin coatings can also be applied by electro-plating, and most tins are made by coating iron with a very thin layer of tin in this way (see ELECTROPLATING).

The strength and hardness of metals can be controlled in two ways, alloying and heat treatment. A metal is usually at its softest and weakest when pure and can be strengthened by alloying (mixing) with another metal. Pure copper is soft and weak, as also is pure tin, but if the two are melted together they make bronze, a hard strong alloy. (See ALLOY.) Heat treatment is described in the article IRON AND STEEL and is a method of altering the hardness and strength of a metal by carefully raising its temperature, after which it is quenched, or cooled. Different metals need different heat treatment.

There are separate articles on the various important metals.

METAMORPHOSIS. Biologists use the term metamorphosis to describe changes in the shape and structure of living organisms. Although all organisms change as they grow, metamorphosis usually describes the striking changes seen in some animals, such as insects and amphibia, as they develop by stages. The changes usually happen in a short space of time.

Complete metamorphosis takes place in the butterfly, moth, bee, wasp and other highly developed insects. The butterfly grows in four main stages, from egg, larva (caterpillar), pupa to adult. Frogs and toads also metamorphose (develop) from their egg or spawn. Insect larvae and tadpoles look completely different from their adult forms and often live in a different environment. For instance, a tadpole swims with its tail and breathes through gills. An adult frog has lungs and legs and lives both on land and in water. This means that the young do not compete with adults for the same food or living space.

There are illustrations of metamorphosis in the articles BUTTERFLY and FROG AND TOAD.

METEOR AND METEORITE. Meteors, which are often called "shooting stars", are really small particles which can be seen flashing across the sky at night. Meteorites are lumps of rock and iron which fall from space to the surface of the Earth.

Meteors are often no bigger than grains of sand, which come into the Earth's atmosphere from outer space. They move very fast, and the friction of the air makes them so hot that they are completely vaporized into gases before they reach the surface of the Earth. It is because they get so hot that they send out the light which makes them visible at night.

A few meteors can be seen every night. On some nights of the year there are showers of meteors, and if the sky is clear many hundreds

Courtesy, Norman Lockyer Observatory, Sidmouth
A meteor or "shooting star" passing the group of brilliant stars which are known as the Pleiades.

can be seen. There are many more which are too faint to be seen. Several thousand million meteors strike the Earth's atmosphere every day.

The meteors in a shower all seem to spread out from the same point in the sky (called the "radiant"). This is an optical illusion. Really they move along almost parallel paths, and the appearance of spreading out from a point is just an effect of perspective. (See DRAWING.)

Most of what is known about meteors has been discovered by tracking them with radar (see RADAR). Meteors can be seen and photographed only on a clear night, but radar can be used even if the sky is cloudy, and in the daytime as well. The shooting star trail of a meteor at night is first visible when the meteor has fallen to about 160 kilometres from the surface of the Earth, and may go on being visible until the meteor has fallen to as low as 30 kilometres, by which time it is completely vaporized. The speeds of meteors vary from about 15 to 80 kilometres a second.

Astronomers have discovered that meteors are usually fragments of the material of comets (see COMET). Sometimes a comet breaks up completely during its journey round the sun; sometimes it just leaves some material behind and goes

on as before. In either case the fragments continue to move along the orbit, or path, of the comet as a meteor stream. When the Earth in its own orbit round the Sun crosses a meteor stream, then a shower of meteors can be seen. If the parent comet has not broken up, but is still moving in its orbit, astronomers can often tell which comet a meteor stream comes from.

Here is a list of the meteor showers most easily seen, with the times of year when they appear, and the comets which some of them come from. Most of the showers are named after the constellations from which they seem to spread out.

Name of shower	Date when shower is brightest	Parent comet
Quadrantids	January 3	
Lyrids	April 21	
Eta Aquarids	May 4	Halley's Comet
Delta Aquarids	July 29	
Perseids	August 11	Comet 1866 III
Orionids	October 20	Halley's Comet
Taurids	November 10	Encke's Comet
Leonids	November 16	Tempel's Comet
Geminids	December 13	

Meteorites

Meteorites are pieces of iron and rock which fall to Earth from interplanetary space. Being much larger than meteors, meteorites do not burn up completely in the atmosphere. They vary in mass from a gram or so to many tonnes. It is unlikely that meteorites have anything to do with meteors. They seldom fall during meteor showers. It is probable that meteorites, like asteroids (see SOLAR SYSTEM), are bits of material left over from the stuff of which the planets were formed.

A meteorite which falls with a brilliant flash of light is sometimes called a fireball. If it makes a bang as it falls, as most meteorites do, it is also called a bolide. Meteorites fall because the Earth's gravitational pull draws them down as they pass through space near the Earth (see GRAVITATION).

The largest meteorite ever found weighs about 60 tonnes. It still lies where it fell, at Grootfontein in South West Africa. Many smaller meteorites have been found. They may be seen in exhibitions at most science museums.

There are several famous craters made by meteorites which fell in prehistoric times. The one called Meteor Crater in central Arizona (United States) is a little over a kilometre across and 180 metres deep. Many small bits of meteorite material have been found near it, but no single large piece has been discovered. The original large meteorite probably exploded when it hit the ground. The Ahnighito Meteorite, the next largest, was found by the explorer Peary in Greenland in 1897. In 1908 in Siberia a meteorite flattened trees over many kilometres.

There are two main kinds of meteorites, stone meteorites and iron meteorites. The stone meteorites, which are also called aerolites, may contain a little iron too, but are mostly rock. The iron meteorites, also called siderites, usually have some nickel in them as well. There are also some stony-iron meteorites, which are made of mixtures of rock and iron. The outer surface of a newly fallen meteorite usually has a black crust, produced by the heat of friction as the meteorite falls through the air to Earth.

The biggest meteorite craters on Earth are similar in some ways to the craters on the Moon, and for this and other reasons most astronomers believe that the craters on the Moon were formed by falling meteorites (see MOON).

METEOROLOGY.

Meteorology is primarily the study of the workings of the atmosphere and the forecasting of the weather. For this the meteorologist needs information on the atmosphere and weather. This is provided by observers on the land, on ships at sea, by instruments carried up through the atmosphere by balloon, and more recently by weather satellites.

From all these observations meteorologists know that the air near the Earth's surface near the equator is very warm but that at the poles and at great heights it is cold. In order to prevent the equatorial areas getting even hotter and the polar areas even colder, the atmosphere moves, shifting heat from equatorial areas to the poles and from near the Earth's surface to high levels. This movement is known as the *general circulation*. When the air is moving it is affected by the spinning of the Earth and so itself tends to move in swirls, somewhat like whirlpools, rather than in straight lines. These swirls are found very often in the middle latitudes. Meteorologists know they are there by measuring the pressure exerted by the air rather than by measuring directly the air speed and direction—a more difficult task. The meteorologist can work out the speed and direction of the wind and, to some extent, the areas of rising air, from the distribution of pressure, which is easily and accurately measured in millibars by a barometer. How-

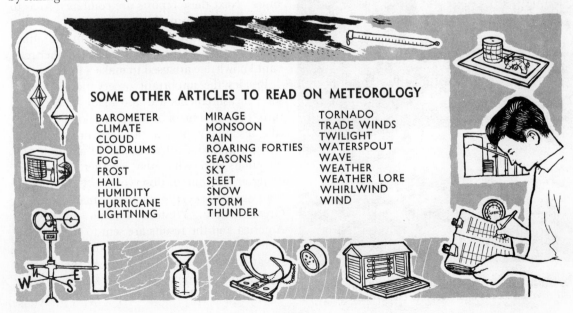

SOME OTHER ARTICLES TO READ ON METEOROLOGY

BAROMETER	MIRAGE	TORNADO
CLIMATE	MONSOON	TRADE WINDS
CLOUD	RAIN	TWILIGHT
DOLDRUMS	ROARING FORTIES	WATERSPOUT
FOG	SEASONS	WAVE
FROST	SKY	WEATHER
HAIL	SLEET	WEATHER LORE
HUMIDITY	SNOW	WHIRLWIND
HURRICANE	STORM	WIND
LIGHTNING	THUNDER	

ever, the upward and downward movement of air, which is the basis of all weather, cannot be measured regularly. From these studies, the meteorologist knows that, in the northern hemisphere, surface *low* pressure areas represent areas of air swirling anti-clockwise and rising. These are called *cyclones* or *depressions*. Surface *high* pressure areas represent areas of air spiralling clockwise and sinking, and these are known as anticyclones. Both types of swirl are usually over 1500 kilometres in diameter and cyclones tend to move at 2 to 18 metres per second.

Within the cyclonic swirls air is rising and therefore cooling and allowing clouds—and often rain—to form. This lifting of air usually occurs at what is known as a *front*, a zone dividing masses of air which are usually quite different from one another in temperature and humidity (dampness) despite being within the same cyclonic swirl. Within the anticyclonic swirls, the air usually moves much more slowly than in the cyclones and the general sinking of air usually results in little cloud and rain and often long sunny periods.

In the countries roughly midway between the equator and the poles one of the main tasks of the meteorologist is to forecast the occurrence and movements of cyclones and anticyclones and

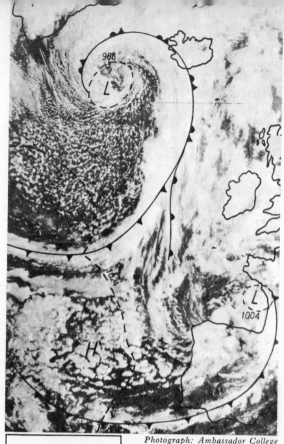

Photograph: Ambassador College

Warm Front	▲▲▲▲
Cold Front	▲▲▲▲
Occlusion	▲▲▲▲

This satellite picture shows a typical depression and the fronts associated with it.

also the weather that they carry. This task has three main parts. The first is to measure the weather conditions in different places at set times. Next these reports are combined so as to make maps of air movement and weather over a large area and at several heights in the atmosphere. Lastly all these maps and any other relevant knowledge are used to make a forecast.

Besides the important observations of pressure, measurements are also made of temperature, the amount of rainfall or snow, visibility (the distance a person can see), humidity, the amount and kind of cloud, wind strength and direction, and what the weather is actually doing at the time of observation. Full observations are made every six hours at many places in Great Britain, Western Europe and North America and the results are sent to the national meteorological services in these areas. Some observations are received hourly. As the weather measurements are received by the forecasting office, they are plotted on maps. Each observing

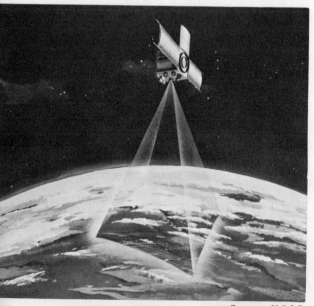

Courtesy, U.S.I.S.

Weather satellites in Earth orbit survey cloud cover and transmit the information to the forecasters.

point, whether on land or sea or at a great height in the atmosphere, has its measurements neatly marked round its position on the map.

Then the meteorologist draws in *isobars* (lines joining equal pressure readings) on the map of surface conditions and slightly different types of lines to describe air movement in higher parts of the atmosphere. Fronts are also drawn on the surface weather map if they exist.

With these maps as a basis the meteorologist uses his knowledge and experience to forecast what sort of weather they should give over a period of 24 hours and also for longer periods.

Crown copyright

Weather ships like this keep station at sea, making meteorological observations.

Increasingly this is done by computers which, when programmed by the meteorologist produce the forecast maps. This saves meteorologists a lot of repetitious work which must be done at high speed if the weather forecast is to be of use.

METER. Meters are measuring instruments. The commonest are the gas and electricity meters in houses, speedometers in cars and thermometers for measuring temperature. Ammeters and voltmeters measure electric currents, a cyclometer measures the distance travelled by a bicycle and a barometer measures the air pressure.

The gas meter, a metal box with pipes to lead the gas in and out, usually has five dials like clock-faces, each marked from 0 to 9 and with one hand, or pointer. Four of the dials are in a row and when read from left to right show the volume of gas in cubic feet. (The fifth dial is used for testing.) The meter has an upper chamber containing two valves controlling the supply of gas and has also two lower gas-tight chambers.

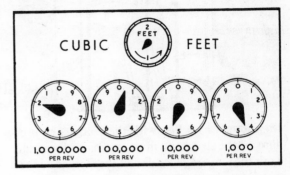

A gas meter reading 204,400 cubic feet.

Each lower chamber contains bellows so connected that as one fills with gas the other empties, pushing out the gas inside it. Movement of the bellows works the valves and also turns the pointers round the dials. The volume of the bellows is exactly known so the volume of gas passed through the meter is shown on the dials. The slot-meter has an attachment which opens the inlet valve when a coin is put in and closes it when gas to the value of the coin has been supplied.

An electricity meter has dials and pointers like those of a gas meter, but they measure the number of units of electricity used. These units are

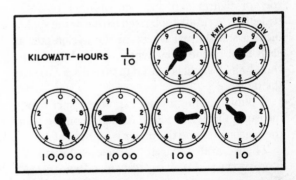

Electricity meter reading 57,788·6 kilowatt-hours (units).

explained in the article ELECTRIC POWER. The meter contains a small electric motor whose moving part—a thin aluminium disc—can usually be seen through a glass window. The speed of

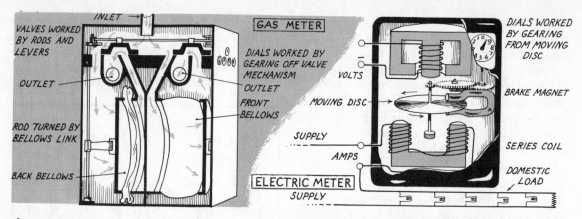

GAS METER

VALVES WORKED BY RODS AND LEVERS

INLET →

DIALS WORKED BY GEARING OFF VALVE MECHANISM

OUTLET

OUTLET

FRONT BELLOWS

ROD TURNED BY BELLOWS LINK

BACK BELLOWS

ELECTRIC METER

SUPPLY

DIALS WORKED BY GEARING FROM MOVING DISC

VOLTS

MOVING DISC →

BRAKE MAGNET

SUPPLY

SERIES COIL

AMPS

DOMESTIC LOAD

the motor varies first with the voltage, or pressure, of the electricity in the mains and secondly with the amperage, or size, of the electric current flowing to lamps and fires in the house. Therefore the speed depends on the power in watts (volts multiplied by amperes) and the number of turns the motor makes depends on the energy in watt-hours (watts multiplied by hours). The shaft of the motor is connected to the pointers of the dials by gearing.

There are several kinds of meters for measuring the flow of liquids such as water. The simplest contains a little wheel fitted with vanes or paddles rather like a windmill. The greater the flow of liquid, the faster the wheel turns. The wheel shaft is connected by gearing to pointers and dials which read in gallons.

The cyclometer of a bicycle is fixed on the front forks and has a slot in which appears a row of figures showing the number of miles travelled. A small knob fixed to one of the spokes flicks a star-shaped wheel on the cyclometer at each turn of the front wheel. The shaft of the star-shaped wheel is geared to turn discs carrying the figures.

A photographer uses an exposure meter which measures the brightness of the light coming from the person or scene the meter is pointed at.

There are separate articles AMMETER; BAROMETER; GALVANOMETER; PYROMETER; THERMOMETER.

METHODISTS

are people who belong to the church that was founded by John Wesley and George Whitefield (see WESLEY, JOHN).

In 1729 Wesley became the leader of a few young men at Oxford University who met together several times a week to pray and read the Bible. They decided to live *methodically,* according to the rules laid down in the Bible. As well as meeting for prayer they visited the poor and went to preach to people in prison. Of these young men the brothers John and Charles Wesley and George Whitefield all became clergymen of the Church of England. The Wesleys went to America to preach to the colonists and Red Indians, and Charles was also secretary to the Governor of Georgia. Whitefield went independently and built Orphan Houses in the colony.

When they returned to England the Wesleys began to feel that their teaching was not succeeding because it did not reach the ordinary people. One night in 1738, while he was attending a religious meeting, John suddenly felt his heart "strangely warmed" and realized that, through Jesus Christ, God came near to each person and took away each person's sins. A few days earlier Charles had had the same sort of experience and they set out to preach the good news. Their followers were called Methodists.

The England of the 18th century was not a happy country for everybody. A great many people were poor, depressed and hopeless. They had little or no education and in order to forget their misery they got drunk. Religion had no meaning for them. It was to these people that Wesley and his followers came with their good news. They preached that God was not a far-off Being, but cared for each individual person and would help each one to find happiness, both on earth and in heaven. When the Methodist preachers were forbidden to preach in the churches they spoke in the open air. People learned the hymns that Charles Wesley wrote— hymns of faith and hope and love. Miners in Bristol, smugglers in Cornwall, shepherds in the Lake District and the hordes of workers in London all thrilled with new faith in Jesus Christ and felt they could make a fresh start, with sins forgiven. They formed societies, and small groups drawn from the societies met together to share in prayer, in fellowship and in helping their neighbours. Methodist preachers covered enormous areas of the country on horseback, founding societies, preaching and helping to improve the living and working conditions of the people. John Wesley travelled as much as 4,000 miles a year in this way. The Industrial Revolution (see INDUSTRIAL REVOLUTION) had started and people had begun to flock into the new factory towns where they often lived and worked in dreadful conditions. Many social reformers (people who tried to improve things) were Methodists.

In the last 100 years Methodism has spread all over the world. Even during his lifetime John Wesley said, "The world is my parish" and today the Methodist Church has millions of followers in more than 120 countries.

During the life of John Wesley and for some years afterwards the Methodists did not fully break away from the Church of England. However, during the early years of the 19th century the separation became complete. Various divisions also took place among the Methodists themselves and several different types of Methodist churches were formed. However, in 1932 the Wesleyan Methodists, Primitive Methodists and United Methodists combined together and became one church, called the Methodist Church. Its ministers are specially ordained but many lay preachers—people who are not so ordained—are trained to give part-time service to the church, especially in preaching. In 1969 the Methodist Conference voted in favour of reunion with the Church of England.

METHUSELAH. The name Methuselah is commonly used to describe anyone of exceptional age, as in the saying "old as Methuselah".

In the fifth chapter of the Book of Genesis it is recorded that Methuselah was the son of Enoch and the grandfather of Noah. He is described as being 969 years old when he died and is thus the oldest person mentioned in the Bible.

METRIC SYSTEM. One of the great changes made in the French Revolution at the end of the 18th century was that of a new system of weights and measures which is now called the international metric system.

The French chose the *metre* as their unit of length. Originally it was supposed to be one-ten-millionth of the distance along the Earth's surface between Pole and equator. Later its length was fixed by international agreement as the distance between two marks on a certain bar of platinum and iridium. In 1960 a more exact definition fixed the metre's length as 1,650,763.73 times the wave-length of the orange light given off by the gas krypton 86. A metre equals 39.37 inches. The yard is exactly 0.9144 metre.

The metric system is based on ten, like our number system. One-tenth of a metre is a decimetre, one-hundredth of a metre a centimetre and one-thousandth of a metre is a millimetre. Ten metres make one decametre, one hundred metres one hectometre and one thousand

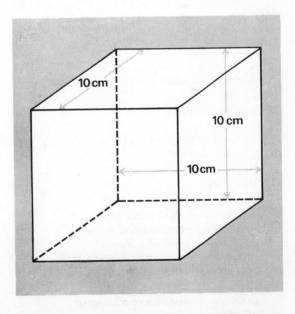

This box holds *exactly* 1 litre; 1 litre of water has a mass of *approximately* 1 kilogram.

metres one kilometre. This makes sums in metric units easy to do, especially with the use of decimals (see DECIMALS).

The same prefixes are used with other metric units : for example, one kilogram is one thousand grams. The kilogram is a unit of mass, that is, the amount of matter in an object. In everyday speech the word weight means mass, but in science weight has a different meaning (see GRAVITATION).

The metric system was soon taken up by other countries and is used by scientists everywhere in its modern form which is known as the SI, or International System of Units. The English-speaking countries were the only ones where it was not in everyday use. In 1968, however, the British government decided that the United Kingdom should change to the metric system by the end of 1975. A Metrication Board was set up to plan the changes and to prepare the public for them.

The full range of prefixes will not normally be used : the unit chosen depends on custom. A measurement which will appear as 900 millimetres in an engineering drawing will be 90 centimetres in dressmaking instructions and 0·9 metre on a navigational chart. (See also WEIGHTS AND MEASURES.)

EVERYDAY METRIC UNITS

Length

millimetre (one thousandth of a metre)	mm
centimetre (one hundredth of a metre)	cm
metre	m
kilometre (one thousand metres)	km
international nautical mile (1852 metres)	n mile

Area

square centimetre	cm²
square metre	m²
hectare (ten thousand square metres)	ha

Volume

cubic centimetre	cm³
cubic metre	m³

Capacity

millilitre (one thousandth of a litre)	ml
centilitre (one hundredth of a litre)	cl
decilitre (one tenth of a litre)	dl
litre (one thousand cubic centimetres)	l
hectolitre (one hundred litres)	hl

Mass

gram (one thousandth of a kilogram)	g
kilogram	kg
tonne (one thousand kilograms)	t

Speed

metre per second	m/s
kilometre per hour	km/h
knot (international nautical mile per hour)	kn

Power

watt	W
kilowatt (one thousand watts)	kW

USEFUL EQUIVALENTS

10 centimetres is about 4 inches
5 miles is about 8 kilometres
4 hectares is about 10 acres
4 litres is about 7 pints
1 gallon is about 4½ litres
5 kilograms is about 11 pounds

MEUSE RIVER.

Through the hilly country of northeast France, across the lower slopes of the Ardennes and the plains of Belgium, the River Meuse flows to join the great delta of the Rhine which forms a large part of the Netherlands. After entering Belgium the Meuse is joined at Namur by its tributary the Sambre and flows eastwards through the Belgian coalfields to Liège. Iron from Lorraine in France is brought along the Meuse valley to the steelworks of Liège. The river then turns north and enters the Netherlands near Maastricht, now becoming the River Maas. From this point to the sea it is bordered by dykes, or built-up banks. These are at first to prevent river floods from spreading over the land, but lower down they keep out the sea. Through most of its course in Belgium and the Netherlands, the river is much used by barge traffic.

The position of the Meuse near the French, Belgian, German and Dutch frontiers gave it great military importance. Fortresses to guard its crossings were built at Verdun, Sedan, Namur and Liège and saw heavy fighting in both world wars.

MEXICO.

The republic of Mexico is more than eight times the size of the British Isles. It is bordered on the north by the United States and stretches southeast for about 1,930 kilometres. Mexico's southern neighbours are Guatemala and Belize. On the west is the Pacific Ocean and on the east the Gulf of Mexico and the Caribbean Sea.

Most of Mexico consists of a broad central

plateau, or tableland, which is highest in the south and rises to between 910 and 2,440 metres above sea level. This central plateau is flanked on both sides by mountain ranges separating it from the hot coastal lowlands. The highest mountain, Pico de Orizaba, or Citlaltepetl, near the east coast, is a snow-capped cone 5,700 metres high. It and most of the other great peaks such as Popocatepetl mountain and Ixtacihuatl were once volcanoes. Volcanic activity still occurs. In 1943, the volcano of Paricutin burst into existence in a cornfield outside Mexico City, and reached a height of 455 metres within a year. As in most volcanic countries, earthquakes are quite common in Mexico, especially near the Pacific coast. The other main features of Mexico are the long narrow peninsula of Lower California, the highlands of Chiapas in the southeast and the low-lying Yucatan peninsula.

Although the southern half of Mexico lies within the tropics, the height of the land in most places keeps the climate fairly cool. There are three main kinds of climate, depending on the height, and all three can be met in one day by motoring from Mexico City—which is more than 2,130 metres above sea level—down to the hot sea coast. Above 1,830 metres is the *tierra fria* ("cold land"), with cool nights and even some frosts, growing oak trees which give place to pines and firs on the higher slopes. Wheat, maize and beans are cultivated in these regions. Lower down is the *tierra templada* ("temperate land"), where coffee is grown. Below about 910 metres lies the *tierra caliente* ("hot land"), a hot and rainy region with forests of tropical trees festooned with flowered climbing plants and with a dense undergrowth. This region, which includes the coastal belts, is always warm and when the fertile land is cleared tropical crops such as cotton, cocoa, rice, rubber, sugar, bananas and pineapples can be grown. The Mexican summer, from June to October, is the rainy season.

With such wide differences in climate Mexico has a huge variety of plant life. There are some valuable kinds of trees in the *tierra caliente*, such as ebony, mahogany and rosewood, but one of the commonest plants of Mexico is the *maguey*. This is a fleshy-leaved plant which is often taller than a man and is sometimes called the century-plant because it is supposed to flower once in 100 years. The juice is squeezed from its thick fleshy leaves to make a spirit drink called *pulque*, which has always been popular with the people of Mexico. The common tomato first grew in Mexico and this may also be true of the maize plant and the cocoa tree.

FACTS ABOUT MEXICO

AREA: 1,972,547 square kilometres.

POPULATION: 50,829,474.

KIND OF COUNTRY: Independent republic.

CAPITAL: Mexico City.

GEOGRAPHICAL FEATURES: A high plateau, open to the north and bounded on the east and west by mountain ranges which meet in the south. Along the coasts are narrow lowland strips.

CHIEF PRODUCTS: Maize, wheat, coffee, cotton, sugar, rice, tobacco, chicle gum (for chewing gum), timber, silver, lead, zinc, copper, iron ore, petroleum, coal.

CHIEF EXPORTS: Cotton, sugar, coffee, shrimps, petroleum, electrical machinery.

IMPORTANT TOWNS: Mexico City, Guadalajara, Monterrey, Ciudad Juarez, Puebla, Merida, Torreon, San Luis Potosi, Veracruz, Tampico, Mazatlan, Mexicali.

EDUCATION: Children should attend school between the ages of 6 and 14, but almost a quarter of the population can neither read nor write.

Mexican animals include jaguars, pumas, monkeys, sloths, tapirs and ocelots (there are separate articles on each of these animals). Among the many kinds of birds are parrots, macaws, toucans and mocking-birds. Snakes and lizards are common but the most remarkable creature is the axolotl, which looks like a newt tadpole about 20 centimetres long and is found in a lake near Mexico City. (See AMPHIBIAN; SALAMANDER.) In some parts of Yucatan and Chiapas the blood-sucking vampire bats are so common that it is difficult to keep horses.

During the three centuries of Spanish rule a certain amount of Spanish blood was introduced into Mexico, but there are few Mexicans of pure Spanish descent, except those who have come to live in the country recently. Most people in the country are of pure American-Indian or mixed Spanish and Indian blood.

As a result of the Mexican revolution which began in 1910, most of the old wealthy families that once ruled the country lost their lands, but there is still a rich governing class which controls a good deal of power by owning *haciendas* (large estates), factories or business firms. Most of the country people are poor peasants and millions of them live in villages of thatched huts grouped beneath the trees beside earth roads. The huts are almost bare inside, with a few straw mats called *petates* on which the family sleep, a charcoal stove for cooking and a few pots and pans. The food consists chiefly of *tortillas* (pancakes of maize flour) and beans flavoured with a kind of hot pepper called chili. The peasants wear cotton trousers and loose shirts with a *sarape*, or small blanket, over the shoulders and wide straw hats. Their women wear loose cotton blouses, full skirts and the traditional *rebozo*, or shawl, in which they carry everything—including their babies—on their backs. Once a week they load their vegetables, pottery, leather-work or other wares on their mules or in baskets to be carried to the nearest market place.

A little over a third of the working people are engaged in agriculture, although about seven-eighths of the country is too dry, too rocky or too steep for farming. About half the land that *can* be cultivated is divided into *ejidos*, or plots of land shared by a number of families, but there are still many peasants without land who earn wages by working on large farms. Maize—the chief crop—beans and coffee are grown on naturally watered land, and wheat, cotton, sugar and vegetables on irrigated (artificially watered) land. Henequen, or sisal hemp, from which rope and twine are made, is grown in northern Yucatan. Tobacco of good quality is another Mexican crop, and chicle, which is used for making chewing gum, is obtained from the sapodilla trees in the Yucatan forests. Much of the land can be used for grazing, and there are large herds of beef cattle, especially in the north.

Most Mexicans speak Spanish and are Roman Catholics. Children are supposed to attend the schools, which are free, between the ages of 6 and 14, but schooling is not easy to arrange in the remote country districts. For the same reason many Indians in remote areas do not speak Spanish. In many villages the school is a place where the parents as well as the children go to learn. There too they get advice on health and farming methods. English is the second language among educated people. Association football—spelt "futbol"—is the most popular game.

The Mexicans are an artistic people and some of their modern painters such as Diego Rivera, José Clemente Orozco and David Alfaro Siqueiros are world-famous. Their work is especially notable for their large wall-paintings telling the story of the Mexican people's fight for independence. The compositions of the leading musician, Carlos Chavez, are intended to express the soul of the common people of his country.

The capital of the republic is Mexico City which lies in a valley at the southern end of the central plateau. There was an Aztec city here before the Spaniards came but the Spaniards rebuilt it (see AZTECS). The great cathedral, the largest in Latin America, stands on the site of the chief Aztec temple, and at this point several main streets fan out from the central square known as El Zocalo or the Plaza Mayor. The city, which has many clusters of high white skyscrapers, is the centre of Mexico's road and rail networks and produces about half the manufactured goods of the country. Most of the other important cities are also on the central plateau.

Paul Popper

Upper left: One of the modern buildings of the University of Mexico. Upper right: A lassoing competition. Lower left: Fishermen on Lake Patzcuaro. Lower right: Gathering cactus leaves for making the spirit drink called *pulque*.

Guadalajara is the second city of Mexico and has many buildings dating from the Spanish colonial period. The chief ports on the Atlantic coast are Veracruz and the oil port of Tampico. Mazatlan is the chief Pacific seaport.

Mexico is very rich in minerals. It produces as much silver as either Canada or the United States, although most of the richer mines are almost used up. Much lead is also mined, as well as sulphur, zinc, gold, copper and mercury. Mexico has enough iron and coal to make sufficient steel for its own use, the chief steelworks being at Monterrey. The mines used to belong to foreign companies but most of them have been taken over by Mexican firms. There are important oil fields in the eastern coastal lowlands, and all the oil wells belong to the state. Sulphur is a very important product.

Since World War II the government has made great efforts to provide water power for making electricity by building dams across the rivers. The water from the artificial lakes formed behind the dams is often used for irrigation. The electric power is used in factories and mines, and Mexican factories provide many of the goods used in the country. These goods include textiles, clothing, footwear, furniture, building materials, soap, glass and pottery. The chief manufacturing areas are Mexico City and the surrounding district, Monterrey and the towns on the railway between Mexico City and Veracruz.

In such a mountainous country the difficulty of getting from place to place has hindered progress. The Mexican railways were built by British and United States companies in the late 19th century and have been greatly improved and extended. Mexico is connected by rail and road with the United States and thousands of American tourists visit Mexico every year, bringing a great deal of money into the country. Although the chief towns and ports are linked by roads, many of the roads are still of unpaved earth. Mexico has a small merchant fleet, most of whose ships are oil tankers. Air transport has made great strides and there are first-class airports at Mexico City, Guadalajara, Monterrey and Mazatlan, as well as many smaller airfields and landing grounds in remote places. Even so, there are hundreds of lonely villages that can be reached only on horseback or by donkey.

History

The ancient civilizations of Mexico, although not as old as those of Egypt or Mesopotamia, almost certainly began many centuries before the time of Christ. Most of them were influenced by the Maya people of Central America, about whom you can read in the separate article RACES AND PEOPLES. Remains of the temples, pyramids and other buildings of ancient Mexico are to be seen near the town of Oaxaca in the south and at Mitla near by, and also at Cholula near Puebla and at Teotihuacan not far from the capital city, as well as at Chichen-Itza in Yucatan. The pyramid-building people called the Toltecs were the forerunners of the Aztecs, who set up their capital in about 1325 where Mexico City stands today.

The Aztecs were a warlike people, but they were no match for the few hundred well armed Spanish soldiers under Hernan Cortes who arrived in 1519 (see CORTES, HERNAN). Within two years Cortes and his men conquered the Aztec lands, and for the next three centuries Mexico, under the name of New Spain, was part of the Spanish Empire. The Spaniards tried to convert the Mexicans to Christianity but generally were more interested in obtaining the great wealth of gold and silver from the Mexican mines. The land was divided into huge estates and the Indians of Mexico became mere slaves.

New ideas came to Mexico as a result of the French Revolution. In 1808 Napoleon invaded Spain and drove the Spanish king from the throne. People in Mexico began to talk about revolution. The first rising was attempted in 1810 by the Indian peasants. Their cry was *Tierra y Libertad* ("Land and Liberty") but the rising was soon put down. When Mexico finally gained its independence in 1821, the power was in the hands of the creoles—the name given to people of Spanish blood born in Mexico—and the peasants were no better off.

The history of Mexico since its independence has been exciting but full of trouble. What is now Texas was then part of Mexico, and the people of Texas wanted to join the United States. This caused a war with the United States (1846–1848) which Mexico lost. As a result, Mexico had to give up not only Texas but also Arizona, California and New Mexico. In 1857 there was a civil war when the big landowners and the army opposed the new laws which aimed at splitting up the huge estates and making all the people in the country obey the same laws. In 1861 the victorious rebel forces entered Mexico City under the Indian leader Benito Juarez, but in the following year the country was invaded by French troops who came to obtain payment of Mexico's debt to France. The French created an empire in Mexico, with Maximilian of Austria on the throne, but he was shot by the Mexicans when the French troops were withdrawn to Europe in 1867. Juarez returned to power but died before he could finish his reforms.

In 1876 General Porfirio Diaz seized power and ruled as a ruthless dictator until 1911. During these years much was done to develop the wealth of the country. Factories, mines, railways, harbours and roads were built with the help of money from abroad. The country prospered but the peasants remained poor, landless and uneducated.

Then came the revolution of 1910, which has

continued to influence the nation's development ever since. Diaz was overthrown and for some years after that the story is one of strife and disorder, with one military leader after another holding power. The three chief objects of the revolution have been to reduce the power of the church, to obtain land for the peasants and to develop the country for the benefit of its people and not of foreigners. In 1917 a new constitution promised great reforms to the workers and peasants as regards working hours, wages, education and the right to own land. Like many great movements, the Mexican Revolution has made mistakes and has not fulfilled all its promises. Even today the aims of the revolution have not all been achieved, but many huge estates have been broken up and thousands of Indians resettled on their own land. In 1938 the oil fields belonging to foreign companies were taken over by the Mexican government.

The rapid growth of the Mexican population has made it difficult to find employment for all the people and schools for all the children. Many workers prefer to go to factories and farms in the United States for higher wages.

Mexico is a federal republic; that is, it has a central government but is made up of a number of states which manage their own affairs. It is officially known as the United States of Mexico. The members of the congress, or parliament, are elected by the people.

MICA is the name given to a group of minerals. The most important types used in industry are muscovite (potash mica) and phlogopite (amber or magnesia mica). Mica is found in nearly all igneous rocks (those that were once molten) and is unlike all other minerals in that it splits in only one direction. Because of this it can be split into sheets that are sometimes less than 0·025 millimetre thick. These are tough and elastic and do not break easily. At the same time they are so soft that they can easily be scratched with the fingernail. In colour they vary from being clear and transparent, as in the best muscovite, through red, yellow, green and brown to the black of some phlogopites which contain much iron.

Other less important kinds of mica are biotite,

Camera Press

Stone warriors guarded the ancient capital of the Toltecs.

sericite and lepidomelane. These do not easily split into sheets and they are used for grinding into powder. Lepidolite and zinnwaldite (lithia micas) and roscoelite (vanadium mica) are used in industry because they contain lithium or vanadium and not for the same purpose as other micas. Vermiculite (hydrated biotite) is a form of mica with special properties and nowadays it is usually looked upon as a separate material.

More than 170,000 tonnes of mica are produced every year and well over two-thirds of this comes from the United States and India. Other important producing countries are the U.S.S.R., South Africa, Brazil and Argentina. Wherever possible mica is mined in large blocks and the larger the block the greater its value. After mining the blocks are sorted for quality and then split to the desired size with sharp knives.

The micas do not crack or melt in great heat. Sheet mica is therefore ideal for the windows of stoves and lamps and for the peep-holes of furnaces. Its most important use is as an insulator for electrical appliances, for it does not conduct an electrical current (see ELECTRICITY). Powdered mica is white and glittering and is often sprinkled on toys or on stage scenery to give a frosted effect. It is also used in the preparation of paint and wallpaper and for dusting roofing felt. It is a poor conductor of heat and is put round boilers and pipes to prevent loss of heat.

MICHAELMAS DAISY.

Michaelmas, or the feast of St. Michael, falls on September 29, and the garden flowers called Michaelmas daisies were given their name because they are in full bloom at that time, although they often appear in July and may go on to November.

Like all the daisies, they belong to the Compositae family. They can be tall or short, sturdy or slender, with flowers single or double, varying from an inch or more across to the size of small buttons. The outer florets are all shades of mauve and purple, or sometimes reddish or white. The disc, or inner florets, are generally yellow. The plants may be as much as eight feet high, or as little as eight inches, and are usually bushy, with leaves up to nine inches long. Some Michaelmas daisies have only one flower at the end of a branch, while in others the flowers grow in clusters.

Radio Times Hulton Library

Michaelmas daisies.

Because the flowers look like stars, their genus, or group, is called *Aster,* from the Greek word for "star", and another common name for them is starwort.

All kinds of Michaelmas daisies except one come from America, but it is chiefly in Great Britain that they have been cultivated as garden flowers. They are hardy plants with strong, spreading rootstocks, and are almost always grown in herbaceous borders.

MICHELANGELO BUONARROTI

(1475–1564). In Italy during the 15th and 16th centuries many brilliant artists lived and worked. Among them were Leonardo da Vinci, Raphael and Titian (all of whom are described in separate articles), but perhaps the greatest of all was Michelangelo Buonarroti. In sculpture and painting no one could equal his achievement, and he was also a fine architect and a poet.

Michelangelo was born in Florence in 1475, the son of a poor gentleman named Ludovico Buonarroti. While still a boy he determined to be an artist in spite of his father's wishes, and when he was only 13 he went to study in the workshop of the foremost painter of the city. Later he attended a school of sculpture which had been set up by Lorenzo dei Medici.

In 1496 Michelangelo left Florence and went to Rome, where in spite of his rugged looks and stern, unsociable temper it was not long before his genius won him the favour of various rich men who wanted him to work for them. One of the statues that he carved during this first stay in Rome was a figure of the Madonna—the mother of Jesus—holding the dead body of her Son across her knees, in which he beautifully showed the grief and heaviness of the scene.

Michelangelo's father was meanwhile urging him to come home to help his family, and in 1501 he did so and spent four years in Florence. It was then that he set to work on his most magnificent statue, the colossal figure of David, the Jewish hero of the Old Testament. It was carved out of a huge block of marble which another sculptor had begun to carve 40 years before and which had lain unused ever since, and when it was finished the best artists of Florence debated where it should be set up. They

Royal Academy, London

Madonna and Child, an unfinished carving by Michelangelo.

finally decided that it should stand on the terrace of the palace of the city rulers, and there it remained until 1882 when it was put into the Academy of Fine Arts for protection.

In 1505 Pope Julius II called Michelangelo back to Rome to design and carve a great monument to himself, which he wanted made during his lifetime. Michelangelo eagerly planned a noble and magnificent piece of sculpture, but before he could get far with the work the Pope demanded instead that he should paint the pictures on the great ceiling of the Sistine Chapel in his palace, the Vatican. With some bitterness and unwillingness—for he always said that painting was not his business—Michelangelo eventually agreed, and began the work in 1508. At first he engaged others to help him in this gigantic scheme, but their work dissatisfied him and he wiped out all they had done and completed the painting single-handed. For four and a half years he laboured, lying on his back on scaffolding nearly 100 feet above the chapel floor. The painting covered 10,000 square feet, and Michelangelo divided it into nine main panels, taking his subjects from the Book of Genesis. He painted the beginning of the world, the creation of the sun and moon, the division of light from darkness, the division of the waters from the dry land, the creation of man and woman and the beginning of sin.

As soon as he had finished, he went to work again on the monument, but he had several times to change his scheme and interrupt his work, and when it was eventually finished many years later it was not as he had originally intended it.

The rest of Michelangelo's life was spent partly in Rome and partly in Florence. Among his sculptures were monuments to members of the Medici family in their chapel in Florence. In Rome, he was asked to do another painting in the Sistine Chapel, this time on the wall above the altar. On the ceiling he had painted man's beginning in the dawn of the world; 21 years later in this picture, "The Last Judgement", he painted man's last moment on the earth when he is judged by his Creator.

As an old man Michelangelo never ceased work. As well as continuing painting and sculpture, he wrote fine poetry, full of deep feelings;

National Gallery, London

Madonna and Child with Saint John and Angels, another of the many works Michelangelo left unfinished.

and at the age of 72 he became chief architect of the great church of St. Peter's in Rome. He was nearly 90 when he died in 1564.

Two of Michelangelo's paintings can be seen in the National Gallery in London.

MICROPHONE. To change sound into electric current so that it can be sent through telephone wires or broadcast by radio or in a public address system, microphones are used. There are several different kinds. The *carbon microphone,* invented in 1878 by David Hughes, is the type used in a telephone mouthpiece and is described in the article TELEPHONE.

The *moving-coil microphone,* sometimes used for broadcasting, has a thin diaphragm, or circular sheet of metal, which vibrates when struck by sound waves. Vibration means that the middle of the diaphragm moves rapidly in and out. The amount of movement depends on the loudness of the sound and the rapidity depends on the pitch. A low-pitched (deep) note causes a slower vibration than a shrill note. To the

Courtesy, B.B.C.

The lip microphone is held close to the speaker's mouth. It is a type of ribbon microphone which does not pick up background noises and is used for outside broadcasts.

diaphragm is fixed a coil of fine wire which is arranged close to the poles, or strongest points, of a magnet. When a coil of wire is moved near a magnet a current of electricity flows in the coil. Vibration of the diaphragm therefore creates in the coil an electric current that matches the loudness and pitch of the sound.

The *crystal microphone* depends on what is known as the piezo-electric effect. Some kinds of quartz crystals when squeezed (*piezo* is a Greek word meaning "press") produce an electric voltage, or pressure, and can therefore be attached to a diaphragm and made to give a varying electric current. In the *ribbon microphone* used in broadcasting, the sound falls on a strip of aluminium foil hanging between the poles of a powerful magnet and makes the strip vibrate, thus causing a varying electric current to flow in it. Generally the varying currents produced by microphones are very feeble and have to be amplified (magnified) before they can be used. The article RADIO explains how this is done.

The ribbon microphone is said to be bi-directional because it picks up sound coming from two directions only. Unless the speaker is directly behind or in front of the microphone he cannot be heard properly and if he moves to one side the listeners think he is disappearing into the distance. This effect is used in radio plays.

MICROSCOPE.
A microscope is an instrument for making small things look bigger. The ordinary magnifying glass described in the

Douglas F. Lawson

Eggs of the large cabbage white butterfly, photographed through a microscope at a magnification of 65×. A dark top to an egg and a dark spot in its centre are signs that the caterpillar is about to hatch out.

Courtesy, W. C. McCrone, Armour Research Foundation

Under the microscope many substances reveal a previously hidden beauty. (1) A form of insecticide. (2) Vitamin K. (3) Sugar. (4) A high explosive.

article Lens is sometimes called a "simple microscope". The word microscope is usually kept, however, for the "compound microscope", a bigger and more complicated instrument.

The idea of the compound microscope, which was invented in 1590, is to use one lens to form an enlarged image of the object being examined and then to look at that image through a second magnifying lens. In practice, groups of lenses are used instead of single ones.

At the bottom end of the brass body tube of the microscope is a group of lenses called the *objective*. The objective focuses, or brings together, the rays of light from the object so as to produce a much-enlarged image of it about half way up the tube. At the top of the tube is a

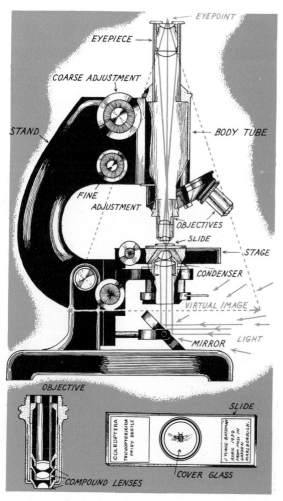

A compound microscope.

second group of lenses called the *eye-piece*, which magnifies the object still further. Below the objective is a *stage*, or platform on which the object is placed. Generally there are several sets of objectives which can be swung into place according to whether a high or low magnifying power is required. Different eye-pieces can also be used.

The tube can be moved up and down by screws so that the object can be brought exactly into focus, thus giving the sharpest and clearest image. Usually the object is carried on a glass slip called a *slide*, which is placed on the stage of the microscope. Parts of animals or plants may be cut into very thin slices (thinner than cigarette paper), stained to make the details stand out more clearly, and then mounted in a clear gum on a slide with a very thin cover slip of glass over them. They can then be viewed in light coming up through the slide from beneath. The light is reflected by a mirror carried below the stage and concentrated by a group of lenses called the *condenser* carried in the stage so that the object on the slide is very brightly lit.

The magnifying power of a microscope is usually given as a number followed by the multiplication sign. A power of 100 × makes a pin 1 millimetre thick look 100 millimetres thick. The power depends on the power of the eye-piece and that of the objective and is obtained by multiplying the two together. Eye-pieces usually vary from 5 × to 20 × and objectives from 6 × to 70 ×. A microscope with these lenses would therefore give a least magnification of $(5 \times 6) = 30 \times$ and a greatest magnification of $(20 \times 70) = 1,400 \times$.

At a magnification of 1,000 × the red cells of the blood look about 6 millimetres across. Many germs can be seen clearly as rods or dots. The way in which skin, muscle, nerve and other parts of the body and of plants are made up can all be seen quite plainly. Above 1,500 ×, however, a compound microscope is no good because the wavelength of light is about one two-thousandth of a millimetre, which prevents objects smaller than that from being distinctly seen, whatever lenses are used.

This difficulty is overcome by the electron microscope. Instead of light rays, the electron

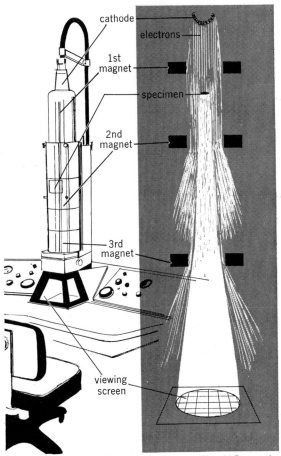

cathode

electrons

1st magnet

specimen

2nd magnet

3rd magnet

viewing screen

Photos, Courtesy, Westinghouse Electric Corporation

microscope uses a beam of electrons—an ordinary electric current in a wire consists of the movement of these tiny particles (see ELECTRON). Instead of lenses, it uses powerful electro-magnets for focusing the beam. The electron beam can be focused by either electric or magnetic fields. Although itself invisible, the beam affects a fluorescent screen or a photographic film and can thus produce a visible image.

The electron microscope can produce pictures with a direct magnification of 20,000 ×. The films can then be enlarged to give magnifications up to 100,000 ×. In one special kind of electron microscope—the field emission microscope—the magnification may be so great as to make it possible to see the arrangement of the individual atoms forming the molecules of a substance (see MOLECULE). This is done by applying a high voltage to a metal tip inside a vacuum tube, so that electrons stream from the tip to form a magnified pattern of it on a screen.

In most microscopes a person looks at the magnified image of the object. But in an electron microscope he looks at a magnified picture of an object. This picture is made by electrons on a coated screen similar to a television tube. Electrons from a lamp cathode pass through the specimen being studied. Magnets spread these to cover a wide area so that on the viewing screen there is a large image of a very small part of the specimen. The two pictures below, taken with an electron microscope, are of iron surfaces magnified about 7,000 times. The tiny whiskers (left) are actually only about 1 millionth of a millimetre high; and the rust crystals (right) are so close together that there are about 160 million to the square centimetre.

Courtesy, Westinghouse Electric Corporation
Adjusting an electron microscope.

Douglas F. Lawson

Above: *Aspergillus amstelodani*, one of the kinds of fungus that cause mould. At a magnification of 400×, tiny air-borne spores can be seen floating from the "flowering heads". Right: Crystals of potassium ferricyanide, a chemical used by photographers. The magnification of this photograph is 55×.

MIDAS. According to a Greek story a king named Midas once helped the Greek god of wine Bacchus and in return Bacchus offered to give him whatever he most wanted. Midas asked that everything he touched should be turned to gold and was overjoyed when his request was granted.

However, the gift soon proved to be a curse. When he picked up a piece of bread to eat it became gold. He lifted his glass to drink and the wine turned to molten gold as soon as it touched his lips. Finally he prayed to Bacchus for deliverance and the god told him to bathe in the Pactolus River in Asia Minor. Midas did so and lost his magic touch but the river's sands have ever after been golden.

Another story of Midas is that he judged a musical competition between the gods Pan and Apollo. He gave the prize to Pan, whereupon Apollo was so angry that he changed the king's ears into those of a donkey. Midas hid his ass's ears under a turban so the secret was known to none but his barber. Finally the barber, unable to keep the story to himself any longer, dug a hole in the ground and whispered into it what he had seen. Immediately a clump of reeds sprang up in the hole and whenever they stir in the breeze they can be heard whispering: "Midas has ass's ears, Midas has ass's ears. ..."

MIDDLE AGES. History is a long and continuous story with no sharp divisions, but historians have to divide it up as a matter of convenience to make their studies easier. European history is often divided into three main parts: ancient history (covering classical Greece and Rome); mediaeval history or the middle ages; and modern history. The middle ages are usually taken as starting in the 5th century A.D. when the Roman Empire in western Europe finally came to an end. The end of the middle ages is more vague. For English history the Battle of Bosworth in 1485 is often taken as a convenient date; in European history, the discovery of America by Christopher Columbus in 1492 is

MIDDLE AGES

"The Patriarch Jared", a · 12th-century window in the south transept of Canterbury Cathedral. During the middle ages men expressed their firm belief in God and their devotion to the Church in their art and architecture. Many of the finest cathedrals and abbeys in western Europe were built at this time, the most skilful craftsmen and artists being employed to build and decorate them. The great churches were the centre of life and worship for mediaeval religious communities and were visited by thousands of pilgrims.

sometimes used in a similar way. During the 15th century several great changes came about which, taken together, can be considered as marking the end of the middle ages. These were the invention and speed of printing, the growing influence of the Renaissance and its ideas, and the decline in the power of the church.

The earliest part of the middle ages is sometimes called the dark ages, because the barbarian tribes who invaded and settled in the lands of the former Roman Empire were less civilized than the Romans and because there are few written records of their history and way of life. In time new civilizations grew up, a blend of the old Roman traditions, the customs of the new people, and the increasing influence of the Christian church.

The most important single characteristic of the middle ages is that all western Europe had one common religion, under the popes at Rome. In 800, the pope crowned Charlemagne Holy Roman Emperor. This was an attempt to make all Europe united once more, as it had been under the Romans, but this time under a Christian ruler. Many of the important quarrels in the middle ages were between the emperors and the popes. This weakened the power first of the emperors, then of the popes as well. At the same time new states such as France and England were coming into being with strong governments of their own. These new, tough and quarrelsome states ended any idea of a Europe united under a pope or emperor.

It is wrong to think that the men of the middle ages were less advanced than the Romans. Their achievements were different. The Romans had fine roads and an efficient system of government, but the middle ages gave us splendid cathedrals, literature and poetry and the earliest forms of our modern universities. For hundreds of years farming and trade were more primitive than under the Romans, because political conditions were so unsettled, but in time cities grew in size, and trade and industry flourished, so that goods were sent all over Europe.

More about the way people lived in the middle ages can be found in the articles AGRICULTURE; CHIVALRY; FEUDALISM; MANOR; MONKS AND FRIARS; PILGRIMAGES.

MIDDLE EAST. The part of the world at the eastern end of the Mediterranean, where Asia and Africa meet, is called the Middle East. The Middle East countries are Turkey, Cyprus, Syria, Iraq, Persia (Iran), Lebanon, Israel, Jordan, Egypt, Saudi Arabia, the two states of Yemen, Oman, and the Persian Gulf states—of which the chief are Kuwait, Bahrain and Qatar. The Arab states of Libya, Tunisia and even Algeria and Morocco, which are in North Africa, are often regarded as belonging to the Middle East because they are so closely involved with its affairs. "Middle East" is a very loose description, and some people think that Turkey and Persia, cut off from the rest by mountain barriers, are not part of the Middle East.

Throughout history, armies have fought to control this area, which has been described as a land bridge between Europe, Asia and Africa. For centuries the Middle East was the natural corridor for trade between Europe and eastern lands such as India. In 1869 the cutting of the Suez Canal opened a short sea route through the Middle East to India, China and Australia. The air lines joining the western world to the East pass through the Middle East.

The most important fact about the Middle East is that it produces more than a quarter of the world's petroleum and has far larger oil reserves than any other area. Most of the oil and petrol used for driving the ships, lorries, buses and motor cars of Great Britain and western Europe comes from the Middle East, chiefly from the Persian Gulf states and from Persia, Iraq and Saudi Arabia. The United States and the U.S.S.R. also use Middle East oil. These other countries are therefore keenly interested in Middle East affairs.

Most of the people of the Middle East are Arabs belonging to the Moslem religion, although Israel is Jewish and Lebanon is half Christian. A thousand years ago the Arabs had a great empire of their own, but this was overcome by the Mongols in 1258. Then for centuries the Middle East was part of the Ottoman (Turkish) Empire. Great Britain and France overthrew Turkish rule and from 1918 onwards the new countries of the Middle East one by one became independent.

Most of the countries of the Middle East are Arab and they often have similar aims and policies. The Arab states opposed the setting up of the state of Israel (see ISRAEL) and fighting has broken out on several occasions. The most serious fighting was during the June War of 1967, after which the Suez Canal was closed. The Arabs have continued to oppose Israel and countries in the Middle East have found it hard to maintain stable government and peace.

MIDDLESEX disappeared as a county for the purposes of local government on April 1, 1965, when most of it became part of Greater London. This article deals with the history of the county.

The name Middlesex first appeared in a charter of 704 A.D., and it meant the land between South Saxons (Sussex) and the East Saxons (Essex). For a time it was overrun by the Danish invaders, until the Saxon kings recaptured London and the surrounding country in the 10th century. Middlesex grew in importance as London grew, and it saw the coming and going of many famous men. The rebel barons stayed at Staines in 1215 on their way to Runnymede where King John was forced to grant Magna Carta. (See MAGNA CARTA.)

In the Civil War in the 17th century, both Royalist and Parliamentary armies were encamped in Middlesex, and in 1685 James II's troops camped on Hounslow Heath before setting off to crush the Duke of Monmouth's rebellion.

In 1768 and 1769 the electors of Middlesex became famous all over the country when they voted for John Wilkes as their member of parliament. Wilkes was a great popular leader, but a rather disreputable man, and the government refused for many years to let him take his seat in the House of Commons, although the voters elected Wilkes four times running.

Hampton Court was built by Cardinal Wolsey, who gave it to Henry VIII. It was a royal home for several centuries. (See HAMPTON COURT.) Syon House and Osterley Park, both near Brentford, were remodelled in the 18th century by the architect Robert Adam. At Twickenham the villa of the poet Alexander

Pope survives, and not far away from it is Strawberry Hill, the home of the 18th-century writer Horace Walpole.

MIDGE. There are several kinds of midges, some being biting insects while others are quite harmless. Those that gather in swarms and perform a kind of flying dance in summer, generally near water and often above a small bush, do not bite. They are small, two-winged flies, very beautiful when seen under a microscope or through a strong magnifying glass.

Most of the larvae, or grubs, of these midges live in water. The best known is the one called the bloodworm, which can generally be found in such places as old water-butts. Another group of very similar midges have grubs which feed in the tissues of plants and cause the lumps called

A bloodworm larva, or grub, and the midge it turns into.

galls to form. These are therefore known as gall midges.

The many biting midges are much smaller than these other kinds. Mostly they suck the juices of plants or insects, but some suck blood and can cause quite painful wounds.

MID GLAMORGAN is the name proposed for a new county formed in the reorganization of local government in Wales. The new county will include the boroughs of Merthyr Tydfil and Rhondda and also parts of Brecknockshire and Monmouthshire.

Livingston new town

curlew

Penicuik House, converted 18th century stables

Royal Highland Show Ingliston

The Prentice Pillar Roslin Chapel

Borthwick Castle

Edinburgh Castle

Newhaven harbour

MIDLOTHIAN is a county in the south of Scotland. It is bordered on the north by the broad estuary, or mouth, of the River Forth, known as the Firth of Forth, and by the city of Edinburgh (see EDINBURGH), and on the northwest by West Lothian; on the southwest by Lanarkshire and on the south by Peeblesshire and Selkirkshire; on the southeast by Roxburghshire and on the east by Berwickshire and East Lothian.

In the south of Midlothian are the Pentland Hills, mostly grassy or heather covered, and to the east are the Moorfoot Hills. The River Esk flows into the Firth of Forth in Midlothian, and so does the River Almond, which first winds through a cultivated plain.

In the lonely uplands of Midlothian are heather-clad hills with plantations of fir, pine, alder and birch trees. There flow the small streams which the Scots call burns, with waters browned by peat, and small rivers stocked with trout. In the rich farmlands of the Midlothian plains are woods of oak, beech and chestnut.

Curlews live in the uplands and flocks of wild geese pass overhead on their migratory journeys Many waders and sea birds frequent the shores of the Forth.

In recent years the county's former major industries of mining and paper making have become less important, and many coal mines and paper mills have closed. Of the four mines that remain in operation, two, Monkhall and Bilston Glen, are able to produce more than 1,000,000 tonnes of coal a year. Many new industries have been started in the county. They include precision engineering, printing, making crystal glass, plastics, knitwear, clothing and tyre making. Several types of farming are carried on in Midlothian. Some farmers grow oats, barley and potatoes, others raise dairy cattle or sheep.

The new town of Livingstone lies on the border of Midlothian and West Lothian. The River Almond flows through the centre of the town which is set in pleasant wooded country. Its population will eventually be about 70,000.

Dalkeith is an old market town between the North and South Esk rivers, which become a single river a little beyond the town. Dalkeith

Palace, which used to be the home of the Dukes of Buccleuch, is now partly used by a computer firm. South of Dalkeith is Newbattle Abbey, which is built on the site of a monastery founded in 1140. It is now used as an adult residential college.

Musselburgh is an old town on the Firth of Forth. Golf has been played there since at least 1672, and the Royal Company of Archers have competed since 1603 for the Musselburgh silver arrow, said to be the oldest prize in the world.

The Roman historian Tacitus wrote of the campaigns of Agricola, the governor of Britain in the 1st century A.D., in what is now Midlothian. Between the rivers Forth and Clyde traces can still be seen of the forts built to protect the area from the wild tribes farther north.

The many castles, churches and mansions of Midlothian suffered much destruction during the wars between England and Scotland in the middle ages. A reminder of later history is Borthwick Castle, near the Moorfoot Hills. It was built in 1430 and for a time in 1567 was the home of Mary Queen of Scots and her third husband, the Earl of Bothwell. The castle has been rebuilt, but the marks of Oliver Cromwell's bombardment in 1650 can still be seen.

In the village of Roslin, southwest of Dalkeith, is a remarkable chapel, founded in about 1450. It is richly ornamented with carving and has a pillar, called the Prentice Pillar, covered with designs of leaves and flowers. It is said that the apprentice, or learner, who designed it was murdered by his jealous master. Near by are the ruins of Roslin Castle, parts of which are said to have been built in the 14th century.

The Scots poet William Drummond (1585–1649) is buried in the churchyard of the ruined Norman church at Lasswade. He was born near by at Hawthornden and is often known as Drummond of Hawthornden.

In the Pentland Hills is a tiny village called Swanston where Robert Louis Stevenson, the author of *Treasure Island,* took his holidays for several years. He was interested in the stories of the struggles between the Covenanters, who wanted a Presbyterian Church in Scotland, and Charles II, who was trying to make the Scots accept the Anglican Church. Stevenson wrote a book on those times called *Pentland Rising.*

Near the village of Mid Calder, not far from the border with West Lothian, is Calder House, built on the site of an old fortress. Here in 1556 John Knox first administered the sacrament of Holy Communion according to the Protestant fashion after the Reformation.

MIGRATION is a word meaning "movement", and many mammals, birds, fishes and insects regularly move from one place to another at certain times of the year. The kind of migration most easily seen is that of birds, and bird migration has been known for a very long time. About 2,500 years ago the prophet Jeremiah wrote about the regular arrival of the turtle dove, crane, swallow and stork. In England the best known bird migrant is the cuckoo, which stays for the spring and summer before flying away to other lands.

Why and how birds migrate is a mystery which scientists do not fully understand. Some specimens of migratory birds are caught, rings are put on their legs and they are then released. If the same birds are found in another country later in the year and their rings identified, it is known from which country they came. But how they find their way and what causes them to go to certain places at certain times is not known.

Swallows, martins and many other birds that live on insects come north in the summer because they can catch many insects in the long, sunny days. When the days get colder and shorter they go south to warmer places where insects can still be found. It is hard to know, however, why the tree pipit goes to spend the winter in Africa while its cousin the meadow pipit can manage well enough to stay in western Europe. There are also winter migrants to western Europe: the best known are probably the redwing and the fieldfare. Many others leave the far north in the cold weather and visit the shores of Great Britain. These include many wading birds, ducks and gulls. Even the commonest birds may migrate to some extent. (See BIRD.)

Among the mammals that migrate, one of the strangest is the lemming, a small rodent that lives in northern Europe. Every few years lemmings move in enormous numbers, swimming rivers,

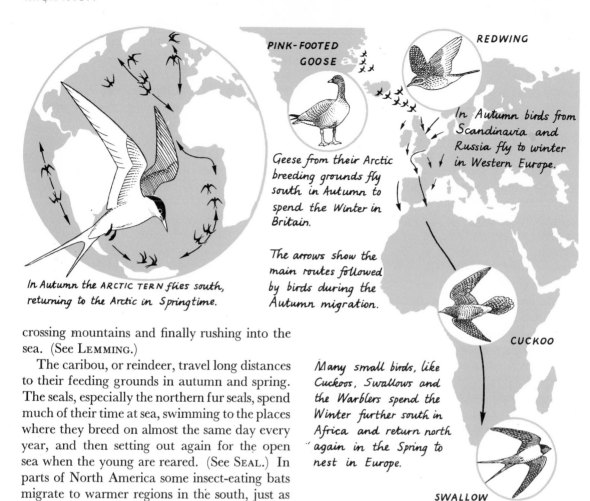

PINK-FOOTED GOOSE

REDWING

Geese from their Arctic breeding grounds fly south in Autumn to spend the Winter in Britain.

In Autumn birds from Scandinavia and Russia fly to winter in Western Europe.

The arrows show the main routes followed by birds during the Autumn migration.

In Autumn the ARCTIC TERN flies south, returning to the Arctic in Springtime.

CUCKOO

Many small birds, like Cuckoos, Swallows and the Warblers spend the Winter further south in Africa and return north again in the Spring to nest in Europe.

SWALLOW

crossing mountains and finally rushing into the sea. (See LEMMING.)

The caribou, or reindeer, travel long distances to their feeding grounds in autumn and spring. The seals, especially the northern fur seals, spend much of their time at sea, swimming to the places where they breed on almost the same day every year, and then setting out again for the open sea when the young are reared. (See SEAL.) In parts of North America some insect-eating bats migrate to warmer regions in the south, just as swallows do.

Many African mammals also move about during the year to get water or to find just the right kinds of plants they need.

The eel is probably the most interesting of migratory fishes. It spends its life in fresh water until it grows up, and then it travels to the sea and sets off for the Sargasso Sea, a fairly still area in the centre of the North Atlantic. Here the eggs are laid and hatch into tiny creatures nothing like eels, while the parent eels die. The young ones make their way back to the rivers from which their parents came. (See EEL.)

With the salmon things happen the other way round, for the eggs are laid in rivers and the young salmon go to the sea, mostly at the age of two or three years. Nobody knows just where they go, but they find plenty of food and grow quickly. They spend one or two years in the

sea before returning to lay their own eggs in the river where they hatched. (See SALMON.)

Besides eels and salmon, such important sea fish as herrings, sardines and pilchards also have regular movements according to the season, and these are closely watched by fishermen.

The locust is the most important and most dangerous of migratory insects. In various parts of the world, especially in the Middle East, great swarms of locusts are hatched and afterwards they spread into other lands, where they do much damage by devouring crops.

Much more attractive insect migrants are several kinds of butterflies. Some come from the continent of Europe to Great Britain. The handsome red admiral would soon die out in Britain if adult butterflies did not arrive regularly from warmer countries. The painted lady is another

Top: David and Katie Urry—Bruce Coleman; above: Jane Burton—Bruce Coleman; centre right: C. J. Ott—Bruce Coleman; below right: J. C. Taylor—Bruce Coleman

Top: A flock of pink-footed geese over Loch Leven in Scotland. Geese are strong fliers and have been recorded at heights of up to 1,500 metres while migrating. Above: Swallows in Africa, after their long flight from their summer homes in Europe. In the background are lesser flamingos. Centre right: Barren ground caribou in Alaska seek out a patch of snow as relief from flies. Caribou move south each year to escape the bitter northern winter. Below right: Migrating butterflies drinking in Guiana. More than 200 species of butterfly migrate.

lovely butterfly which migrates. It breeds in southwest Europe and flies northwards from there. In parts of the tropics great swarms of butterflies migrate, and hundreds of thousands of them stream by, sometimes for weeks at a time. The best known migratory butterfly is the monarch of North America. (See BUTTERFLY.)

MIKADO is an old Japanese word that means "emperor". Nowadays, however, the Japanese usually call their emperor *Tenno Heka*, or Son of Heaven.

According to legend the first emperor, Jimmu Tenno, came to the throne in the 7th century B.C. and was descended from the sun goddess. His descendants also were thought to be divine and therefore to have a sacred right to rule. However, by the 12th century A.D., the real rulers of Japan were the military governors, called *shogun*, who ruled in the emperor's name. For centuries the emperors were powerless, shadowy figures who lived a sheltered secluded life at Kyoto surrounded by their court nobles.

Then in 1867 the emperor was restored to his position as supreme ruler of the country. He was still regarded as a being of divine origin and his right to rule was still sacred. Every Japanese person owed him the kind of reverence that is usually given only to God. To serve the emperor was supposed to be the main purpose of all his subjects. This emperor-worship, as it is sometimes called, helped to make Japan strong and united, but it did not encourage a democratic type of government.

Since World War II, in which Japan was defeated by the United States and Great Britain, there have been changes in the position of the emperor. He is still the head of the state and he is still treated with great respect by the people, but he has given up his claim to be of divine origin.

MILAN is the second largest city in Italy and stands in the centre of the fertile north Italian plain. The Simplon and St. Gotthard tunnels link it with the rest of Europe and make it Italy's most important railway junction. About 75 miles to the south lies the port of Genoa.

Milan stood on the route of all the northern

invaders of Italy and so was destroyed over and over again. For this reason there are few beautiful old buildings except the Church of St. Ambrose, begun by him in the year 386 but completed in the 12th century. In the centre of the city is the huge Gothic cathedral, which has more than 100 spires and more than 3,000 statues. All around there are new blocks of big marble-faced buildings and skyscrapers, but one of the most famous features of the city is the Galleria. This is an arcade, or covered passage, opening off the cathedral square. It is

Courtesy, Italian State Tourist Office

The Pirelli building in Milan is one of the most splendid in the city.

made up of two streets in the form of a cross, all roofed by glass and with a tall glass dome in the centre. Luxurious shops line the arcade, and much business is done in the cafés there.

From the cathedral roof, the country round Milan looks like a huge garden divided into plots by poplar and mulberry trees. This land grows Italy's best crops and the mulberry trees feed the silkworms for one of Milan's chief industries, the spinning and weaving of silk. Other important industries are the manufacture of heavy machinery such as railway engines and of motor cars, aircraft, furniture, paper and glass. Milan also has steel mills and important printing works. As coal is scarce in Italy, most of the factories in Milan depend on electricity made by water power from the swift streams of the Alps.

During the middle ages and the Renaissance (see RENAISSANCE), Milan was ruled by a few families of great landowners, among the most important of whom were the Visconti and the Sforza. These families brought many of the great Italian artists to work in Milan, chief among them being Leonardo da Vinci. The remains of his great painting "The Last Supper" can be seen on one of the walls of the refectory (dining hall) of the convent of Santa Maria delle Grazie. The city is rich in works of art and has for long been a great centre of Italian artistic and literary life. Its great opera house, La Scala, can seat 3,600 people and is famous all over the world. Not far from the opera house is the Poldi-Pezzoli museum, containing many fine pictures and old weapons and armour.

In 1500 the French captured Milan and then for 350 years it was under foreign rule. The Spaniards and Austrians followed the French. In 1796, Napoleon Bonaparte made Milan the capital of his Cisalpine Republic and in 1805 he was crowned King of Italy in the cathedral. The Austrians came back after Napoleon's defeat in 1814, but the Milanese had tasted freedom and Milan became the centre of resistance to foreign rule. At last in 1859, after the Battle of Magenta, the city welcomed Victor Emmanuel, the first king of united Italy. Although Benito Mussolini founded his Fascist party in Milan in 1919 (see ITALY), the city became a centre of resistance to Fascism and to German occupation in World War II. As an industrial city and rail centre it suffered severely from bombing.

The population of Milan is about 1,700,000.

MILFORD TRACK.
The beautiful Milford Track, from Lake Te Anau to Milford Sound, was the first discovered route between the southern lakes and the fiordland on the southwest coast of the South Island of New Zealand. The track passes through magnificent bushland, lake and mountain scenery. The actual walk is very rough and covers a distance of about 34 miles but visitors can travel another 60 miles by launch along the lake and on Milford Sound.

From the shores of Lake Te Anau, the first part of the journey is made by launch to the north end of the lake 40 miles away. The Clinton River is crossed and the Milford Track begins, passing first through the bush-clad Clinton Canyon, 14 miles long and with the Pariroa Heights towering 5,000 feet above. This canyon is the groove which an ancient glacier (ice river) carved out of the solid rock. Ten miles' walking brings the traveller to Pompolona Huts, where he rests for the night.

Next the track crosses McKinnon's Pass, 3,400 feet above sea level, named after the explorer who first crossed it in 1888. On all sides grow evergreen trees which, as the track becomes higher, gradually give way to mountain flowers and alpine lilies, among them the *Ranunculus lyalli*, the world's largest buttercup. Its leaves are as big as dinner plates and many a traveller has quenched his thirst from the rain-water lying in the hollow of a leaf.

Near Quinton Huts, the next overnight stopping-place, are the 1,904-foot Sutherland Falls. (See the separate article SUTHERLAND FALLS.) Then the track follows the Arthur River for some six miles, skirts Lake Ada and ends a short distance farther on at the head of Milford Sound. Finally the traveller goes by launch down the Sound, with splendid peaks rising steeply from the water's edge. The launch passes Anita Bay, where greenstone—a semi-precious stone something like jade—is found on the beach.

Nowadays the trip from Lake Te Anau to the head of Milford Sound can be made by a motor road that passes through the Homer Tunnel east of Milford.

MILK.
Although milk is made up mainly of water it contains nearly all the food substances needed by the body. That is why children in Britain are encouraged to drink some every day.

Milk looks white because it contains a protein (body-building substance) called casein. Through a microscope floating globules (small drops) of fat can be seen in milk. The layer of cream which floats on the top of milk is made up of fat globules. As well as casein and fat, which can both be seen, milk also contains a special sugar which is invisible because it is completely dissolved in the watery part. This milk sugar, called *lactose*, is another very important food, although it is not as sweet as ordinary sugar. Minerals, particularly calcium and phosphorus (which are important in forming bones and teeth) and most of the vitamins essential for life and health (see VITAMIN) are also contained in milk.

Milk is produced by all female mammals to feed their young for the first part of their lives. All young mammals, from whales to babies, have milk for their first food. Because milk is good for grown-ups as well as for babies and children, people have kept animals for their milk from very early times. In many countries goats are kept for milk, and both goats' and sheep's milk is used for cheese-making. In eastern countries buffaloes are milked.

In Great Britain and the Commonwealth the animal most used for milk is the cow. Each cow in England and Wales produces an average of 850 gallons of milk in a year, which is enough to fill 6,800 pint bottles. There are also prize animals which give much more.

Farms which keep cows for their milk are known as dairy farms. About two-thirds of the milk produced in Britain is drunk fresh. The rest is made into cheese and butter. About half the cheese and one-eighth of the butter eaten in Britain are home-produced. (See BUTTER ; CATTLE ; CHEESE ; DAIRY FARMING.)

Bacteria and Pasteurization

Besides being an ideal food for babies and other young mammals, milk is also an ideal food for many bacteria, or germs. Some of these cause disease, and if they get into milk, either from a diseased cow or from people dealing with the milk, they make it dangerous to drink.

Since the 1930s veterinary officers in Britain have tested cows for tuberculosis, and cattle there are practically free from the disease. It is also government policy to get rid of brucellosis, a rarer cattle disease that can cause undulant fever in human beings.

Fortunately most bacteria do not cause illness, but they do spoil milk. Some kinds of bacteria grow in milk very rapidly and change the sugar in the milk into an acid known as lactic acid, which has a sour taste. The lactic acid also alters

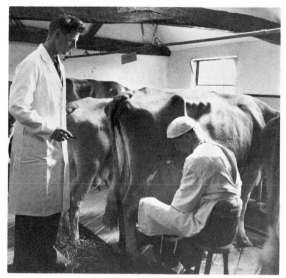
Courtesy, Milk Marketing Board
Milking a cow by hand is a skilful operation.

the casein, causing it to curdle, or thicken. Any other acid, such as vinegar, will curdle milk in the same way. One drop of sour milk contains many millions of bacteria, which, however, are harmless and help in making cheese and butter.

Although yoghurt—a form of soured milk— has recently become popular in Britain, most milk is drunk fresh. There are several ways of making it keep and remain fresh. First of all, as far as possible, bacteria must be prevented from getting into it. This means that all the containers into which milk is poured, such as buckets, cans and bottles, must be absolutely clean, because bacteria thrive in dust and dirt. Even careful cleaning, however, does not remove all the bacteria, and those which remain must be killed by sterilizing the containers. This means steaming them or putting them in very hot water, or using a special chemical substance. Another way of keeping out bacteria is to cover containers full of milk to prevent dust or flies from falling into it. Flies are particularly dangerous as they carry enormous numbers of bacteria. There are always some bacteria in milk, and if the milk is kept in a warm place they soon increase.

The way to keep milk fresh is to keep it in a cool larder or a refrigerator. Bacteria can only grow slowly in cold conditions.

Most bacteria can be killed by heating, and some people boil their milk in hot weather to make it keep longer. Boiling spoils the taste of milk, however, and it is possible to heat it to a rather lower temperature and kill the bacteria without spoiling the milk. This very important process is called *pasteurization*, after Louis Pasteur, the French scientist who discovered the existence of germs. (See PASTEUR, LOUIS.) Most countries have very strict laws to make sure that milk is pasteurized properly before being sold. Nearly all the milk sold in Great Britain is pasteurized.

The Morning Bottle of Milk

Large cities like London must have milk brought to them from as far away as 250 miles, because there are not enough farms near by to supply all the milk needed. The placing of bottles of milk on the doorstep is the end of a long series of processes carried out by farmers, transport workers and scientists. The time taken from the cow to the doorstep varies from one to two days according to the distance the milk has to be transported.

First of all, the cows on the dairy farms are milked morning and evening, usually by machine but sometimes by hand on small farms. The cows' udders are carefully washed before milking and utensils are cleaned and sterilized.

The milk, which is warm when it leaves the cow, is immediately transferred into large re-frigerated vans and cooled to 4°C. Some milk is still collected in churns which contain about 80 pints and are also cooled.

Every morning a road tanker empties the bulk vat or a lorry collects the churns for delivery either to a milk depot or direct to a dairy. The use of refrigerated bulk tankers means that milk can now be transported over much greater distances without any deterioration in quality.

Either at the country depot or at the town dairy the milk is pasteurized by raising its temperature for a short time in closely controlled conditions. Pasteurization kills nearly all bacteria. There are several kinds of pasteurizer, but all are elaborate machines made of stainless steel, which heat the milk to the correct temperature and then cool it at once to 4°C. The cold pasteurized milk is put into bottles by automatic filling machines which also seal the bottle tops. Sometimes waxed paper cartons are used and there is a machine which folds specially treated paper to form pyramid-shaped cartons. The bottles and cartons are then placed in a cold store until they are taken round in vans to the houses.

It is important to put empty milk bottles outside the door because the milkman collects them and returns them to the dairy. There they are passed through large automatic machines which wash and sterilize them so that they can be used again.

The use of electrical equipment has made milking more hygienic and efficient. Several cows can be milked at one time.
Courtesy, Milk Marketing Board

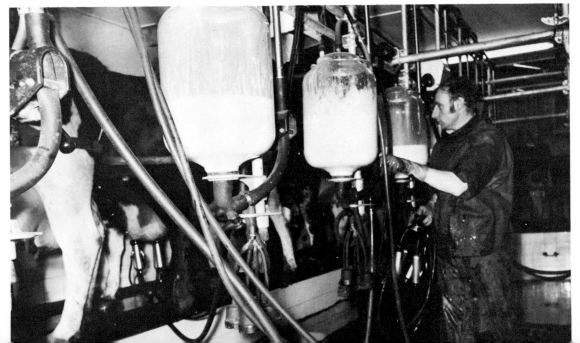

THE DAIRY FARM

Your morning milk was once grass. After eating a quantity, the cows lie down and slowly chew the cud so that it can be easily digested. A cow may eat as much as 150 lb of grass in a day. Half is for her own needs, the rest to make milk.

Milk production is protected by legislation. Ministry of Agriculture officials visit the farms regularly to advise on milk handling and to inspect the cows, dairy buildings and quality of the milk. Here you see an animal being subjected to a test by a veterinary officer.

In the cowshed the udders and teats of the cows must be thoroughly washed before each milking. Automatic machines have now replaced hand milking and these quickly draw off the milk into closed containers, keeping it pure and clean.

The quantity of milk from each cow is carefully recorded and, in the farm dairy (which is quite separate from the cowshed), the warm new milk is strained, run into churns and at once cooled. This picture shows an in-churn cooler.

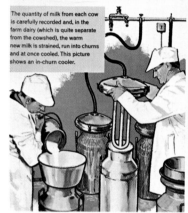

Cleanliness in the farm dairy is of the utmost importance. After milking, the equipment is cleaned with hot water and special detergents and disinfectants. The cowsheds, too, are thoroughly cleaned, ready for the next milking.

The churns are taken to a roadside platform near the farm. Here they wait for the collecting lorry to take them to the milk depot or bottling plant. Washed and sterilised empty churns are returned when the full ones are collected.

FARM TO DOORSTEP

The churns are taken by lorry to a depot or bottling plant. Here the milk is tested for freshness, weighed, and tipped into a large tank. Empty churns are thoroughly cleaned.

Laboratory tests are made at every stage of milk processing to ensure that the milk is pure and clean. Regular tests are also made to check the efficiency and cleanliness of the equipment.

At the country depots milk is cooled and then pumped into large insulated road or rail tankers. These take the milk to bottling plants in the larger towns and cities.

On arrival at the bottling plant the milk is checked by the laboratory staff before being pumped into large tanks. Here it is kept cool until it passes through the pasteurisation plant.

Bottles are thoroughly cleaned in large bottle-washing machines. The clean bottles are then automatically filled with milk in high-speed machines. They are at once sealed with metal-foil caps and transferred to crates.

The crates of milk are loaded on to the delivery vehicles and the milkman makes his regular delivery of milk to homes, schools, hospitals and other establishments.

Courtesy, Milk Marketing Board

MILKY WAY. The Milky Way is a wide, cloudy band of light that shines right across the sky. It can easily be seen on a clear night. Its outlines are very irregular and some parts are much brighter than others. One part near the constellation Southern Cross (see CONSTELLATION and SOUTHERN CROSS) is so black that it is called the Coal Sack.

In 1609 the Italian astronomer Galileo made and used one of the newly invented telescopes. With it he discovered that the Milky Way really consists of many millions of separate stars. To the naked eye it looks like a cloud, because the stars of the Milky Way are so far from us that they cannot be seen distinctly.

Astronomers think that the Milky Way contains 100,000,000,000 stars or more. Our own Sun is one of these (see SUN). The stars of the Milky Way are spread out in a flat disc shaped like a Catherine Wheel. Our Sun, with the Earth and the other planets of the Solar System (see SOLAR SYSTEM), lies out near the edge of the disc. When we look at the disc we see it edge on, which is why it looks like a band of light. The dark parts like the Coal Sack are not gaps between the stars, but vast clouds of dust and gases which hide the light from the stars behind them.

The Milky Way is one of the great groups of stars called galaxies (see GALAXIES). It is sometimes called *the* Galaxy, to distinguish it from the others. Galaxies are so big that astronomers do not measure distances across them in kilometres, but in light-years. A light-year is the distance that light travels in a year, which is about 9,470,000,000,000 kilometres. The Galaxy is over 60,000 light-years across, and the Sun lies about 25,000 light-years from the centre.

MILL, John Stuart (1806–1873). This great British philosopher and economist (see PHILOSOPHY and ECONOMICS) began learning Greek at the age of three and by the time he was eight had read many books in that language.

He was born in London on May 20, 1806, and was the eldest son of James Mill. From a very early age the young John spent most of his time with his father who, being a historian and philosopher, taught John never to accept an idea without first considering all the evidence for and against it. His father also taught him Greek, Latin, philosophy, logic (see LOGIC) and history. As a boy, John's only recreation was going for long walks with his father during which they discussed philosophy.

As John grew up he was greatly influenced by the philosophy of Jeremy Bentham. Bentham belonged to a group of philosophers who were known as the Utilitarians. They believed that a good act was one which gave pleasure, and that the best act was one that gave the greatest pleasure to the most people. Mill accepted these ideas and set them out in an essay called *Utilitarianism*. They were behind his keen interest in politics and made him anxious to improve the conditions in which the working classes lived and worked. These ideas also made him support the demand that women should be educated and that they should have the right to vote.

Although he was not a socialist, Mill was interested in the theories that were then being worked out by the early socialists. (See SOCIALISM.) In his essay *On Liberty* he discussed the question of how much the rights of individual people should be limited by laws.

Mill was member of parliament for Westminster (London) from 1865 to 1868 and was connected with many reforms, some of which made him very unpopular. He was not very keen on party politics, but he generally supported the Liberals. When he was defeated in the general election of 1868 he retired, without regrets. He went to Avignon in southeastern France, where he spent the rest of his life reading, writing and making a study of wild flowers.

MILLET. The group of grain crops known as millets are not so much grown in Europe as they

Millet has been grown by men since prehistoric times.

used to be. In *Grimm's Fairy Tales*, for instance, millet is often mentioned as one of the commonest of the peasants' crops. The common millet, however, is still found in eastern Europe and in Russia, as well as in the Middle East and the United States.

The other important millets are foxtail or Italian millet, grown in parts of Asia; Japanese millet, also grown in Asia; finger millet, grown in India and Africa and given its name because the grain is carried in short, finger-like spikes; bulrush or pearl millet, also grown in India and Africa; and great millet, sometimes called sorghum, which grows in many countries of Africa and Asia. In South Africa it is known as Kaffir corn. (See SORGHUM.)

Millets need a hot growing season, but they ripen very quickly and most of them can be grown in countries which have only a few hot summer months. The great advantage of millets is that they will grow in poor soils and with less rain than any other grain crops. Bulrush millet is one of the crops that can be grown closest to the Sahara desert. Millets do not produce much grain, but they provide some food in places where other crops could hardly be grown at all.

Millets can also be kept longer in store than other crops in hot climates. Finger millet in East Africa can be stored unthreshed in native granaries (grain stores) for up to eight years and still be good to eat. This is of great importance to people who have to lay up a reserve of food in case the rains fail one year.

MILNE, Alan Alexander (1882–1956).
A. A. Milne wrote many different kinds of books and plays, of which one of the most popular was *Mr. Pim Passes By*, but most people think of him first as a writer of children's books. Christopher Robin, his own son, comes into the four best known books. In the first of them, a book of poems called *When We Were Very Young*, Christopher Robin is only about three or four years old. One of the poems is "Vespers", which ends:

> Little Boy kneels at the foot of the bed,
> Droops on the little hands little gold head.
> Hush! Hush! Whisper who dares!
> Christopher Robin is saying his prayers.

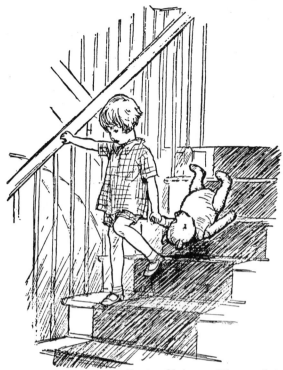

Courtesy, Methuen and Company Ltd.
One of Ernest Shepard's illustrations for *Winnie-the-Pooh*.

In the next poetry book, *Now We Are Six*, Christopher Robin is older.

Winnie-the-Pooh and *The House at Pooh Corner* are story books, in which Christopher Robin's toys come to life. Among them are Eeyore, Kanga, Tigger, Piglet and, chief of all, Winnie-the-Pooh himself, the Bear of Little Brain who was so fond of honey.

After Christopher Robin grew up A. A. Milne did not write any more books for children. He made a play, however, out of parts of Kenneth Grahame's book *The Wind in the Willows*. It is called *Toad of Toad Hall*.

MILNER, ALFRED MILNER, VISCOUNT (1854–1925).
Lord Milner was a statesman devoted to the interests of the British Empire. After experience as a lawyer and journalist he became a civil servant and served in England and Egypt with great ability. In 1897 he became Governor of the Cape Colony and High Commissioner for South Africa. This was not long after the Jameson Raid (see JAMESON RAID) and feelings between British and Boers were still bitter. Milner

concluded that the grievance of the British and other "Uitlanders" who had settled in the Boer republic of the Transvaal must be remedied, by force if necessary. He met Paul Kruger, the President of the Transvaal, to discuss a settlement, but neither would give way and in October 1899 the Boer War began. (See BOER WAR.)

In the war, the Transvaal and the Orange Free State were conquered and Milner became Governor of both of them. Helped by a team of brilliant young men from Oxford University, who became known as "Milner's kindergarten", he did valuable work in building up the two countries after the destruction of the war. Nevertheless, Milner was still determined that the British should control South Africa and he was disappointed when the government decided to grant self-rule to the two countries.

Milner's skill and ability were used by the government to settle difficult questions in World War I. He died of sleeping sickness in 1925.

MILTON, John (1608–1674). John Milton
is usually thought of as the greatest of all English poets except Shakespeare. His most magnificent poem is *Paradise Lost,* which tells the story of God's dealings with mankind, from the creation of the world.

Milton was born in London and went to St. Paul's School, where he was so eager to learn that, he said, "From the twelfth year of my age I scarce ever went to bed before midnight." At 16 he went to Christ's College, Cambridge, and when he left after more than seven years he settled down to continue studying in a Buckinghamshire village called Horton. Already he knew that he wanted to write a great poem and he believed that to do this he must be not only a learned man but also a good one.

Although he was not ready yet to begin his great task, Milton did write other poems while he lived at Horton. Among them were probably "L'Allegro" and "Il Penseroso". "L'Allegro" described the things that a cheerful man likes and "Il Penseroso" the things a serious man likes. Also written at Horton were *Comus,* in praise of purity and beauty, and "Lycidas", a beautiful, sad poem lamenting the death of Edward King, a fellow-student who had been drowned.

An engraving of John Milton made in 1670.

In 1638 Milton went to travel abroad for over a year, mostly in Italy, and when he came home he set up a small school in London. In 1643 he married, but the marriage was not a happy one. A year earlier the Civil War between parliament and the king had broken out, and Milton was a strong supporter of parliament. He wrote many pamphlets attacking those whom he believed to be the enemies of freedom, but his most famous pamphlet, *Areopagitica,* protested against a law which parliament itself had passed. This law said that books must be censored before they were published, and it angered Milton and roused him to plead for freedom to write and to read without restriction.

Under Oliver Cromwell's rule Milton held an important government post, but his eyesight was failing and two years later he was completely blind, his great poem still not written.

Milton's wife died in 1652, and though four years later he married again his happiness was short lived for his new wife died after two years.

In 1663 he married for the third time.

Milton expressed his thoughts about being blind in this sonnet :

> When I consider how my light is spent,
> Ere half my days, in this dark world and wide,
> And that one talent which is death to hide,
> Lodg'd with me useless, though my soul more bent
> To serve therewith my Maker, and present
> My true account, lest he returning chide,
> Doth God exact day-labour, light denied,
> I fondly ask; but patience to prevent
> That murmur, soon replies, God doth not need
> Either man's work or his own gifts, who best
> Bear his milde yoke, they serve him best, his state
> Is kingly. Thousands at his bidding speed
> And post o'er land and ocean without rest.
> They also serve who only stand and wait.

However, blindness and difficulty did not hold Milton back from the masterpiece he had planned for years. He began *Paradise Lost* in earnest in 1658 and by 1665, or perhaps earlier, it was finished. In it Milton told how Satan fell from heaven through pride and then persuaded Adam and Eve to turn away from God too. He described their penitence and how they were shown that, through Christ, God would eventually win men back to Him. It was the noblest subject Milton could find and for it he used an appropriate poetic style, with rich and dignified language. These lines come in Satan's defiant speech when he finds himself in Hell, defeated :

> What though the field be lost?
> All is not lost; the unconquerable will,
> And study of revenge, immortal hate,
> And courage never to submit or yield :
> And what is else not to be overcome?

In contrast is the description of the bower of Adam and Eve in the Garden of Eden :

> Each beauteous flower,
> Iris all hues, roses, and jessamine
> Reared high their flourished heads between, and wrought
> Mosaic; underfoot the violet,
> Crocus, and hyacinth with rich inlay
> Broidered the ground, more coloured than with stone
> Of costliest emblem; other creatures here
> Beast, bird, insect, or worm durst enter none.

After *Paradise Lost* Milton wrote *Paradise Regained*, a shorter poem about Christ's temptation in the wilderness. His last great poem was a tragedy called *Samson Agonistes*, which he modelled on the Greek plays of classical times.

MINCE PIE. Pies filled with mincemeat have been traditional Christmas food in England since at least the 16th century. The early mince pies are supposed to have been made in the form of a hay-rack to represent the manger in which the baby Jesus was laid. In those days the mincemeat inside the pies was a mixture of minced meat, preserved fruits—especially plums—spices and wine. Nowadays lean meat is hardly ever put into mincemeat, although the hard fat known as suet is still used in grated form, while the plums have been replaced by raisins, currants and sultanas. Mincemeat is now made from currants, raisins, sultanas, suet, candied lemon peel, lemon juice, grated apple, brown sugar, mixed spice and nutmeg. Some housewives add a little brandy.

MINE. In war explosive charges called mines are used on land and at sea to blow up the enemy. Early land mines were placed in tunnels dug under enemy positions and these were still used in World War I. In World War II there were two main kinds, *anti-personnel* mines that exploded when a man trod on one and *anti-tank* mines to explode beneath a tank or lorry. The first kind contained a few ounces of explosive and the second ten pounds or more. They were laid, or buried, a few inches below the surface.

The two main kinds of mines used at sea are *moored* and *ground* mines. Moored mines are round or egg-shaped, with spikes or horns sticking out which explode the mine when hit by a ship. The mine is buoyant, but it is moored (anchored) at the right depth below the surface by a strong wire rope fixed to a sinker on the sea bed. The mine and the sinker are laid together and they separate on entering the water. The sinker has wheels so that it can be pushed like a truck along rails on the deck of the minelayer, which is a submarine or surface warship built to lay mines.

Ground mines lie on the bottom of the sea, being laid from submarines or aircraft. When

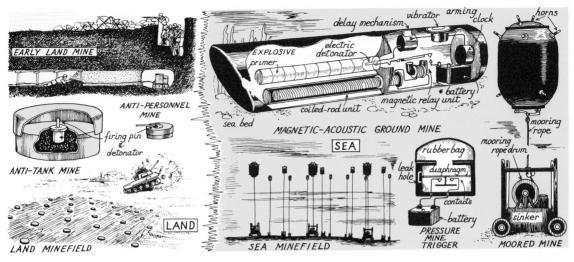

EARLY LAND MINE

ANTI-PERSONNEL MINE

firing pin & detonator

ANTI-TANK MINE

LAND MINEFIELD

LAND

delay mechanism *vibrator* *arming clock* *horns*

EXPLOSIVE *electric detonator* primer

coiled-rod unit *magnetic relay unit* *battery*

sea bed

MAGNETIC-ACOUSTIC GROUND MINE

SEA

leak hole

SEA MINEFIELD

rubber bag *diaphragm* *contacts* *battery*

PRESSURE MINE TRIGGER

mooring rope

mooring rope drum

sinker

MOORED MINE

laid from aircraft they may use parachutes to prevent their falling too fast and breaking up on hitting the water. They are usually cylindrical and may contain 1,000 pounds or more of explosive. Ground mines may either be exploded by the magnetic effect of a ship passing over them or acoustically; that is, by the vibration and noise of the ship's propeller. Some mines are designed so that they are cocked, or made ready, by the ship's noise and exploded by its magnetism. Another type is the pressure mine which depends on the fact that in fairly shallow water the pressure in the water beneath a moving ship is slightly reduced.

The so-called "land mines" which did much damage in air raids on Great Britain in World War II were really large bombs, although they were designed to work as ground mines when dropped in the sea.

Both land and sea mines are often laid as minefields, consisting of a pattern of several rows. To clear a passage through a minefield is slow and dangerous work. Land mines can be found by prodding the ground with a bayonet or spike, or by means of mine detectors which make a buzzing noise in earphones when brought near the metal casing of a mine. Sea minefields are swept, or cleared, by special ships called minesweepers which cut the mooring ropes of moored mines by dragging wires through them. Special machinery for making a loud underwater noise and for creating a powerful magnetic effect is used by mine-sweepers to explode acoustic and magnetic mines. Pressure mines are much more difficult to sweep. Both land and sea mines may contain devices to explode them if they are disturbed, which makes the work of sweeping dangerous.

MINERALS. There are two meanings of the word "mineral". If a mineralogist (a person who studies minerals) uses the word he means a substance that is found in the Earth's crust and that has a definite chemical composition and, usually, a continuous crystal structure (see CRYSTAL). Thus to a mineralogist substances like coal and limestone are not minerals because their composition varies, although they may be formed of individual minerals; but to a mining engineer any substance that is mined is a mineral. The rest of this article is about the kind of minerals studied by a mineralogist. (See COAL; LIMESTONE.)

A distinction must be made between a mineral and a rock. A mineral is different from a rock because its chemical composition is always the same. Specimens of the same kind of mineral always have the same quantities of the same elements, but specimens of the same kind of rock may be made up very differently from one another. Rocks are usually formed of mixtures of several minerals.

Many minerals were originally formed in what are called igneous rocks; that is, the rocks that were solidified from molten magma (a pasty mixture of mineral substances) or lava (see ROCK). The minerals crystallized from the

D. L. Weide, Dept. of Geology, University of California

Most minerals appear in the form of rocks. Quartz, feldspar, biotite and hornblende crystals are present in the piece of granite (top left). A section cut, polished and magnified 1½ × (top right) shows crystals which are pink and white (feldspar), smoky (quartz), black (biotite and hornblende). Below: A thin section magnified 12 × shows quartz (white and grey), feldspar (blue-grey), biotite (green and brown). The brown crystal at the centre is hornblende.

molten mass as it cooled. In this way were formed the micas, feldspars, hornblende and quartz that are found in granite (see MICA; QUARTZ). Other minerals were formed by heat and pressure in metamorphic rocks (the rocks that were changed through the action of great heat and pressure). An example of a metamorphic mineral is garnet, which was produced from shale.

As a result of the erosion, or wearing away, of the igneous rocks, many minerals are not found in their original rocks but in the form of deposits elsewhere (see EROSION). As the rocks are worn away their minerals are freed and particles float away in streams and rivers, forming deposits of sandstone, shale and conglomerates (mixtures)

wherever the water drops the particles. Sandstone, for example, is a collection of particles, mainly of quartz, that have become cemented together (see SANDSTONE).

Other minerals were deposited from solution in veins along cracks in the ground by hot water from cooling rocks. Often they were accompanied by quantities of valuable metals. Stalactites and stalagmites are formed by the depositing (mostly) of calcite (see STALACTITE AND STALAGMITE). When salt water evaporates minerals are deposited in a definite order. First come the calcium and magnesium carbonates to produce beds of limestone, next comes the calcium sulphate, producing gypsum and hydrite, then sodium chloride, producing rock salt, and finally the potassium salts.

Small quantities of foreign matter (substances other than the mineral itself) may sometimes be present in a mineral substance. For example, the brilliant green of the emerald is caused by traces of chromium oxide that have got into the beryl of which the emerald is composed. Marble is often coloured by the presence of foreign matter. Iron salts give the beautiful colourings to ruby and topaz, while manganese colours the amethyst. These foreign substances occur in only very small quantities and change the chemical composition only slightly, but they make marked changes in the colour and appearance of the minerals.

When a mineral forms, the molecules and atoms attract one another along certain definite lines. If there is no interference, the result is a definite, regular form of crystal. (See CRYSTAL.) However, if a magma solidifies in a cramped space, its crystals cannot always take on their regular outward form, although the constant internal form can be discovered by the use of a special petrological microscope.

The crystal form, together with other characteristics such as colour and brightness and the internal crystal structure as discovered by a microscope, help the mineralogist to identify mineral specimens. He sometimes completes the identification by studying characteristics such as hardness, specific gravity (see DENSITY), solubility (ability to be dissolved) and behaviour when heat is applied. If he is still uncertain, a complete chemical analysis must be made, and X-ray equipment is also used to help identification (see X-RAY).

MINERVA was a goddess worshipped in Rome and among several peoples of ancient Italy. She was the goddess of all arts and skills, especially weaving and spinning, and cobblers, carpenters, artists, poets, doctors and schoolmasters all looked to her as their patron. She was the goddess of schoolchildren, too, and on her festival day they had holidays.

People came to think of Minerva as being the same as the Greek goddess Athena, who was also goddess of arts and crafts, and of wisdom. (See ATHENA.)

MINIATURE PAINTING. Miniatures are very small and delicate pictures. The word "miniature" today can mean anything that is unusually small, but when it was first used to describe paintings it had nothing to do with their size, but referred to the kind of paint that was used in them. In Latin this paint was called *minium*, and it was the type of red paint used in the decoration of the manuscripts written in the middle ages. A manuscript often contained little portraits of the patron who was paying for it to be written out, and it was from such portraits that the art of miniature painting grew

Courtesy, Victoria and Albert Museum

"A Lady in a Masque Costume" by Isaac Oliver.

up. However, it only began to be generally practised in England in the 16th century.

Hans Holbein, a German artist who spent some time in England, set the fashion for it and he was followed by Nicholas Hilliard and his pupil Isaac Oliver. They painted beautiful portraits of members of the court of Queen Elizabeth I and of King James I, and also designed the splendid gold settings which sur-

By Gracious Permission (left) of H.M. Queen Elizabeth II; Courtesy, (right) Victoria and Albert Museum

Left: "Mary, Queen of Scots" by the 16th-century French artist François Clouet. François succeeded his father, Jean, as painter at the French court in 1540. Right: "Mrs. Pemberton", by the younger Hans Holbein, is thought to be one of the finest miniatures ever painted. Also 16th-century, it measures only 5 centimetres across.

211

MINIATURE PAINTING

Courtesy, (top and bottom left) Victoria and Albert Museum, (top right) Wallace Collection, (bottom right) Phillip Falk, Esq.

Top left: "Self-portrait" by Thomas Flatman (1635–1688), one of the many English miniatures painted in the 17th century. Top right: "The Painter's Family" by Peter Adolf Hall is an example of the 18th-century continental style. Bottom left: "An Unknown Lady" by Jeremiah Meyer. Right: "Mr. Bigland" by Richard Cosway. Both artists were fashionable in 18th-century England.

rounded the pictures. In these graceful miniatures all the tiny details of the embroidery, lace or jewellery worn by the sitters were shown.

Miniatures were first painted with water colour mixed with gum, on the backs of playing cards or on thin skin (usually chicken skin) stretched over the card. Later they were painted with oil colours on copper, wood, ivory and even marble. A famous painter of miniatures in the 17th century was Samuel Cooper, whose sitters included Oliver Cromwell and Prince Rupert. In the 18th century the artist Richard Cosway painted miniatures on ivory.

Although miniatures in England have almost always been portraits of people, the miniature painting of eastern countries like Persia and India also included illustrations of scenes from books and folk tales, often very beautiful.

212

MINING means the procedures used to extract minerals and other raw materials from the Earth. Only some of the rocks of the Earth's crust contain enough useful minerals to be worth working and these rocks are called *ores*. The quantity of useful mineral in an ore may vary widely. For example, an ore of iron can contain from 20% to 60% of iron while a gold ore often only contains a few parts per million of the precious metal. The main tasks of the mineral engineer are: firstly, prospecting to find a suitable ore; secondly, mining to extract the ore from the Earth's crust; and thirdly, mineral processing to separate the valuable parts from the waste material.

Metallic ores are often found in almost vertical lodes, or veins, that vary in thickness and direction while coal and some other materials, such as rock phosphate, are found in more regular horizontal beds. Iron and copper ores sometimes form big irregular shaped masses that can be many cubic kilometres in size. In the course of geological time the lodes, veins and beds of ore are exposed to wind, frost and rain. They are slowly worn away and the broken fragments are carried down by streams and rivers to form new soft *alluvial* deposits in the river valleys.

In days gone by the prospector was usually a lone individual who searched for mineral deposits with simple tools: he was especially successful in South Africa, North America and Australia. Nowadays, however, prospecting is generally carried out by a team of experts consisting of geochemists, geophysicists, geologists and mineral engineers. A large area is first studied by the examination of aerial photographs and from this study the geologist can select the few best places for further work.

Magnetic ores of iron or nickel can often be detected by a magnetometer, which is an instrument that is sensitive to magnetic fields. This instrument can be carried in an aeroplane, in a helicopter or in a motor car. Some metallic ores are heavier than the surrounding rocks and the greater gravitational pull can be detected by sensitive balances; other ores may be found as a result of their special electrical properties or by measuring the speed at which sound waves pass through them. Radioactive ores can be detected by Geiger counters. (See GEIGER COUNTER.)

Rocks suspected of containing the desired minerals are collected for assaying and testing. If the results of these tests are favourable then samples from deep within the ore body must be obtained by drilling. The boreholes are drilled using a hollow steel rod armed with a diamond cutting edge. A cylindrical core of the rock collects inside the tube and can then be brought to the surface for more intensive testing and analysis.

When a suitable ore body has been found, and it has been shown to be an economic proposition, the ore must be removed from the Earth's crust by mining. Almost three-quarters of all mining operations take place above the ground.

Alluvial and Open-pit Mining

Large amounts of alluvial tin ore in Southeast Asia and Nigeria are mined by dredges which suck or scoop up the sand and gravel from the bed of a river or a large pool. Sometimes powerful jets of water are used to break up the ore in an open pit by a system called hydraulicking. This system is widely used for mining china-clay in Cornwall and rock phosphate in Florida.

Open-pit methods are used when the mineral deposit comes to the surface of the ground as an "outcrop" or lies just beneath the surface. Any soil or "overburden" is removed and then the ore is worked in the manner described in the article QUARRYING. The ore is broken by explosives and loaded into lorries or on to conveyor belts by mechanical diggers.

Underground Mining

The ore body is reached through shafts or adits (tunnels) dug from the surface. Ore at a shallow depth beneath the surface is usually reached by a sloping tunnel but when the ore lies deeply buried it is best reached by a vertical shaft. Such a shaft must be large enough for the miners and their equipment to reach the required depth and must also be used for hoisting the ore to the surface. From the bottom of a shaft a number of horizontal tunnels (or cross-cuts) are cut into the ore. Each crosscut is connected with the ones above and below by further small shafts called raises and winzes. In the ore a

MINING

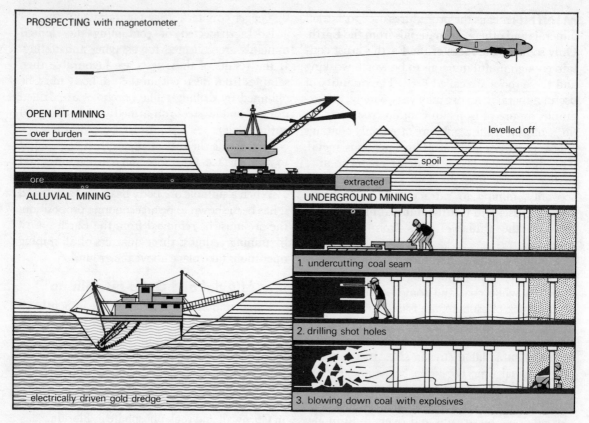

PROSPECTING with magnetometer

OPEN PIT MINING

over burden

levelled off

spoil

ore

extracted

ALLUVIAL MINING

UNDERGROUND MINING

1. undercutting coal seam

2. drilling shot holes

electrically driven gold dredge

3. blowing down coal with explosives

"stope", or working place, is dug out or removed by explosives and the space that is left is supported by timber props or by leaving pillars of unworked ore.

The operation of excavating the ore is called stoping. Holes are drilled into the ore with pneumatic drills: the holes are filled with explosives which, on being fired, bring down a quantity of the ore.

Moving this broken ore from the stope to the surface is one of the major tasks of the mining engineer. This task tends to become more difficult with time since the distance from stope to shaft gradually increases. Ore may be moved up to 10 kilometres before reaching the shaft. Delivering the ore to the shaft bottom is usually done by conveyor belt or in trucks hauled by electric or diesel locomotives. The final stage of a deep-mine haulage operation is to lift the ore up the shaft, sometimes at hoisting speeds as high as 12 to 15 metres a second.

Every deep mine has at least two shafts. Air enters the mine through the "downcast" shaft and is drawn through the mine by fans situated at the top of the "upcast" shaft. This air ventilates the mine and since the rock temperatures slowly increase with depth the air is also often used to cool the mine workings.

In the deepest mines (which are over 3,000 metres deep) the natural rock temperatures often exceed 50°C and the ventilation air has to be cooled by large refrigerators.

Mineral Processing

Very few ores can be used in the form in which they are extracted from the mines. The operations required to prepare an ore for sale are called mineral processing. Firstly the different components of an ore must be freed from each other, generally by breaking the ore into small fragments in crushers and grinding machines. The different minerals are then separated into distinct groups by using differences in the properties of the various groups. These properties include size, shape, colour, density, magnetism and chemical activity.

Since only small fractions of the usual ores are ultimately sold there are large amounts of waste produced from almost all mining operations. Only rarely is it possible to put the waste back into the hole from which it was initially obtained. Great çare is taken to dispose of this waste material in such a way that it is not a danger to health or the environment.

You can read about coal mining in the article COAL. There are separate articles on the important metals and minerals.

MINK.
One of the most prized furs for making coats comes from the mink, a relative of the weasel, which is found in Europe, including

The mink is at home both on land and in the water.

much of Russia, and in North America. Minks are rather like weasels in appearance and have rich brown fur. They spend much of their time in water and live in holes along the banks of brooks and rivers, swimming and diving skilfully to catch shellfish, frogs and fish. Minks are fierce hunters and chase rabbits, mice and rats. Sometimes they climb trees to kill small birds and steal their eggs.

When attacked by other animals, minks fight savagely and also give off a strong and disagreeable smell, like their relatives the skunks. Minks have from four to six young once a year.

The common mink of North America, which has the most valuable fur, is up to 18 inches long, with a bushy, tapering tail about half as long as its body. It has a white patch on the underpart of its jaw and splashes of white on its chest. The European mink is much like the American one, but is smaller and has a white upper lip. It is found in Finland and Poland as well as Russia.

Before mink fur is ready for market, the coarse outer hairs must be pulled out. The farther north minks live, the richer and more shining is their fur. They are specially bred on large mink farms in Canada, the United States and Great Britain. (There is an article FURS.)

MINNOW.
The minnow is a good looking little fish which is a member of the carp family and lives in ponds, lakes and streams where the water is clean and the bottom usually sandy or gravelly. It rarely grows larger than four inches and its body is silvery-fawn, the upper half being much darker. Down its sides the fish has a series of wide vertical lines.

Minnows breed from May to July. At this time of the year the markings are more pronounced and the male fish has white spots on its head. Minnows like to spawn in fairly swiftly moving streams which have a gravel bottom. Large shoals take part in the spawning migration, the males moving upstream before the females. The eggs are sticky and can sometimes be found under stones in small clumps of 10 to 20 eggs. They are also to be found scattered amongst the finer gravel.

Minnows are found all over Great Britain except northern Scotland. They are widely distributed in Europe and are also found in parts of Siberia. They are very useful fish, serving as food for trout, pike and eels. In Germany they are often used to feed trout in fish farms. Fishermen use them as bait to catch other fishes.

Minnows have tiny scales and rather flat, tapering bodies.

MINOTAUR. According to Greek mythology, the Minotaur was a terrible monster, half man and half bull. It was the child of Pasiphaë, the wife of Minos, king of Crete, and to hide it, Minos shut it up in a maze called the Labyrinth. Every year he forced the Athenians to send him seven boys and seven girls who were put into the Labyrinth to starve or be eaten by the monster. In the end the Minotaur was killed by the hero Theseus with the help of Minos' daughter Ariadne. (See THESEUS.)

MINSTREL. In the middle ages bands of musicians travelled the roads. They attended feasts, entertained people at inns and after arriving at a nobleman's castle were often invited to go up into the minstrel's gallery in his hall to play and sing to him and his guests while they ate.

Their favourite instrument was the viol (a stringed instrument played with a bow). They also had tambourines, harps, guitars, bagpipes, horns and trumpets. They sang of ancient heroes like King Arthur as well as ballads about heroes of their own times. They carried news from place to place, and made up ditties about political happenings. It was from a popular minstrel's song that John Ball took his text when he preached at the outbreak of the Peasants' Revolt (see PEASANTS' REVOLT) in 1381 :

> When Adam delved and Eve span,
> Who was then the gentleman?

Kings, great lords and cities kept their own troupes of minstrels, who had a higher position in society than those who served no master and wandered about to find employment. William the Conqueror's chief minstrel, Taillefer, was given the privilege of leading the Norman attack at the Battle of Hastings. Tradition has it that when King Richard the Lion Heart was imprisoned in an Austrian castle on his way back from the Crusades it was his minstrel, Blondel, who discovered where his prison was. Blondel went round the castles and outside them sang a song that he and Richard had composed together. At last when he heard the song being continued from inside a castle he knew that he had found the King.

Minstrels provided amusement in the days when there were no printed books. By the 16th century many of them turned to acting plays and became known as players.

MINUET. From the middle of the 17th century to the end of the 18th century the minuet was a very fashionable dance. It is believed that it was earlier a French country dance, but in 1650 began to be danced in Paris and then at the French court. After that it became extremely dignified with slow movements, elaborate curtseys from the ladies and elegant bows from their partners.

Composers wrote special music for it and then began to include the same kind of music in pieces that were not intended to accompany dancing. Haydn introduced it into his chamber music and symphonies. Beethoven also used it and developed it into the scherzo.

The name "minuet" comes from a French word which is connected with our own word

In noblemen's houses all over Europe, minstrels sang and played their instruments to entertain the guests at table.

"minute", meaning "tiny" or "dainty". The steps of the minuet are in fact dainty, delicate and small.

MIRACLE is the name given to some very unusual happening for which there seems to be no ordinary cause. So, if a dead man suddenly returned to life, a river began to flow backwards or a bird started talking, we should call these things miracles, for they are against the ordinary laws of nature. If we could find a natural explanation, if the man were found merely to have fainted, if an earthquake had altered the bed of the river or if the bird proved merely to be mimicking sounds it heard (as parrots do) and not to be talking sense, we should no longer say that these things were miracles. We had merely *thought* they were miracles because we had not examined them well enough to find out their causes. To be a miracle the event must be something we cannot explain, however hard we try.

Some people, especially those who do not believe in God, claim that miracles cannot happen, because they believe that the laws of nature can never be changed. Therefore they explain some miracles as false stories or as honest mistakes that were made by people who did not understand what they thought they saw. If there seems good evidence that something extraordinary really *did* happen, their explanation would be that it was due to a law of nature we have not yet discovered, just as eclipses (see ECLIPSE) seem to be miracles to those who do not understand how the sun and moon move.

However, those who believe in an almighty God, who Himself has made the laws of nature, do not find difficulty in admitting miracles, for they cannot believe that God is tied down by His own laws. Just as men can, for special purposes, allow exceptions to rules they have made, so can God. If God is really almighty, then He must be able to work miracles if He chooses, and most believers in God think that He sometimes does so. The Christian faith is based upon the miracle of Christ's rising from the dead, and Jews, Moslems and Hindus also believe in miracles, not only in the past but also to-day. (Thus many Christians accept as miracles the sudden cures of serious illnesses at Lourdes in France, when pilgrims go to pray there, for doctors cannot explain some of these cures.)

This does not mean, of course, that a believer in God is bound to accept as true every story of a miracle. Like other people, he will study the evidence and decide whether it is convincing.

MIRAGE. When a traveller in the desert sees what appears to be a shimmering lake, only to find that it vanishes as he draws near, the appearance is called a mirage. Without going to the desert, we can often see what look like pools of water lying on a road in very hot weather, when we know the road must be dry. In other mirages, distant objects are seen distorted, or misshapen, or sometimes upside down.

All mirages are caused by refraction, or the bending of light as it passes from one transparent substance to another. (See REFRACTION.) In

Light from the sky is bent upwards by hot air near the ground. The boy seems to see a shimmering pool of water.

Rays of light from the ship are bent downwards by cold air so that the boy sees an image of the ship in the sky.

air, the refraction depends on the density, or heaviness, of the air. The air near the ground on a sunny day becomes very hot and expands, or swells, and therefore becomes less dense. Rays of light entering this layer of hot, thin air are bent *away from* the Earth's surface, and so what the traveller sees in the desert (or what we see on the road) is really the brightness of the sky. As the layer of hot air is never quite still, the light passing through it shimmers slightly, causing the appearance of ripples.

Another kind of mirage, which is most common in polar regions, is caused by a layer of very cold (and therefore dense) air lying directly above the surface of the sea. Rays of light entering this layer are bent *towards* the Earth's surface, so that distant objects such as ships beyond the horizon come into view. As the layers of cold air are more stable, or still, the images are clean and sharp in contrast to the shimmering images produced with hot rising air. Layers of warmer air above the cold layer may twist the rays of light so that the distant ship or object appears upside down.

These two effects, which are due to the air being heated by the land and cooled by the sea, may be confused. Thus a remarkable mirage is sometimes seen in the Strait of Messina between Italy and Sicily. Distant cottages take the appearance of wondrous fairy castles in the air. This mirage is called the *Fata Morgana*, taking its name from the witch Morgan le Fay who was supposed to cause it by her magic. The famous mirage at Hastings in July 1798, when the whole of the French coast from Calais to Dieppe some 60 to 70 miles away was seen in clear detail for three hours, occurred on a very hot, still afternoon with a relatively cool sea.

MIRROR. Until the 17th century most mirrors were made of a flat sheet of highly polished metal, and mirrors of this kind are still used by people like explorers who need unbreakable ones. Usually, however, mirrors are now made of glass that has been coated with metal on one side to make it reflect whatever is put in front of it. What is known as plate glass (see GLASS-MAKING) is the best for mirrors because it gives the truest reflections.

The mirrors of the ancient Greeks and Romans were usually made of a sheet of bronze that was highly polished on one side and had a design engraved on the other. The Celts of Britain also had metal mirrors, probably having copied those of the Romans. They were used throughout the middle ages, for although people knew how to make glass mirrors—by backing glass with metal—their glass was too impure to give a good reflection.

In the 16th century, however, the Venetians discovered how to make better glass and built up a great industry that exported glass mirrors all over Europe. It was not until the early part of the 17th century that they began to be made in England. In the second half of the century, however, the Duke of Buckingham's factory at Vauxhall, London, became famous for its mirrors. The old method of backing the glass with tin foil and mercury continued to be used until 1835 when J. F. von Liebig, a German chemist, discovered a process known as silvering. This process consists of putting a film of silver on one side of the glass.

Mirrors have three main uses—for looking into, for the decoration of rooms and for optical

Mirrors are usually made of high-quality clear glass. One side of the glass is coated with a thin, smooth coat of highly reflective material. At one time silver and an amalgam of tin and mercury were the only materials used for this purpose. Today aluminium is used on some mirrors. Using vacuum techniques, almost any reflective material can be used to make mirrors.

5th century B.C. Greek mirror
Courtesy The Metropolitan Museum of Art
Gift of J. Pierpont Morgan, 1917

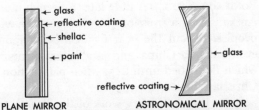

glass
reflective coating
shellac
paint

glass

reflective coating

PLANE MIRROR   ASTRONOMICAL MIRROR

son   daughter   mother

Mirrors reflect light at the same angle at which they receive light. A mother and daughter (above right), who are not standing in front of the mirror and therefore cannot see themselves, can be seen by the son. The diagram (right) shows why this happens. The angle at which light is reflected from the mother to the mirror is equal to the angle at which that light is reflected to the son: $\angle A = \angle A'$. The same is true for the girl's reflection: $\angle B = \angle B'$. The images of all three people appear to be behind the mirror. If the mother is two feet in front of the mirror, her image will appear to be two feet behind the mirror. If the son is eight inches in front of the mirror, he will, in his reflection, appear to be eight inches behind the mirror.

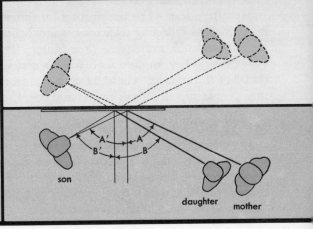

son

daughter   mother

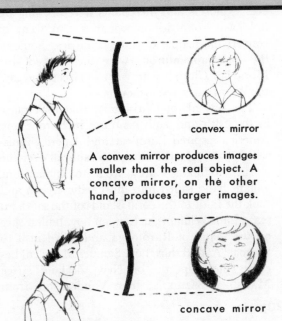

convex mirror

A convex mirror produces images smaller than the real object. A concave mirror, on the other hand, produces larger images.

concave mirror

The great telescope atop Mount Palomar has a 200-inch concave mirror. It was made of 30,000 pounds of glass. The mirror helps astronomers view the extremely distant planets and stars.

instruments such as reflecting telescopes. The old metal mirrors were mainly for looking into and can be compared to the hand-mirror from a woman's dressing table or the small mirror in her handbag. They were often carried on a girdle round the waist or in a pocket. New uses were found for mirrors when the glass mirrors of the 17th century became available. They were put into elaborate frames and were used as much for decoration of the living rooms as for dressing purposes in the bedrooms. During the 18th century mirrors became an outstanding feature of interior decoration.

Their uses for dressing were developed too. Mirrors on swivel-stands that allowed changes of position were introduced, first as separate pieces to stand on a table and then combined with a table to make dressing tables.

Men have learned to use mirrors for instruments such as reflecting telescopes, searchlights, sextants and film projectors. (See LIGHT; REFLECTION.) They are also used for less serious purposes in fun-fairs, where distorting mirrors turn people into all sorts of shapes and sizes!

MISSIONARY. Ever since men followed Christ during His life on earth there have been Christian missionaries, or people who have spread the good news of God. Other great religions have also had their missionaries, especially the religion of the Moslems (see ISLAM).

The book of the Acts of the Apostles in the Bible tells how the first missionaries set out to spread the word of God. St. Paul, the greatest of them, suffered many dangers. He was shipwrecked, imprisoned and finally put to death for his faith. Yet he succeeded in setting up churches all over Asia Minor and in many Greek cities, which in turn sent out their missionaries. (See PAUL, SAINT.) Christianity had spread to most parts of the Roman Empire before the emperor Constantine the Great (311–337) became a Christian, and then it spread even more easily.

Many later missionaries were holy men called monks. In the 5th century St. Patrick took Christianity to Ireland from France and in the 6th century St. Columba carried it from Ireland to western Scotland, where he set up a monastery on the island of Iona. At the end of that century St. Augustine came from Rome to convert the people of southern England. Soon afterwards monks from Iona converted the people of northern England. (See PATRICK, SAINT; COLUMBA, SAINT; AUGUSTINE OF CANTERBURY, SAINT.) By the end of the 7th century the Christian faith had spread all over the British Isles, and Benedictine monks from England were going out to Germany. The greatest of them was St. Boniface, who died a martyr's death. (See BONIFACE, SAINT.) A little later a French monk, Anskar, led a mission to the Scandinavian peoples. About the year 635 Christian monks even went to China and established a mission which flourished until 845, when persecution of Christians began.

Later the missionary work of the church was carried on by friars, rather than by monks, and among the friars the Franciscans and Dominicans did most. (See MONKS AND FRIARS.)

The discovery of "new" countries and of new routes to "old" countries that were made in the 15th and 16th centuries took Europeans to many countries whose people were pagans. (See PAGANS.) It was the members of the Society of Jesus, known as Jesuits, who undertook much of the missionary work in these lands. St. Francis Xavier, one of the Jesuits, travelled to India, Japan and Malaya, while others went to Canada and South America and many other countries. (See JESUITS; XAVIER, SAINT FRANCIS.) Wherever explorers and merchants were opening up unknown countries missionaries also went to convert the people of those countries. Some of the most adventurous were members of the Moravian Church who went to Greenland and the West Indies (see MORAVIANS).

The revivals of Christianity that took place in the 18th and 19th centuries in Europe and America inspired European and American missionaries to take the Christian faith all over the world. William Carey went to India; one gallant band sailed into the Pacific Ocean and took the faith to the coral islands of the southern seas; John Williams, a London boy, built a ship on the island of Rarotonga and sailed in it to Samoa. A Yorkshire boy, Samuel Marsden, became the "apostle of New Zealand" (see MARSDEN, SAMUEL). John Vanderkemp from

Courtesy, London Missionary Society

The death of John Williams on the island of Eromanga, New Hebrides, November 20, 1839—from a 19th-century print.

the Netherlands and John Philip from Aberdeen went to South Africa, where they fought to protect the rights of the African peoples. Two young Welshmen, David Jones and David Griffiths, went to convert the people of Madagascar. By 1807 Christian missionaries had returned to China, where Robert Morrison translated the Bible into Chinese.

Towards the end of the 19th century large numbers of women took up missionary work, especially as nurses and teachers. Mary Slessor, a Scotswoman who went to Nigeria, is among the most famous. (See SLESSOR, MARY.)

Missionaries have always tried to civilize and educate people, as well as to teach Christianity. Some, like Robert Moffat and his famous son-in-law David Livingstone, have also been great travellers and explorers. (See LIVINGSTONE, DAVID.) Pioneer missionaries in Africa include James Mackay and James Hannington in East Africa, George Grenfell in the Congo and Birch Freeman in the Gold Coast, now called Ghana. Others like Albert Schweitzer (see SCHWEITZER, ALBERT) have built hospitals and trained native doctors and nurses. All over the world missionaries were the first to care for people suffering from leprosy. (See DAMIEN, FATHER.)

Other missionaries have been great teachers.

By translating the Bible into native languages they have sometimes been the first people to write down native languages. Wherever they have gone they have set up schools and colleges. William Carey, the 18th-century Baptist missionary, founded a college at Serampore in India.

Missionaries are often discouraged or driven out of some countries but there are enough Christians in those countries to carry on the Christian churches there. Churches in many parts of the world, apart from Europe and the United States, engage actively in missionary work.

MISSISSIPPI–MISSOURI RIVERS. The central trunk of the greatest river system of North America is the Mississippi. Together with its tributaries, this river drains the United States between the Rocky Mountains and the Appalachians. The longest tributary is the Missouri, which comes from the northwest to join the Mississippi just above St. Louis. The Mississippi itself rises in the hills west of Lake Superior and flows south to the Gulf of Mexico. The chief eastern tributary is the Ohio, which rises in the Appalachians and joins the Mississippi at Cairo, below St. Louis.

From the sea to the farthest source of the Missouri is about 6,212 kilometres. This makes the

Mississippi-Missouri among the longest river systems in the world, the Nile and Amazon being even longer.

Although first discovered by Europeans in 1541, the Mississippi was not properly explored until the end of the 17th century. French explorers were then quick to see the importance of the river, which could be used by boats for more than 2,000 miles from its mouth up to the Falls

of St. Anthony near what is now Minneapolis.

Below St. Louis, where great quantities of mud are brought in by the Missouri, the slope of the river is only about an inch in a mile. The valley gets wider and flatter and the river winds slowly through it in huge curves. When swollen by heavy rain or melting snow, the Mississippi overflows its banks and floods wide areas of land. In recent years much has been done to control flooding by building dams and basins to hold back the water in the upper reaches and by building high banks called levees to prevent overflowing. The rich flood-plains of the lower Mississippi have long been used for growing cotton and about 100 miles from its mouth is the great city and port of New Orleans. (See NEW ORLEANS.) Hundreds of millions of tons of mud are brought down the river each year and this has formed a fertile delta where sugar is grown.

After leaving the Rocky Mountains the Missouri flows through prairie country where there are cattle ranches. It then runs through the maize-growing lands known as the "corn belt"

with the great meat-packing towns of Omaha and Kansas City.

The rivers are still used for the transport of heavy cargoes, which are carried in large barges pushed by powerful diesel-engined tow-boats. In the old days there were many passenger steamers on the Mississippi and even "show-boats" that went from place to place to give theatrical shows. The American writer Mark Twain spent his boyhood at Hannibal on the Mississippi and his book *The Adventures of Huckleberry Finn* gives a wonderful idea of the mighty river.

MISTLETOE. The mistletoe is an evergreen bush, pale green in colour, with thick and leathery leaves that grow in pairs. It is what is known as a parasite, which means that it lives on other plants, which are then known as hosts. The most usual host of the English mistletoe is the apple tree, but it also grows on the hawthorn, poplar, willow, lime, mountain ash, maple and —very rarely—on the oak.

The mistletoe flowers come out in February and March and are small and yellowish. They grow in groups of three, the males on one plant and the females on another. The white berries, which are attractive to birds, are filled with a sticky pulp, so a bird, after eating one, wipes its

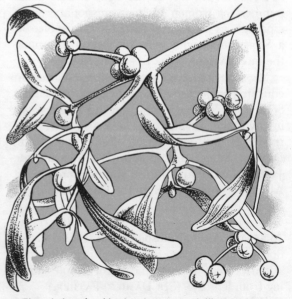

The mistletoe's white berries are much liked by birds.

beak on the tree and leaves the seeds in cracks in the bark. They then send out sucker roots which grow through the bark. Mistletoe draws some, but not all, of its nourishment from the tree on which it grows and generally dies at the same time as its host.

There are many superstitions and legends about the mistletoe. One is that it will bring happiness, safety and good fortune as long as it does not touch the ground. This is probably why it is hung up in English homes at Christmas time and is supposed to bring luck to those who kiss under it.

The Druids, who were the priests of the Celts of Britain and Gaul, are said to have worshipped the oak and when they found mistletoe growing on it they thought it must have great powers.

MITE. The mites are arachnids, which means that they are related to spiders and are not insects. Only recently have scientists begun to understand the importance of mites, and perhaps the reason for this is that they are very small, the largest being no more than 1/25 of an inch long, while the smallest are invisible to the naked eye.

For the most part, mites have a rounded body on which are a number of long bristles. There is little sign of a head, though they have sucking mouth-parts. Some have eyes, others are blind. Like spiders, mites have four pairs of legs. The young mite is called a nymph, and has only three pairs of legs when it hatches. It moults several times while it is growing and by the time it is adult it has four pairs of legs.

There are enormous numbers of different kinds of mites all over the world, and they feed upon almost every kind of food. Many of them are parasites—that is, they live on another creature—and some of these cause diseases. Some live in fresh water, and a few in the sea.

The larger relation of the mite is the tick, which is a parasite found on such animals as dogs and sheep. (See Tick.) The cheese-mite can be seen with a magnifying-glass on an old cheese. The snout-mites, with a false head or snout, live in cold, damp places under moss or decaying wood.

The spinning-mites produce silk from their mouths, and the red spider, which sometimes covers whole bushes or the trunks of trees with a glistening web of silk, is one of them. The harvest-bug is the nymph of a spinning-mite.

MITHRAS. Most people think of Mithras as the god of the Roman soldiers, probably from reading about him in *Puck of Pook's Hill*, Kipling's story of a boy and girl who are carried back to the 4th century A.D. and make friends with one of the Roman soldiers guarding Hadrian's Wall. This soldier worships Mithras.

Mithras, god of the morning, our trumpets waken the Wall!
"Rome is above the nations, but thou art over all!"

The worship of Mithras started in the Middle East, especially in Persia and Babylon, long before the 4th century A.D. In Persia, where his worship was strongest, he was regarded as the god of light and truth, and also as the supporter of armies and the guardian of crops. In the West, people of the Roman Empire began to worship him about 2,000 years ago but his worship did not become widespread until the 2nd century A.D. It appealed to soldiers because it emphasized the virtues of courage and fidelity, and to merchants because of its emphasis on honesty and the need to keep one's word. Soldiers and merchants spread Mithraism throughout the Roman Empire. Two well-preserved Mithraic temples have been found in England in recent years. One was excavated in 1951 outside the fort of Carrawburgh near Hexham on the Roman Wall. It still contained the original statues and altars (just as they had been left by the Roman soldiers), as well as remains of the wooden stalls where the congregation sat. In 1954 a temple was found near Cannon Street Station, London. Excavation showed that it had been dismantled and its statues buried under the floor—probably when Christianity was declared the official Roman religion by the Emperor Constantine in the early years of the 4th century A.D. The statues are now in the Guildhall Museum, London.

After this triumph of Christianity, Mithras and the other pagan religions of the time gradually disappeared.

MOBILE.

A mobile is really a piece of sculpture made of flat shapes joined by wires; it hangs from the ceiling and moves round as it is blown by a draught of air. Mobiles were invented by an American sculptor, Alexander Calder, who started to make them soon after 1930. They are generally made out of wire and metal, card, glass or wood, and are so delicately balanced that they revolve in the air. This is rather like a piece of sculpture coming to life and as it moves creating new shapes and patterns. Mobiles have been made to represent fishes or to suggest birds in flight, while others are just pleasing shapes.

You can make a mobile out of stiff cardboard and wire. The wire should be galvanized and strong enough to be springy, so that it keeps its shape when bent, but not too thick to bend by hand.

First, cut a sheet of stiff card into interesting shapes and sizes, all of which should have some family likeness. Circles, ovals and triangles are good shapes to use. Then cut or punch a small hole near the edge at a point vertically above the centre of gravity, so that the shapes will hang straight. This hole is used to fix the shapes to the wire bars. (To find the centre of gravity, let the shape hang freely from a pin. Hang a piece of cotton with a weight on the end from the pin and mark the line of this across the shape. Repeat this by suspending the shape from any other point near its edge. Where the two lines cross is the centre of gravity.)

Cut a piece of wire for the lowest bar, about eight inches long. It looks more attractive if it is gently bent into a curve. Care is needed because wire, once it is bent too sharply, cannot be straightened again. Now bend each end of the wire with pliers to form two small loops and hang the card shapes from these loops by nylon thread. The shapes should hang freely below the wire bar. Make the lowest bar of the mobile first and put a loop in the wire bar to join it to the bar above. This loop must be at the centre of gravity of the bar, which can be discovered by hanging the bar from a loop of thread. Make a mark at the point where the bar hangs level. Then with the pliers make a loop by bending one arm through a full circle.

Make the next arm in the same way and add a cardboard shape to one end. The other end is joined to the loop of the lower arm either by a piece of hooked wire or by nylon thread if you want the arms to move independently. Go on building up the mobile in this way until the final arm is added. This is made in the same way as the others except for attaching the cardboard shape, in which you have to punch two holes close to each other. Thread the wire through both holes and then bend it back. This fixes the shape firmly to the arm and acts as a rudder for the whole mobile. This rudder need not be the top shape but it is often easier to leave it until last.

When the mobile is finished and hangs evenly you can paint it. Black, with a few shapes painted in bright colours, looks very effective. The colours should be carefully thought out, as in a picture. Bright colours look more attractive than soft pastel shades. When painted, the mobile can be hung from a hook so that it turns with every breath of air.

Mobiles are among the most interesting forms of modern sculpture and are taken seriously by artists. One of Calder's best-known mobiles, "Lobster Trap and Fish Tail", hangs in the Museum of Modern Art in New York. Most of his mobiles have as their subject nature in movement; some include representations of trees and snow. In the history of sculpture there is no more direct or poetic expression of nature's rhythm.

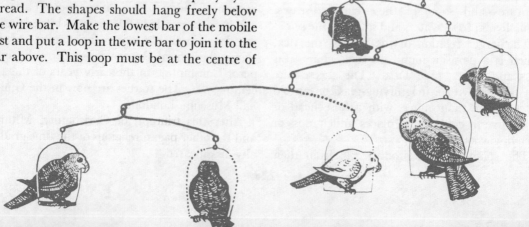

MOCKING BIRD. The mocking bird of America was given its name because it imitates the songs and notes of other birds. ("Imitate" is one meaning of the word "mock".) Some mocking birds can perfectly imitate the song of the bluebird, the call of the bird known from its cry as the whippoorwill, the scream of the jay and even the call of the eagle.

The mocking bird is found all over the United States and as far south as Mexico. It belongs to a family of American birds which includes the thrashers. It is rather like a thrush in appearance. It is dull-coloured, being ash-grey above and dirty white below with a black tail edged with white. The cock and hen are much alike and are 9 to 11 inches long.

Besides its power of mimicking other birds, the mocking bird has a fine song of its own. It is an attractive and lively bird, haunting gardens and parks and even the streets of towns. The nest, which is large and untidy, is made of twigs, leaves and roots and is built in a bush or a low tree. The hen bird lays three to six eggs, often bluish-green speckled with brown, but varying in colour.

MODEL AEROPLANES. The making of model aeroplanes, or aeromodelling as it is sometimes called, is closely linked with the design of full-size aircraft. The founders of several well-known firms in the aircraft industry started by building and flying models, and it is agreed by experts that the hobby provides an excellent grounding in the principles of flight. Models are often used by aircraft designers to try out new ideas or to show the working of them, and although the detailed requirements of model and full-size aircraft differ widely, the basic principles on which they work are the same.

Aeromodelling is an excellent hobby for the boy or girl who likes making things, and is one that can be enjoyed both in and out of doors. It teaches the modeller how to read and understand working drawings and gives training in the correct use of a wide range of materials. Patience and the ability to accept disappointment are needed as well as craftsmanship, for even the best flier sometimes suffers damage to his models or loses them.

Since 1903, when the first successful aero-

Courtesy, R. G. Moulton

A simple control line trainer for engines of up to 1 cc is the "Kitty Wasp" (top). Below it is a perfect scale model of a Grumman Baby veteran sailplane built from a kit.

plane flight was made, tremendous progress has been made in the design of aircraft. The advance in aeromodelling materials and methods has been almost as great. Early modellers had to make do with materials which were often unsuitable but today there is a special industry to supply their needs. Prefabricated kits (sets of finished parts) can be bought which include everything needed to make a model aeroplane, and all the modeller has to do is to put the various parts together correctly.

The introduction of balsa wood in the early 1930s was an important event in the history of aeromodelling. The extreme lightness of this wood and the ease with which it can be shaped make it ideal for modelling. Thus it soon took the place of the heavier materials which had previously been used. (See BALSA.) Models used to be made from ash, spruce or cane which were used in the early full-size aeroplanes, and the fact that such models flew at all is a tribute to the skill of the modellers.

There are many types of model aircraft, but the beginner will find it best to start with the simplest type of all, which is the hand-launched

☐ Read about BUILDING A MODEL ORNITHOPTER in the blue pages of volume I

glider made of sheet balsa. The parts are shaped to outline, leaving them a little oversize, and then smoothed down with sandpaper to the correct size.

One of these small models can be made in an hour or two and gives practice in the shaping and joining of materials. This experience is valuable when tackling more difficult models. Very fine sandpaper is used to produce a smooth finish, which is preserved by coating the wood with "dope". Dope is a general term for a liquid substance which dries quickly to leave a thin protective film. This proofs the surface against damp and keeps it smooth.

The finished glider may not look very remarkable but it will be found to fly for well over a minute in suitable conditions. At this stage, long flights are not the aim, but the making and flying of a simple glider model can teach the beginner about the conditions which control flight.

Next come the general-purpose and high-performance types of glider better known as sailplanes. In some cases these are made with solid wooden fuselages (bodies) but the wing, tailplane and fin are built up. A number of thin wooden spars (strips) run from end to end and specially shaped ribs are spaced out along them, using a blunt leading (front) spar and a sharp trailing (rear) edge to give the correct "wing section" or aerofoil. This built-up method gives much lighter models than the use of solid balsa. The whole framework is covered either with strong tissue paper or lightweight silk. Finally, one or two coats of dope are applied. These not only strengthen the fabric and make it waterproof but also cause it to shrink so that it is tightly stretched.

Sailplanes may be made very big and models with a wing span (width) of 3 to 4·5 metres are quite common, but the usual span is about 1·5 metres. Such models can fly for several minutes and the world record for model sailplanes is more than 12 hours. To make these long flights, however, the model needs to meet the up-currents of air called "thermals" (see GLIDING).

Another type of model aircraft has the general features of the sailplane but is driven through the air by a propeller, or airscrew as it should

The Aeromodeller

This lightweight model plane, powered by a very small internal combustion engine, is designed for free flight.

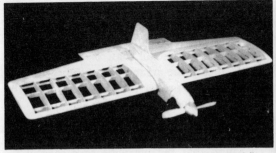

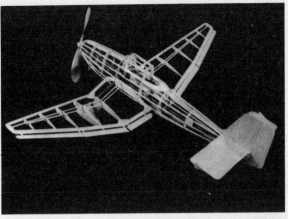

The Aeromodeller

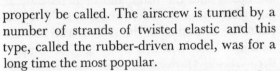

Above: Framework of a power-driven "flying wing". In flight this model will be controlled by two thin lines. Right: Framework of a Stuka dive bomber. This rubber-driven model can be built from an inexpensive kit.

properly be called. The airscrew is turned by a number of strands of twisted elastic and this type, called the rubber-driven model, was for a long time the most popular.

Another type of model aeroplane which has become very popular since World War II is the power-driven model, in which a small internal combustion engine takes the place of the rubber motor. These tiny engines, with cylinders as small as a thimble, develop surprising power.

The development of these engines has made much longer flights possible and has brought about great changes in the hobby. Most of the models seen on any flying field are power-driven.

There are several ways of flying power-driven models, ranging from simple free flight to control-line flying, in which the model is attached to two thin lines and answers the control of the pilot on the ground. Speed flying is a further development of the control-line machine and speeds of well over 280 kilometres an hour are quite common with expert fliers.

Power-driven models can also be controlled by radio. The degree of control can range from movement of the rudder only to a system giving proportional control of ailerons, elevators, flaps, rudder, undercarriage and engine through movement of sticks on the radio transmitter. Some of these models have exceeded 300 kilometres an hour; others have reached 6,500 metres; and the duration record for a radio-controlled glider is over 15 hours. These advanced methods have introduced new attitudes to the hobby, particularly since the model may be carrying equipment costing up to £200.

Another interest centres on the highly detailed exact-scale models made possible by reliable radio control. One development of the scale model is the "pylon racer". This class involves up to four realistic models racing round a triangular course at over 160 kilometres an hour. Strict specifications and standard fuels ensure that competitors are closely matched.

Another form of radio-controlled model is the slope-soaring glider which rides the up-currents on the windward side of a steep hill. Simple rudder-only controlled gliders can soar for hours.

The model aircraft movement in Britain is controlled by the Society of Model Aeronautical Engineers based in London, which arranges contests and organizes clubs. There are a large number of aeromodelling clubs and the beginner is advised to join one in his district, for much can be learned from the more experienced members.

MODEL BOATS. One of the earliest model boats known was found in an Egyptian tomb about 4,000 years old. The ancient Egyptians believed that the spirit of a dead person needed help in crossing the Nile River so they buried "spirit ships" in the tombs. In the middle ages ship models were often hung in churches as thanksgiving offerings from sailors. One of the oldest of these, dating from about 1450, was found in a church at Mataro near Barcelona (Spain). These church models, although sometimes not true to scale, give a lot of useful information about old ships. A model is "true to scale" if each part of it is reduced to the same extent compared with a real ship. Thus if the real ship is 350 feet long and has a beam (width) of 35 feet, a model built to the scale of one-hundredth must be not only 3 feet 6 inches long but must have a beam of just over 4 inches.

In 1607 the famous Elizabethan shipbuilder Phineas Pett made a toy ship for Prince Henry, and later he made another for Prince Charles, aged four. It was originally mounted on a "carriage with wheels resembling the sea" and can be seen in the Ashmolean Museum at Oxford. Samuel Pepys, who was Secretary to the Admiralty and about whom there is a separate article, had a whole collection of models illustrating ship construction and design. Many models from 1660 onwards have been kept and are to be seen in museums, a very fine collection being in the National Maritime Museum at Greenwich, near London.

Model Yachts

Yachting was introduced into England in the reign of King Charles II and soon became popular with the wealthy. Then model yachts were made and races were sailed between them, not only by young people but also by grown-ups. The early model yachts were just like the real ones but after a while it was found that if a model were built true to scale it was top-heavy and floated too deep in the water. To overcome this, the underwater body must be made rather fuller, or fatter, than that in the full-sized craft,

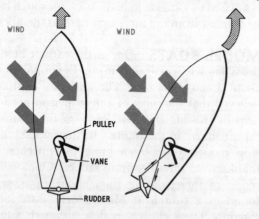

The vane steering gear is set so that the vane points directly into the wind when the model boat is on course. If the boat strays off its course, the wind will turn the vane and this will automatically put the rudder over until the boat is heading in the right direction once more.

and the ballast in the form of a lead keel must be carried as low down as possible.

The development of the aeroplane has had a great effect on the sail plan of the yacht, by which is meant the arrangement and size of the sails. The sails propel the yacht in much the same way as the wing lifts the aeroplane. By studying the air-flow over aeroplane wings and applying the results to the sails of a yacht, it has been found that the big wide sails carried by yachts of the early 20th century are not the best. By making the sails tall and narrow, the yacht will sail faster to windward (that is, when pointing nearly into the wind) and be practically as fast when running before the wind. This has led to the discarding of the gaff rig with its huge topsail and long bowsprit in favour of the simpler Bermuda or Marconi rig with tall narrow triangular sails. (See SAILING.)

Model yacht clubs have their sailing lakes in most cities and large towns. For racing, model yachts are divided into classes as follows: 36-inch Restricted Class, 50-inch Marblehead Class, 10-rater Class (about 6 feet long) and "A" Class (about 7 feet). Far the most popular is the Marblehead. The "A" Class, weighing 50 to 80 pounds and standing some 9 feet out of the water, are too big and powerful to be handled by children. Recent developments include radio control in yachts of 36 inches or longer, and multihulled racing with catamarans and trimarans. (See CATAMARAN.) There are published designs for all classes and for smaller models, though anything less than 24 inches long cannot be expected to sail really well. Much can be learned, however, from even the smallest and simplest model if it is properly designed. The Model Yacht Association controls racing in Britain.

Model Power Craft

Before about 1920, nearly all model steamers and power boats were driven by steam engines or electric motors, but since that date miniature internal combustion engines have become increasingly popular.

To make a fair-sized model of an ocean liner or large warship the scale must be very small, and although such a model may look well on the water the details and fittings are so fragile that they suffer badly when the model is handled at the pond-side. Therefore the smaller ships are a better choice for modelling, as the scale reduction is less for a model of any chosen size. Also, the hull shape of a small ship is more suitable for modelling because the beam and depth are greater, as compared with the length, than they are in a big ship. Even so, it is sometimes advisable to increase the beam or depth (or both) of a working model above true-scale size. Naval destroyers are popular with model-makers because of their high speed and bold appearance, but they are so narrow and of such shallow draught that a true-scale model would be quite unstable. However, the model will look all right if the extra beam and depth are added carefully.

Good subjects for modelling are small cargo vessels, cross-Channel steamers, coasters, tugs and trawlers. When it is driven by a petrol or diesel engine a model of this kind looks and

A model boat on the Round Pond in Kensington Gardens.

sounds like the real thing on the water, especially if lit up inside with small electric bulbs.

Most model power boats nowadays are radio-controlled and designed either for high speed or accurate steering and not intended to look like full-sized boats. In competitions, speed events are held over triangular courses and steering events over courses marked by buoys laid out in tricky patterns. Other contests for radio-controlled models include balloon-bursting competitions, offshore racing in the open sea, and

endurance racing aimed at covering the greatest number of laps of a course in a given time. The sport is controlled in Britain by the Model Power Boat Association.

Non-working models, which are not designed to float but are accurate representations of full-sized ships, attract many people. They may be full-hull models or modelled only above the waterline, and can be anything from an inch to several feet long. The larger the model, the more detail must be included. With very small models, much detail can be omitted to leave an instantly recognizable ship if the work is skilfully done.

MODELLING AND CASTING. The art of making things with clay by moulding it into shapes is called modelling. While clay is damp it is soft and pliable and can easily be shaped either with the hands or with simple tools, but when it dries it becomes hard and solid. When an article has been modelled out of clay, it is first left to dry naturally and then put into a kiln, which is a special kind of oven that can be heated to a very high temperature, where it is "fired", or baked, until it is thoroughly hard. Articles that are going to be fired have to be made hollow, or else they would crack during the firing. Bowls and jars, therefore, are good things to make by modelling, and it is also possible to make a model of the head of a person or an animal as long as it is left hollow inside.

There is another rather different way of using clay, however, and this is for making objects that are to be "cast" into some more permanent material such as plaster or metal. Suppose an artist wants to make a plaster model—or plaster cast, as it is called—of a horse. First he makes a model of the horse out of solid clay, shaping it just as he wants his finished cast to be. Next he makes a solid mould round the clay model (there are several methods of doing this that he can choose from) and when this is done he takes the clay out from inside and pours the liquid plaster into the mould. It fills up the space where the clay had been, and when it has set hard the mould is taken off it, leaving a plaster cast exactly like the original clay model.

Casting from a clay model in this way is quite a complicated process, but you will find a

☐ Read about MAKING A MODEL CATAMARAN in the blue pages of volume 17

description of some of the ways it can be done farther on in this article. There is a different type of plaster casting, however, which is much simpler, and instructions for it are given in the article PLASTER CASTING.

Modelling

One of the traditional methods of modelling a hollow object with clay is by *coiling*. It consists of rolling the clay into long "snakes" with the palms of the hands and then coiling them round on top of each other like a rope, building up the model from the bottom section by section. As each coil is placed on the top of the one before, the clay is firmly pressed together to form one piece. The coiling method is a simple one to use for making a round bowl or jar, but making something as complicated as a model of a head or figure requires considerable skill. Each section has to be made as accurately as possible because the clay dries quickly when it is used in this way, and does not leave much time for alterations.

However, if an artist is modelling a portrait of someone's head, he wants all the details to be accurate and so needs more time for alterations. Instead of coiling the clay he can use a method

Keystone

Modelling a head at the Slade School of Fine Arts, London.

like the one used by the great Italian sculptors of the 15th and 16th centuries. First of all a wooden post is made in the shape of a dunce's cap upside down—about 5 centimetres across at the top, tapering down to about 1 centimetre

at the bottom. The post is fastened to a board with a nail and then a length of cord or thin rope is wound round the post to form the rough shape of the head. Then the clay is put on and shaped over the rope, which forms a foundation for it, and when the model of the head is completed it is left until it is firm but not dry. Finally the post is taken off the board and withdrawn from the middle of the coil of rope, and the rope is pulled out to leave the clay head hollow. The head is then dried thoroughly before being fired in a kiln.

The tools used in modelling are simple polished wooden sticks, some flat and some round, and other tools with stiff wire ends for cutting the clay. Most of the moulding and shaping, however, is done with the flat of the hand and the thumb. The artist can produce a great variety of rough and smooth surfaces in the clay according to how he works it into the shape he wants.

Casting

When a clay model is to be used as a base for casting in plaster or metal, it is made solid and not hollow and it has to have a strong support inside it to hold the weight of the clay. This support is called an armature and it is usually constructed of wood and lead piping. Lead is used because it will bend, and the armature is bent so that it is exactly the right shape for the figure—of a head, for example, or a man on a horse—that the artist is planning. The clay is put on over the armature and gradually the complete clay model is built up.

It is then that the process of casting itself begins, with the making of a solid mould round the clay. There are several ways of doing this, one of which is glue moulding.

The clay model is covered first with a layer of paper and next with a layer of fresh clay about 2 centimetres thick. An outer "shell" of plaster is then put over this, made in several sections so that it can easily be taken apart and put together again. This is very important because when the plaster has set hard it is taken apart and the layers of clay and paper are removed from the model. The next step is to put back the plaster shell round the model, and this

□ Read about WORKING WITH CLAY in the blue pages of volume 5

time there is an empty space all round between the model and the shell where the layers of clay and paper were before. Into this empty space is poured special melted "casting glue" or gelatine, through a hole in the top of the plaster shell; after a time the glue sets hard, and then the clay is removed from inside it. The solid glue has formed a mould in the shape of the clay model, and is ready for the wet plaster to be poured into it and left to set. Finally, when the plaster is hard, the mould is taken apart once more to free the finished article. The mould can afterwards be cleaned and used again to make more casts.

Another method of making a mould for a plaster cast is called waste-moulding, because the mould can only be used once. A layer of coloured plaster is put all over the clay model— the artist splatters it on with his fingers—and then a second layer of white plaster goes over this. This outer case, like the one for glue mould-ing, is made with sections so that it can be taken apart after it has set. By this method, however, it is the plaster shell itself that forms the mould : when the clay has been removed from inside it, it is put firmly together again and wet plaster is poured into it through a hole in the top. After this plaster inside has set comes the process of taking off the outer shell. The artist chips off the white outer layer with a chisel and so gets down to the layer of coloured plaster, and this warns him that he must go carefully because he is nearing the cast itself. He then gently chips away the coloured layer and so reveals the finished cast.

Casting a clay model into metal such as bronze is a different process and it can be done only by professional bronze-casters.

MODEL RAILWAYS.
Great Britain led the way in making railways early in the 19th century and also led the way with model railways, al-though these did not become really popular until about 1905.

In the early days, people wanting a model rail-way usually had to build most of it themselves, especially if they wanted one that looked any-thing like the real thing. In the early part of the 20th century, models made in Germany became popular as they were cheap and ran quite well,

although they were rather "tinny" and did not look very real. After World War I British manu-facturers made a great effort to supply the de-mand and by the 1930s really first-class model railways could be bought at a reasonable price.

Before going further it is important to under-stand the word "scale" as used in modelling work. Without a definite scale no true model of anything can be made. Suppose a model of a railway coach is to be made. Measurement of the full-sized coach might show it to be 60 feet long. If it were decided to make the model to a scale of 1 inch to the foot, then everything a foot long on the real coach would be an inch long on the model. Therefore the model coach would be 60 *inches* long. Actually, a scale of 1 inch to the foot is far too big and model railways are generally built on a much smaller scale.

Before World War II the popular scales were those known as Gauge 1 and Gauge 0. The *gauge* of a railway is the distance between the running rails of the lines, being 4 feet $8\frac{1}{2}$ inches in Great Britain and many other countries. Gauge 1, which measures $1\frac{3}{4}$ inches between the rails, is the name given to model railways built to a scale of 10 millimetres to the foot. The slightly smaller Gauge 0, measuring $1\frac{1}{4}$ inches, is to a scale of 7 millimetres to the foot.

However, even a Gauge 0 railway proved too large for most people. Unless it could be laid in a loft or a shed or in a room not wanted for any-thing else, a model of this kind generally had to be put together each time it was wanted and taken to pieces afterwards. The answer was to make models on an even smaller scale, and in the 1930s Gauge 00 was introduced. This is to a scale of 4 millimetres to the foot, with a distance between the rails of $16\frac{1}{2}$ millimetres. On this scale a 60-foot coach becomes 240 milli-metres ($9\frac{1}{2}$ inches) long.

Gauge 00 is still the most popular size and everything for a complete model railway can be bought on this scale. The locomotives are driven by electricity through a controller which allows the operator to start, stop and alter the speed of the train without touching anything on the track. In the late 1950s Gauge TT was introduced, with a scale of 3 millimetres to the foot, but failed to win much support. However, the even smaller

N Gauge, on a scale of 2 millimetres to the foot, was introduced in 1965 and became quite popular. On this, the 60-foot coach becomes 120 millimetres ($4\frac{3}{4}$ inches) long.

The fairground and other railways that carry passengers on a gauge of up to 2 feet are not strictly model railways but miniature ones. They require professional engineers and staff to operate them.

Making a Model Railway

Most boys begin with a train set, having a circle of rails, an engine and a few coaches or wagons. The lengths of track can be clipped together and the circle is usually laid on the floor. As more track and equipment are bought it is better to mount it all on a *baseboard* which can be stood against the wall when not in use. The simplest baseboard is the material chipboard sold by timber merchants. It is possible to have two boards, hinged so that they fold against one another, but it is then necessary to remove some of the taller fixed equipment before folding. The ideal to aim at is to have the baseboard supported on legs and erected permanently in a room, loft or garden shed.

The kind of railway built depends on personal taste, but it is advisable to think about this before buying too much equipment. Does the owner want a system representing the modern British Rail, or something recalling the age of steam? Again, some boys like to have crack expresses running from a large terminus, while others prefer a quiet branch line winding through picturesque scenery with hills, tunnels and rivers. Whatever the aim, the main thing is to have a clear picture of what you want and to plan it thoroughly before building it.

When a line has beeen planned a choice must be made of the kind of track and points to be used. The orginal track of the train set is still suitable, although the curves are rather sharp. For a permanent layout built on a baseboard it is better to buy flexible track, which can be bent to any shape without the need for sharp curves.

Its metal rails are fixed to a special fibrecard base which, when cut with a sharp knife, allows the rails to be bent into a smooth even curve.

Philip J. Kelley

Station and locomotive yard on a Gauge 00 model railway. This layout is designed to be operated to a timetable.

Track laying is only the beginning of what is for many people the most delightful of all hobbies. There are stations to be bought or built; as well as signals, signal cabins and the dozens of things seen on the real railways. It is surprising what can be done with cardboard!

MODEL THEATRE.

The model theatre was one of the most popular toys in England during the 19th century. Children had probably been making models of real theatres—as they still do today—ever since the first theatre was built; but in about 1811 an organized trade grew up and toy theatres complete with the plays to act on them appeared for sale in the shops. They did not really begin as toys, however, for the things that were sold at first were "souvenir" sheets of pictures of the popular actors of the day, dressed in the costumes of their favourite parts—rather as photographs of film stars are sold today.

At this time there was of course no cinema, radio or television and the theatre was a popular entertainment with everyone. Children of ten years and upwards, especially boys, often went to the theatre and enthusiastically followed the new dramas and the favourite stars. The souvenir sheets of actors and actresses soon grew more and more detailed, until children could buy pictures of figures for every important new play, showing all the characters in all their different costumes and sometimes in various attitudes as well. Sheets of miniature scenery and of the "stage fronts" of the big London theatres were also published.

The sheets were sold for "a penny plain, or twopence coloured"—and this phrase became so well known that it is often quoted. Robert Louis Stevenson described them in one of his essays. The "twopence coloured" sheets were painted by hand in wonderfully bright colours, but most children bought their plays "plain" and painted the sheets at home. The sheets had to be stuck on to cardboard and the figures cut out with a pair of scissors, and then the characters were clipped on to strips of tin or wood by which they could be slid on to the stage and moved about. Finally a model stage was set up and then the play could be performed in the drawing-room or nursery with the children speaking the parts. The juvenile drama, as it was called, flourished for more than 50 years and 300 different plays were adapted for toy theatre performances. The plays became more and more complicated until sometimes 20 or more sheets were needed for a complete production. Even at a penny a sheet this made plays quite expensive, and so after about 1830 most of the publishers reduced their prices to a halfpenny plain and a penny coloured. This meant that the quality of the pictures, which had often been beautifully drawn and printed, was less good.

Every play published was a faithful adaptation of a play actually performed on the London stage, and the toy theatre plays are now of very great historical interest, because they have preserved in their sheets the costumes and scenery of many old plays that are now quite forgotten. The sheets of the early publishers are very rare and there are collections of them in the British Museum and the London Museum.

By the end of the 19th century the toy theatre had nearly disappeared, for the sheets had become poorly printed and the plays, which had been the same since the toy theatre first became popular, now seemed out of date and old-fashioned. Most of the firms making them died out, though a few carried on business.

The toy theatre is, however, not only an interesting old Victorian toy, but can still be excellent fun today. Among the new plays published for the toy theatre since World War II is *The High Toby* by J. B. Priestley, with scenery and characters designed by the artist Doris Zinkeisen. This is a story about highwaymen, with plenty of horses and coaches which can be shown very effectively on a model stage.

Making Your Own Theatre

Many boys and girls like to make their own model theatres, write their own plays and draw their own scenery and characters. You can do this quite effectively and without having to spend much money, even if you are not an expert artist. You become your own producer, playwright, scene painter and cast, and in doing so you also get to know a great deal about how things work on the real stage.

You will have your own ideas about writing

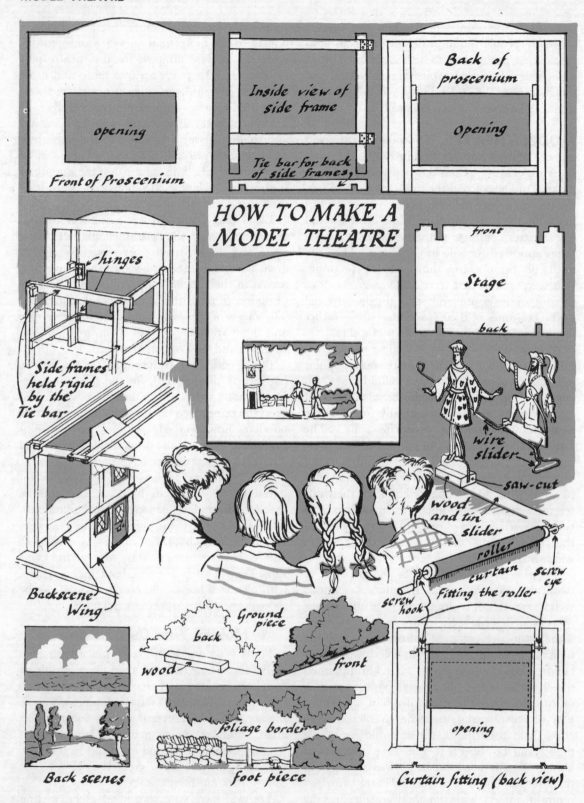

Front of Proscenium

opening

Inside view of side frame

Tie bar for back of side frames,

Back of proscenium

Opening

HOW TO MAKE A MODEL THEATRE

hinges

Side frames held rigid by the Tie bar

front

Stage

back

wire slider

saw-cut

wood and tin slider

roller

curtain

screw eye

screw hook

Fitting the roller

Backscene Wing

Ground piece

back

front

wood

foliage border

foot piece

Back scenes

opening

Curtain fitting (back view)

the play, but whatever kind you do it is really best to keep the dialogue quite short. Romantic plays in bright costume and stories of imaginary characters and creatures go better in a model theatre than ordinary realistic dramas in the costume of the present day; religious plays such as nativity plays are also very suitable. It is a good idea to think of the effects that can easily be put on a model stage : a procession over the stage, for instance, is easy because all you have to do is slide the figures slowly across, but it would be hard with your still cardboard figures to show a rough fight between two characters. When the play is being performed, you can show which character is supposed to be talking by gently moving the slider that pushes it on.

For the scenery, use thick cardboard and either paint straight on to it or stick paper sheets on before painting. The characters should be on fairly thin cardboard glued to small blocks of wood and slid flat along the stage. Strips of tin make good "sliders" for moving the characters—make them fairly long so that your hand will not show when you move the figures about.

The stage itself can be made in various different ways—all that is really necessary is a framework that will hold the scenery up, and thin wood is a good material to use. The "frame" round a stage as you look at it from the audience is called the proscenium, and for your model stage a suitable size for the proscenium might be 50 centimetres wide by 40 centimetres high. These are the measurements of the outside of the frame : the inside of the frame, which is the proscenium opening, could then be 30 centimetres wide by 20 centimetres high. In the old toy theatres the proscenium was always highly decorated with painted marble columns and plush curtains and with boxes on either side.

The floor of the stage should be 50 centimetres wide, so that it gives you plenty of room that is hidden from the audience at either side (these side parts of the stage are called "wings") and about 45 centimetres from front to back. It is best to have it raised about 6 centimetres above the level of the table the theatre is to stand on, and a few wooden blocks underneath will do this. The scenery at the back and at the wings can be held up by an overhead grid of wooden

slats, about 25 centimetres above the stage level, supported by upright slats at the four corners of the stage.

For the lighting of your model stage you can use ordinary electric light bulbs like those in reading lamps on either side of the stage or you can make a special installation, or arrangement, of miniature torch bulbs. The best way to copy real theatre lighting is by using miniature bulbs. These can be wired in rows on to pieces of wood to form what are called battens and fixed to the grid above the stage, some at the back and some at the front so that they light the stage all over. One set can be used as footlights, placed level with the stage and in front of it. Thin sheets of coloured gelatine can be bought, and by putting these in front of the bulbs you can produce lighting of several different colours.

For a stage of the size described above you might need one set of footlights (about 9 lamps) and two top battens (9 lamps each). Torch bulbs are usually either 2·5 or 3·8 volts and you can draw your power either from batteries or from the mains through a transformer (see TRANSFORMER). The transformer costs more, but it is far more satisfactory in the long run. It is essential, however, that your electricity supply is A.C. A switchboard for this lighting installation should have about three switches or dimmers, which can sometimes be made from the volume controls of old wireless sets. This low voltage lighting is quite harmless but one with the lamps connected direct to the mains should not be used as there is a risk of dangerous electric shocks.

MODERN DANCE is a name given to a method of dancing which was started by Rudolf von Laban. He founded the Central European School of Dancing in 1911, and many of his early pupils afterwards became famous dance leaders—for example, Kurt Jooss and Sigurd Leeder in Europe, and Mary Wigman in the United States.

Bodily movements in Modern Dance differ from those of the classic ballet (see BALLET) in that they are just natural, everyday actions, although expanded to something "larger than life" for dramatic purposes.

Modern dancing is taught in many schools in

England to help children develop their dramatic and musical abilities and to encourage graceful bodily action.

MOGUL EMPIRE.

In 1526 a prince from western Asia named Baber (the Tiger) conquered northern India and started an empire. Baber was a descendant of great conquerors. On his father's side he was descended from the famous Tamerlane, who had conquered an empire in western Asia and made Samarkand his capital. Through his mother, Baber was descended from Jenghiz Khan, an earlier conqueror of vast territories. (See TAMERLANE ; JENGHIZ KHAN.)

By the time Baber succeeded his father most of their ancestral territory had been lost and he ruled only the small state of Ferghana, in Turkestan. However, it was his great ambition to regain the empire of Tamerlane. He tried to do this but failed, and was even driven out of Ferghana, so he turned his attention to India.

From Kabul (in what is now Afghanistan) he carried out a series of raids into India and then, in 1526, led his final expedition through the Khyber Pass (see KHYBER PASS) and down into the plains of India. At Panipat, north of Delhi, he defeated Sultan Ibrahim Lodi and entered Delhi, his capital. A harder task awaited him in the following year when, near Agra, he had to meet a mighty force of men called Rajputs, who were the finest soldiers in India. However, in both these battles his enemies relied on elephants, while Baber had archers mounted on swift, light horses that were far more manageable than the lumbering elephants, and put them to flight. After another battle near Patna, Baber took over most of northern India. The empire he started is known as the Mogul Empire.

Baber died in 1530 and thus had little time to establish himself firmly in his new empire and his son Humayun inherited a throne that was far from secure. After ten years of fighting and confusion Humayun was driven out of India and fled to Persia. It was during the flight that his famous son Akbar the Great was born. Thirteen years later, in 1555, Humayun began the reconquest of India but before he could achieve very much he fell from a balcony and was killed. The young Akbar thus had to fight for his throne. He recovered what had been lost and much more, for at his death in 1605 his empire stretched from the Hindu Kush Mountains in the north to the River Godavari in central India. He was a brilliant ruler whose achievements are explained in the article AKBAR, JALAL UD-DIN MOHAMMED. Above all, he realized that he must unite his followers, who were Moslems (see ISLAM), with the people they had conquered, who were Hindus (see HINDUS AND HINDUISM). He therefore abolished the extra rights and privileges that the Moslems had had in the past and he married a Hindu princess. She bore him a son called Salim, who reigned under the name of Jahangir.

Jahangir was an able man but he was idle, cruel and took drugs. Gradually he left the management of his affairs to his strong-minded wife, Nur Jahan. It was during his reign that the English established their first trading posts in India (see EAST INDIA COMPANY). Jahangir died in 1627 and was soon succeeded by his son Shah Jahan, who reigned until 1658. Shah Jahan erected many splendid buildings, the most famous of which is the Taj Mahal at Agra, which he built as a tomb for his wife Mumtaz Mahal. (See TAJ MAHAL.) He did not die until 1666 but spent the last eight years of his life as a prisoner, for his son Aurangzeb had him confined in the fort at Agra and ruled in his place.

Aurangzeb was the last of the famous Mogul emperors. By the time he seized the throne the empire was already becoming weak and he made matters much worse by bringing back the idea of treating his Moslem and Hindu subjects differently, and even went as far as destroying Hindu temples. While he was fighting in the south his Hindu subjects rebelled and when he died in 1707 there was confusion everywhere. The whole country was bankrupt and famine was widespread. His successors could do nothing to stop the ruin and the empire broke up into many separate kingdoms. Persians and Afghans invaded India, and by this time several European countries had established colonies there.

The Mogul emperors continued to rule at Delhi for another 150 years, but they never had any real power and their rule never extended beyond the city. In 1857, when the Indian soldiers mutinied against the East India Company (see

INDIAN MUTINY), they declared Bahadur Shah to be once more the emperor of India. When the mutiny was suppressed, the British tried Bahadur Shah and banished him to Burma.

MOHAMMED (?570–632) founded the religion of the Moslems, which is called Islam (see ISLAM). He was born about A.D. 570 at Mecca in the country that is now Saudi Arabia.

He was the son of Abdullah and his wife Aminah, and thus belonged to the Hashimi section of the Koreish tribe. His father died before he was born and his mother died when he was six. After this happened he was brought up by his grandfather and later by his uncle. At that time Mecca was a centre of the Arabian caravan trade and in his youth Mohammed seems to have accompanied Meccan traders to Syria and southern Arabia and perhaps farther afield. He also seems to have worked as a shepherd. When he was 25 he married Khadija, a wealthy widow who had employed him to conduct a caravan to Syria. It was not until he was 40 that Mohammed began to receive the divine revelations that led to the foundation of the religion of Islam.

According to tradition he received the first revelation on a mountain called Hira where he had retired to meditate, or think quietly. The archangel Gabriel summoned him to go out and preach that there was only one God, the God of all the universe, and that he (Mohammed) was his prophet who was to reform the world and stop people worshipping idols, as the Arabs did at that time. Mohammed's family and a few friends believed in his mission but the leaders at Mecca opposed his teaching and in 622 he was in such danger that he and his few followers fled to Medina, farther north. His flight is known as the Hejira and the Moslem calendar is dated from it. Settled in Medina, Mohammed built a mosque (see MOSQUE) and began to preach to the tribes, trying to persuade them to adopt his new faith, which he called Islam. In English this word means "submission" (to God). He made little progress at first but two years after his flight he won a great victory over the Meccans at the Battle of Badr. Mohammed and his followers had started raiding Meccan caravans while they were returning from Syria and one of these attacks led to the battle. Although the Meccans defeated him the next year they did not take advantage of their victory and went home.

After his victory Mohammed was treated with much greater respect, and so many tribes accepted Islam and gave up worshipping idols that he was able to gather a great army for an attack on Mecca. Faced with this powerful array of troops, Mecca surrendered without a battle and Mohammed entered the town in triumph. He went straight to the Ka'aba, a shrine of the old religion, and broke down its idols, turning it into a shrine of Islam. Ever since that day it has been the most important shrine in Islam. The next year, A.D. 632, Mohammed himself led the people of Medina on their pilgrimage to the Ka'aba in Mecca, but his health was failing and on his return to Medina he died at the age of 62.

From the year 610 until the year of his death Mohammed believed that he heard recitations from heaven which were collected together and make up the holy book of the Moslems, which is known as the Koran (see KORAN).

In the 100 years after Mohammed's death the religion he had started spread over great areas of Asia and into Europe, for the Arabs conquered an empire that included Spain in the west and stretched to the borders of China in the east.

MOLE. The small mounds of earth often seen on fields and golf courses and occasionally in gardens are thrown up by the burrowing activities of moles. The British mole is a small insect-eating mammal covered with soft black fur like

The British mole is 15 centimetres long, with a tail of 2 centimetres. It has broad, spade-like front feet.

velvet. The fur does not lie down in any particular direction, so the mole can easily move forward or backward in its narrow burrows.

The mole has a short tail, a movable, sensitive snout and tiny eyes buried in its fur. It has eyes, but they seem to be almost useless. The mole's front feet have developed almost into spades and are most efficient for digging tunnels.

The food of moles is mostly worms and grubs, which they find by making regular tours of the complicated tunnel systems they dig out for themselves. They have very large appetites.

Young moles are naked and pink when born. They are brought up in nests in specially built chambers that are higher than the tunnels leading to them in order to protect them from floods. The mole is often trapped, for it is one of the few British animals whose fur can be used for making and trimming clothes.

This mole is also found in other parts of Europe. In North America lives the star-nosed mole, so called because of the star-shaped group of fleshy growths around its nose. Golden moles live in Central and South Africa, and in Australia is the marsupial mole, which is, however, not related to the common mole.

MOLECULE.

The smallest particle of a substance that can exist and still remain the substance is called a molecule. A molecule is built up of atoms. The molecule of an *element* consists of atoms all of the same kind but the molecule of a *compound* contains atoms of two or more kinds. The molecule of the element hydrogen contains two hydrogen atoms; the molecule of the compound water contains two atoms of hydrogen and one atom of oxygen; but the more complicated compound chlorophyll, which makes plants green, has a molecule made up of 136 atoms of five different elements. (See ATOM; ELEMENT.)

A water molecule (written H_2O by the chemist) can be divided only by decomposing the water into hydrogen and oxygen. These are both gases and are quite different from one another, and from the original water.

Scientists have been able to find out how the atoms are actually arranged in solid materials, that is, what we would see if there were microscopes capable of showing atoms. There are several different types of arrangement.

Whether a substance is a solid, a liquid or a gas depends on the behaviour of its molecules. A solid keeps its shape because its molecules are tightly packed, or joined together to make a rigid framework. In a liquid, the molecules are not in fixed positions but can slide over one another, so that the liquid, while continuing to occupy the same volume, readily alters its shape. In a gas, the molecules are so scattered that they can move freely, so that the gas expands, or spreads, to fill any container. Also a gas, unlike solids and liquids, can be compressed into a much smaller space. At ordinary temperatures, oxygen molecules move at about 450 metres a second and those of hydrogen nearly four times as fast, although they cannot travel far without colliding with another molecule.

The movement of the molecules in a substance depends on how hot it is. If all the molecular energy could be removed from an object, then its temperature would be "absolute zero" (about $-273°C$) and its molecules would be at a standstill. When a substance is warmed, its molecules move faster. The molecules in a solid occupy fixed positions and can only vibrate; the higher the temperature of the solid the greater the vibrations of its molecules. In a hot iron the molecules are vibrating so rapidly that we can actually feel their movement when we touch the iron, which we say "feels hot". When a kettle of water is boiled, the molecules of water dash about more and more violently until they can no longer hold together as a liquid, but escape as a gas—steam.

Molecules are very tiny indeed; in a gas, for instance, molecules are scattered about like currants in a cake but there are about 80,000,000,000,000,000,000,000 molecules of air in an average size balloon (with a volume of about 3 litres). The largest molecules are probably not much bigger than one thirty thousandth of a centimetre long and it is just possible to see photographs of them in an electron microscope (see MICROSCOPE). The largest molecules are those of certain substances in plants and animals, such as haemoglobin, which is the red colouring of blood. Even larger molecules are found in viruses; each virus is one enormous molecule covered with a sheath of protein. For some types of virus the central molecule is D.N.A.—deoxyribonucleic acid, while for others it is R.N.A.—ribonucleic acid.

Scientists often have to refer to the mass of a molecule, but this is an impossibly tiny figure. Instead a scientist gives the *molecular weight*. This is an historical term whose present meaning is "relative molecular mass". It is the mass of one molecule of the substance compared with the mass of one atom of hydrogen. The actual values used are determined by saying that the mass of the C^{12} isotope of carbon, about 12 times the mass of the hydrogen atom, has an *atomic weight* of exactly 12. This makes the atomic weight of hydrogen approximately 1 (actually 1·00797). The atomic weight of oxygen is 16. Ammonia (NH_3) has a molecular weight of 17 because its molecule is made up of one atom of nitrogen (atomic weight 14) and three atoms of hydrogen (atomic weight 1).

Many of the substances now synthesized, or artificially built up, by chemists—such as plastics, artificial rubbers and silicones—have complicated structures consisting of long chains or sheets of atoms. The properties and behaviour of such a substance depends largely on the pattern in which its atoms are joined together. Thus to make polythene ("poly-ethylene"), ethylene molecules are made to link together in chains.

The idea that matter was composed of molecules came from the Italian scientist Amedeo Avogadro (1776–1856).

MONACO is one of the world's smallest countries, a strip of land on the southeast coast of France covering an area of only 1·9 square kilometres. It lies at the foot of the Maritime Alps by the sparkling blue waters of the Mediterranean. The capital, also called Monaco, is an old town built on a rocky peninsula in the south and contains the ancient fortress, the Prince's palace and the modern cathedral. The peninsula shelters a small harbour used by yachts and pleasure craft and surrounded by the town of La Condamine with its many shops and hotels. On a rocky ridge north of the harbour is Monte Carlo, famous for its great casino and luxury hotels set amid beautiful gardens. (See MONTE CARLO.)

Although under French protection since 1861, Monaco is an independent state and has been ruled since the 15th century by princes of the Grimaldi family, which originally came from Genoa. The Prince governs with the help of a council of state and an elected national council. The French language is spoken. Monaco has its own coinage, law courts, police and small army. It is the only European country without customs duties and passport regulations. Its people pay no taxes, as enough money to run the state is obtained from tourists and from the profits of the gambling casino. The Monégasques, as the people of Monaco are called, are not allowed to gamble there.

There are quite a large number of factories in Monaco making textiles, plastics, chemicals, perfumes, machinery and instruments.

The population of Monaco is about 23,000 of whom only about 3,000 are Monégasques.

MONAGHAN is a county in the province of Ulster, belonging to the Republic of Ireland, not to Northern Ireland. There is more about Monaghan in the article ULSTER.

MONARCH is an English word which comes from a Greek word meaning "a man who is the sole ruler" of a state. The original Greek word did not always mean that he was a king; it merely stressed the fact that he was the *sole* ruler. However, as time went by the word "monarch" came to mean a "king" or an "emperor", and as rule by a king or emperor was hereditary—that is, it passed from father to son or daughter or other descendant—so monarchy came to mean hereditary rule by one person.

In early civilizations monarchs were often worshipped as gods. For example, in ancient Egypt the pharaohs were thought to be either the sun god or his sons. In the later period of the Roman Empire the emperors were often worshipped while they were alive as well as after they died. During the middle ages a slightly different idea about monarchs grew up. Kings were no longer thought of as divine, but in some countries they *were* thought to be God's representatives on earth. Because they were thought to have been appointed by God, their subjects had a holy duty to obey them at all times and rebellion was therefore considered sinful. This idea continued until the 17th century, when it became known as the Divine Right of Kings, and James I of England wrote a book defending it.

In England, however, even in the middle ages it was generally believed that monarchs ought to govern in accordance with the law of the land. Thus King John had to grant Magna Carta, whereby he promised to govern according to the laws and customs of England (see MAGNA CARTA). In the 16th century the idea spread that kings held their power *on behalf of* their people and that they could be dethroned if they did not use this power for the *good* of their people. In the 17th century, when Charles I tried to rule without consulting parliament, the Civil War broke out and not only did he lose his throne but also his head. (See CIVIL WAR; CHARLES I.) All British monarchs who reigned after this knew that they must pay attention to the wishes of their people, and as their people wanted to be governed more and more by the representatives they sent to parliament, the monarchs had to give up more and more of their political power. As a result there developed in Britain what is called a *constitutional monarchy*.

In a constitutional monarchy the monarch does not rule according to his own ideas but according to the constitution, which is a set of laws and customs about how the country shall be governed. In such a system the monarch does not actually rule at all, if by the word "rule" is meant "govern the country personally". In a constitutional monarchy parliament contains the elected representatives of the people and expresses their wishes through the laws it makes. The cabinet (which is made up from the majority party in parliament) governs the country and depends for its power on the approval of parliament. The monarch is the symbol of the unity of the country, being completely outside party politics and not seeking to exercise political power. (See CABINET; KING; PARLIAMENT.)

MONET, Claude (1840–1926). If you look closely at a piece of material such as tweed you will see that it is made up of tiny threads of different colours woven together—a piece that looks a plain greenish colour when you see it at a distance may really have blue, brown, yellow, and even orange and red threads in it. The painter Claude Monet realized how the eye "mixes up" tiny scraps of colour from a distance in this way. Therefore when he wanted to give certain impressions, or ideas, of colour and light in his pictures he painted in tiny dots of different colours to gain the effect he aimed at, whether it was brilliant dazzling light or soft mistiness.

Monet was born in Paris and studied painting under the guidance of well-known artists of the day. However, he did not want to paint in the way that was then thought correct and soon began to try out his own ideas. In 1863 a picture of his called "Impression—sunrise" was shown in an exhibition in Paris, and this title was what gained for Monet and his friends the name "Impressionists." The Impressionist painters wanted to paint the *look* of things at particular moments, not necessarily what they really were. For example, if some trees in the distance looked a bluish colour because they were far away, they painted them blue and not green.

Often Monet painted the same scene at different times of the day and at different seasons of the year, to show how the various kinds of light could change the look of it. He painted as many as 17 pictures of the front of Rouen Cathedral. For many years the public did not like his work, but he persevered until at last people began to try to understand him and to buy his pictures. By 1891 he was a prosperous artist.

There are pictures by Monet in London at the National Gallery and at the Tate Gallery.

MONEY consists of paper notes and metal coins. The British system of money used to have 20 shillings in the pound and 12 pence in the shilling. It was replaced on February 15, 1971 by decimal currency, with the pound divided into 100 new pence. The £10, £5 and £1 banknotes remain in use, with the same value as before, and there are decimal coins with the value of 50 pence (written 50p), 10 pence (10p), 5 pence (5p), 2 pence (2p), 1 penny (1p) and ½ penny (½p).

Florins (two-shilling pieces) have the value of 10p. Shillings have the value of 5p. Sixpences were used for some time after decimalization, with a value of $2\frac{1}{2}$p. The old penny, halfpenny and threepenny pieces ceased to be used and as there were no exact equivalents to these among the decimal coins, their value was shown in an official table of conversions.

The 50p, 10p and 5p coins are minted in cupronickel. The 10p coin weighs twice as much as the 5p. The 5p and 10p coins are the only new coins with milled edges. The 2p, 1p and $\frac{1}{2}$p are minted in bronze and their weights are also related; for instance, 1p weighs twice as much as $\frac{1}{2}$p. (You can read more about this currency in the article DECIMAL CURRENCY; see also COINS AND COIN COLLECTING.)

Money is used as a measure of value, as a means of storing wealth and for buying and selling goods. Just as metres are used to measure a person's height and kilograms his weight so money is used to measure the value of his coat, his books and his bicycle. When we say that money measures the value of an object we are really saying that it measures the value of one object as compared with the value of another; that is, the terms on which they could be exchanged, or "swopped".

Let us forget money for a moment and think only of the exchange of goods. Suppose a loaf and a bar of chocolate are considered to be of equal value, people could exchange them without loss by either owner. If, however, a loaf came to be considered more valuable than a bar of chocolate then the owner of loaves would suffer a loss if he continued to exchange a loaf for a bar of chocolate. (The reasons for such a change in value are explained in ECONOMICS.)

Now to return to money. As it is obviously impossible to carry on this *exchange of goods* every time we want something, this is where *money* comes in. When you go to the sweetshop you take money, not a loaf of bread, to pay for your chocolate. Money thus represents, or stands for, the value of the chocolate. We have already said that one type of goods may come to have less value than another type which originally had the same value. Therefore, because money stands for the value of goods, the value of money also can change. In that way money is not like the measures of height and weight—metres and kilo-

grams—which always remain the same. Nevertheless, it is still a measure of value.

Metals such as silver, copper and cupronickel are not the only things that can be used for money. Among primitive, or backward, people cattle or shells may be used. Whatever is chosen should be something that has a value and keeps its value. Strawberries, for example, would be no use because they would rot. Blocks of stone would not rot but they would be no use either—because they have so little value that people would have to carry tons of stone when they went shopping. The ideal substance for use as money should be scarce, but not too scarce, able to stand up to wear and tear and always be of the same quality. Gold and silver are therefore ideal. Diamonds are so rare that they would have to be cut up into impossibly small pieces, and in any case they vary so much in quality that people using diamonds as money would have to decide what value to put on each other's money before they could buy and sell.

Buying and selling is often done without the handing over of actual money, for cheques are used instead. (How this works is explained in the article BANKS AND BANKING.) However, it is always possible to demand that a debt should be paid in actual money.

Since gold and silver ceased to be used, the value of the coins themselves has had little to do with their value as metal, and it is quite obvious that a piece of paper cannot of itself be worth £1. The pieces of money we use now merely represent gold and silver. Their value is guaranteed by the government.

Each country has its own money, or currency, as it is usually called. Therefore when people travel from one country to another they have to change their currency into that of the country they are visiting. The value of each currency in relation to others may vary. However, when British people go to France they usually know how much French money they will get in return for, say, £1.

MONGOLIA. In the heart of east Asia lies the independent republic of Mongolia, which few people from western lands have visited. Mongolia is an immense plateau, or tableland, separating Siberia in the U.S.S.R. from China. It is about ten times the size of England and Wales. Most of Mongolia is more than 910 metres above sea level and there are mountain ranges in the western part. Several tremendous earthquakes have occurred in the mountains during the 20th century, forming great cracks in the earth and causing huge landslides. The southern boundary of the republic passes through the Gobi Desert (see GOBI DESERT). The northern part of Mongolia is more fertile and most of the people live there. There is little rainfall and the climate tends to extremes, with bitter winters, scorching summers and great differences between night and day temperatures. There are patches of forest on the mountain slopes and good pasture in some of the valleys.

The people are Mongols, belonging to the yellow race and with high cheekbones and black

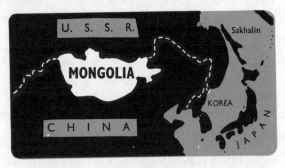

hair. They are wonderful horsemen and fierce fighters. Many of them are still nomads, or wanderers, living in round tents called yurts made of camel-hair felt stretched on a wooden framework. They move between their summer and winter grazing grounds herding horses, camels, sheep, goats and cattle. Their meals are mostly mutton and cheese, both highly flavoured. The men wear a long reddish robe with a bright sash, hats like upturned saucers and high leather boots with pointed toes. The women wear skirts and jackets of brilliant brocade and dress their hair with silver and turquoise ornaments. The children must attend school between the ages of 8 and 12. The Mongolians have their own language and many of them are Buddhists of the same kind as the people of Tibet, but religion is controlled.

Although the chief products of Mongolia are

wool, hides and skins, horns and horses, the republic contains coal, oil and gold and within recent years great progress has been made in developing the mines and oilfields. The chief coal mines are at Nalaikha near Ulan Bator, which is the capital. Ulan Bator has been changed from a town of untidy shacks into a modern city that has a university, libraries, museums and a theatre for opera and ballet. The people who live there are beginning to wear western dress rather than their old national dress. Ulan Bator is connected by air and by rail with Siberia and China, and on the old caravan routes of Mongolia lorries and motor cars now mingle with camels, horses and ox-carts.

History

In the 12th and 13th centuries the Mongols conquered most of Asia, Russia and eastern Europe. (See the article JENGHIZ KHAN.) In the 14th century the Mongolian Empire crumbled away and China itself became a strong nation. Gradually the Chinese increased their power and at the end of the 17th century Mongolia accepted Chinese rule. The Chinese influence was stronger in that part of Mongolia south of the Gobi Desert, now called the Inner Mongolian Autonomous Region of the Chinese Republic. (Autonomous means "self-governing".)

After the Chinese revolution in 1911 the people of northern Mongolia (the present republic) declared themselves independent and came under Russian influence. The Chinese made attempts to regain control of the country but in 1924 the Mongolian People's Republic was formed with its capital at Ulan Bator. The

FACTS ABOUT MONGOLIA

AREA: 1,565,000 square kilometres.
POPULATION: 1,285,000.
KIND OF COUNTRY: Self-governing republic.
CAPITAL: Ulan Bator.
GEOGRAPHICAL FEATURES: A vast steppe tableland from 900 to 1,500 metres high, with some peaks over 4,000 metres. In the south is the Gobi Desert.
CHIEF PRODUCTS: Livestock and animal products.
IMPORTANT TOWNS: Ulan Bator, Choybalsan, Sühe Baatar, Tsetserlig, Jirgalanta.
EDUCATION: Children must attend school between the ages of 8 and 12.

C. R. Bawden

Scenes in Ulan Bator, capital of Mongolia. The felt tents called yurts can be seen behind the woman and child.

government followed the pattern and the methods of those in the U.S.S.R. and other Communist countries and Mongolia was shut off from the western world. China did not recognize the independence of Mongolia until 1946. In recent years much has been done to encourage industry by building electric power stations and factories, and also to cultivate the land for growing grain instead of using it all for pasture. Both these tendencies have caused the Mongols to lose something of their wandering habits.

MONGOOSE. The mongoose is a small, flesh-eating mammal, rather like a ferret in size and shape. There are many species, or kinds, which live mostly in Africa, though some are found in Asia and one species, or kind, in southern Spain. They are slender animals with rather long, pointed noses, and their fur is often rough.

Some mongooses are famous for killing snakes, including poisonous ones. They are so nimble and sharp sighted that they can dodge the snake's head as it strikes, but if a poisonous snake does get its fangs into a mongoose the little animal may be killed.

Mongooses feed mostly on rats, mice, lizards, worms, insects and snails, and some eat much fruit and vegetable matter. Many mongooses are fond of eggs, which they take between their forefeet and throw hard on the ground to smash them. Some mongooses live in swampy places and feed on crabs.

Two well-known African mongooses are the Egyptian mongoose and the meerkat, which lives only in southern Africa and is often kept as a pet. The best known kind, however, is the Indian mongoose. Rudyard Kipling wrote a story about an Indian mongoose called Rikki-Tikki-Tavi (because of the chattering noise he made) who was kept as a pet by an English family in India.

Many years ago mongooses were introduced into Jamaica and other parts of the West Indies to kill the rats which had become a serious pest there. Unfortunately they soon left the rats alone and ate birds, poultry and useful snakes instead.

The mongoose is a slender, sharp sighted, nimble creature.

Top row: Arabian baboon, black howler monkey, potto. Bottom row: Black and white colobus monkey, tarsier.

MONKEY. It can be seen at first glance that monkeys are more closely related to human beings than are most other animals. Their faces are not so very unlike those of human beings and they have hands and feet.

Monkeys belong to the group of animals known as *primates*. Man, the apes—the gorilla, chimpanzee, orang-utan and gibbon—and the lemurs are also primates. The apes are without tails and, except for the gibbons, are bigger than monkeys. (See APE; CHIMPANZEE; GIBBON; GORILLA; ORANG-UTAN.) Lemurs live mostly in the island of Madagascar. A few kinds are found in Africa, Asia and the East Indies.

Monkeys are very varied in appearance and habits. The largest are the baboons and the smallest are the marmosets. They are generally divided into two groups: the Old World monkeys of Africa, Asia and the Pacific, and the New World monkeys of South and Central America.

Old World Monkeys

Many Old World monkeys have pouches in their cheeks in which they store food to be eaten later. No New World monkeys have these pouches, nor do they have the bare patches of skin on their hindquarters that Old World monkeys have. The main groups of Old World monkeys are the baboons, the grinning monkeys or guenons, the colobus family, the langurs and the macaques.

Baboons are strange-looking creatures with bright-coloured markings on their faces and hind quarters. Most monkeys live in trees, leaping from branch to branch, but baboons spend most of their lives on the ground. (See BABOON.)

The guenons, which all come from Africa, are probably the commonest monkeys in European zoos, as they thrive on fruit, nuts and vegetables. Some guenons are very handsome, particularly the diana monkey, which has grey, black, white and chestnut fur. Other guenons are the mona, green and white-nosed monkeys.

The colobus monkeys are also very striking-looking. They live in the tropical African forests and feed on leaves. A black and white colobus monkey with long fur and a very long tail is sometimes seen in zoos, although colobus monkeys generally do not do well in captivity.

The langurs, like the colobus monkeys, have no thumbs. Langurs are leaf-eating monkeys found from the Himalaya Mountains right down to

Borneo. They have long tails and thin bodies. The Indian langur, or hanuman, is allowed to roam where it likes, for it is looked on as a sacred animal by the Hindus. In Hindu legend Hanuman was the monkey god who sprang across the sea from India to Ceylon to help to rescue Sita, the wife of the hero Rama.

The macaques are a group of rather plain monkeys found over a large part of Asia, including China and Japan. The commonest and hardiest kind is the greyish-brown rhesus monkey, which has a short tail. Rhesus monkeys go about in large bands. The only kind of macaque that is found outside Asia is the rock ape of Gibraltar and northwest Africa.

Perhaps the oddest-looking monkey of all is the proboscis monkey of Borneo. The males have very long noses which hang down in front of their mouths. This kind is seldom seen in a zoo.

New World Monkeys

The New World monkeys of America have much flatter noses than those of the Old World, and the group also includes the only monkeys whose tails are prehensile; that is, that can be used for gripping.

The best known American monkeys are the capuchins, which used to be seen sitting on barrel organs in the street. The name capuchin was given to these monkeys because the hair on their heads looks a little like the cowl, or hood, worn by Capuchin friars.

Capuchins have prehensile tails, but these are not as well developed as that of the spider monkey, which uses its tail almost like a fifth hand. Near the end of the tail there is an area so sensitive that as it reaches out to grasp a branch or pick up a fruit it almost seems to have an eye in it. There are several kinds of spider monkeys and all live in the forest trees. They are most common in the Amazon area, but one kind is found as far north as Mexico. They are among the largest American monkeys. Their limbs are very long and they look all arms and legs, from which they get the name spider monkey. They do well in captivity and make gentle, affectionate pets. Some kinds are entirely black and others are greyish or brown.

The woolly monkeys are rather like spider monkeys, but not so thin and spidery in appearance. They have thick, woolly fur.

Howler monkeys, the biggest of all American monkeys, are almost impossible to keep in captivity anywhere because they are more temperamental than most kinds and are very fussy about food. They get their name from the howls which they utter from the tree-tops.

The smallest of all monkeys are the dainty marmosets, which have claws instead of nails, except on their big toes. They may have as many as three babies at a time, while most monkeys have only one. (See MARMOSET.) The squirrel monkeys are not much bigger than marmosets; in fact the word "squirrel" describes their size rather than their general appearance.

The douroucoulis or night apes, a group rather like the squirrel monkeys, are the only monkeys that are nocturnal; that is, they sleep by day and search for their food (insects and small birds) by night. They have small ears, large eyes and long tails which are not prehensile.

Lemurs and Tarsiers

In Madagascar there are many varieties of lemurs, large and small. Lemurs are less intelligent than monkeys. Most of them live in trees and come out at night to search for their food, which generally consists of fruit, birds and eggs, reptiles and insects.

The best known lemurs are the galagos or bush babies of East Africa. The smallest of these is about 12 centimetres long, with a 17 centimetre tail. The largest is more than 30 centimetres long, with a tail about the same length. They are pretty little animals with soft woolly fur, long tails, large eyes and big ears which they can fold close to their heads. At night they are quick and acrobatic.

The pottos are a kind of lemur which live in West Africa. The ordinary potto has large staring eyes, a stump of a tail and a reddish-brown coat. Pottos have no first fingers.

In Madagascar lives the curious aye-aye, a kind of lemur about the size of a cat, with a very long, thin third finger on each hand. At night the aye-aye goes in search of wood-boring grubs and, having gnawed through the wood that covers them, picks them out with its third fingers.

☐ Read about BUSHBABIES AS PETS in the blue pages of volume 1

The lorises have great staring eyes and soft fur, but no tail. They live in trees, moving slowly from branch to branch instead of leaping. The slender loris lives in the forests of Madras in India and in Ceylon, and the larger slow loris lives in parts of India and the East Indies and in the Malay peninsula.

The tarsiers, which live in the East Indies, are related to lemurs and monkeys and are very interesting to scientists, as their heads are held erect and their eyes look forward in the same way as those of human beings. They have disc-like pads on their fingers and toes which enable them to cling to branches.

MONKEY PUZZLE is the name given to an evergreen tree whose stiff, arching branches are closely covered with spiral rows of spiny leaves. This tree, it has been said, would puzzle a monkey to climb, and so it is generally known as the monkey puzzle. A more correct name for it is the Chile pine. It grows in large forests on the mountains of Chile and Patagonia in South America, where it is an important timber tree.

Jane Burton

The monkey puzzle is an evergreen tree whose branches are thickly covered with spiny leaves.

It was introduced into England late in the 18th century.

The genus, or group, of the monkey puzzle is *Araucaria*, from *araucanos*, its name in Chile. It is the only member of its genus that is hardy enough to grow in most English gardens. The monkey puzzle grows up to 30 metres in height. Male and female cones are produced on different trees, and ripe seed cones are as large as a man's head. They contain starchy seeds which can be eaten and taste like chestnuts. The timber resembles common pine timber, or deal, except that it is without resin.

Another tree of the *Araucaria* genus is the Norfolk Island pine, a very handsome tree which grows on Norfolk Island, north of New Zealand, and is sometimes grown in gardens in Cornwall.

MONKS AND FRIARS. The word "monk" comes from the Greek word *monakhos* which means "single" or "solitary", and the word "friar" comes from the Latin word *frater* which means "brother". Both monks and friars are members of religious orders, or brotherhoods, and they are known by the general word "religious". In the present article the noun "religious" is used whenever monks and friars are referred to together, and the words "monk" and "friar" wherever it is necessary to talk about them separately. All religious submit themselves to strict discipline and lead lives of prayer and self-sacrifice.

There have always been people who felt that they could get nearer to God by withdrawing from ordinary life, giving up ease and comfort and expensive food and clothing. Christian saints have sometimes made themselves live extremely hard lives, partly because they were ready to suffer anything for God's sake and partly because doing difficult and painful things helped them to control their selfish desires. Other religions also, especially Buddhism, Hinduism and Taoism, have their monks and holy men.

Christians who become members of a religious order all take the vows of poverty, chastity and obedience; that is, they swear not to have money for their own use, not to marry and to carry out faithfully whatever work they are given. Before taking these vows they go through a period of probation, or trial. This period is known as the noviciate, and while they are going through it they are novices. (The word "novice" comes from the Latin word *novus* which means "new".) The noviciate enables them to know what the life of a religious is like. During this period they make up their minds whether they wish to live such a life, and the novice-master (the religious in charge of the novices) decides whether they are suitable for it. The three vows of poverty, chastity and obedience are taken only at the *end* of the noviciate when both the novices and the order which they wish to enter are certain of each other. The vows are taken at first for

A Franciscan Friar

three years only and then they are renewed for life if both the religious and his order agree.

When they become novices the religious put on a special dress, or "habit", which consists of a long tunic reaching to the floor, a short cloak (scapular) covering the shoulders and a hood. They wear this type of dress for the rest of their lives. In choir they also wear a cowl, which is a cloak with wide folds and sleeves. Different orders wear habits of different colours and, as you will see, some orders have come to be known by the colour of their habits.

Monks

In the 3rd century A.D. a number of Christians began to leave the company of their fellow men to live solitary lives as hermits in the Egyptian desert. (See HERMIT.) However, although they lived strict lives and devoted themselves to prayer and the study of religion, they were not monks. Monks live together and according to what is known as a Rule: in spite of its name this is not just one rule but a set of

rules which state how the members of the order are to live and what kind of work they are to do. The different orders have different Rules. The desert hermits sometimes lived near one another and met together for prayers, but they were not organized in any way and each lived according to his own conscience. However, one of the hermits, St. Pachomius, built a monastery near the River Nile, installed his followers in it to live as members of a community and gave them a Rule to guide their lives. This first Christian monastery was built about A.D. 320 and by the time Pachomius died, about 346, nine monasteries for men and two for women were living according to his Rule. (See NUNS.)

The idea spread. Before long St. Basil founded a monastery in Asia Minor (now the main part of Turkey) in which the monks lived together and did all kinds of manual and charitable work, living according to the Rule he laid down. The monasteries of the Orthodox Eastern Church today still regard St. Basil's monastery and his Rule as their model. (See ORTHODOX EASTERN CHURCH.) The idea of monasteries was brought to western Europe by St. Athanasius (a friend of Pachomius) when he went to Rome in 340. Monasteries sprang up in Rome, then all over Italy and before long in Gaul (see GAUL). St. Patrick, who became the patron saint of Ireland, studied at the monastery on the Isle of Lerina, now called St. Honorat, a tiny island off the coast of southeastern France. (See PATRICK, SAINT.) In Ireland itself many monasteries were opened and the Irish monks played a leading part in the spread of Christianity through northern and central Europe. However, none of the monks of western Europe had well-organized orders and, as yet, nobody had started a model that was copied in western Europe as St. Basil's monastery had been copied in eastern Europe.

It was St. Benedict who started the first great order of monks in western Europe. (See BENEDICT, SAINT.) He was born about 480 into a noble Italian family and when he was a young man went to live as a hermit in a cave at Subiaco, east of Rome. Gradually other people joined him and he established his first monastery. About 525 he moved to Monte Cassino, farther south, and started the famous monastery that has been there ever since even though it has been destroyed several times. It was here that he wrote down his Rule and put it into practice. Some time after this monks living under the Rule of St. Benedict became known as Benedictines. Because of the black habits which they wear they are often also called "Black Monks".

Benedict stated how the monastery should be organized and how the monks should spend their time. The abbot, or head of the monastery, was to be elected by the monks and would remain abbot until he died. The monks were to spend part of each day in church, part in reading religious books and part in doing the necessary domestic and manual work of the monastery. The monastery had its own workshops and fields, and was thus a little community that did everything for itself.

Pope Gregory the Great was himself a monk from this monastery and in 596 he sent a party of monks under St. Augustine to convert the people of England to Christianity. (See AUGUSTINE OF CANTERBURY, SAINT.)

As the years passed, some of the black monks began to forget the Rule of Benedict and became slack in their ways. In any case, although each monastery had been founded according to the Rule, there was no one man in charge of them all. Each monastery was therefore free to go its own way and develop customs that Benedict had never intended. However, in the 10th century the monks of Cluny in eastern France began to follow Benedict's Rule strictly and persuaded those of many other monasteries to do the same. Another great change was made: the Abbot of Cluny became the head of many monasteries and could therefore see to it that all the monasteries under his control followed exactly the same form of worship and the same way of life.

In 1098 there was founded at Cîteaux, north of Cluny, a new order of monks known as Cistercians. They were called "White Monks" because their habit was made of white undyed wool. The Cistercians, who took their name from *Cistercium*, the old Roman name for Cîteaux, started their new order because they wanted to live in a stricter way than the Cluniacs. They built their monasteries in lonely places and their abbeys were severely plain, un-

like those of the black monks who emphasized the glory of God by adorning theirs with rich and beautiful carvings. The Cistercians started very strict rules about food and silence. They all did manual work and came to be famous sheep farmers. Fountains Abbey and the other Yorkshire abbeys of the Cistercian order in England sent great amounts of wool to foreign countries. One of the most outstanding Cistercians was St. Bernard of Clairvaux. (See BERNARD, SAINT.)

Friars

By the end of the 12th century many people felt that the monks, shut up in their monasteries, were too far removed from the life of the ordinary people. Towns were becoming bigger and their inhabitants lacked religious teachers and were beginning to hold false ideas about Christianity. Apart from these problems, novices were being chosen carelessly and their training had become slack.

St. Francis and St. Dominic saw that a new type of order was needed and in 1209 St. Francis started the Order of Friars Minor (usually called Franciscans) and in 1214 St. Dominic began to form the Order of Friars Preachers, usually called Dominicans. (See DOMINIC, SAINT; FRANCIS OF ASSISI, SAINT.) You will have noticed that the members of these orders were friars, not monks. This meant that they did not live shut off from the world in monasteries but continued to mix among people in order to help them. The friars made the vows of poverty, chastity and obedience in the same way as the monks. When a monk took the vow of poverty it meant that he could not have money or possessions for his own use. His order as a whole, however, *was*

A Dominican Friar

permitted to have money and possessions. In the orders of friars even the orders were not permitted to have possessions—other than the houses they lived in and the chapels they worshipped in—and their members had to depend on begging if necessary.

The Franciscans have always made a point of preaching to the poor and of helping them in sickness. During the Black Death (see BLACK DEATH) no fewer than 10,000 Franciscans died because they caught the disease from the people they nursed. The Franciscans are often called Grey Friars because they originally wore a grey habit although they now wear brown. The main work of the Dominicans has always been teaching, for they believe that if people are taught properly they will hold correct beliefs. Sometimes they teach through very carefully prepared sermons and sometimes through the ordinary methods of school and university. Their greatest teacher, St. Thomas Aquinas, is still recognized as one of the greatest thinkers in the history of the Christian Church. (See AQUINAS, SAINT THOMAS.) The Dominicans are often called Black Friars because of their black cloaks. They gave the name "Blackfriars" to a road, a bridge and an area of the City of London, where they settled in the 13th century.

Other Monks and Friars

Apart from the Benedictines and Cistercians, the chief orders of monks in the Roman Catholic Church are the Carthusians and the Trappists. The Carthusian Order was founded by St. Bruno in 1084, and its members are scarcely ever permitted to speak to one another, each living, working and eating in his own cell. They have a long walk together outside the walls of the monastery once a week, during which they talk. Apart from this, they meet only at services in the church and at meals on feast days.

The Trappists follow an even stricter life and are never permitted to talk to one another. Originally founded (in 1664) as an extremely strict abbey, they joined the Cistercians after the French Revolution. The Trappists not only returned to the full strictness of the Rule but also added extra severities to their way of life, such as the rule against talking. Their correct name is

A Trappist Monk

the Reformed Cistercians of the Strict Observance and they take their more usual name from their first monastery, La Trappe, in Normandy.

Apart from the Franciscans and Dominicans, the main orders of friars are the Carmelites and the Augustinian Hermits. The proper name of the Carmelites is the Order of Our Lady of Mount Carmel. They are also known as White Friars, from their white cloaks, and gave their name to Whitefriars Street in the City of London, where they settled about 1241. The order was founded in Palestine about 1154 by St. Berthold. The Carmelites spend much of their time in prayer, study and parish work and in missionary work abroad. One of their most famous members was St. John of the Cross.

The Order of Augustinian Hermits was formed in 1256 in central Italy, where various collections of hermits were living under several different Rules. The Pope united them into one order and, as they were going to live under the Rule of St. Augustine of Hippo (on whom there is an article), they became known as Augustinian Hermits. The name "Hermits" is not really correct, for they live in a community and have the same sort of life as other friars. As well as the orders of monks and friars the Roman Catholic Church has other religious orders whose members do not live a community life. The Society of Jesus, whose members are called Jesuits, is perhaps the best known example of such an order. (See JESUITS.)

Anglican Orders

There are several orders of monks and friars in the Anglican Communion (see the separate article ANGLICAN COMMUNION). The Anglican orders are organized in much the same way as the Roman Catholic orders, and their members take the three vows of poverty, chastity and obedience. The Society of St. John the Evangelist, with headquarters at Oxford, was founded in 1866 and is thus the oldest order in the Church of England. Its members are often called the Cowley Fathers, for the order was founded in the parish of Cowley, in Oxford. It specializes in missionary work abroad, especially in India and South Africa. The Community of the Resurrection was founded in 1892 and has its headquarters at Mirfield in Yorkshire. Its members run a training college for men who wish to become Church of England clergymen, and undertake missionary work in South Africa and the West Indies. The Society of The Sacred Mission was founded in 1894 and has its headquarters at Kelham, in Nottinghamshire. The Order of St. Benedict, a much smaller order, lives at Nashdom Abbey, near Burnham in Buckinghamshire.

The Society of St. Francis is an order of friars who live near Dorchester in Dorset. They began their work in 1921, helping the poor.

Life in a Benedictine Monastery

In some ways Benedictine life has changed little for hundreds of years. This is not surprising, for the monks have always lived under the same Rule, that of St. Benedict. As the main purpose of the monks is to worship God through prayer the life of the monastery is ordered according to the times of the religious services. (These are described in a later paragraph, and together are known as the Divine Office.) Although the times of some of the services have

changed the same sort of services are held as in the past. The monks still wear the famous black habits like those of the monks of St. Benedict.

Today each monastery is governed by an abbot who has been elected for life by the monks. He has a deputy called the prior. The abbot has considerable authority but has to govern according to the Rule of the order and according to the laws of the Roman Catholic Church. When a monk takes the vow of obedience this means obedience to the will of God and obedience, also, to the abbot of his monastery. The individual has to give up his own life and learn to become one of a community; he could not do this if he pleased himself.

The abbot appoints monks to be in charge of

A Benedictine lay-brother

different aspects of the life of the monastery. The *cantor* or *precentor* is chief singer and keeper of the library. He arranges the services and chooses what is to be said or sung. The *sacrist* tends the altars and looks after the church. The *cellarer* orders the food and other goods needed by the monastery and keeps the accounts. Cooking is the work of the *kitchener*. The sick and aged monks are cared for by the *infirmerer*. (These last three jobs are often done by lay-brothers, who are not priests.) A *guest master* looks after visitors and travellers. Novices are in the charge of the *novice-master*.

The monastery has special names for some of its rooms. The *chapter house* is the room where meetings are held and the *refectory* is the dining room. The *cloister*, usually on the sunny side of the church, is a covered walk which is often built round the four sides of a square lawn. The monks sometimes work in the cloister and sometimes walk round it for exercise. Apart from the buildings with special names there are, of course,

A Carmelite Friar

the church, the kitchen and cellar, the hospital and the guest house. As we are talking of a Benedictine monastery the church is likely to be very beautiful, for the Benedictines believe that everything connected with worship must be beautiful in order to show the greatest honour to God. The church will probably contain rich decorations and carvings, and the singing will be practised with great care.

Since the Vatican Council of 1962 to 1965, the monastic Office, or service, has been shortened in most abbeys. There is a Morning Office at 6 a.m. followed by private prayer and private Masses. After breakfast the High Mass is celebrated and is followed by work, study or teaching until dinner. During meals one of the monks reads aloud to the others, first a chapter of the Bible, then part of a history or the life of a saint. After dinner, there is time for talking, walking or quiet relaxation. Vespers follow in the later afternoon and after supper, which is taken about 7 p.m., there is another short period of recreation followed usually by Compline, the final Office of the day, and then the monks go to their cells. From this time until the end of Morning Office nobody is permitted to talk.

MONMOUTHSHIRE was the name of a former county on the border between England and Wales. After local government reorganization in 1974 most of Monmouthshire, including Newport, became part of the new Welsh county of Gwent. The rest of Monmouthshire joined the counties of Mid Glamorgan and South Glamorgan. (See GWENT and GLAMORGAN.)

Monmouth is one of the six dioceses (districts under a bishop) in the Anglican Church in Wales. The area is bordered by the estuary of the River Severn to the south and on the east by Gloucester and Hereford and Worcester. To the west is Glamorgan and to the northwest the former county of Brecknockshire. The Welsh name for the former shire of Monmouth is Sir Fynwy.

The largest region of Monmouthshire is the Plain of Gwent, extending from the uplands—including Sugar Loaf Mountain—in the northwest, to the hill country of the Forest of Dean in Gloucestershire to the east. Between these two hilly regions the rivers Usk and Wye flow in a north-to-south direction to the Severn estuary.

Monmouthshire includes part of the great south Wales coalfield and the deep and steep valleys of the Rhymney, Sirhowy and Ebbw Rivers. Roads and railways have been built to follow these valleys.

Along the coast of the Severn estuary is a belt of flat land and much of this, locally called "levels" and "moors", is below high water level. Sea walls have been put up to protect it from flooding and a system of wide ditches, known as "reens", has been dug to drain the area. A reminder of the terrible floods of 1606, when about 2,000 people were drowned, are the stones built into many churches to mark the height which the waters reached.

Monmouthshire has large industrial areas, but the plain of the Usk is good farming country and the county has much woodland. The Wye is renowned for its beauty, particularly the bend of the river where the ruins of Tintern Abbey stand. In the Wye Valley grow serrate-leaved wintergreen (with notched leaves), stone bramble, lily of the valley, Solomon's seal and upright spurge. Unusual plants, including the white beak-rush, also grow in Treleck bog. The marshy "levels" are the homes of many water-plants and water-fowl, and salmon and trout swim in the rivers.

Monmouth, the former county town, is at the junction of the Wye and Monnow. An English king, Henry V, was born there and is sometimes known as Henry of Monmouth. The town

Monnow Bridge at Monmouth

UTRIQUE FIDELIS

miners at Llanhilleth

transporter bridge across the Usk at Newport

Tintern Abbey

1949, with modern housing and a traffic-free centre.

Other industrial towns of Monmouthshire are Rhymney, Tredegar, Ebbw Vale, Nantyglo, Abercarn, Pontypool, Mynyddislwyn and Bedwellty, all of which were once concerned with coalmining. At Ebbw Vale, Llanwern and Griffithstown are iron and steelworks.

Ironworks and wire-making works were established in Monmouthshire in the 16th century but the main coal and iron industries date from the 18th century. Pit coal was used to smelt iron—that is, to extract it from iron ore by melting—and iron, steel and tinplate production became the county's main industries. Before this, a lacquer works had been established at Pontypool and flourished until the middle of the 19th century.

This industrial development brought people from all parts of Britain to seek work, and as a result the Welsh-speaking people of Monmouthshire became outnumbered. Most of the people speak English with fewer than one person in thirty speaking Welsh.

The coal-mining parts of Monmouthshire suffered severely in the time known as the depression during the 1930s, when many people could not find work. After World War II, however, many new industries grew up. They include the making of glass, explosives, aluminium, nylon yarn, toys, rubber goods, clothing, motor parts, agricultural tools and furniture.

While western Monmouthshire is the industrial area, eastern Monmouthshire is the agricultural region. Much wheat is grown in the fertile areas along the Severn and the banks of the Usk. In the past many cattle and sheep were reared in the county, but now more attention is paid to milk production. Besides Monmouth and Usk, Chepstow on the Wye, near the Severn estuary, and Abergavenny on the Usk are market towns.

Monmouthshire in the Past

When the Romans invaded Britain the land of Monmouthshire was occupied by the warlike tribe of Britons called Silures, who were led by the great chief Caratacus. After resisting the Romans for several years, Caratacus was captured and taken to Rome, but the Emperor

was also the birthplace (probably in 1100) of Geoffrey of Monmouth, who collected and wrote down the legends of King Arthur.

Usk, a market town north of Caerleon, has the remains of a Norman castle overlooking the town. Adam of Usk, born in the town some time in the middle of the 14th century, was a lawyer who wrote a Latin chronicle (history) of the last years of the reign of Richard II and the first years of the reign of Henry IV. The great naturalist Alfred Russel Wallace, who with Charles Darwin explained the theory of evolution, was born at Usk in 1823. (See EVOLUTION; NATURALISTS.)

The largest town in the Monmouth area is Newport, which stands near the estuary of the Usk. It has large docks for seagoing ships and imports iron ore for the steelworks near by. To the north is Cwmbran, a new town established in

Claudius, who was impressed by his dignity and bravery, released him.

The Romans built Isca (Caerleon) which became the base for the Second Augustan Legion. (A legion is a large division of soldiers.) The plan of the fort has been uncovered, together with its water pipes, bath house and amphitheatre, all of which can be seen today.

The Romans built a town with shops, baths and temples for the Silures, 15 kilometres east of Caerleon. They called it Venta Silurum and it was the only non-military town in Roman Wales. Today it is the town of Caerwent. Less important Roman settlements were established at Usk, Monmouth and Abergavenny.

Before the days of the Norman kings, Monmouthshire was the Welsh kingdom of Gwent. There was a good deal of fighting between the Normans and the Welsh, the archers of Gwent becoming famed for their skill with the longbow. The Normans built many castles in Monmouthshire and made it into March Lordships. (This kind of march is the borderland between two countries.) In order to prevent fighting and to keep the roads open between one country and another, the kings of the middle ages used to put the borderlands in charge of strong noblemen.

The marches were made into the county of Monmouthshire in 1536, and, as it was a border county, the difficulty about whether it was English or Welsh arose. It was not definitely separated from Wales in 1536, but in 1543, when a new system of justice called the Court of Great Sessions was set up for Wales, Monmouthshire was treated differently from Wales by being joined to the Oxford Circuit in England. (A circuit is the journey of a judge in a particular district to hold courts.)

During the 17th century the more extreme Protestants were known as Puritans, and two Welsh Puritan leaders came from Monmouthshire. One was William Wroth, who was born in 1570 in Abergavenny and became vicar of Llanvaches. However, his bishop disliked his Puritanism, and with the aid of Walter Craddock Wroth established the first Nonconformist church in Wales at Llanvaches, about half-way between Newport and Chepstow.

During the hard times which followed the Napoleonic Wars, and particularly in the 1830s, some of the coal-miners and iron-workers of Monmouth became very discontented with their lot and joined the Chartist movement, which aimed at getting better conditions for working men. (See CHARTISTS.) On November 3 and 4, 1839, a large number of Chartists marched to Newport and made an uproar. Troops on guard fired into the crowd, killing 22 people. Three of the Chartist leaders (including John Frost, who had been mayor of Newport) were transported, or sent abroad, for life, but were pardoned more than 15 years later.

MONMOUTH'S REBELLION. In 1685 the Duke of Monmouth led an unsuccessful rebellion against James II.

Monmouth was born at Rotterdam in the Netherlands on April 9, 1649, and was the son of Charles II (then in exile) and Lucy Walter. Soon after Charles was restored to the throne in 1660 his handsome young son came to England and soon became popular. As he grew up people began to call him "the Protestant Duke" to distinguish him from the king's brother, the Duke of York, who was a Roman Catholic. York was heir to the throne, for Charles had no legitimate children, but he was very unpopular because few people wanted a Roman Catholic king. In 1683 there were plots against the throne and Monmouth thought it best to flee to the Netherlands in case he should be accused of taking part.

On February 6, 1685, Charles died and the Duke of York succeeded him as James II. On June 11 Monmouth landed at Lyme Regis (Dorset) with a few followers and claimed that he was the rightful king. By the time he reached Taunton (Somerset) he had an army of some thousands of men and had himself proclaimed king. However, his men were mostly peasants armed only with scythes and they had to fight against James's trained soldiers.

The rebels made a night attack on James's army camped at Sedgemoor (Somerset) but were driven off and slaughtered. Monmouth escaped but later was captured, disguised as a shepherd, in a ditch near Ringwood in the New Forest. He was beheaded on Tower Hill (London) on July 15, 1685. The other rebel prisoners were tried before Lord Chief Justice Jeffreys on his notorious Bloody Assize (see BLOODY ASSIZE).

A rising in Scotland at the same time as Monmouth's rising in England also failed.

MONSOON.

A monsoon is a seasonal wind blowing inland in summer and out to sea in winter. The monsoons are most important in India and China but they blow over all southeast Asia, in northern Australia, West Africa and parts of western America.

In the hot summers the air over these tropical lands grows tremendously hot. It expands, or swells, and the air pressure therefore falls. The air over the comparatively cool seas is at higher pressure and when it flows in to the low-pressure area over the land the monsoon begins. In India it is said to "break" because it starts so suddenly —as a southwest wind begins to blow over the coast near Bombay. This wind is laden with moisture from the Indian Ocean and brings drenching rain to much of the country. Bombay has as much rain in July as eastern England receives in a whole year, and June is nearly as wet.

In winter, when the air over the land cools and areas of high pressure form, dry winds blow out to sea and little or no rain falls. Bombay then seldom has any rain at all for five months.

The difference in rainfall between the two seasons in other monsoon countries is not so great as in India. In all of them the heavy summer rains often cause the rivers to flood. However, if the rains are late or poor, as they sometimes are, the food crops such as rice may fail and widespread famine be caused.

MONTCALM, LOUIS-JOSEPH DE MONTCALM-GOZON, MARQUIS DE (1712–1759).

The French General Montcalm had a commission in the army at 15 and was made a captain at 18. He distinguished himself in Germany and Italy and at the battle of Piacenza (1746) was wounded five times before being taken prisoner.

In 1756 he was made a major-general and given command of the French troops in Canada, where the struggle between Great Britain and France was reaching its height. During the next two years Montcalm won victories at Oswego, at Fort William Henry and also at Ticonderoga.

In 1759 Montcalm had to defend Quebec

Paul Popper

MONTE CARLO has a warm agreeable climate. It is sheltered from north winds by the southernmost slopes of the Alps.

against the brilliant young British general James Wolfe. (See WOLFE, JAMES.) For more than two months Montcalm beat off attacks near the city, but in the end he was outwitted. Wolfe and his army sailed up the St. Lawrence River, disembarked under cover of darkness and stormed the city by scaling the steep cliffs called the Heights of Abraham. The French were taken by surprise. In the battle that followed both Wolfe and Montcalm (who had behaved with great gallantry) were mortally wounded. The British capture of Quebec put an end to French rule in Canada. In 1828 a monument in honour of both generals was erected in Quebec by Canadians of French and British descent.

MONTE CARLO.
The famous pleasure resort of Monte Carlo forms the northeastern part of the little country of Monaco, on which there is a separate article.

In 1861 François Blanc of Homburg (Germany) obtained permission to set up gambling tables at Monte Carlo. His casino (the name for a gambling house) and its beautiful gardens attracted visitors from all parts of the world.

Monte Carlo has several luxurious hotels and its warm agreeable climate makes it a pleasant place in which to stay. There is a theatre famous for its ballet and orchestras and in the summer there are yacht races and other sports on the Mediterranean. There are also many carnivals, among them the joyous festival of roses.

MONTEVIDEO
is the capital of the South American republic of Uruguay. It lies on the north bank of the estuary of the Plata River and is an important port at the entrance to this great waterway. In 1520 the Portuguese explorer Ferdinand Magellan sailed into the estuary. One of his sailors saw a cone-shaped hill rising from the flat coast and called out *"Monte vide eu!"* ("I see a mountain!") This gave the name to the town that later grew up round this hill, which is now known as the Cerro.

The old part of the city stands on a rocky headland. Between the headland and the Cerro to the westward is an almost circular bay. In 1901 breakwaters, basins and docks were built to make the bay into a harbour through which

Paul Popper
Independence Square is the centre of Montevideo's life.

passes most of the foreign trade of Uruguay.

Montevideo is a clean city with wide streets and squares and many fine buildings. Most of the modern houses are white, with gaily painted shutters, and gardens. Within the city there are several beautiful parks and the oldest of them, the Prado, has rose gardens in which nearly 800 kinds of roses are grown. Along the coast there are a number of sandy beaches where there is splendid bathing. Many people live near these beaches in bungalows and blocks of flats and travel by bus to work or to school. Yachting and football are popular sports. The beaches are a summer resort for many people from Argentina and Brazil as well as for Uruguayans.

Much of the industrial part of Montevideo lies near the Cerro, where there are factories for canning meat and making textiles, shoes, soap and other goods, many of them run by the state. The main railways and roads of Uruguay all fan out from Montevideo, which has its airport at Carrasco about 20 kilometres away.

The city of Montevideo was founded by the Spaniards in 1726, the first settlers being people from the Canary Islands and from Galicia and Andalusia in Spain. It was captured by British troops in 1807 during the campaign against the Spanish possessions in America but was abandoned when the British expedition against

Buenos Aires was defeated. The Spanish troops were driven out in 1814 by Argentine forces but rivalry between Argentina and Brazil over the possession of Uruguay continued to hamper the growth of Montevideo for another 50 years. It became the capital of Uruguay in 1828.

The population of Montevideo is about 1,280,000, so that it contains something like one-half of the people of Uruguay.

MONTFORT, Simon de (c. 1208–1265).

For most of Henry III's long reign his barons disliked the way he governed the kingdom. They hated the favour he showed to foreigners, and his habit of spending money he could not afford in seeking foreign kingdoms for his relatives. The barons were particularly angry when, in 1255, Henry tried to buy the Mediterranean kingdom of Sicily for his son, Edmund.

So in 1258 the barons insisted that, in future, Henry should govern as they wished through a Council they had chosen. Their leader was Simon de Montfort, Earl of Leicester. He was a French nobleman who had only come to England in 1231 as one of Henry's foreign favourites, and in 1238 he had married Eleanor, the King's sister. Simon, who was a masterful man, soon quarrelled with the other barons, and many ceased to help him. In 1263 King Louis of France tried, but failed, to settle the quarrel. Then civil war began, and in May 1264 Simon defeated the royal army at Lewes (Sussex) and captured Henry III and his son, the future Edward I. But Edward later escaped.

Simon ruled as he pleased until 1265, when he and his followers were killed at the Battle of Evesham. He is remembered as the first to have attempted to limit the power of monarchy and foster that of parliament, through his supporters, the county knights and burgesses.

MONTGOMERY OF ALAMEIN, BERNARD LAW MONTGOMERY, 1ST VISCOUNT (born 1887).

The most successful British general of World War II was Montgomery. A careful and thorough strategist, he defeated the German army in North Africa, commanded the Allied landings in Normandy in 1944 and led the northern wing of their forces across France and into Germany. Montgomery was the son of the Bishop of Tasmania and was strictly brought up by his mother. The children had to stand

Peter Skingley of Planet News

Three comrades in arms—Montgomery with Winston Churchill and General Eisenhower at the Alamein Reunion in 1951.

like soldiers while their rooms were inspected, do lessons and attend chapel—all before breakfast. Bernard Montgomery was educated at King's School, Canterbury, and at St. Paul's School, London. He then went to the Royal Military College (now the Royal Military Academy, Sandhurst) and joined the Royal Warwickshire Regiment as an officer in 1908. In World War I he was twice wounded and won the D.S.O.

When the British army was forced to retreat to the French coast in 1940, during the early part of World War II, Montgomery skilfully withdrew his division to the Dunkirk beaches. He then held commands in Great Britain and soon became known for his unusual methods. Middle-aged staff officers had to go for runs with the rest of the troops. When Montgomery lectured he gave the audience two minutes in which to cough, and after that woe betide anyone who coughed during the lecture!

In August 1942 the British Eighth Army had been driven back over the Libyan desert to the last defences before Cairo by the forces under Field Marshal Rommel, a brilliant German soldier. Montgomery was sent to command the Eighth Army and soon the soldiers knew the slight, wiry general wearing the black beret of the Royal Armoured Corps, for he drove round to see them all and promised them victory. Then at the Battle of Alamein Montgomery drove Rommel's forces headlong across North Africa to Tunisia. (See ALAMEIN, BATTLE OF.) Like most of his victories, this one depended mainly on two things. The first was thorough preparation, for Montgomery would not attack until troops, guns, air support and supplies were ready, and until he had full information about the enemy. The second reason for Montgomery's success was that he made himself known to his troops and made each man feel that he had an important part to play.

Montgomery returned to the United Kingdom in the early spring of 1944 to command the 21st Army Group (1st Canadian and 2nd British Armies), which was preparing to reconquer northwest Europe from the Germans. He commanded the 21st Army Group until the end of the war. However, during the actual landings, which began on June 6, 1944, and the earlier battles in the beachhead, he commanded all the Allied troops. He was made a Field Marshal in September 1944. He was later made a Viscount and became Chief of the Imperial General Staff. In 1951 he became Deputy Supreme Commander of the Allied Powers in Europe. He resigned from this post in 1958.

MONTGOMERYSHIRE was the name of a county on the eastern border of Wales which after local government reorganization in 1974 became part of the new county of Powys (see Powys). This article describes Montgomeryshire as it was until 1974.

Montgomery's eastern border is with the English county of Salop, to the north are the former counties of Denbighshire and Merioneth and to the south the former counties of Radnorshire and Cardiganshire. The region is a land of mountains and river valleys. Among the rivers are the Vyrnwy and the Dovey, while the sources of both the Severn and the Wye are in the Plynlimon mountains. Parts of the Berwyn Mountains, which rise to 825 metres, the Kerry Hills, and, on the Salop border, the Breidden Hills and Corndon Hill, stand in Montgomery.

A great dam built near the source of the Vyrnwy in 1888 forms an artificial lake. The water is carried through pipelines to Liverpool, 95 kilometres away. Near Llanidloes the Clywedog Reservoir was built in 1967 to control the flow of the Severn. Its dam, 65 metres high, is one of the highest in Britain.

Birds such as the curlew live in the mountainous parts. In the lowlands there are wild duck and, in winter, flights of geese. There are salmon and trout in the Wye, the Severn and the Dovey.

Montgomeryshire is mainly agricultural, well known for its cattle, sheep and red clover, but has some light industries. The towns are small. Montgomery, near the English border, is the old county town, but most business is carried on at Welshpool and Newtown.

Newtown, on the Severn, near the border with Radnor, is a lively market town, growing rapidly under a government expansion programme. Welshpool, north of Montgomery, also has a large market where cattle are sold. At Welshpool is Powis Castle, parts of which were

Lake Vyrnwy

Old Market Hall Llanidloes

clock tower Machynlleth

Powis Castle Welshpool

built in the 12th century. It is the seat of the Earl of Powis.

At Machynlleth in the valley of the Dovey is a building which is claimed to have been the place where the Welsh hero Owen Glendower held a parliament in the early part of the 15th century. (See GLENDOWER, OWEN.) Llanidloes is an ancient town on the Severn.

There are many remains of prehistoric people in Montgomeryshire. The Breidden Hills are said to have been the scene of the last stand of the British king Caratacus (Caradoc) against the Roman invaders in A.D. 51. Along much of the eastern boundary of the county runs the ancient earthwork known as Offa's Dyke. It was probably built in the 8th century by Offa, king of the Mercians, to mark the extent of his conquests.

MONTH. The year is divided into 12 periods known as months; some of them have 31 days, some 30 days, and one—February—has 28 days, except in Leap Years when it has 29. (See LEAP YEAR.) However, months have not always been divided up in this way and there have not always been 12 of them in the year. The word "month" is connected with the word "moon", and when the ancient peoples first made calendars a month was measured by the length of time from new moon to new moon—this is about $29\frac{1}{2}$ days. The month then began when the new crescent moon was first seen in the sky at sunset and the lengths of the months were either 29 or 30 days. The article CALENDAR explains why this did not produce an accurate calendar and why, therefore, the system was dropped. Our present months, with their different numbers of days, do not correspond to any movements of the heavenly bodies.

Sometimes when people use the word "month" they mean any period of 28 days—which may easily occur in two different months so far as the calendar is concerned. Therefore, whenever it is necessary to distinguish between the two uses of the word, the months as shown on the calendar are often spoken of as calendar months.

The names of the months came from those that the ancient Romans used, and as they spoke Latin all the English names are taken from Latin. Some of the original Latin names were given in honour of gods and goddesses, some in honour of famous people and some according to the order in which the months occurred. The last method of naming has had a very interesting result for us today—because September, October, November and December are Latin words meaning 7th, 8th, 9th and 10th, whereas they are actually the 9th, 10th, 11th and 12th months of our year. This curious situation arises from the fact that in the earlier period of their history the Romans used a calendar in which there were only ten months in the year, the first month being March. Thus the months we know as September, October, November and December really were the 7th, 8th, 9th and 10th months. About 700 B.C. the calendar was reformed by Numa who added two months at the beginning of the year, January and February. The old names of the previous ten months were continued, however, and so have come down to us.

January takes its name from Janus, a Roman god who had two faces and looked in two directions at the same time. This was probably intended to express the idea that January looks backward to the old year and forward to the new one.

February got its name from the Roman god Februus, who presided over ceremonies of purification held at that time of the year.

March took its name from the god Mars, who was thought to look after both the agricultural and the military activities of the Romans. As this is the season when people, plants and animals begin to receive the new life that comes with spring, it is easy to understand the connection between Mars and the month.

It is not certain that the name April had a Roman origin, but it probably came from the Latin word *aperire*, which means to open—describing the season at which plants open and grow after the winter. May was probably named after the goddess Maia, originally a Greek goddess whose name meant "mother" or "nurse". Probably again there was the idea of the growing crops. June may have been called after the goddess Juno, who looked after women, but this is by no means certain. July commemorates Julius Caesar who made many alterations to the calendar of the Romans. (See CALENDAR; JULIUS CAESAR.) August commemorates Augustus Caesar, the first of the Roman emperors (see AUGUSTUS CAESAR).

MONTREAL. Although it is in Canada, Montreal is the largest French-speaking city in the world after Paris. It is also the largest city in Canada and its chief port and commercial centre. In the province of Quebec, it is situated on Montreal Island in the St. Lawrence River. The port of Montreal is nearly 1,600 kilometres from the Atlantic, but it is nevertheless nearer to the port of Liverpool than New York is. Montreal's great harbour stretches for 25 kilometres along the river. It is ice-free from May to November and huge quantities of wheat are loaded into ships there. Montreal is also Canada's greatest railway junction and has a busy airport at Dorval, southwest of the city. The chief manufactures are engineering and electrical goods, tobacco, textiles, shoes and cement.

J. Allan Cash from Rapho-Guillumette

Skyscrapers in a variety of modern shapes beautify Montreal, Canada's largest city.

Montreal takes its name from Mont Réal (French for "Mount Royal"), which rises 230 metres behind the city. On the top is a huge cross which is lit up at night.

In 1535 Jacques Cartier sailed up the St. Lawrence and reached an American Indian village called Hochelaga where Montreal now is. In 1611 Samuel de Champlain set up a trading post there, and in 1642 Paul de Chomedey de Maisonneuve started a Roman Catholic mission named Ville Marie de Montréal on the island. The French in Montreal held out against the British for a year after the capture of Quebec by James Wolfe in 1759 but all Canada came under British rule at the peace of 1763. Even today, however, about two-thirds of Montreal's people speak French and are of French descent.

The population of Montreal is about 2,743,000.

MONTROSE, JAMES GRAHAM, MARQUESS OF (1612–1650). Apart from Oliver Cromwell, the Marquess of Montrose—a Scottish nobleman—was the most skilful soldier of the Civil War. (See CIVIL WAR; CROMWELL, OLIVER.)

He first came into prominence in 1637 when he helped to draw up a document known as the National Covenant. At that time King Charles I was trying to make the Church of Scotland use the Prayer Book of the Church of England and adopt the same type of organization as that Church. The Scots refused to make these changes and drew up the National Covenant, which stated that the Church of Scotland must remain free from the Church of England. Nearly all the leading nobles of Scotland signed it, and the King was forced to give in.

However, Montrose soon found himself unable to agree with the Scottish leader Archibald Campbell, Marquess of Argyll, who was seeking power for himself and was trying to make everybody in Scotland become Presbyterians (see PRESBYTERIANS). Montrose did not wish to see Argyll all-powerful, nor did he approve of forcing people to become Presbyterians. He finally broke with Argyll and the Covenanters when they gave their support to the Puritans (see PURITANS) in England, who agreed to try to force all the people of England and Ireland to accept their form of religion. After the Civil War broke out in England in 1642 between the King and the Puritans, Montrose sided with the King. He constantly asked the King to let him raise an army in Scotland to fight against Argyll, who was helping the Puritans of England against the King. Charles could not make up his mind, so Montrose joined him in England and in 1644 was at last given permission to attack Argyll.

Disguised as a groom, with only two followers, Montrose made his way into the Highlands of Scotland to rally the clans. He never had a permanent base, never had guns other than those he captured and had to keep on raising fresh troops—apart from the Irish Macdonalds who joined him and stayed with him for some time—because the Highlanders often went home after a battle. In spite of these and other difficulties he fought brilliantly and won six battles (Tippermuir, Aberdeen, Inverlochy, Auldearn, Alford and Kilsyth). Successful at last, he summoned the Scottish parliament to meet on October 20, 1645. This never happened as the defeat of the King at Naseby in England compelled Montrose to go to his help, but on the way he was surprised and defeated at Philiphaugh, near Selkirk, by much larger forces.

In September 1646 he escaped abroad but returned in 1649 to try to win Scotland for the

Montrose was one of the ablest soldiers of the Civil War.

young Charles II, who was living in exile on the continent of Europe. (Charles had taken the title of king when his father Charles I was executed by Cromwell and the Puritans in January 1649.) However, Montrose failed to raise the clans and was sold to Argyll by Macleod of Assynt, with whom he had taken refuge. On May 21, 1650, he was hanged in Edinburgh.

MONTSERRAT. The British colony of Montserrat lies in the Caribbean Sea. (See WEST INDIES.) It has an area of 39 square miles and lies southwest of Antigua in the Leeward Islands. Montserrat is volcanic, rising to 3,000 feet.

It has a warm climate with plentiful rainfall. Hurricanes may occur. The chief products are cotton, limes, bananas and vegetables, and there are factories processing cotton, making syrup and distilling rum. The population is about 14,000, of whom some 3,000 live in Plymouth, the capital and only port.

Montserrat was not easily visited before the completion of Blackburne airfield in 1956. Discovered by Christopher Columbus in 1493, the island was named after a mountain in Catalonia, Spain, which has a famous monastery. It is governed by a council under an administrator who is appointed by the British government.

MONUMENTS. The word "monument" means a memorial, something which keeps alive the memory of a person, or of an event, or of a time in history. The pyramids in Egypt, for example, are monuments to the kings of far-off times who are buried within them. In Rome huge arches, known as triumphal arches, were set up in honour of the victories of Roman generals in war, and there is a famous triumphal arch—the Arc de Triomphe—in Paris, commemorating the victories of Napoleon's armies. In nearly every town and village in Great Britain there is a very familiar kind of monument—the war memorial which honours the memory of soldiers, and often civilians as well, who were killed in war. Many war memorials are stone pillars or crosses, and the most famous one in Britain is the stone monument called the Cenotaph in Whitehall, London.

Some of the monuments in public places have been set up in memory of individual people, like the memorial to Queen Victoria, which stands outside Buckingham Palace, or Nelson's Column in Trafalgar Square. Most of the statues of people in streets and public places are monuments of this kind.

Tombs and Temples

Because the word "monument" means something that serves as a reminder of past times, it is used in some of the structures of stone and earth that were made by the people of prehistoric ages and ancient civilizations. The prehistoric stone monuments in Britain belong to two different types. They are either graves or temples. The graves were originally covered by mounds of earth but these have long since been washed away by rain or ploughed up by the farmers of later times, and what is left now is the stone room or chamber in which the bodies of the dead people were placed. Stone monuments like this are often called megaliths, from the Greek words *megalo*, meaning "large", and *lithos*, meaning "stone". They have been found all over the world and were built by people who lived nearly 4,000 years ago, between 2000 B.C. and 1800 B.C.

Some of the graves are called gallery graves because the actual burial-place is made in the shape of a long low room or gallery. Gallery graves were built of large slabs of stone set upright, with other slabs forming the roof.

Another kind of tomb is the passage grave, so called because the burial chamber is connected to the outside by a long low passage. Often the mound which covered a passage grave was surrounded by a circle of large stones. Like the gallery graves, the passage graves were used for more than one burial, but they were built rather later by people who had already begun to use metal. One of the finest examples of a passage grave in Britain is Maeshowe in the Orkneys. It has a great central chamber with a domed roof, and three smaller rooms opening off it in which the bodies were placed.

Open-air temples, made of large stones set on end, are not so common as tombs but they are found in northern France and southern England. They consist of one or more circles of stones surrounded by a ditch and an earth bank. The

Courtesy, British Tourist Authority

The monuments of Westminster Abbey include some to famous writers in Poets' Corner. Among those shown here are Tennyson, Longfellow, Ben Jonson, Samuel Butler, John Milton, Edmund Spenser, Thomas Gray and Matthew Prior.

most famous ones in England are Avebury and Stonehenge, both of which are described in separate articles. Like the churches of modern times, temples such as these, built in the late Stone Age or early Bronze Age (about 1800 B.C.), were rebuilt and added to from time to time, and in some of them graves have been placed close to the stones, just as today people are buried close to a church. We do not know what gods were worshipped in the stone temples, nor what the ceremonies that took place in them were like.

Memorials in Churches

Some of the oldest memorials in churches in Britain date from the 12th century A.D. In those days rich and distinguished persons were laid to rest in stone coffins and often the coffins were buried in the floors of churches so that the lids became part of the pavement. At first there were no words on them and they were decorated simply with a cross and circle which was cut or carved in the stone. Later on, the dead man's

name was sometimes carved on them, and a design showing what his occupation had been in life. Thus men-at-arms were shown by weapons, priests by a chalice and staff (the chalice is the cup used in the Communion service) and merchants by articles of their particular trade.

From the 13th century onwards thin sheets of brass began to be used as memorials. Designs were cut into the metal and outlined with black, or sometimes decorated with coloured enamel. The brass sheets were then set in level with the stone flooring of the churches. Brasses, as they are called, went on being made until the 17th century and there are many of them still to be seen in churches.

Towards the end of the 13th century a new kind of memorial began to be made. A life-sized figure of the dead person was made in stone or metal and placed on top of the tomb in the church. Figures like these are called effigies. The earliest effigies look rather stiff and unnatural but later on the figures were made more life-like, and sometimes knights in armour were represented in alert, cross-legged positions, as if ready to spring to life in an instant. Usually, however, they were shown in repose, their heads resting on their helmets, hands clasped in prayer, a lion or a dog crouching at their feet. In the 15th and 16th centuries figures of the dead person's children were sometimes carved kneeling in groups round the tomb.

The most usual kind of monuments to be seen in churches nowadays, however, are not in the floor or on tombs but on the walls. Tablets and plaques of metal, wood or stone of various kinds are set in the walls of many churches and cathedrals to commemorate people who lived in the district or who were associated with the church.

MOON. In ancient times the Moon was often worshipped as a goddess and even when people ceased to worship it their superstitions about the Moon lingered on. It used to be thought that the old Moon had a bad influence, while the new Moon and the full Moon were considered lucky. People therefore chose the times of new and full Moon for beginning important activities. Even today some believe that the Moon influences the weather, though probably that is not true. But the Moon does affect the tides of the sea, whose rise and fall are caused mostly by the pull of the Moon and Sun. (See TIDES AND CURRENTS.)

The Moon is a satellite of the Earth. As the Earth moves round the Sun, the Moon in turn revolves round the Earth. (See SATELLITE; SOLAR SYSTEM.) The Earth weighs 81 times as much as the Moon. The pull of gravity at the Moon's surface is only one-sixth as strong as that on the Earth's surface (see GRAVITATION), so that a man on the Moon's surface—if unencumbered by a space suit—could jump six times as high as he could on Earth. But as the Moon has almost no atmosphere and no moisture, no one can live there without a space suit.

Strange effects result from this lack of air and water. No noise is made when a meteorite falls on the Moon's surface, because there is no air to carry the sound waves. There are no rains, no oceans, no smells. The most powerful telescopes make the Moon appear as it would to the naked eye if it were only 300 kilometres away. The Moon's average distance from the Earth is actually 384,400 kilometres and its diameter 3,476 kilometres.

Surface of the Moon

Study of the Moon with artificial satellites began on September 13, 1959, when the Russian instrument capsule Lunik 2 became the first man-made object to reach the Moon's surface. Other Russian and American unmanned spacecraft photographed the Moon from orbit or landed and transmitted pictures from its surface. In December 1968 the American Apollo 8 spacecraft took three men in orbit round the Moon. The historic first manned landing on the Moon on July 20, 1969 by Apollo 11 was followed by several others, during which astronauts began the scientific exploration of the Moon. Unmanned spacecraft have also returned samples of rock from the Moon. (See APOLLO PROGRAMME; SPACE EXPLORATION.)

Only one side of the Moon is visible from Earth. This is because it makes one turn on its axis in the same length of time that it takes to make one journey round the Earth, so that the same side of the Moon always faces the Earth. We can actually see slightly more than half the Moon's surface (about four-sevenths altogether) because of slight wobbles in the Moon's motion as seen from the Earth. The hidden side appears to be similar to the visible side.

When the Italian scientist Galileo made a telescope in 1609, one of the first things he observed through it was the Moon. He saw its craters and mountains, and the dark markings called *maria* (Latin for "seas"). The *maria* are not really seas, however. In 1647 the German astronomer Johannes Hevelius made a map showing many details of the Moon's surface. The biggest markings were named by the Italian astronomer Giovanni Riccioli, who published a map in 1651. Some of the mountains were named after those on the Earth, such as the Alps and Apennines. The craters were named after scientists and philosophers, including Riccioli himself. Many craters on the hidden side of the Moon, which was first observed by the Russian Lunik 3 in 1959, have now been given names.

The Moon's craters show up most clearly when they cast long shadows. The "seas" of rock or dust always appear dark.

The thousands of craters which can be seen scattered over the surface of the Moon are generally much larger than similar craters on the surface of the Earth. The largest known crater is on the hidden side of the Moon. The Bailly Crater, which is about 290 kilometres across, is the biggest that can be seen from the Earth. At the other extreme, there are some craters less than 1 metre across.

It is not certain how the craters were formed, although there has been much discussion about it. Most scientists believe that many of the craters were formed by the fall of meteorites.

FIRST QUARTER

NEW MOON

FULL MOON

RAYS OF LIGHT FROM THE SUN

EARTH

LAST QUARTER

Yerkes Observatory; University of Chicago Press

Half the Moon is always dark, as shown by the inner circle in the diagram. The outer circle shows the Moon as seen from the Earth. When it is between the Earth and the Sun (A), no Moon is seen. As the Moon moves to (B) "the new Moon" is seen. By the time it reaches (E), completing half of its journey, it is a "full Moon."

(See METEOR AND METEORITE.) Because there is no air or water on the Moon, the crater walls have not been worn away by wind and waves like the walls of meteorite craters on the Earth.

The Moon has no light of its own and shines only because it reflects the Sun's light. As it turns on its axis only once in a journey round the Earth, each part of its surface has first about two weeks of darkness and then about two weeks of sunlight. Of the lighted half of the Moon, only that part which is turned towards the Earth can be seen by us. When the Moon in its travels comes between the Earth and the Sun's rays, it is almost entirely invisible because its lighted half is turned towards the Sun and its dark half towards the Earth. This is the time of "new Moon". A few days later, a thin crescent Moon is seen in the western sky, but the whole disc is seen faintly because lit by Earth-shine (light reflected from the Earth). This appearance is sometimes called "the old Moon in the new Moon's arms". The crescent waxes, or grows larger, as more of the Moon's lighted surface is turned towards the Earth. At "full Moon" the whole of the lighted surface can be seen, after which the Moon wanes, or grows smaller, until it becomes a thin C-shaped crescent. The Moon takes a lunar month ($29\frac{1}{2}$ of our days) to go through these phases. Ancient calendars (see CALENDAR) reckoned by lunar months.

Man's knowledge of the Moon has increased greatly with the progress of lunar exploration. When Apollo 11 landed in the Sea of Tranquillity in 1969 astronauts Armstrong and Aldrin

Keystone
The Copernicus crater photographed in 1966 by the unmanned American space-craft Lunar Orbiter 2. The smaller dark crater in the foreground is about 13 miles across.

Courtesy, NASA

This photograph of the near side of the Moon was taken by Apollo 12 and shows the area around the crater Kepler. Kepler is about 35 kilometres in diameter and its rim throws long shadows across the lunar surface.

set up three experiments: a reflector for laser beams to measure accurately the distance from the Earth, a device to measure the solar radiation reaching the Moon, and a seismometer to measure moonquakes and meteorite impacts. Over 20 kilograms of Moon rock were brought back for study by scientists all over the world.

Apollo 12, which landed in the Ocean of Storms, carried more experiments, some of which were powered by a small nuclear generator. This equipment continued sending information back to Earth after the astronauts had returned.

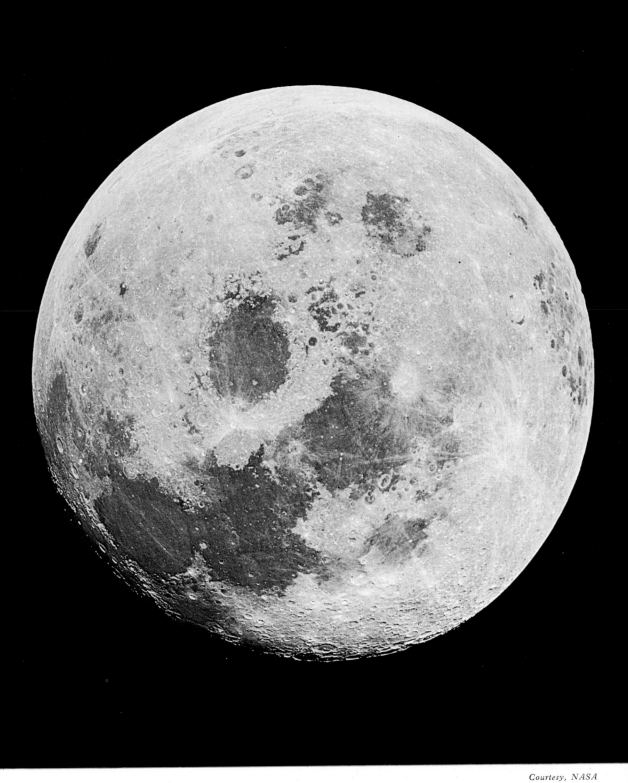

Courtesy, NASA

The full Moon seen by the astronauts in Apollo 11 as it returned to Earth. The dark areas are the lunar seas, or *maria*.

267

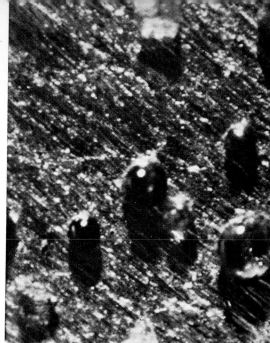

Courtesy, United States Information Service

Left: Surveyor 3's foot pad photographed by the Apollo 12 astronauts, showing clearly how the spacecraft bounced on landing. There is no rain or wind to erode marks in the lunar dust. Right: The Moon's surface is covered with glassy spheres made by meteorite impact. The largest shown is 0.4 millimetres in diameter.

Almost 30 kilograms of rock were collected.

On later flights the astronauts used an electrically-powered lunar roving vehicle so that they could explore a larger region around the spacecraft than would be possible on foot. During several Apollo missions used spacecraft were deliberately crashed on to the surface of the Moon. Seismometers placed there by the astronauts registered the shocks caused by the impact for more than an hour, much longer than scientists had expected. (Seismometers are instruments used on Earth to record earthquakes.) The instruments also recorded many natural Moonquakes. Some of these are caused by falling meteorites, but others originate deep within the Moon.

The Apollo Moon flights revealed the presence of gravitational irregularities on the Moon. These areas were called mascons and were thought to be masses of dense material lying roughly 50 kilometres beneath the surface. The magnetometer left behind by Apollo 12 revealed that the Moon's magnetic field was tiny compared with the Earth's, but that it was stronger than had been expected.

Examination of the samples of rock brought back to Earth by the first two manned Moon flights showed that the surface consisted mainly of oxides of silicon, magnesium and iron. Many of the fragments resembled basalt rocks found on Earth. The crystalline rocks were dark grey and contained small, round holes. The glass-like "marbles" found on the Moon's surface were of various colours, from colourless to grey, green, brown and red. The structure of the rock samples showed that the Moon had once been volcanically active. Those brought back by the crew of Apollo 11 were thought to be at least 3,500,000,000 years old and the dust which covers most of the Moon is still older. There was no evidence of life on the Moon, past or present, but water vapour may occasionally exist.

The great age of the rocks indicated that the Moon had probably never been a part of the Earth which had later split away. Nor was it likely that the Moon had once been an independent planet which had been captured by the Earth's gravitational pull. In either of these cases, scientists thought, the Moon's surface would have been in a molten state more recently than was shown by the rocks, because of the immense release of energy. It seemed that the Moon might have been formed out of the same cloud of dust as the Earth but lost its atmosphere and ceased its surface activity much more quickly because it was less massive.

MOORE, Henry Spencer (born 1898).

The best known works by this English sculptor are the large forms that are known as reclining figures. Many of them are recognizable as human beings, but they look almost as if a person were slowly changing into a prehistoric monster or into a huge stone polished smooth by wind and weather.

Moore was born at Castleford in Yorkshire where his father was a miner. Henry always intended to be a sculptor and when he was about ten the stories he was told about Michelangelo strengthened his resolve. His imagination was fired when he discovered the primitive art and sculpture of the African Negroes and the Aztecs of Mexico. When he came to London to study at the Royal College of Art he spent most of his weekends at the British Museum looking at ancient sculpture. In 1925 a travelling scholarship took him to Italy for six months, and in the splendid frescoes of Masaccio he found simple monumental figures which seemed more wonderful than anything he had seen.

It became Moore's aim to create simple and powerful sculpture. At times this led him to make completely abstract sculpture; that is, sculpture that does not copy other things but uses shapes and sizes suitable to the material in which it is made, whether stone, wood or metal. By the

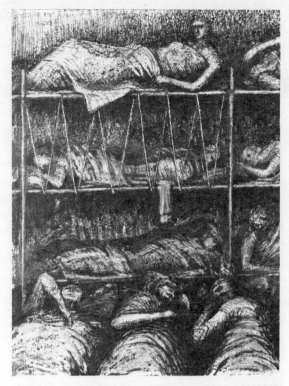

Courtesy, Marlborough Fine Art (London) Ltd.

Above: In World War II many Londoners were allowed to spend the night on the platforms of Underground railway stations, sheltered from German air raids. This reproduction of a Henry Moore drawing depicts the scene. Below: This reclining figure sculptured by Moore in elm is somewhat larger than life size.

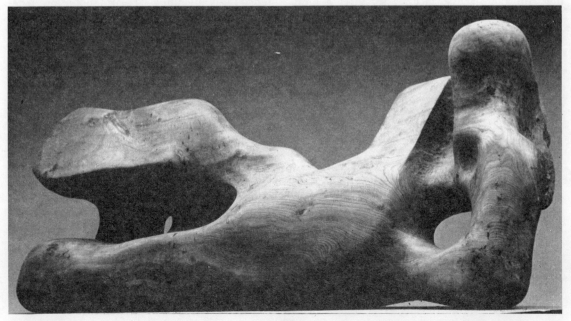

late 1930s Moore's work was becoming widely known. During World War II he made many drawings of people in London sheltering from the air raids—mysterious, impersonal, sleeping figures rather than people wrapped in blankets.

After the war Moore rapidly became world famous for his sculptures in stone and metal. These smooth rounded forms, some recognizably human with huge limbs and small heads, others abstract and pierced with holes, became familiar at exhibitions in many countries. Later he lived in Italy near the great Carrara marble quarries and his latest works, exhibited in London in 1968, were immense abstract carvings in polished marble—shapes felt simply as shapes, "not as description or reminiscence", as Moore said.

MOORHEN.

Another name for the moorhen is the waterhen, which is really a better name as it is a water-bird. The moorhen is about 33 centimetres long and has brownish-black plumage with white feathers along its sides and under its tail. Its bill is yellow with a red patch at the base. The legs are green with red round the tops and the toes are very long.

Moorhens are found on all types of wet ground, but they like to keep under cover. On land they walk with long strides and jerk their heads and tails. When rising off the water they first run along the surface. They utter a loud croaking sound when alarmed. They eat mainly

The moorhen.

the seeds and fruit of plants growing near the water, but also some small animals.

The nest of the moorhen is made of dead reeds or sticks and is usually found among plants on the water's edge or in the branches of trees or bushes. The hen bird lays from 5 to 11 buff-coloured eggs marked with brown spots. The young birds are covered with black down and can swim soon after they are hatched.

Moorhens are found all over the British Isles and also live in the continent of Europe, in Asia, Africa and America, where they are called gallinules. There are various other species, or kinds, in South Africa and Australia.

MOORS

are the Moslem peoples of northwest Africa. The word Moor comes from Mauri which was the name given by the Romans to the inhabitants of Mauretania (now Morocco and Algeria) which they conquered in 25 B.C. Mauretania was invaded by the Arabs in the 7th century A.D. and they finally conquered it in 702. They converted the Mauri to the Moslem religion. (See ISLAM.)

Soon afterwards the Moorish Arabs were asked by a ruler in southern Spain to help him in a rebellion against King Roderick of Spain. They came across and captured Gibraltar, which takes its name from their leader Tarik ibn Ziyad (*Jebel Tarik*, meaning "Tarik's mountain"), defeated Roderick and in 711 overran all southern Spain. The Moors then pushed onwards into France and in 732 captured Bordeaux, but were later driven out of France again. They established themselves in Spain, however, and set up a kingdom there. Under the Moors, Spain became the most civilized country of western Europe. They introduced the study of such subjects as astronomy, geography, chemistry and natural history, and their capital Cordova became a centre of learning for Christians as well as Moslems. Many of the beautiful Moorish buildings in Spain are still to be seen, including the magnificent Alhambra, a splendid palace and fortress built by the Moorish kings in the 13th and 14th centuries near the city of Granada. (See ALHAMBRA.) After the 10th century, however, the power of the Moors in Spain gradually declined as the Spaniards slowly reconquered their country. Granada was the last Moorish stronghold and when it surrendered in 1492 the Moors became Spanish subjects until the last of them were driven out of the country in 1610.

Today the name Moor is loosely used for all the Arab peoples of Morocco and also for those living farther south in the Atlas Mountains and in the Sahara as far south as Timbuktu.

The Moors are not black people, as the word "blackamoor" suggests. Although usually bronzed by the sun, they belong to white stock and the men are handsome, fine-featured, bearded and distinguished in appearance. Their manner is dignified and polite but beneath it there is a strain of brutality. The Barbary pirates were Moors and during the 16th, 17th and 18th centuries they preyed on European shipping off the North African coast with barbarous cruelty (see BARBARY PIRATES). Any sailor captured by the pirates was either put to death or made to toil for the rest of his life at the oars of the pirate craft called galleys. The Barbary pirates practised slavery for 300 years and their slave markets survived until about 1850 when they were closed under pressure from European countries.

MOOSE and ELK.

The largest living member of the deer family is the moose. It is also the largest wild animal in North America, which is the only region where it lives. When full grown, a bull moose may be nearly 2 metres high and may weigh as much as 635 kilograms. It has enormous, leaf-shaped antlers, sometimes measuring nearly 1·5 metres across, which are shed each year. The cow moose and the calf have knobs on their heads instead of antlers. Their bodies are covered with coarse, brownish hair.

Moose live during the summer in thick, damp forests, and with their heavy, humped shoulders and large square heads they can charge through the thickest undergrowth. On their own ground they can also outrun the swiftest horse. They eat leaves, bark, tender shoots and water plants, and gather moss with their fleshy, overhanging upper lips. Late in the summer the bull moose battle savagely together for the cows. They utter bellowing roars, which hunters imitate with birchbark horns to lure them to their deaths.

In winter moose collect in small herds and, by trampling down the snow, form an open space known as a "moose-yard" to move about in. The young, one to three in number, are born in spring. They may stay with their mothers until they are about three years old.

Hunting moose is a popular sport in North America, but since they are becoming very rare,

Courtesy, Canadian Government Travel Bureau
This bull moose is wading in search of water plants.

both the United States and the Canadian governments have passed strict hunting laws to protect them and have set aside areas of country in which it is forbidden to kill them.

The European moose is known as an elk. It is found in western Russia, northern Germany and in the Scandinavian countries.

The American elk, generally known in zoos as the wapiti, is related to the European red deer rather than to the moose. A giant deer known as the Irish elk once lived in the British Isles, but became extinct (died out) a long time ago.

MORAVIANS,

or Moravian Brethren, are followers of the religion that was started in Moravia (part of the country now called Czechoslovakia) in 1457 by some of the followers of John Huss.

Huss was rector (head) of the University of Prague in the early 1400s. His religious views were strongly influenced by the writings of John Wycliffe (see WYCLIFFE, JOHN), an Englishman who criticized the church. Agreeing with Wycliffe's criticisms, Huss tried to bring about reforms in the church and as a result was burned at the stake in 1415. Some of his followers settled at Kunwald on the borders of Moravia and Silesia and at a conference in 1457 formed a church fellowship called "The Unity of Brethren". In 1467 they chose bishops to rule their church and aimed at living strictly according to the teaching of the New Testament.

During the 16th century the movement spread and links were made with other Protestants. They started many centres in Poland and Prussia, but owing to war and persecution they were forced to flee from their lands between 1620 and 1630. They were led by their bishop, Johann Amos Comenius (also called Komensky), one of the most learned men of his age who is still famous for his books on education.

In 1724 some Moravians went to Germany and settled on the estate of Count von Zinzendorf, who allowed them to build the town of Herrnhut, not far from Dresden. When persecution started again he sent some of them to Georgia, in the United States. The Englishman John Wesley, who founded the Methodists, met Moravians both in England and the United States and was greatly impressed by the way in which they felt near to God and trusted in Him.

There are about 353,000 Moravians today.

MORAY was the name of a former county in the northeast of Scotland which after local government reorganization in 1975 became part of the new Grampian region (see GRAMPIAN). This article describes Moray as it was until 1975.

Moray's boundaries are with the Moray Firth to the north, with the former counties of Banffshire and Nairnshire to the east and west and with the mountains of Inverness to the south. It has an area of 1,370 square kilometres.

The rivers of Moray all flow northeast and water the fertile lowlands of the Laigh of Moray. The best known of these rivers is the Spey—said to be the fastest-flowing river in Scotland—which rises to the west of the Cairngorm Mountains in Inverness. It is famous for its salmon fishing. The beautiful River Findhorn enters the sea north of the town of Forres at Findhorn Bay. The River Lossie is a quiet-flowing river which rises in the Dallas Hills and joins the sea at

Lossiemouth. To the west of Forres and near the county boundary with Nairn is a former stretch of moorland, now largely planted with trees, which is the "blasted heath" of Shakespeare's play *Macbeth*. Macbeth, king of Scotland from 1040 to 1057, came from Moray.

Northwest of Forres is Culbin Forest. Formerly it was called Culbin Sands, a sandy waste beneath which a mansion, a church and several farms were buried in a great sandstorm in 1694. After 1926, however, it was planted with Corsican pines by the Forestry Commission.

The former county town of Moray is Elgin, an ancient royal burgh on the Lossie. In it are woollen mills, most of whose goods are exported. Forres is also an ancient royal burgh, Lossiemouth is a fishing port and the port of Elgin, while Grantown-on-Spey is a holiday town among the woods of Strathspey at the foot of the Cairngorms. Rothes, also on the Spey, is a centre of the distilling, or whisky-making trade.

Burghead on the Moray Firth is a fishing port where the interesting old custom of "burning the

Gordonstoun School

Elgin Marbles

"burning the Clavie"

forestry at Culbin

Clavie" is carried out each January. The Clavie is a barrel full of tar that is set on fire and carried to the top of a headland called Doorie Hill.

Moray is chiefly an agricultural region. Almost anything can be grown in the Laigh of Moray, but barley, rather than wheat, is the chief crop. Forestry is important in Moray, which is the home of the Scots fir, and soft fruits are now grown. Cattle, particularly the Aberdeen Angus breed, are kept in large numbers.

Probably the best known of the old buildings of Moray is Gordonstoun House, north of Elgin. It is now a school and its most famous pupils were the Duke of Edinburgh and his son Charles, Prince of Wales.

In the middle ages there were several Earls of Moray who played important parts in the history of Scotland. Thomas Bruce, the 7th Earl of Elgin (1766–1841), brought the wonderful Greek sculptures known as the Elgin Marbles from the Parthenon in Athens to the British Museum in London. James Ramsay MacDonald (1866–1937), the first Labour prime minister, was born at Lossiemouth.

MORE, Sir Thomas (1478–1535).
Sir Thomas More was a lawyer, scholar, statesman and writer who was brave enough to oppose King Henry VIII and was executed for doing so.

He was born in Milk Street in the City of London on February 7, 1478, and was the son of Sir John More, a lawyer who later became a judge. The young Thomas was educated at St. Anthony's School in Threadneedle Street and then in the household of Thomas Morton, archbishop of Canterbury. After that he studied at Oxford University and then at Lincoln's Inn, London, where he became a lawyer. By 1518 his fame as a lawyer and his reputation for both humour and wisdom attracted the attention of Henry VIII, who made him a member of the Privy Council. In 1523 he became Speaker of the House of Commons and soon afterwards Chancellor of the Duchy of Lancaster. The King obviously enjoyed his learned humour and even took to visiting his house without previous notice. Finally, in 1529, More succeeded Cardinal Wolsey as Chancellor and thus held one of the most important posts in the land.

Henry and his Chancellor were already not in agreement, for More could not agree with Henry's desire to end his marriage to Queen Catherine and marry Anne Boleyn. When in 1532 the King took away from the clergy their right to make church laws without his consent, More resigned his office and retired into private life at his house in Chelsea.

However, Henry could not afford to be opposed, even silently, by so important a man. In 1534 he ordered More to take the Oath of Supremacy, acknowledging the King as head of the English Church, the title which parliament had given him. More refused, as this was against his conscience, although he was willing to swear to accept the children of Anne Boleyn as heirs to the throne. He was then imprisoned in the Tower of London and finally beheaded on Tower Hill on July 6, 1535. More died with great courage and calmness and his execution shocked all Europe. He was made a saint by the Roman Catholic Church in 1935.

Of Thomas More's many books the most famous is *Utopia*, which describes a perfect city state as More imagined it and showed up the evils of England and Europe in his day.

MORMONS
belong to a church whose members are found mostly in the state of Utah in the United States. The correct name of their church is the Church of Jesus Christ of Latter-day Saints (that is, Christians of Jesus Christ's last day on Earth), but they are usually called Mormons because they take part of their religion from the Book of Mormon. They believe that this book contains an account of the first inhabitants of America, which was originally written on tablets of gold.

Joseph Smith, the founder of Mormonism, said that he had been told in a vision about tablets of gold in a hillside near his home at Palmyra, New York state, and that he had special means to understand the writing on them, and thus to write and publish the Book of Mormon in 1830.

Mormons accept many Christian beliefs but think that Christians went astray soon after the death of Jesus, and that the authority then lost was restored to Joseph Smith. They stress the

The Mormons travelled across the great plains, through Indian country and over mountain passes to their new home.

importance of education and recreation. They believe in life after death and that their marriages continue in heaven for ever. If anyone dies unbaptized, another can be baptized on his behalf and thus put him right with God.

Mormons help each other through a scheme known as the Church Welfare Programme, which protects members against need and unemployment. Every month there is a fast day and the money which is saved by not eating is given to the poor.

The Mormon Church was founded by Joseph Smith in 1830 in New York state. However, its members were persecuted so they moved westwards to Ohio and then to Nauvoo, Illinois. Persecution continued and in 1844 Joseph Smith and his brother were killed by a mob.

One reason for the persecution of the Mormons was their belief that a man could have more than one wife. In 1890, however, they gave up this belief.

Brigham Young followed Joseph Smith as president of the church and in 1846 led about 15,000 Mormons to find a new home in the Rocky Mountains. In July 1847 they reached Salt Lake City in what is now the state of Utah and began to cultivate the land. At that time the country belonged to Mexico but the Mormons set up a government of their own and in 1896 Utah became a member of the United States of America.

There is now more than one Mormon church organization. There are no paid clergy, but at 12 every boy considered worthy becomes a deacon and many later become priests.

MOROCCO is a kingdom in northwest Africa about three times the size of England and Wales. Bounded on the southwest by Spanish Sahara and on the south and east by Algeria, Morocco has coastlines both on the Atlantic and the Mediterranean. The fertile plains of the Atlantic coast stretch inland to the foot of the ranges forming the Atlas Mountains, which run in a northeasterly direction across Morocco into Algeria. (See ATLAS MOUNTAINS.) Between the slopes of these ranges there are many fertile valleys and high tablelands, and some of the peaks are snowclad for most of the year. In the north is a coastal range of mountains called the Rif, while in the south stretches the Sahara Desert, with its beautiful oases. (See OASIS.)

Morocco has mild winters and hot dry summers. The climate is harsher inland and the rainfall is less towards the south. There are fine forests of cork trees and evergreen oaks, with firs and cedars on the higher slopes. The plains are

FACTS ABOUT MOROCCO

AREA: 458,730 square kilometres.
POPULATION: 15,579,000.
KIND OF COUNTRY: Independent kingdom.
CAPITAL: Rabat.
GEOGRAPHICAL FEATURES: There is a fertile plain on the Atlantic coast: the Mediterranean coast is mountainous. The Atlas mountains cross the country from southwest to northeast.
CHIEF PRODUCTS: Wheat, barley, citrus fruits, dates, olives; phosphate, coal; iron ore, manganese ore, zinc, lead, cobalt.
IMPORTANT TOWNS: Rabat, Casablanca, Marrakesh, Fès, Meknès, Tangier, Oujda, Tetuan, Kenitra, Safi.
EDUCATION: Children must attend school between the ages of 7 and 13.

Left: A mud fort in southern Morocco. Right: The Oum-er-Rbia, one of the rivers that water the fertile coastal plain.

covered with bushes or thorny shrubs. Gazelles are plentiful and although lions have disappeared there are still panthers, monkeys, wild boars and jackals.

The people of Morocco are mostly Berbers, which is a name given to the inhabitants of North Africa by the Arabs who conquered them in the 7th century A.D. Some of the Berbers have kept their own languages but the coastal tribes speak Arabic which is the official language. In east

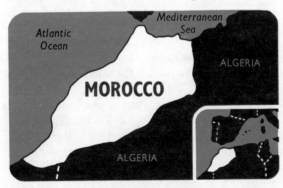

Morocco the people are mainly Arabs and there is Sudanese blood in the south. All these people are Moslems and the king is their spiritual leader as well as their ruler. In the towns of Morocco dwell a large number of Jews. There are also some Christians, most of them French and Spanish.

The chief occupation is farming. Important crops are barley, wheat, millet, linseed, olives, oranges, lemons, almonds and dates, and there are many vineyards and market gardens. Cattle,

sheep, goats and camels are bred. The chief mineral is phosphate, which is mined at Khouribga and Youssoufia in the northwest for use as fertilizer. Iron and manganese are also mined and there is some coal and petroleum (oil), but electricity is mainly made from water power.

The capital of Morocco is Rabat, a city on the Atlantic coast. (See RABAT.) Casablanca, some 80 kilometres southwest, is a much larger city and is Morocco's chief port. At Fès, one of the old capitals, is the Karueein, which is the largest mosque (Moslem temple) in Africa, and also the mosque of Moulay Idris, which is considered so sacred that non-Moslems and animals are not allowed in the streets leading to it. (See MOSQUE.) Other Moroccan cities are Marrakesh, another ancient capital, situated in a huge palm grove; Meknès, where there are a number of beautiful buildings; and Tangier at the western entrance to the Straits of Gibraltar. Morocco is famous for its leather. Carpets are also made there, and goods of many kinds in factories in Casablanca. The country has good roads and there is a railway linking the main towns with Algeria.

History

The northern part of Morocco was once part of the Roman province of Mauretania, and there are Roman remains at Volubilis near Meknès. After the Roman rule crumbled in the 5th century A.D. there was no settled government until the Berbers were united under one of the descendants of the Prophet Mohammed in about 800.

From then on, there was a succession of Moslem rulers, of whom the greatest were Moulay Ismail (17th century) and Moulay Hassan (19th century). Nevertheless in spite of their efforts a large number of tribes continued to rebel and the country remained in an unsettled state. In 1904 Great Britain agreed to recognize French power in Morocco in return for French recognition of British power in Egypt. The French set up a protectorate over Morocco in 1912. The protectorate included a Spanish zone along the north coast, and Tangier became an international city ruled by British, French and Spanish officials.

Until 1925 the French protectorate was governed by Marshal Louis Lyautey (1854–1934), who modernized the country and subdued the rebellious tribes, the Sultan of Morocco being little more than a religious leader. In 1936 there began a movement for Moroccan independence and in 1956 France recognized Morocco as an independent country and Spain soon afterwards did the same. In 1957 the Sultan took the title of King of Morocco. Tangier is now part of Morocco, and Ifni, a Spanish possession on the Atlantic coast, passed to Morocco in 1969.

MORRIS DANCING.

In many parts of the world there are spring-time customs which include dances performed by picked teams of young men. The performers are carrying on a very ancient rite, or ceremony, which in Europe was once part of the religion there before the coming of Christianity. The rite was at one time designed to ensure increase in the crops and the flocks and it went on as a custom after the people became Christians. The young men-dancers have different names in different countries. In England they are known as Morrice, or Morris, dancers.

The Morris dancers wear white clothes, decorated with ribbons and flowers and bells, and dance with white handkerchiefs and sticks. So do the "Volants" of Navarre, the Calusari of Romania and the Russallia of Macedonia and similar groups in Austria, Germany, Italy and even in India.

These young men are sometimes found associated with a "monster"—a dragon or a hobby horse—and often have clowns and other characters to help to amuse the onlookers.

There are several types of Morris dancing in England. In Lancashire the group of Morris men once pulled a rush-cart and were urged on by a "whiffler" carrying a whip. In Derbyshire, where the dancers were accompanied by a black-faced clown and a King and Queen, they were divided into two sides—each side being recognized by their distinctive hats. The dance was most widespread in the Cotswold area of the English midlands. It was their form of Morris which attracted the attention of Cecil

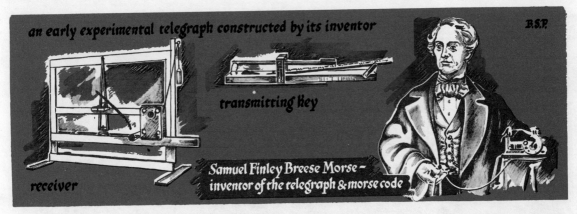

an early experimental telegraph constructed by its inventor

B.S.P.

transmitting key

receiver

Samuel Finley Breese Morse ~ inventor of the telegraph & morse code

Sharp when he saw the "side" from Headington Quarry, near Oxford, led by William Kimber in 1899. Such traditional dancers as Kimber of Headington, William Wells of Bampton-in-the-Bush and Sam Bennett of Ilmington helped Cecil Sharp to establish the present folk dance revival.

MORSE, Samuel Finley Breese (1791–1872). The inventor of the electro-magnetic telegraph and of the morse code used for telegraphic messages was an American artist named Samuel Morse. He became interested in science while at college, but decided to become a painter and went to London to study.

In 1832, on his return from a second visit to Europe, Morse gave up painting and set to work to invent a telegraph. For years he had little money and made his own models and parts. At last in 1837 he was able to exhibit a working telegraph instrument in New York. For some time no government would take an interest in the invention but in 1844 a telegraph line was set up between Baltimore and Washington (about 60 kilometres). Later, Morse became interested in the first attempts to lay a telegraph cable across the Atlantic.

Morse's invention was based on the discovery made in 1820 by the Dane, H. C. Oersted, that a magnetic needle pivoted so as to swing freely was deflected, or twisted, when a wire carrying an electric current was brought near it. Morse made an instrument in which the electric current, when turned on, worked an electro-magnet which caused a pencil to mark a moving strip of paper. The electric current was supplied from a battery and was turned on and off by means of a simple tapping "key". When pressed down the key caused the current to flow and when released it shut off the current. Thus long or short taps on the key caused the pencil to make long or short marks on the paper. Each letter of the alphabet was represented by a different combination of long and short signals, and this "morse code" for sending messages is given in full in the article SIGNALLING. The tapping key was connected to one end of the telegraph wire and the receiving instrument to the other. (See TELEGRAPHS.)

MORTGAGE. Houses and land are usually very expensive, and often a person who wants to buy a house or some land has not got enough money and so has to borrow some. The man who lends the money, however, wants to make sure that he will not lose it, and so he usually asks for a mortgage over the land.

The effect of a mortgage (pronounced "mawgij") is to give the lender the right to take possession of the land or to sell it if the borrower fails to repay.

MOSAIC. Children at the seaside often decorate their sandcastles by sticking coloured stones or shells on them to make pictures or patterns. Exactly the same idea is used in making mosaic, but instead of sand wet plaster or cement makes the base, and instead of shells small cubes of coloured stone, pottery or glass about the size of a knob of sugar are stuck close together on to the plaster. Patterns or pictures in mosaic can be used to decorate the floors, walls or ceilings of buildings.

A mosaic in the apse of the Cathedral of S. Apollinare in Classe, Ravenna.

The ancient Greeks made a kind of mosaic for the floors of their houses. They began by using pebbles, mostly black and white ones, the black ones set into the floor to make a background and the white ones forming the pattern or picture. Sometimes there were red, yellow and green pebbles too. Later on small cubes were cut from stone (or sometimes glass) and were used instead of the pebbles. They made a much smoother surface and could be set closer together.

The Romans also often made their floors from mosaic, sometimes coloured and sometimes black and white. Many examples of mosaic pavements have been discovered on the sites of former Roman camps, such as at Lullingstone Park in Kent and at Colchester in Essex. Pictures and scenes with figures of people and animals were combined with beautiful patterns.

When mosaic came to be used in the decoration of Christian churches, it was put on the walls or ceiling and not on the floor. This meant that the mosaic no longer needed to be so hard-wearing, and instead of stone brilliantly coloured glass and gold cubes were used to form magnificent pictures of saints and holy scenes. There are some world-famous mosaics made during early Christian times (probably the 6th century A.D.) at Ravenna in Italy. In the church of San Vitale there the red, purple, green and gold colours of the mosaic pictures shimmer like the feathers on a peacock's breast.

After about the 13th century mosaic came to be less and less used in churches and painting took its place. In recent times, however, mosaics have been made again for the walls, floors and ceilings of public buildings in several countries.

MOSCOW is the capital of the Union of Soviet Socialist Republics (U.S.S.R.). It is also the capital of the Russian Soviet Federated Socialist Republic, which is the largest of the 15 republics of the U.S.S.R.

In 1156 Prince Yury Dolgoruky built a wooden fortress on the north bank of the River Moskva. This area, triangular in shape and now surrounded by high walls of pinkish brick, is the centre around which the city has grown and is called the Kremlin, which means "citadel" or "fortress". Within the Kremlin are many old buildings including a cathedral, golden-domed

Novosti

Tchaikovsky Street, Moscow. The capital has excellent roads, rail and underground transport systems.

churches and palaces, some of which are used as government offices and others as museums.

As Moscow spread, new walls were built to protect the people and this caused the city to grow rather in the shape of a cobweb, with the main streets fanning out from the Kremlin and the cross streets arranged round it in circles. On the northeast side of the Kremlin is a wide open space usually called the Red Square (strictly speaking it should be "Beautiful Square") which is used for big celebrations, demonstrations and army reviews. Facing the square is a stone mausoleum (tomb) which contains the body of the Russian leader Lenin (about whom there is a separate article). In the tower above the central gate to the Kremlin is a famous peal of bells set up by an Englishman in 1625. Twice daily the tune of the "International"—the song of world socialism—is played on these bells. At the south end of the Red Square is St. Basil's Cathedral, completed in 1560 and one of the finest examples of Russian architecture. It has nine great domes, all differently shaped. It is now used as a museum.

Moscow contains buildings of several different styles. In the suburbs are to be seen wooden houses like those in the Russian countryside. Nearer to the centre are the stately dwellings with pillared doorways built by wealthy citizens in the days before the Russian Revolution of 1917. Since the 1920s many blocks of flats have been built for the workers. There are a number of skyscrapers including the Moscow University building which is 240 metres high. The Central Lenin stadium in Moscow seats more than 100,000 people, and the Dynamo stadium is another huge sports-ground. Among the famous theatres are the Bolshoi opera and ballet and the Moscow Art Theatre, which was founded by the famous Russian producer Stanislavsky.

Moscow has long been an important industrial centre. Most of the factories are on the outskirts of the city and include iron and steel works and factories making motor cars, machinery, electrical goods, chemicals, textiles (fabrics and materials) and footwear. Moscow is the chief railway centre of the U.S.S.R. and has 11 main lines connecting it to all parts of the country, with 9 passenger and 11 goods stations all linked

by a circular railway. For transport within the city there is a "metro" or underground railway, the first part of which was built by British engineers and which has very spacious and grandly decorated stations. Moscow is connected by a canal with the Volga River to the north, and has other canal links so that it can be reached by small seagoing ships from five seas—the Baltic, White, Caspian, Azov and Black Seas. The city has three port areas for shipping. The main airport is at Vnukovo, 27 kilometres southwest of the city centre.

Moscow was the capital of Russia until 1712, when the Tsar (Emperor) Peter the Great chose St. Petersburg instead (see LENINGRAD). When the French invaded Russia in 1812, Napoleon's army occupied Moscow on September 2 but the city was set on fire on the following night. Most of the food and supplies were burnt and Napoleon was forced to retreat. Moscow was rebuilt and increased in importance, but only in 1918, after the Communist revolution, did it again become the capital city. In World War II the German invaders approached to within about 30 kilometres of Moscow and often bombed the city, but it was not badly damaged.

The population of Moscow is about 7,000,000.

MOSES was the man who formed the Hebrew tribes into a nation and who was chosen by God to reveal His laws to the nation. With God's help he led the Hebrews out of their slavery in Egypt, laid the foundations of the Hebrew nation and gave its people laws for worship and for daily life. In the Bible the Book of Exodus tells the story of his early life as well as what he did later, while the Book of Numbers tells only of his later life.

Moses was born in Egypt at a time when the Hebrews were slaves in that country. When they had first come to Egypt from Canaan many years earlier their kinsman Joseph (see JOSEPH) was chief minister to the Egyptian king and they had been given the fertile land of Goshen, northeast of Cairo. However, later kings feared them and turned them into slaves. One of these kings ordered that all new-born Hebrew boys were to be killed. Therefore when Moses was born his

The princess took pity on the baby when she heard it cry.

mother hid him as long as she could and then put him in a little boat among the rushes on the bank of the River Nile. His sister Miriam waited to see if anybody would find him and take pity on him. At last the king's daughter came to bathe and seeing the little Moses was obviously attracted by him. Miriam asked if the princess wanted a Hebrew woman to look after him and was told to go and find one. Miriam returned with her mother—the mother of Moses also—and the child was put in her care. When he was older he went to live in the princess's house as her son.

One day when Moses was a young man, he saw an Egyptian overseer beating a Hebrew slave. He killed the Egyptian and had to flee. He went to the land of Midian and found shelter with a man called Jethro. He married Jethro's daughter Zipporah and worked for many years as a shepherd.

One day he came to the sacred mountain of Horeb and heard God speaking to him out of a burning bush. God told him to return to Egypt and ask the king to set free the Hebrews. Moses was afraid but God insisted that he should go. God did the miraculous things that are described in the fourth chapter of the Book of Exodus and

also arranged for Aaron (Moses' brother) to meet Moses as he was journeying to Egypt.

Together Moses and Aaron asked the king to free the Hebrews. When the king refused, Moses and Aaron turned all the water of Egypt into blood, and then brought a plague of frogs. At this the king agreed to let the Hebrews go, but changed his mind as soon as the plague of frogs stopped. More plagues followed and it was the tenth—in which the eldest son of every Egyptian family died, including the king's eldest son— that made the king agree to free the Hebrews. Moses gathered them together and they started on their journey. To this day, in a ceremony known as the feast of the Passover, Jews still celebrate their escape from Egypt. (See PASSOVER and HAGGADAH.)

However, their problems were not over—the king sent his army after them and the Israelites found themselves trapped between that and the Red Sea. Moses called to the Lord for help and the waters of the sea divided. The Hebrews passed through safely but the Egyptian army was swallowed up as the waters closed again.

After this the Hebrews wandered across the desert. Many catastrophes happened and each time the people blamed Moses for their miseries. However, God was on his side. When there was nothing to eat He provided quails and manna (see QUAIL; MANNA), and when there was no water He told Moses to speak to the rock in Horeb and water would come out of it.

When they arrived at Mount Sinai Moses was told by God to go up the mountain, and was given the Ten Commandments on tablets of stone. (See TEN COMMANDMENTS.) While Moses was up the mountain the Hebrews got tired of waiting and made a golden calf to worship. When he came down and discovered what was going on he was so angry that he threw down the tablets, which broke. Again he went up Mount Sinai and was given new tablets. This time they were carefully preserved. A great chest called the ark of the covenant was made for them and was put in a special tent called the tabernacle. As the Hebrews continued their journey Moses made rules for worship and daily life.

At last they came in sight of Canaan, the Promised Land, but Moses died after seeing it from the top of Mount Nebo. It was Joshua who led the Hebrews across the River Jordan, conquered Jericho and settled the people in Canaan, which later came to be known as Palestine. (See JOSHUA.)

MOSHESH (?1790–1870).

Chief Moshesh (in African, Moshoeshoe) was a great leader of the Basuto people in South Africa. He was a chief's son and as a young man gathered about him the remains of the tribes broken up by the invading Zulus under King Chaka (see CHAKA). Moshesh and his people made a stronghold on a high, flat-topped mountain called Thaba Bosiu west of the Drakensberg Mountains. He ruled firmly, forbidding witchcraft and alcoholic drink. European traders could enter his country but were not allowed to buy land. He invited missionaries to work among the Basutos but gave them no control over affairs.

Later in life, Moshesh had disputes with the Boers (South African Dutch) who had settled in the Orange Free State. These disputes led to war with the Boers. The Basutos suffered heavy losses but were still unconquered when Moshesh sent a message to the British in the Cape Colony: "Let me and my people rest and live under the large folds of the flag of England." This request was granted by Queen Victoria and Basutoland was in 1868 taken under British protection. When Moshesh died he was buried on the summit of Thaba Bosiu.

MOSQUE.

The word mosque comes from the Arabic word *mesjid* meaning "a place of adoration", and mosques are the buildings in which the services of the religion called Islam, or Mohammedanism, take place. (The religion is described in the article ISLAM.) The founder of Islam was the prophet Mohammed, and the oldest and most holy mosque is at his birthplace, the city of Mecca in Saudi Arabia. This mosque is called the Haram and has no roof, but most mosques do have roofs which are often ornamental and beautiful, with domes and minarets reaching up into the sky. Sometimes the domes are rounded at the top, but often they are rather pointed and end in a spike. The minarets are tall narrow towers or spires, gracefully shaped and sometimes decorated with patterns of coloured marble.

Inside, all mosques have certain special features. In the wall facing the holy city of Mecca is the *mihrab* or prayer niche. It is usually a round recess or alcove with an arch over it, which directs the prayers of the congregation towards Mecca to honour Mohammed's birthplace. Next is the *mimbar* or pulpit, usually placed close to the *mihrab*. It is ornately decorated, with a flight of steps, or sometimes two, leading up to a small platform with a canopy over it, from which the preacher (the *imam*) gives his Friday sermon. A third general feature is a low railed wooden platform where the reader (the *khatib*) sits to recite the Koran, or holy book, to worshippers sitting cross-legged all round him.

Every mosque, too, has just outside it or near the doorway a tank where the worshippers wash themselves ceremonially before praying. Usually the face, the hands and the feet are washed, and

Paul Popper
The minarets are slender spires encircled by galleries.

the worshipper says his prayers barefooted but always with his head covered. Women are normally expected to say their prayers in their own homes but in some of the larger mosques there are places for them, either on a strip of floor specially reserved for them or in a balcony surrounded by a thick screen or lattice.

There are no professional priests belonging to a mosque and the *imam* who gives the weekly sermon is usually occupied in an ordinary job during the week. So also is the *muezzin*, who cries the call to prayer five times daily from the minaret.

MOSQUITO.
Among the insects of the order Diptera (two-winged flies) are mosquitoes. They are small, slender, long-legged flies with fringes of short, scale-like hairs on the edge of their wings. Most kinds also have a similar fringe on each of the wing veins. The females have long antennae, or feelers, covered with hairy whorls, or rings. The males have plume-like or bushy antennae.

Mosquitoes are found all over the world, even in the Arctic. For a long time little was known about them except that they bit people and caused irritating lumps to appear on their skins.

In 1878 a Scottish doctor called Patrick Manson showed that certain species, or kinds, of mosquitoes carry the tiny worms that cause elephantiasis, a tropical disease. Later in the century Ronald Ross, an Englishman, and Giovanni Grassi, an Italian, proved that the germs of the disease called malaria are also carried by mosquitoes. Finally, an American medical team under Walter Reed proved that yet another species of mosquito spread the disease of yellow fever. (See also MALARIA; ROSS, SIR RONALD; YELLOW FEVER.)

Only female mosquitoes bite people and suck their blood. The female mosquito has a long part called a proboscis which has piercing organs arranged round a sucking tube. When the mosquito bites it injects a liquid into the blood which infects the blood and also makes it easier for the insect to suck it up. Male mosquitoes feed on plant juices, and sometimes females do too.

The tropical genus, or group, *Anopheles* con-

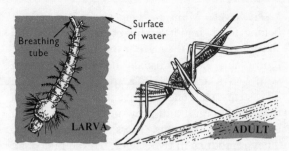

tains several species of malaria-carrying mosquitoes. An *Anopheles* mosquito has black spots on its wings. When at rest it stands with its head down and its proboscis and body in a straight line. The mosquito that carries yellow fever belongs to the genus *Aedes*. It has white stripes round its legs and crosswise on its back.

There are a number of species, or kinds, of mosquitoes in Great Britain, of which *Culex pipiens* is the most common. However, all of them are harmless.

Wherever they live, mosquitoes begin their lives in water, generally fresh water. The females lay from 40 to 400 eggs, sometimes singly and sometimes in raft-like masses, in places such as ponds, pools in the desert or rain barrels. Within a week small legless larvae, or grubs, hatch out. They wriggle so actively through the water that they are usually called wrigglers. Very few species can breathe under water so they live at the surface, taking in air through breathing tubes on their tails. Some larvae feed by sweeping bits of animal and plant material into their mouths with the feathery brushes on their heads. Some eat other mosquito larvae. As they grow the wrigglers shed their skins, and eventually become pupae, more fully developed grubs in the last stage of growth before adulthood.

Mosquito pupae are called tumblers and also have to live near the surface to breathe. They are active but do not eat. After a few days their skins split and the full-grown mosquitoes crawl out. Usually they die after a few weeks.

People in tropical countries keep mosquitoes away at night by hanging fine nets known as mosquito nets round their beds.

MOSS.
Tiny plants can be found on the ground or on trees in almost any shady wood, growing so close together that they look like

green velvet. Many of them are mosses, which belong to an important plant group called the Bryophyta, and they are some of the simplest land plants. Mosses usually have upright stems with leaves arranged in a spiral round them. The stems are generally not more than one to three inches high and grow in close tufts which look like little cushions. Mosses have no flowers. They reproduce in two stages. In the first stage an egg is fertilized and grows into a tiny new plant attached to the parent. From it there then grows a long delicate stalk at the end of which is a case containing spores, or tiny cells. These little stalks with the flask-shaped spore-cases at their ends can be seen at certain times of the year, especially in the spring, growing out of the moss cushions. When ripe, the spore-case splits or opens by a lid-like structure and the hundreds of spores, which are very light, float away on the wind. From the spores new moss plants grow. This is the second stage.

Wherever there is moisture for some part of the year mosses will be found. They grow near the tops of the highest mountains, on the trees of hot, wet, tropical forests and far north in the Arctic. Most mosses prefer damp sheltered places but some grow on walls and rocks, and in dry weather they can become quite dry and brittle, although a shower of rain quickly revives them. Mosses are often the first plants to grow on rocks or bare sand. From the lower part of the stem grow a number of root-like structures which hold grains of wind-blown soil and also water, so that in time a layer of soil is built up.

Mnium is a moss with rounded leaves and a delicate vein running down the centre of each leaf. It forms loose, dark green clumps on earthy banks free from dead leaves. On heaths and moor a stiff, sharp-leaved moss called *Polytrichum* is common. It has brown, spore-bearing heads and is one of the largest British mosses.

A very important moss is *Sphagnum*, the bog moss. It has tiny holes in its leaves through which it sucks up water. When bog moss grows in a pool, the dead plants sink to the bottom and fresh ones grow on top, until the pool is filled in. Over the years the layer of dead moss grows thicker and peat is formed. (See PEAT.)

The word moss is frequently given to plants that are not mosses at all. Irish moss, or carrageen, is a seaweed; Iceland and reindeer mosses are lichens; and Spanish moss is a plant bearing flowers and is closely related to the pineapple. (See LICHEN; SEAWEED; SPANISH MOSS.)

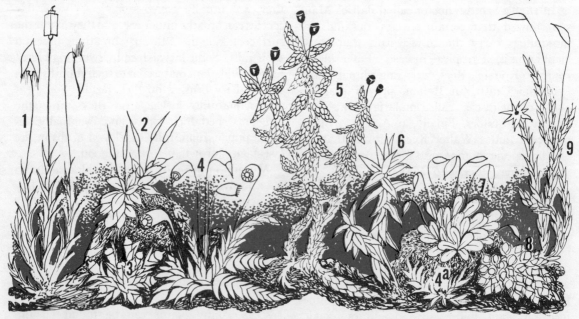

Some British mosses. (1) *Polytrichum commune*, found on heaths and moors. (2) *Tortula muralis*. (3) *Grimmia apocarpa*. (4) *Brachythecium rutabulum* with spore capsules and (4a) without spore capsules. (5) *Sphagnum palustre* or bog moss. (6) *Atrichum undulatum*. (7) *Mnium punctatum*. (8) *Bryum argenteum*. (9) *Aulacomnion palustre*.

MATHEMATICAL PUZZLES

by Paul Bethell

Colouring a Map

If a map is divided into districts (such as counties) and you have to colour it so that no district is the same colour as one next to it, what is the least number of colours needed? This is of practical importance to map printers, who long ago found that four colours are enough.

The problem was not considered by mathematicians until the German mathematician August Möbius drew attention to it in 1840. Even now there is no strict mathematical proof that no more than four colours are ever needed. Clearly you do not need a different colour for each district. Only if two districts are separated by nothing more than a line must they be coloured differently.

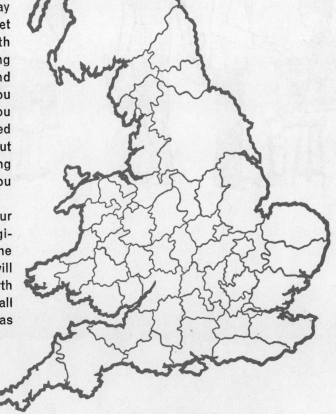

If you start colouring a plain map of the counties of England and Wales you may find that, with only four colours, you "get stuck" and cannot continue without a fifth colour. But by starting again and following a different scheme, you will always find that you can do the job with four. If you then add some imaginary counties you may find that they cannot be coloured differently from those next to them without a fifth colour. Once again, by starting afresh and using a different scheme, you will find that four colours suffice.

A practical way of showing that four colours are enough is to draw three imaginary districts, each having a boundary line with both the others. Obviously they will need three colours. You can draw a fourth district having boundary lines with all three, but you cannot draw a fifth that has boundaries with all the others.

The Seaside Couples

Our artist has drawn six married couples at the seaside. He says that you can pair off the husbands and wives simply by looking at his drawing. Can you?

In the seaside couples puzzle the clues to the relationships were contained in the picture. The clues can be given in words, and the undergraduates puzzle that follows is an example. Before trying it, however, read the following exercise in simple logic.

If you are told that there are three school children, Jane, Harold and Chris, only one of whom goes to the William Austin School, and you know that Jane goes there, then Harold and Chris must go elsewhere to school. If there are three men, Adams, Bruce and Collins, one of whom is bald, and you know that Bruce and Collins are not bald, then Adams must be.

The Undergraduates

Smith, Brown, Jones, Robinson and Green are at five different Oxford colleges—Balliol, Brasenose, Merton, Trinity and Magdalen. Smith and Jones have never set foot in Balliol and Smith has no friends outside his own college except at Brasenose. Jones stroked his college crew in the races during Eights Week, but they were bumped by Magdalen. No undergraduate's name begins with the first letter of the name of his college. Brown's father would have preferred his son to go to Magdalen. Green's parents have never been to France. Smith played rugger for his college against Merton and Magdalen, and Robinson represented his college at squash against Balliol.

Which man is at which college?

Mr and Mrs Evans

How old was Mr. Evans when he married 18 years ago, if he was then three times as old as his wife but is now twice as old as she is?

(You can do this without the use of algebra or equations by trying various numbers to see if they fit the case. Nobody in Britain is allowed to marry under the age of 16.)

The Cyclist's Problem

A cyclist wishes to ride to a seaside place and to reach it at a certain time. If he rides at 15 miles an hour he will get there an hour too soon, but if he rides at 10 miles an hour he will arrive an hour too late. What is the distance?

(This problem too can be solved by trying various distances for the answer.)

Weeding the Garden

Peter and Adrian agreed to weed the borders on each side of granny's garden. Peter starts first and has weeded 4 feet on the south side when Adrian comes out and says that they had agreed that Peter should take the north side. So Peter starts again on the north border. Adrian finishes the south side and then moves across and weeds 8 feet for Peter, thus finishing the job.

If the borders on each side are the same length, which boy weeded the greater length of border, and by how much?

The Gambler

Racke the gambler has a good day at the races and returns with £12 in his pocket. To his friend he says, "I'll bet half the money I have on me on the toss of a coin—heads I win; tails I lose." His friend agrees, they toss up and the loser pays. They agree to repeat the bet under the same conditions, and continue doing this. Racke's friend says he forgets how often they tossed up, but he remembers that Racke won exactly as many tosses as he lost. Did Racke end up richer or poorer than he started?

If there are three children in a family and their ages are 5, 7 and 12, then their average age is (5+7+12) divided by 3, or $\frac{24}{3}$, which is 8. Thus the average of any number of quantities is obtained by dividing their sum by their number. Try this problem:

Six Boys at Margate

Six boys spend a day at Margate. Five of them spend 9*s.* each, but Bob, who gets more pocket-money than the others, spends 5*s.* more than the average amount spent by the six. How much does Bob spend?

(This can be done by trying various amounts for what Bob spends. But it is quicker to use algebra in the form of an equation, by putting the problem as "let x shillings be the amount Bob spends." The way of doing this is shown in the answers at the end.)

There is no trick in the next problem, which is perfectly simple. Yet many people get the answer wrong through being careless. You have been warned!

The Bookworm

A set of *Children's Britannica* which had been kept in its bookcase in the tropics while the children were at school in Britain was found to have been damaged by bookworms. One greedy worm had bored a straight hole from the first page of volume 1 to the last page of volume 12. If every volume has a one-inch thickness of pages and two covers each one-twentieth of an inch thick, how long was the hole bored by the worm?

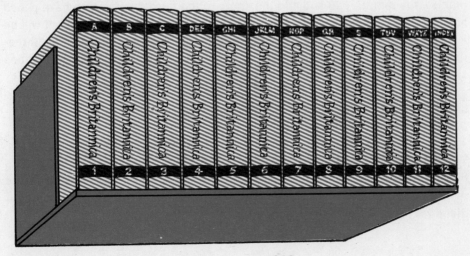

Finding a Number

Ask someone to think of a number. Tell him to multiply the number by itself, and then to subtract 1 from the result. Tell him next to divide the remainder by one less than the number he thought of, and to give you the result. If you subtract 1 from that, you will always have the number he thought of.

Your friend can have pencil and paper to help him with this trick, which is here given with an example. Tell your friend to:

Think of a number	(15)
Multiply it by 12	(180)
Divide the result by 4	(45)
Multiply this by 7	(315)
Divide by 3	(105)
Divide by the number thought of	(7)
Add the number thought of, and tell you the result	(22)

If you subtract 7 from this, the remainder is always the number thought of.

For this trick you need three dice. Tell a friend to throw all three so that you cannot see how they land.

Now tell him to multiply the spots on the first die by 2 and add 5; then to multiply this number by 5 and add the spots of the second die; and next to multiply the result by 10 and add the spots of the third die. (He can have pencil and paper to work out these sums.) Ask him to tell you the final result. It will be a three-figure number. Subtract 250 from it; this will give you another three-figure number, each figure of which corresponds to the number thrown and does so in the correct order.

For example, suppose he throws 4, 2, and 6. The first step is $4 \times 2 + 5 = 13$; the second step is $13 \times 5 + 2 = 67$; and the third step gives $67 \times 10 + 6 = 676$. Subtracting 250 from this leaves 426.

(If you have not got three dice, you can use an ordinary pack of playing cards. Throw out all the cards of one suit—say diamonds. Then from the other suits throw out all cards except the 2, 3, 4, 5, 6 and the ace, which counts as 1. The remaining cards must be arranged by suits in three packs of six, which your friend may shuffle as he pleases.)

The Explorers

Four explorers enter a desert. Each carries enough food and water to last one man for five days. They can march 30 miles a day. What is the greatest distance from the edge of the desert at which the leader can plant a flag and then return? (They do not make "depots", or dumps of food and water, for use on the return journey.)

The Family Crossing

Mr. and Mrs. Brown wish to cross a river with their two sons and a trunk. Each parent weighs 10 stone; each son weighs 5 stone and so does the trunk. The boat can carry only 10 stone. Everyone in the family can row. Can you see how the crossing can be made in 11 trips?

If you can solve this, try the crossing of a river by three men and three boys in a boat that can carry only one man or two boys. (Fifteen trips are needed.)

Most puzzles about dividing something into shares under particular conditions can be solved only by trying likely answers and seeing if they fit. There are no formulas, or rules, that can lead you to a quick solution. The puzzle about sharing out the jar of balsam is a very ancient one.

The Jar of Balsam

Three thieves stole a jar containing 24 ounces of priceless balsam. When they got back to their den, they wished to divide the balsam into equal shares, but the only vessels they had were one that would hold 5 ounces, one that would hold 11 ounces and one that would hold 13 ounces. How was the division made?

The Chests of Gold

A rich merchant died leaving 21 chests, some of which contained gold pieces, to be divided between his three sons. His will directed that each son was to receive not only the same amount of gold but also the same number of chests, and that no gold pieces were to be moved from one chest to another. When the sons examined the chests, they found 7 full of gold pieces, 7 half full and 7 empty. How was the division made? (It is possible in two ways.)

Like the puzzle about the chests of gold, the chain puzzle also comes from the East. It is concerned with joining instead of dividing and it repays a little study before you jump in to give an answer.

The Endless Chain

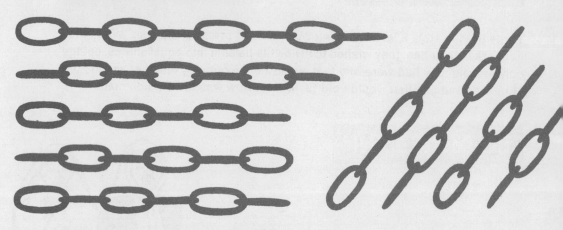

A man had nine lengths of silver chain and wished to have them joined into a single endless chain. The lengths are shown in the drawing. One had 8 links, one had 7 links, three had 6 links, two had 5 links, one had 4 links and one had 3 links—a total of 50 links. The man found that it would cost 3 shekels to open one link and reclose it by welding. He also found that he could buy a 50-link endless chain of the same quality for 26 shekels in the bazaar. What was his best course of action?

The Four Shapes

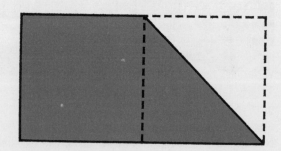

The figure shown in the diagram has been constructed by drawing a square, alongside which is a halved square. Draw it on squared paper and cut it out. Then see if you can divide it into four pieces each of the same shape and size.

How Many Moves?

The next puzzle is rather like the game of patience played with cards. Seven cards are arranged as shown on the left. You have to bring them into the arrangement shown on the right (the ace counting as 1). Cards may be moved only by sliding one next to the empty space into the space. You can see that only three starting moves are possible; either the ace, the 3 or the 4 being moved. What is the least number of moves needed to obtain the new arrangement?

The Orchard

It is said that the great English scientist Sir Isaac Newton (1642–1727), when sitting in the garden at Woolsthorpe Manor in Lincolnshire, saw an apple drop from a tree. He wondered what made it fall straight downwards, and this led him to work out the theory of gravitation. When he was in rooms near the Great Gate of Trinity College, Cambridge, Newton had a small garden there which he carefully tended. There are still apple trees at Woolsthorpe, and Newton's love of gardens probably led him to invent this puzzle:

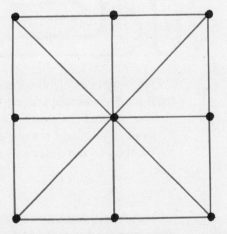

Plant 9 trees in straight rows so that there are ten rows with 3 trees in each row. (Notice that the obvious arrangement in the diagram gives only eight rows, so something a bit cleverer is needed.)

The String and Pins

Get a really long piece of string—six feet is not too much—and tie the ends together, thus forming an endless loop. Then ask a friend to lay out the string on a table or wooden floor. He may arrange it in coils of the most complicated pattern he likes; the only condition is that all parts of the string must touch the table (or floor) and that no part may cross another. You now offer to put in six pins *without hesitating*, in such a way that when the string is taken at any point and pulled away, no pin will catch up in the loop.

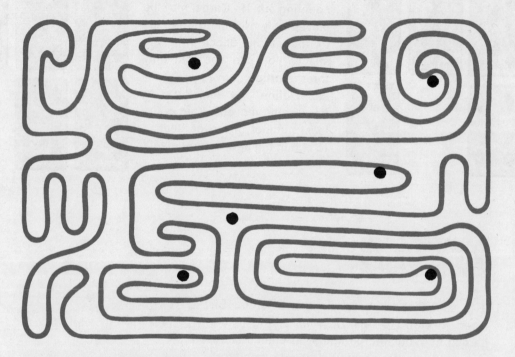

This is quite easily done and it can be most impressive. There is no need to trace the loop before putting in the pins. All that is necessary is to count the number of times the string is crossed when the pin is moved in from the outside. If this number is odd the pin will always lie inside the loop; but if it is even the pin must be on the outer side of the loop and the string, when pulled away, will clear it.

Although this puzzle may seem to have little to do with mathematics, it is a simple example in topology, which is the study of what happens to geometrical figures when they are bent or twisted. Topology is one of the newest branches of mathematics.

The Sheep Pens

The drawing shows eleven sheep in a square field. Can you divide the field into pens by drawing four straight lines to represent fences, so that each pen contains only one sheep? (Fences may cross one another.)

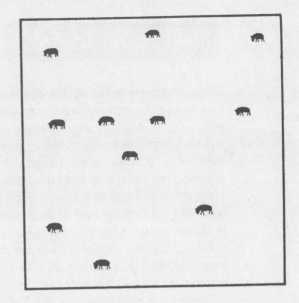

The Cottages and Wells

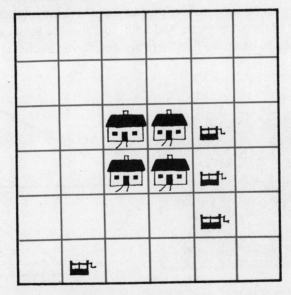

A farmer had a square piece of land on which there were four cottages and four wells. When he died, his will directed that the land was to be divided equally between his four sons. The four plots were to be the same size and the same shape, and each was to include one cottage and one well. Can you see how the dividing lines were drawn? (There is only one way.)

Right-angled Triangles

It is useful to know something about right-angled triangles and their properties. One corner of a right-angled triangle is square. Most people know that a triangle with sides 5, 4 and 3 units long is right-angled, with the 90-degree angle (or square corner) opposite to the hypotenuse, or longest side. It is often used by builders, who make up a set-square from wooden laths 5, 4 and 3 feet long for checking the squareness of foundations and corners.

An important fact about right-angled triangles is that the square of the hypotenuse is equal to the sum of the squares of the shorter sides. The proof of this is the famous theorem of Pythagoras, which was sometimes known as *pons asinorum* ("asses' bridge") because the stupider pupils never managed to get past it. In the 5, 4, 3 triangle, $25 = 16 + 9$. This relationship can be used to check whether a particular triangle is right-angled.

Clearly, if a triangle with sides 5, 4 and 3 units long is right-angled, then so must be one with the sides doubled (10, 8, 6); likewise 15, 12, 9 (sides trebled); and 20, 16, 12 (sides quadrupled). All these are the same shape and form a family of what mathematicians call "similar triangles".

Obviously there is an infinite number of shapes, or families, of right-angled triangles. But if we consider the families that have all their sides an exact whole number of units in length, and limit ourselves to those with a long side of not more than 50 units, we find there are only seven such families. They are:

long side	short sides	
5	4	3
13	12	5
17	15	8
25	24	7
29	21	20
37	35	12
41	40	9

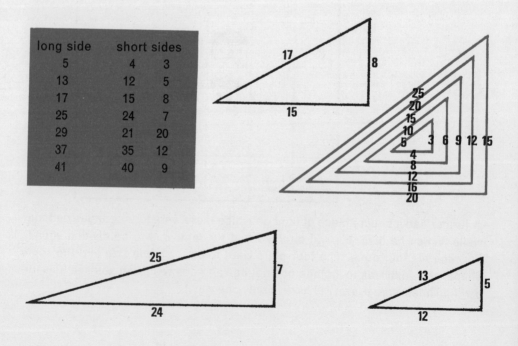

The properties of right-angled triangles are widely used in mathematics, and not only in geometry. Many puzzles are based on them. Here are a few:

The Long Way Round

I wish to drive from Anchester to Brockhurst, which lies due east of it. But the direct road is blocked; and I am forced to make a dog-leg journey through Copley, which lies 12 miles north of the direct road. Copley is nearer to Anchester than to Brockhurst. On reaching Brockhurst, I find I have driven 28 miles. What are the distances between the three places?

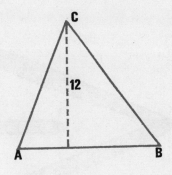

The Mainsail

A sail has the measurements shown. What is the distance AB from throat to clew? (The bottom left-hand corner is square.)

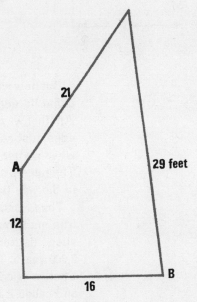

The Wasp and the Fly

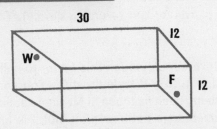

A room is 30 feet long, 12 feet wide and 12 feet high. On the centre line of one of the smaller walls and 1 foot from the ceiling is a wasp. On the centre line of the opposite wall and 1 foot from the floor is a fly. What is the shortest distance the wasp must move if it crawls all the way to catch the fly?

Drawing a Straight Line

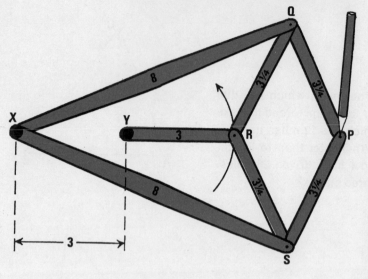

How do you draw a straight line? Most people will answer, "by using the straight edge of a ruler", and this is the method always used in geometry. The great mathematician Euclid, who lived about 300 B.C., in his book *Elements* described a straight line as "a line which lies evenly with the points on itself". In the same book, Euclid included among his "postulates"—that is, things taken for granted—the statement that it is possible "to draw a straight line from a point to any point". And of course it is—provided you have a ruler with a straight edge!

But how was the first ruler made? Probably by taking a strip of wood, sighting along its edge, and shaving it down until all points on the edge were in line. Another way would be to use a tightly stretched string as a guide to forming the edge, just as a gardener uses a line to guide him when trimming a border. But when we use a ruler, all we really do is to use one straight edge to trace another. The ruler is strictly a device for *copying*; it is not a true mathematical instrument in the way that a pair of compasses is.

The fact that it is easy to make and use a ruler made it unimportant to seek a true mathematical instrument that would draw a perfect straight line, and no such instrument was invented until Euclid had been dead for more than 2,000 years. The inventor, a French army engineer who became a general, was Charles Nicolas Peaucellier (1832–1913). He produced his instrument in 1864 and called it the *inverseur* ("inversor", or reversing device). You can make one quite easily.

The diagram shows an inversor. Although it is better to make the arms from strips of wood, cardboard will do if it is fairly stiff. (You could use finished metal strips with holes in them, such as those in Meccano sets.) In the inversor shown, the exact measurements are not important, but it is important that the distances between the holes in the long arms (XQ and XS) should be the same. Also, the distances between the holes in the shorter arms (QR, QP, SR and SP) must be the same. You can make sure of this by piling the arms on top of one another when you have cut them out, and pricking through from the top.

Arrange the inversor on a large sheet of paper. Connect the arms by drawing-pins with the points *upwards* at Q, R and S, and by drawing-pins with the points *downwards* at X and Y. It is most important that the distance XY should be the same as YR. When the drawing-pins at X and Y have been pushed in, place the point of a sharp pencil through the hole at P. Support the pencil lightly with the right hand. Then with the left hand move the pin R firmly up or down, and the pencil will draw a vertical straight line.

This result is rather remarkable, for it is obvious that the path traced by R is a circle with centre Y. Thus what we have done is to use a circle to produce a straight line.

The Pantograph

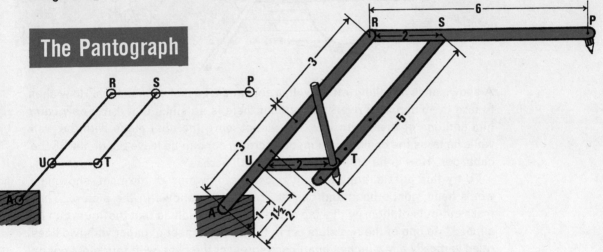

The pantograph is a linkage formed something after the manner of the Peaucellier inversor to make an instrument for quite a different purpose. The pantograph is used for enlarging or reducing drawings and diagrams. In the illustration on the left, if the point T is moved one inch in any direction, then the point P will move in the same direction through a distance which depends on the relation between the lengths AR and AU. If AR is three times as long as AU, P will move three inches.

This principle can be used to make a pantograph, but cardboard strips and drawing-pins are not really good enough for the job and you need to be fairly handy with tools. Wooden strips can be used for the arms AR and RP, but the arms UT and TS should be transparent, or you will not be able to see the drawing you are reproducing. They can be made by cutting them from an old set-square or protractor. The pivots at A, R, S and U need to be a good fit in their holes, as if they are at all loose the pantograph will not reproduce accurately. In the larger illustration, measurements are given. Notice that four sets of holes are marked for the arm UT. Depending on which of them is used, the original drawing will be enlarged to 2, 3, 4 or 6 times the size by the pencil at P. In use, the pivot A is fixed to the drawing board and the pencil at T is traced over the outline of the original drawing. The pencil stub at P may need a small weight on it to make it mark clearly.

Another Ferry Problem

A showman is travelling with a wolf, a goat and a basket of cabbages. He wishes to take them across a river but the boat there is so small that it will only carry him and *one* of them with him. He cannot leave the goat alone with the wolf while he takes the basket of cabbages across, nor can he leave the goat with the cabbages. How is he going to bring them all across?

To try this puzzle, copy on stiff paper the drawings of the boat, showman, wolf's head, goat's head and basket of cabbages shown in the picture. Then make cut-outs of them, with a tab at the bottom of each so that the figure can be slipped into one of the two slots cut in the boat. A sheet of paper with two lines ruled vertically a few inches apart can represent the river, with four slots cut on each bank to hold the figures. Remember that only the showman can row the boat!

Prime Numbers

These are whole numbers that cannot be divided without remainder by any number except themselves and 1; thus 1, 2, 17, 43, and 89 are prime. But 15 is not prime because it can be divided by 3 and 5; in other words 15 has the *factors* 3 and 5. There are tests that can be used to discover whether a number is prime, without going to the trouble of dividing it by all possible factors, but they are very difficult to apply. The great French mathematician Pierre de Fermat (?1601–1665) is believed to have had a quick and simple test for prime numbers but its secret died with him. He once received a letter asking whether the number 100,895,598,169 had any factors. Fermat replied at once that its factors were 898,423 and 112,303. Both these factors are themselves prime numbers.

Some fairly large prime numbers can be constructed from the formula

$x^2 + x + 41$, where x may be any number below 40. (Thus if $x = 5$, we get $25 + 5 + 41$, which is 71 and prime.) There are 664,580 prime numbers up to 10,000,000, and more than 50,000,000 of them up to 1,000,000,000. Euclid proved that the number of prime numbers is infinite. A large prime number is:

170,141,183,460,469,231,731,687,303,715,884,105,727.

The Frenchman Marin Mersenne (who was probably repeating a statement made by Fermat) said in 1644 that this enormous number would be found to be prime, but that was not proved until 1877. Some even larger prime numbers have been found by using automatic computers. One such number, too large to express here in figures, is $2^{4,423} - 1$. (The expression 2^2 means 2×2, while 2^3 means $2 \times 2 \times 2$, or two multiplications. So to find $2^{4,423}$ you have to make 4,422 such multiplications.) Can an even number be prime? No, because it can be divided by 2, but it is almost certain that every even number is itself the sum of two prime numbers. All prime numbers greater than 3 are within 1 of being divisible by 6. For example, the prime number 11 is $12 - 1$, and 12 is 6×2. The prime number 19 is $18 + 1$, and 18 is 6×3. Unfortunately, this fact cannot be used for constructing guaranteed prime numbers, because not every number constructed in this way is prime. But, if any number when divided by 6 gives a remainder other than 1 or 5, that number is certainly not prime.

Perfect Numbers

A number that is equal to the sum of all the numbers which will divide into it without remainder is said to be perfect. Examples are 6, which is $3 + 2 + 1$; and 28, which is $14 + 7 + 4 + 2 + 1$. It is almost certain that no odd number can be perfect and only 12 perfect numbers are known. All these have 6 or 28 as their last figures. If you care to try you can multiply $2^{4,423} - 1$ by $2^{4,422}$. You will probably find that the product is perfect, though nobody has tried this yet. But the whole calculation will take some time! As an easier calculation, you might like to test for yourself whether 496 is a perfect number or not.

An ordinary person with a taste for arithmetic can have much fun from messing about with pure numbers, and may quite possibly make interesting discoveries. The reason is this: in most mathematics theory runs ahead of observation, but with pure numbers it is the other way round. By messing about with them you may observe something that will lead you to a theory, or rule. You might even rediscover Fermat's rule for testing numbers to find if they are prime.

The Bridges of Königsberg

The great Swiss mathematician Leonhard Euler (1707–1783) set this problem. In his day the town of Königsberg (the modern Kaliningrad) in eastern Europe, through which the Pregel (Pregolya) River runs, had its central island linked to the other parts by seven bridges. Start anywhere in the town and, crossing every bridge once and once only, return to the starting-point.

Magic Squares

So-called "magic squares" are constructed by ruling up a square like a chessboard and writing numbers in each small square. The numbers have to be chosen in a particular way. The numbers in each vertical column must all add up to the same sum, and this sum must be equal to that of the numbers in each horizontal row. Also it must be the same as the sum of the numbers across each of the two diagonals (that is, the lines between opposite corners). Numbers should begin at 1 and run consecutively, without any being missed out.

47	58	69	80	1	12	23	34	45
57	68	79	9	11	22	33	44	46
67	78	8	10	21	32	43	54	56
77	7	18	20	31	42	53	55	66
6	17	19	30	41	52	63	65	76
16	27	29	40	51	62	64	75	5
26	28	39	50	61	72	74	4	15
36	38	49	60	71	73	3	14	25
37	48	59	70	81	2	13	24	35

There is really no more magic about such squares than in the figures on a bus time-table. The Chinese used them as charms long before the time of Christ and in Europe in the middle ages they were supposed to protect people against the plague. Magic squares are not particularly difficult to construct. One set of rules, obtained by a Frenchman in Siam towards the end of the 17th century, can be understood by following the magic square of 81 numbers shown here. These rules apply only for squares containing an odd number of small squares, such as 25, 49, or 81.

Put the number 1 in the middle square of the top row.

Work diagonally upwards to the right (that is, northeastwards when north is the top of the paper).

When you reach the top margin, continue at the foot of the next column to the right. (You will need to do this straight away with the number 2, because you have started at the top.)

When you reach the right-hand margin, continue in the left-hand column of the next row above.

When your path would lead you into a square already filled, drop instead to the square below the one you have just numbered. Do this also after numbering the top right-hand square.

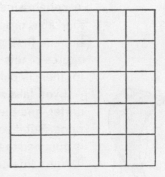

If you follow the rules correctly you will find that the last number fills the middle square of the bottom row. You will also find that the sum of the figures in each row (or in each column or across each diagonal) is half the number obtained by multiplying the number of rows (or columns) by one more than the largest number in the square. You may like to try your hand at making your own magic square in the margin.

The Mystery Area

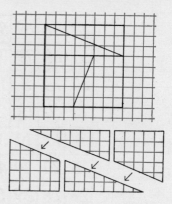

Using squared paper, draw a square with sides 8 small squares long. With a ruler, draw lines dividing this square into the four areas shown in the top diagram. The total area is clearly $8 \times 8 = 64$ small squares. Now cut out the four areas with scissors and rearrange them as in the bottom diagram.

You now appear to have a rectangle of area $13 \times 5 = 65$ small squares. How have you managed to increase the area of the original big square by one-sixty-fourth? To get at the truth of the matter, your drawing, cutting and arranging must be very accurately done.

The Möbius Strip

A certain kind of geometrical figure that anyone can make quite easily has remarkable properties. These properties may have been known to the ancients but the first person to draw attention to them was August Möbius. Therefore figures of this kind are usually known as Möbius strips, although another name for them is paradromic rings. (Paradromic means "running side by side".)

If you take a strip of paper and gum the ends together to form a band like a garter, and then cut the strip lengthwise along its middle, you get two narrower rings. But if you put a half twist in the strip so that the back surface of one end is gummed to the front surface of the other, this is a Möbius strip. Before making it, rule a line down the centre to serve as a guide later. The strip used should be about one inch wide and about one foot long.

The ordinary garter band has two edges and two sides (an inside and an outside). Examine the Möbius ring closely. By marking a pencil cross near one edge and then tracing right round the ring (in either direction) you will find that this remarkable strip of paper has only one edge. What is even more strange, you will find that it has only one surface.

Now cut the Möbius ring along its middle line with scissors. The result is a single ring, not two. If this ring is again cut along its middle it yields two interlocked rings. If the strip is ruled into three before being made into a Mobius ring, cuts along the two lines yield two interlocked rings, not three. And one of these two rings is twice as long as the other.

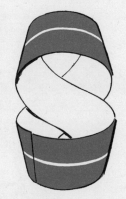

Make another ring, but this time give the strip a complete twist (that is, through 360 degrees) instead of a half twist before gumming the ends. This ring, which will be found to have two edges and two sides, yields two interlocked rings if cut along the middle. See what happens if these two rings in turn are cut along their middles.

The Shunting Puzzle

The diagram shows a railway whose main line ABC is connected by two curved tracks D and E with a short siding at S. The siding S is long enough to take a single wagon, such as V or W, but too short to take the engine L. So if the engine approaches the siding along D or E it must return the same way. (On a real railway a siding would never be as short as this, but for the sake of this puzzle it has to be!)

You can draw the tracks on a piece of paper using ruler and compasses, and cut small blocks of wood or rectangles of cardboard to represent the engine and two wagons, remembering to make the engine longer than a wagon. Mark one wagon V and the other W; then place V on the curve D and W on the curve E. Put the engine on the main line.

The problem is to use the engine to interchange the wagons so as to leave wagon V at E and wagon W at D. On this railway you may not use a "flying shunt" to send a wagon on under its own momentum.

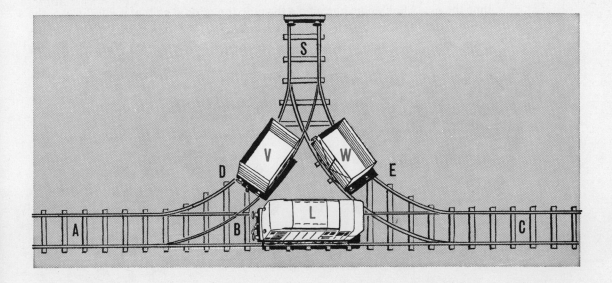

The Tower of Hanoi

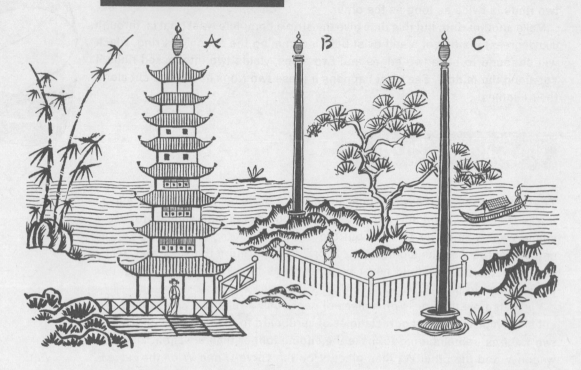

This puzzle consists of three pegs each about two inches high fixed upright on a board. Eight circular discs, each a little wider than the next, are cut out of cardboard. (If you are making these, suitable sizes are $\frac{3}{4}$ inch across for the smallest disc and $2\frac{1}{2}$ inches across for the largest, each disc being $\frac{1}{4}$ inch wider than the next.) Each disc has a hole through the middle so that it will slip over the pegs. To begin with, all eight discs are arranged in order of size on one of the pegs, with the largest disc at the bottom and the smallest at the top. This looks

308

something like one of the towers called pagodas (most of which are Buddhist temples) in Vietnam, where the city of Hanoi was famous for the Pagoda of the Great Buddha.

The puzzle is to move the whole tower on to one of the other pegs, ending with the discs in the same order as they started. There are two rules. Only one disc may be moved at a time; and no disc may ever rest upon a smaller disc. The puzzle can be done in 255 moves.

The same puzzle can be tried with ordinary playing cards to save the trouble of making the board, pegs and discs. Use cards of the same suit from 1 to 8, taking the ace to represent 1. Or if you have no playing cards, use plain cards or squares cut from stiff paper, numbered from 1 to 8. In this case the cards are arranged in order in a single pile, face upwards, with 1 at the top and 8 at the bottom. You must solve the puzzle by unbuilding the pile into three piles, and then building up one of the two new piles with the cards in the correct order. Only one card may be moved at a time and no card may ever lie on top of one with a lower number.

Tracing Networks

The three figures in the illustration are networks of a special type and the problem with each is to draw it without lifting the pencil from the paper and without going along any line twice. The first is the pentagram star, which was used by the members of a brotherhood founded by the Greek philosopher Pythagoras in about 530 B.C. They used it to recognize each other, and later it was used as a sign of health. The middle figure is supposed to be one traced in the sand by Mohammed with his scimitar (sword) without lifting the point from the ground. The right-hand network can also be drawn without breaking the rules.

The Puzzle of the Pins

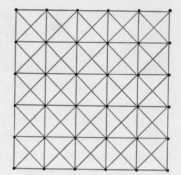

The diagram shows a square ruled into 25 small squares, each of which is crossed by diagonal lines. It can be drawn on a sheet of squared paper and pasted on to soft cardboard. The dots at the corner of each square are positions where pins may be placed. The problem is to take six pins and put them in so that no two pins are joined by one of the straight lines on the diagram. You will find that there is more than one way of doing this.

This puzzle may be varied by drawing the big square so that it is divided into 36 small squares (that is, each side is 6 small squares long) or even into 64 small squares or 100. If 36 small squares are used there must be 7 pins to match, while 64 squares need 9 pins and 100 squares need 11 pins. It is possible to solve the problem in every case. Contrary to what might be thought, increasing the size of the puzzle in this way does not make it more difficult. It is really a kind of chess problem, although much simpler than most.

The Two Jugs

This puzzle dates from the middle ages. A girl is sent to fetch water from a well and given two jugs, one that will hold 5 pints and the other 3 pints. She is told to bring back exactly 4 pints. How does she do it?

Answers

The Seaside Couples

The empty pram must be for the baby carried by 3, so her husband is Mr. 12. Mrs. 11 has a dog lead but no dog, so she must be the wife of Mr. 6, whom the dog is jumping up to greet. Mr. 4 has a tennis racket so his wife must be 10, who is carrying a net of tennis balls. Mrs. 1 is the only person in bathing things, so why is 8 carrying a snorkel and swim-fins unless he is her husband? Mr. 7 is paying the newsboy but not taking a paper because his wife 5 has already taken one. This leaves only 2 and 9, who must be the sixth married couple.

The Undergraduates

Smith is at Trinity, Brown at Merton, Jones at Brasenose, Robinson at Magdalen and Green at Balliol.

To solve this kind of puzzle without getting hopelessly muddled, make a table. From the first clues given, you can put a cross on the Balliol line under Smith and Jones. When you have worked through the clues, the table will look like this.

	Smith	Brown	Jones	Robinson	Green
Balliol	X	X	X	X	
Brasenose	X	X			
Merton	X				
Trinity					
Magdalen	X	X	X		

As there are four crosses in the Balliol line, the fifth space (Green's) must be a tick. And if Green is at Balliol, all the other spaces under his name must be crosses. The rest of the spaces are filled in by the same method.

You can make up your own puzzles of this kind, with as many people to be fitted in as you like. For example, six girls who choose dresses of six different colours, with clues such as "Mary and Doris cannot bear green; red doesn't suit Margaret and Barbara; and the only blue dress Gay likes is too big", and so on. Be careful to give enough clues, but only just enough. The least number of clues needed is half the number of people multiplied by one less than the number of people, and this least number applies only when the clues are arranged in a particular way. One line of the table must have crosses in every space except one, a second must have them in every space except two, and so on. Start making your own puzzle by drawing the table and arranging the crosses. Finally, you can throw in a perfectly useless clue (but not a misleading one) to make the puzzle more of a teaser. In our example, the statement about Green's parents never having been to France is a clue of this kind.

Mr and Mrs Evans

We need to find a two-figure number (Mr. Evans's age at marriage) which is exactly divisible by three, and which when 18 is added to it is exactly divisible by two. Trial shows that 54 will fit, and that no other number will.

This sort of problem is often solved by turning it into algebra. Suppose Mr. Evans was E years old at marriage and that his wife's age was then W years. We can then say $E = 3W$. We also know that $E + 18$ is equal to twice $(W + 18)$, which we write as $E + 18 = 2W + 36$. This second equation (as it is called) can be rewritten $E = 2W + 18$. As we know that $E = 3W$, we can write $3W = 2W + 18$, so W is 18. This gives 54 for E.

The Cyclist's Problem

Sixty miles. Although this answer can be obtained by trying various distances, the use of algebra is much quicker. Call the distance D miles. Then the time taken at 15 miles an hour is $\frac{D}{15}$ hours, and we know that this is 2 hours less than the time taken at 10 miles an hour, which is $\frac{D}{10}$ hours. So we can write $\frac{D}{15} = \frac{D}{10} - 2$, and simplify this by multiplying all through by 30, giving $2D = 3D - 60$, whence $D = 60$.

Weeding the Garden

Adrian weeded 8 feet more than Peter. Choose any sensible length—say 40 feet—for each border. On the south side, if Peter weeds 4 feet, Adrian must do 36 feet. On the north side, if Adrian does 8 feet Peter must do 32 feet. So Peter's total is 36 and Adrian's total is 44 feet, which is 8 feet more than Peter's. Any length you choose for the borders will give this answer. If you choose x feet, Peter's total is $x - 4$ feet and Adrian's is $x + 4$ feet.

The Gambler

Poorer. You might think that Racke would come out all square, but under these conditions he is bound to lose, and the longer he goes on the more he loses. If he calls correctly three times and wrongly three times he will be left with £5 1s. 3d., no matter in what order his wins and losses occur.

Six Boys at Margate

Let x be the number of shillings spent by Bob. Then the average spent by the whole party is $\frac{45 + x}{6}$. But we know that x is 5s. more than this, so we can write:

$$x = \frac{45 + x}{6} + 5$$

Multiplying all through by 6 gives us:

$$6x = 45 + x + 30$$
$$\text{so } 5x = 75$$
$$\text{and } x = 15, \text{ or Bob spent } 15s.$$

The Bookworm

If you stand any book the right way up on the table, with its spine towards you, you will see that its first page is the right-hand one and the last page the left-hand one. Therefore the bookworm did not bore through any of the pages of volume 1, but only through one of its covers, which is $\frac{1}{20}$ inch. The worm went right through the next ten volumes (volumes 2–11), a distance of 10×1 plus $10 \times \frac{1}{20}$, or 11 inches. In volume 12, the worm had to bore only through one cover—$\frac{1}{20}$ inch—to reach the last page. So the total length of hole was $\frac{1}{20} + 11 + \frac{1}{20}$ or $11\frac{1}{10}$ inches.

The Explorers

The expedition carried $4 \times 5 = 20$ man-days of food and water. Call the explorers A, B, C and D. All advance on the first day, camping 30 miles from the edge of the desert. They have eaten 4 man-days of their supplies. On the second day, D turns back and reaches base at nightfall, when the others camp 60 miles from base. Another 4 man-days of supplies have been used. On the third day, C turns back while B and A reach a point 90 miles from base, and 3 man-days of supplies are consumed. On the fourth day, B turns back, C reaches base and A goes on to plant the flag 120 miles into the unknown. Again 3 man-days' supplies are eaten. On the fifth day B continues returning and A starts to return, between them consuming 2 man-days' supplies. On the sixth day B reaches base while A gets half-way back—another 2 man-days' supplies gone. The weary A plods into base at nightfall on the eighth day, having finished the last 2 man-days' supplies.

There is a formula, or rule, for this. If E is the number of explorers and D the number of days for which the supplies carried by each explorer will last one man, the longest possible journey before the leader turns back will be one that lasts

$$\frac{E \times D}{E+1} \text{ days.}$$

In the example given, this is 4×5 divided by $4+1$, which gives 4 days as the answer. But by looking at the formula we can see that if E is a very large number, the formula gives an answer which is as near to D as no matter. The practical result of this is that even if the desert expedition hires 1,000,000 Arabs to carry extra supplies, the leader will never be able to travel for more than 5 days before he must return.

The limit to travel forced upon expeditions by this cast-iron mathematical rule was realized long ago. Explorers sought to get round it by "depoting" supplies, or leaving dumps along the route for use on the return journey. Captain Scott in his expedition to the South Pole (1911–1912), laid out depots and divided his men into First Return Party, Second Return Party and Polar Party.

If the expedition makes depots, the longest possible journey before the leader turns back is given by the formula:

$$\tfrac{1}{2}D(1 + \tfrac{1}{2} + \tfrac{1}{3} + \text{ and so on down to } + \tfrac{1}{E}) \text{ days.}$$

In the case of our desert expedition, the formula would give $2\tfrac{1}{2}(1 + \tfrac{1}{2} + \tfrac{1}{3} + \tfrac{1}{4})$ or $\tfrac{125}{24}$ days, which is rather over 5 days. By increasing the number of explorers to 10 without increasing their loads we get a longest journey before returning of 7 days, and by increasing the number to 100 we get nearly 13 days. But for the leader to march for a month before turning back he would need a party of more than 12,000, and to march for 77 days he would need 6 million million men—or nearly 1,700 times the population of the world.

The Family Crossing

The first trip must be one in which both sons cross. The next moves are: (2) one son returns; (3) Mrs. Brown crosses; (4) other son returns; (5) one son ferries trunk across; (6) he then returns; (7) both sons cross; (8) one son returns; (9) Mr. Brown crosses; (10) other son returns; (11) both sons cross.

The Jar of Balsam

This kind of problem can be solved only by trial. As a first step, fill the 5-ounce vessel from the jar, leaving 19 ounces in the jar. If the 11-ounce vessel is then filled from the jar, 8 ounces remain there and can stay as one thief's share. The situation then, and the pourings that must be done afterwards, are shown in the following lines:

5-ounce vessel	11-ounce vessel	13-ounce vessel
5	11	0
0	11	5
0	3	13
5	3	8
0	8	8

The Chests of Gold

Clearly each son must have seven chests, and since the gold amounts to $(7 \times 1) + (7 \times \tfrac{1}{2}) + (7 \times 0) = 10\tfrac{1}{2}$ chestfuls, a one-third share is $3\tfrac{1}{2}$ chestfuls. Set out the problem like this:

	full chests	half-full chests	empty chests	chestfuls of gold
TOTAL	7	7	7	10½
1st son	3	1	3	3½
2nd son	2	3	2	3½
3rd son	2	3	2	3½

The other answer is to give the first and second sons the share shown above for the first son. The third son will then get one full chest, five of the half-full chests and one empty chest.

The Endless Chain

There are 9 lengths of chain so it seems there must be 9 joins, and as each join means opening and rewelding one link, this will cost $9 \times 3 = 27$ shekels. However, if every link of the 8-link length is opened, these 8 links can be used to join the other 8 lengths at a cost of 24 shekels. Better still, if every link of the 3-link and 4-link lengths is opened, these 7 links will serve to join the other 7 lengths for 21 shekels.

The Four Shapes

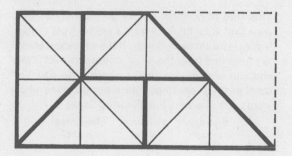

If you divide the figure into 12 equal triangles as shown, then each piece must contain three of them. Cuts are therefore required along the thick lines.

How Many Moves?

The smallest number of moves in which the new arrangement can be obtained is 23. Cards are moved in the order ace, 2, 6, 5, 3, ace, 2, 6, 5, 3, ace, 2, 4, 8, 7, ace, 2, 4, 8, 7, 4, 5, 6.

The Orchard

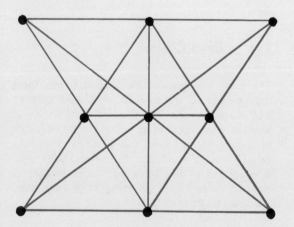

The Sheep Pens

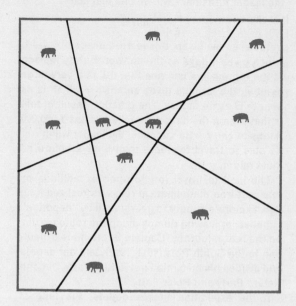

The Cottages and Wells

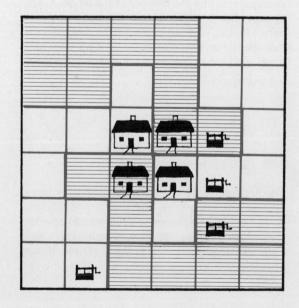

314

The Long Way Round

It looks as if the triangles 15, 12, 9 and 20, 16, 12, both from the 5, 4, 3 family, could be put together to solve this puzzle. However, their long sides add up to 35, and that is too much, as we need 28 for AC + CB. We can get this by placing a 13, 12, 5 triangle alongside the 15, 12, 9 one:

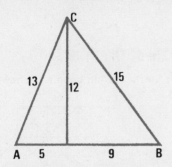

This gives Anchester to Brockhurst 14, Anchester to Copley 13 and Copley to Brockhurst 15 miles.

The Mainsail

AB is the long side of the right-angled triangle 20, 16, 12 of the 5, 4, 3 family. It is also a side of the right-angled triangle 29, 21, 20. So its length must be 20 feet.

The Wasp and the Fly

It looks as if the wasp's shortest path was $1 + 30 + 11 = 42$ feet, but it is not. This puzzle is solved by

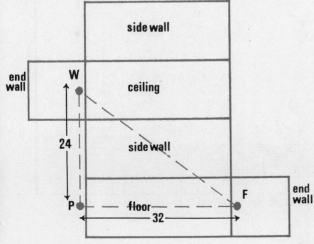

drawing the walls, floor and ceiling on a piece of paper so that when folded it makes a model of the room. When the paper is flattened out, the shortest path for the wasp is seen to be the straight line WF. If you draw the room on squared paper to the scale of 10 feet to 1 inch, you will find that WF is 4 inches long, giving a shortest path of 40 feet.

You can also calculate the answer. Remembering what was said about "the square on the hypotenuse" in right-angled triangles, then $WF^2 = WP^2 + PF^2$. Since WP is 24 and PF is 32 feet long, this is $576 + 1,024 = 1,600$, giving WF a length of 40 feet.

Another Ferry Problem

Showman rows across with goat, leaving it on the far bank. He then returns and picks up wolf. He takes wolf across, but before wolf can attack goat, showman takes goat back to near bank. Before goat can eat cabbages, showman takes them across and leaves them with wolf. Showman returns to fetch goat.

Perfect Numbers

The number 496 is perfect because it can be divided without remainder by 1, 2, 4, 8, 16, 31, 62, 124 and 248, which add up to 496.

The Bridges of Königsberg

A solution is impossible. There is no way of returning to the starting point by crossing every one of the seven bridges once only.

The Mystery Area

If you use paper with large squares and draw and cut along the lines very carefully, you will find that the four pieces do not form a true rectangle. Set the top side of the "rectangle" absolutely parallel with the bottom side (you can do this by laying out the four pieces on a sheet of squared paper). You will then find that a narrow gap lies

315

along the diagonal joining top left and bottom right corners. This diamond-shaped gap is one small square in area.

The Shunting Puzzle

The engine L first pushes the wagon V up the curve D into the siding S. The engine returns and then pushes W up the curve E against V. V and W are then coupled together; L pulls them out to C and pushes them along the main line to B, where V is uncoupled and left. L then takes W along E to S, where W is left. L then returns along E to the main line and takes V to E, leaving it there. L can now go by way of C, B, A, and D to fetch W from S, leaving it at D.

The Tower of Hanoi

For this you must have a system. It is best to number the discs from 1 to 8 (if you are using cards, they are already numbered). Also, letter the pegs (or piles) A, B and C. Now make the rule that odd-numbered discs (or cards) always move round in the direction ABCA while even-numbered ones always move in the direction ACBA. The first move, third move, fifth move and so on for every alternate move must always be made by moving the smallest disc (1) to the next peg in the direction ACBA.

Tracing Networks

For the star, draw the longest lines you can see in the figure five times, one after the other. Similarly, Mohammed's sign can be drawn in four bold sweeps. The third figure illustrated is more difficult, but the trick is to begin at one end of the diagonal that runs across the central square and finish at the other end of it.

The Puzzle of the Pins

An answer for the six-pin square is shown in the illustration.

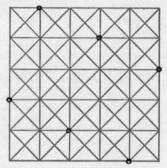

The Two Jugs

The girl fills the 3-pint jug and empties it into the 5-pint jug. She refills the 3-pint jug and from it fills the 5-pint jug, thus leaving 1 pint in the smaller jug. Then she pours away the water from the big jug and empties the smaller one into it. Finally she fills the 3-pint jug and once more empties it into the big one, ending with $1+3=4$ pints.

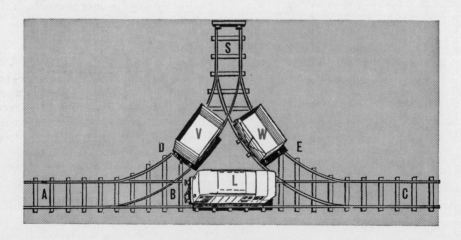